"I've Seen the Best of It"

Books by JOSEPH W. ALSOP

THE 168 DAYS (with Turner Catledge)
MEN AROUND THE PRESIDENT (with Robert Kintner)
AMERICAN WHITE PAPER (with Robert Kintner)
WE ACCUSE! (with Stewart Alsop)
THE REPORTER'S TRADE (with Stewart Alsop)
FROM THE SILENT EARTH
F.D.R.: A CENTENARY REMEMBRANCE
THE RARE ART TRADITIONS

Joseph Wright Alsop (1910–1989).

JOSEPH W. ALSOP

"I've Seen the Best of It"

MEMOIRS

with

ADAM PLATT

W · W · NORTON & COMPANY · *New York London*

Printed in the United States of America.

Selections from *F.D.R.: A Centenary Remembrance* by Joseph Alsop, copyright ©
1982 by Thames and Hudson Ltd., used by permission of Viking Penguin,
a division of Penguin Books USA Inc.

Poem from *The Stilwell Papers* by Joseph W. Stilwell, edited by T. H. White,
copyright 1948, renewed 1975, used by permission of William Morrow and
Company, Inc., Publishers, New York.

All photographs not otherwise credited are from the private collection of
Joseph W. Alsop.

The text of this book is composed in Janson Alternate,
with the display set in Perpetua.
Composition and manufacturing by the Haddon Craftsmen, Inc.
Book design by Jacques Chazaud.

First Edition.

Library of Congress Cataloging in Publication Data

Alsop, Joseph, 1910–1989
I've seen the best of it: memoirs / Joseph W. Alsop; with Adam Platt.
p.   cm.
Includes index.
1. Alsop, Joseph, 1910–1989. 2. Journalists—United States—
Biography. 3. World politics—20th century. I. Platt, Adam.
II. Title.
PN4874.A43A3 1992
070'.92—dc20
[B]   91–13071
ISBN 0–393–02917–4

W. W. Norton & Company, Inc., 500 Fifth Avenue, New York, NY 10110
W. W. Norton & Company, Ltd., 10 Coptic Street, London WC1A 1PU

1 2 3 4 5 6 7 8 9 0

Contents

Photographs follow pages 120, 242, and 368.

Preface

Not long ago, my doctor told me I had lung cancer. The news did not enormously surprise me, since I smoked ninety-five cigarettes a day until not so many years ago. To my more real surprise, the news did not enormously distress me, either. I have had an improbably lucky and satisfying life. I suspect, too, that I am already near that turning point that I have observed in all too many older persons I have cared about, beginning with my mother—the turning point when one has finally lived too long and life itself loses its savor.

Partly for these reasons, I have now refused the pleas of my doctor and his allies to try this, that, or the other which may (or may not) stretch out the time allotted to me. This was the choice faced by my brother, Stewart, when he came down, late in 1971, with a particularly fierce leukemia. He was still vastly enjoying his family, his friends, and, for that matter, his dinner and his customary diversions. His doctors had to admit that their systems of life prolongation would end all forms of enjoyment immediately yet could not work for very long. This seemed a bad bargain to my brother, and today it still seems a bad bargain to me, although my kind doctor-proposed gambles on life prolongation are not quite so horrendous as the gambles my brother rejected. As it turned out, my brother continued to be able to enjoy his life until the very end. I hope for a similar result.

Meanwhile, only one omission worries me any longer. All the scenes of the past I have loved most dearly; all the past episodes that have made me laugh most loudly (and some that have forced me to laugh silently into my sleeve); all the many comedies and occasional tragedies I have witnessed or played a role in; all the dramas I have seen change history a little, or at least teeter on the brink of changing history—all this vast accumulation of uncommonly rich experience will be lost when I reach my term, unless what is most enlightening and amusing, significant and curious can somehow be set down for the record. The longer I have pondered the matter, the more desirable it has seemed to me to rescue selected fragments of this past that will otherwise be irredeemably lost before very long.

From the day I began work as a newspaperman, July 5, 1932, until the day of completion of my only major book, *The Rare Art Traditions*, in July 1982, I must have averaged close to one thousand words a day, all written for publication except in the years of the second big war, when I still wrote but not for publication. The truth is, however, that only a few weeks after I put away my typewriter in July 1982, I came down with a long, obstinate infection that began with a vicious back pain and ended with a double bypass and the insertion of a pig's valve to replace my own aortic valve. The consequence, for causes I do not quite understand, has been near-total writer's block.

The truth is, I am now a very weak man. Since my operation, I have been able to write a little, but it has been very little, and even this has been achieved with agonizing slowness. I cannot meet the present case, however, by writing very little, and that little at molasses speed. So I have chosen a partner, Adam Platt, the son and grandson of old friends and—far, far more important—a man whose writing I have come to admire greatly. The rescue, reorganization, and retelling of my past I leave to him. I will choose what to say; it will be Adam's task to decide how to say it. You can think of this book, therefore, as an extended interview over which I have retained the partial authority of a partner in authorship.

Joseph W. Alsop
Washington, D.C.

Introduction

Joseph W. Alsop died on August 28, 1989, roughly two years after beginning work on these memoirs. He was able, as he had hoped, to enjoy his life to the very end. Although he was a weak man during these last years of his life (the cancer that his doctors feared never metastasized), Joe was able to take a greater hand in the research and composition of this book than he gives himself credit. He wanted these memoirs to be broadly casual in both tone and subject matter. From a long, rich journalistic career spanning over four decades, he chose to remember the people, places, and events that had absorbed him and brought him pleasure. He did not wish to discuss his personal life in any great detail. Nor was he capable, at the end of his life, of producing a thorough historical analysis of his times, although he would have dearly liked to do so.

This, then, is a selective reminiscence. From an objective standpoint, the narrative remains incomplete. Joe chose to end his story with the death of John F. Kennedy, an event that shattered him personally and shook his belief in this country's progress. The Kennedy time in Washington, he liked to say, was the last in which he felt himself to be "a really young man." President Kennedy was both a hero to Joe and a special friend. He had known the president since Kennedy's days in the Congress and had supported his run for the White House in a way that sometimes crossed the usual bounds of journalistic propriety. For Joe, the Kennedy assassination represented the end of a bright time and set a bitter, contentious tone from which he never fully recovered.

Joe's outspoken support for the Vietnam War is covered in an epilogue. This was written to satisfy my editor's desire for completeness in treating a famous career. The 1960s were not kind to traditionalists in this country, and Alsop suffered more than most. Like Dean Acheson, Robert Lovett, and many other members of the postwar foreign-policy establishment he admired, Joe saw the Vietnam conflict in strict balance-of-power terms. Unlike many of these men, he never publicly abandoned the view that the war was part of a much larger global struggle with the Soviet Union and was, therefore, both winnable and worth winning. As opposition to the war grew at home, the tone of his columns became more strident, his private confrontations with old friends more severe. These battles left Joe feeling old, bitter, and depleted. At the very end of his life, he was neither willing nor able to relive them.

In putting together these memoirs, I have drawn from Joseph Alsop's private correspondence as well as from his own journalistic work. Fragments of many of his columns, written with Robert Kintner as well as his brother Stewart, have been reproduced here. The same is true of his books, specifically *The Reporter's Trade*, published in 1958 after Joe and Stewart ended their professional partnership, and *F.D.R.: A Centennial Remembrance*, which appeared in 1982. Portions of magazine articles reproduced here first appeared under the Alsop byline in the *Atlantic Monthly*, in the *New Yorker*, and, with his first partner, Turner Catledge, in the *Saturday Evening Post*. Although Joe did not entirely approve of this pilfering, he condoned it on the grounds that the practice of reworking old material was not uncommon among aged writers of journalistic memoirs.

I am not an historian, and, despite his protests to the contrary, neither was Joe. In checking this manuscript, I have, therefore, relied on the judgment and counsel of a number of professionals. William E. Leuchtenburg, William Rand Kenan Professor of History at the University of North Carolina, read the chapters on Franklin Roosevelt. Professor Nancy Tucker of Georgetown University did the same for the material covering Joe's experiences in China during the Second World War, as did my friend, Lawrence MacDonald of the *Asian Wall Street Journal*. Evan Thomas and Lucius Battle read the chapters dealing with the Truman administration. Robert Silvers, Edwin Yoder, and Arthur Schlesinger, Jr. provided invaluable

comments on the entire manuscript. Dr. Leann Grabavoy Alm-
quist's University of Georgia doctoral dissertation "Joseph Alsop
and American Foreign Policy: The Journalist As Advocate" was
useful as background. Dr. David Wigdor, assistant chief of the Manuscript Division of the Library of Congress, helped me navigate
through Joe's voluminous collection of private papers, and Peter
Braestrup provided background for my epilogue. Finally, Professor
Douglas Brinkley of Hofstra University took time out from his own
hectic schedule to give this manuscript not one, but two thorough
and scholarly readings. Doug brought a writer's touch to this chore,
offering editorial tips as well as factual advice at a time when both
were desperately needed. I am grateful for his help as Joe would
have been, had he lived to see his book completed.

Throughout the long term of this project, the members of the
immediate Alsop family have been helpful, gracious, and uncom-
plaining. John Alsop generally backed up his older brother's memory and helped to fill in a number of gaps in the book's early chapters. Susan Mary Alsop and Stewart's wife Tish gave Joe great moral
support during the last years of his life and provided valuable points
on the manuscript. As executor of Joe's estate, Joseph Alsop (eldest
son to Stewart) gave me access to all of his uncle's old papers and
photographs, photocopied and sent out countless drafts of the manuscript, and offered general counsel whenever it was needed.

Our editors at W. W. Norton & Company, Eric Swenson and
Henning Gutmann, showed patience and perseverance in nursing
the manuscript through various stages of disrepair. Henning, in particular, gave the kind of thorough, hardheaded reading Joe would
have greatly admired and appreciated. Our manuscript editor, Carol
Flechner, set a special standard for correctness and worked well
beyond the usual duties of her post to verify the names, dates, and
facts from Joe's distant past.

Lois and Tom Wallace, literary agents to Joe and me, performed above and well beyond the call of duty in seeing this book to
its completion. Joe Alsop was never an easy man to work with, and
when I broke down or blew up, as happened frequently, they
gamely filled the breach. They offered words of comfort and advice.
They coaxed and calmed. Both Lois and Tom were in on the book's
inception, and both stayed on doggedly until the work was done.
Without their help, these memoirs would not have been written.

Adam Platt
Washington, D.C.
August 1991

"I've Seen the Best of It"

1

My World

The other day, in a secondhand book shop, I happened across a seedy looking, little green paperbound volume called *Women and Repeal*. It recounts the saga—a very genuine saga it was, too—of the repeal of the Eighteenth Amendment quite largely by efforts of the mobilized womanhood of the WASP Ascendancy. Their leader on this occasion was Mrs. Charles H. Sabin, later Mrs. Pauline Davis. (Her second husband, a former secretary of war, created the international tennis competition, the Davis Cup.) Her Women's Organization for National Prohibition Reform beat the tar out of the formerly all-powerful Women's Christian Temperance Union and its formidable boss Mrs. Ella A. Boole, whose pince-nez had gleamed upon scenes of uninterrupted triumph since 1918.

I bought the dingy little book, which I suspect its heroine paid to have written, for several distinctly miscellaneous reasons. To begin with, the former Mrs. Sabin was a leading Washington personage after she became Mrs. Dwight Davis, and there she became an enormously kind older friend when I was assigned to the capital by the *New York Herald Tribune* in late 1935. Then, too, a great number of the ladies mentioned in the little green book were well known to me as my mother's dear friends—although, to be sure, my mother was much too partisan a Republican to approve of complete nonpartisanship, even in the fight against the Eighteenth Amendment as advocated by the ladies battling for repeal.

Furthermore, I am by way of being a very minor member of the ever-diminishing group of survivors of the WASP Ascendancy; and the assault upon Prohibition by the ladies led by Mrs. Sabin was the WASP Ascendancy's last *organized* success. The equation was simple. The belatedly unanimous, belatedly vocal, almost nationwide WASP Ascendancy was organized by Mrs. Sabin in the name of repeal. It thus was firmly added to the nation's near–50 percent of Catholic, Greek, Ukrainian, and other groups known to the politicians nowadays by the silly label "ethnics," and it produced a solid majority for repeal in most states of the Union outside the Bible Belt. So the politicians, instead of trembling before Mrs. Boole, her ferocious ladies, and her Baptist and Methodist allies of the Anti-Saloon League and such like, suddenly found themselves trembling and making obeisance to Mrs. Sabin, assorted archbishops and metropolitans, and city bosses of Irish and Italian stock. The WASP injection gave the extra weight that did the trick.

Nowadays everybody talks about WASPs without thinking very clearly about what is meant. In most cases, however, it is pretty clear that what is really meant is the WASP Ascendancy. Otherwise the label is vastly too inclusive—for example, applying equally to the defeated Mrs. Boole and her cohorts and to Mrs. Sabin and hers. After all, White Anglo-Saxon Protestants, if these qualities were the only tickets of admission, still constituted just about half the total population of the United States when I was a boy and young man.

The WASP Ascendancy, however, was a much narrower group. I don't know quite how to define it without sounding a fool except to say that it really was an ascendancy—in fact, an inner group that was recognizable as a group, on the one hand, because its members tended to resemble one another in several ways, frequently knew one another as friends or at least acquaintances, and might even be related to one another by blood; and, on the other hand, an inner group that was, on average, substantially richer and enjoyed substantially more leverage than other Americans. For those very reasons, too, this group had long supplied the role models followed by other Americans, whether WASP or non-WASP, who were on their way up in the world.

If these others rose far enough, moreover, they had to be really pretty awful not to be promptly absorbed into the WASP Ascendancy. Oddly enough, this absorption was then quite often advertised by ecclesiastical migration. My mother's family, for example, was Scottish on her father's side and basically Dutch on her mother's. Her mother was Theodore Roosevelt's younger sister. Among the Scots in my mother's tribe, the migration began, despite howls of Presbyterian rage from the primitive tribal majority, when one of the tribe's leading males bought a pew in Grace Church (Episcopalian) around 1840 because "all the better people go there." (For the rich former significance of Grace Church, see Edith Wharton's *The Age of Innocence,* the wedding of Newland Archer.)

I do not know how soon thereafter my mother's family's Presbyterian-to-Episcopalian migration was completed or when the various branches of the Roosevelt clan left their Dutch conventicles. But all of them on both sides certainly ended as Episcopalians. I fear, too, that the attraction of the Episcopal Church lay in the simple fact that this used to be almost everywhere the all-but-official church of the WASP Ascendancy. Pittsburgh was, and perhaps is still, the exception that proves the foregoing rule. The same ecclesiastical migration took place there, but Episcopalians were the ones who migrated since the local branch of the ascendancy remained fiercely loyal to its native Presbyterianism—and where Mellons went, there went many more.

I think, as many others have thought (all too often mistakenly), that I have had an exceptionally interesting life as well as a very lucky one. Yet I cannot make any sense of the pattern of my life, nor do I think anybody else can, except by taking note of the trifling-seeming fact that I began as a minor member of this now-vanished group, the WASP Ascendancy.

In its day—although one begins to forget this—the group was highly recognizable, and not just by the fairly extreme but regional New England/New York accent I happen to possess. The recognition signals were often very odd indeed. By my time, for example, not a great many members of the WASP Ascendancy still had what were called "family houses," which merely meant large, rural tribal dwellings going back a century or two. But those who had hung onto these redoubts somehow contrived that all family houses should smell the same. I believe the secret was beeswax, rather lavishly used year 'round to polish floors and furniture, plus a great many flowers from the summer gardens. At any rate, the front door would open, and this splendid scent would waft outward, particularly in summer, for this was before air-conditioning and the summer rule was still in force. It held that all windows were closed and shades were pulled until after dusk, when windows were thrown open again to let in the cool night air. And so the house's smell would tell you just what sort of décor and human atmosphere to expect after you had passed the front door.

But the special smell of the few remaining family houses was in fact a very minor recognition signal of the WASP Ascendancy. To begin with, there were all sorts of dos and don'ts about clothes and shoes. But I shall speak only of those of concern to men, for I cannot to this day tell what outward signs enabled my mother and her friends to choose the five or six other ladies who it "might be nice to know" from the scores of possibilities presented, say, by the teeming decks of a transatlantic liner. I only know that in my young days, even if American ladies came from the very richest, top-most branches of the worldly tree, they were never likely to be mistaken for exceedingly expensive, though not quite successful, takeoffs of their counterparts in Paris.

As for the men, the first rule was to go to London for suits and shoes as soon as you could afford it. If financial strain was then felt, shirts, neckties, and so forth might also be acquired in London or even New York. But if expense was no object, it was preferable to seek these lesser articles from Charvet or Sulka in Paris. The less well heeled, meanwhile, clothed, shirted, and shoed themselves at Brooks Brothers, and so did 90 percent of the young males until the awe-inspiring moment when their fathers would take them to their London tailors—not necessarily in London, for the tailors' and shoemakers' representatives came to the United States twice a year to see to the current wants of their regular customers on this side of the water.

The correct suppliers were by no means the end of the story, however. The dos and don'ts of men's wear were almost endless. I shall offer only a selection. Beginning at the bottom, you couldn't wear saddle shoes. In summer, if you went on a weekend, you had to take along a pair of white bucks, complete with whitening to make them white, a piece of bone to smooth the whitening and make it shiny, and a small bottle of black lacquer to cover the edges of the red-rubber soles and heels. The effect intended was that you had a valet doing all this for you. I fear that my bucks never looked in the least like a valet's handiwork.

Then, at the other end, you could not appear in public without a hat. In four years at Harvard, I never went out onto the street, even on the most beautiful day, without a felt hat on my head, except in spring, when the time came for straw boaters or Panama hats. Panama hats, I may add, were judged by whether they had been woven underwater with very thin reeds. These reeds produced a texture like rough cloth so that the hat could be rolled up and tucked in a suitcase without damage.

In the evening, almost all the men who were dining with friends in town, and quite often men staying at one of the richer houses in the country, automatically "dressed for dinner." "Dressing for dinner," thank God, no longer meant putting on a stiff shirt. By my time, men were allowed soft shirts, preferably silk, although the very young could wear white Brooks Brothers' shirts. However, one still needed a dinner jacket and trousers, with black silk socks and pumps, and, to complete the turnout, a black bow tie, and a fine white—always white—handkerchief, and a cummerbund or waistcoat. Woe to you forever if you ventured a ruffled or colored shirt or necktie of the sort the young wear to what they call "formals" nowadays. Worse than woe to you, too, even if your necktie was black but was seen to be "made up."

Yet the essentials for men only began with the rule that any fanciness introduced into the basic black-and-white pattern of a dinner jacket and trousers was grossly improper. If you were sufficiently unfortunate as to have to wear white tie and tails, a whole series of other strict rules came into severe force. First and foremost, the waistcoat could not show a white line beneath the two side wings of the coat, and it must not be too short to cover amply the top of the trousers. For an evening suit, a double line of braid on the trousers was required, whereas a mere single line of broader braid was needed for a dinner jacket. Again, there would be no departure from the pattern of black and white. It was highly desirable for the stiff shirt and collar, which were absolutely essential with evening dress, to be washed in such a way that, when ironed, the starched linen was glossy. And with evening dress, instead of wearing the patent-leather pumps suitable for a dinner jacket, one needed shoes that laced but that were, of course, once again, of patent leather.

After I retired, when I moved from the big Georgetown house I built shortly after the second war, I was reminded of all the horrors we went through at weddings. If you were a member of the wedding party, you needed as a minimum a top hat, a morning coat, striped trousers, dark socks, and black shoes. Usually, in order to insure uniformity, the groom gave his ushers and best man spats, waistcoats, and neckties, and in the early days the neckties were usually heavy grey silk ascots. Since nobody, except an occasional foxhunter, knew how to tie an ascot, Brooks Brothers, where these vital appurtenances were always bought by the groom, used to send along a special man to each wedding to tie the ushers' ties and to see that all was in order. Finally, the spring weddings—by far the most numerous—called for white linen double-breasted waistcoats and white linen spats. When I moved to a new house in Washington a great many decades later than the period I am speaking of, I was presented with a large brown box with the impatient inquiry, "Do you want to take all this junk with you?" I opened the box and found no fewer than nineteen pairs of white linen spats that I had acquired as an usher at friends' sunlit weddings before the second war. I decided I could do without them.

As for the more casual garments, the aim in town for men was to look a bit like a partner at the Morgan bank since the Morgan partners had their own rather flossy style of haberdashery, which was as much admired as was their bank. To this day, when I dress to go out to an old-fashioned luncheon party in Washington, I do my best to suggest a Morgan partner of 1928.

Gentlemen, meaning members of the WASP Ascendancy or persons who aspired to be members, did not wear brown suits in the city—I have never understood why. Dark grey, navy blue, or even black was required, albeit possibly with a discreet pinstripe, if desired. Black shoes also were essential in town—and no nonsense about it, except that with a dark grey flannel suit, it was possible to wear brown shoes so repeatedly polished for so long a period of time that they all but counted as black. One also wore a silk handkerchief in the handkerchief pocket—and it was rather second rate to keep it just for show, instead of blowing your nose with it in case of need. To round it all out, in those days men still got boutonnières from the florist on festive occasions. I remember I used to buy a yellow carnation every Sunday in New York after I went to work there—on $18 a week—and on Sundays, too, I would put a little Florida Water on my handkerchief, as my father had taught me.

Language, however, was the true empire of the dos and don'ts. Here, very roughly, the rule was that the earliest English name for any thing or any occupation was desirable, and anything later was highly undesirable. So you were buried in a coffin, not a casket, and the coffin was supplied by an undertaker, never a funeral director and (God preserve us) not a mortician. Windows had curtains, not drapes or draperies. "Drapes" remains the most grating word in the language to old WASPs like me. But a close second is the phrase "gracious home." In the first place, one lived in a house, not a home, unless one had been "put away" by one's relations; and, in the second place, it is never good style to use the adjective "gracious."

To continue the list briefly, the unlucky had false teeth, not dentures; and when their lives ended, they died instead of "passing." Then, too, all of the people I am trying to describe really did speak of tomahtoes; and they had a whole series of other required pronunciations, most of which have by now been forgotten by all, including myself. But what I cannot ever quite forget is the feeling that it is wrong to abbreviate. So it grates on my ear to this day when people say they will "phone" me instead of promising to "telephone" me. This sort of thing, I need not point out, always grows up when it is desired to mark off "us" from "them"; and this was the real purpose of all the silly recognition signals that I have just listed and all the many more that I have mercifully forgotten.

All these ethnographic annotations may sound trifling now, yet there is a serious, central reason for giving some space to the WASP Ascendancy. This is, quite simply, its duration. By 1928, the year I graduated from Groton School in Massachusetts, a great ascendancy fortress, the power of this special group and its special place in American life had endured for no less than three centuries, which is a pretty good run by any standard. As I have already indicated, the composition of the group did not remain the same through the centuries in question. Pre-Depression, in the first years I remember, there were indeed plenty of families whose names and fortunes went back to the beginning, or very nearly. The Winthrops, all descended from the first Governor Winthrop of Massachusetts, were still very much on hand, as they are today, for example, and in my youth they were very conscious of it, too.

When I was at Harvard, the daughter of the Boston Mr. Winthrop wished to marry a rather nice man called Standish Bradford, who bore, after all, a well-known *Mayflower* name. The *Mayflower* also reached Massachusetts rather earlier than the *Arbella*, the ship that brought the Winthrops and the second echelon, which established the colony in Boston. But when Dorothy Winthrop engaged herself to Standish Bradford, Mr. Winthrop was heard to grumble that he didn't want his daughter to marry into "that *Mayflower* lot" because too many of them were "a pack of thieves and poor debtors." And Mr. Winthrop only half-meant it as part of his comic turn.

This doesn't seem to me an attractive story, but it is funny rather than being nastily snobbish in the manner of a modern-day story concerning Senator Peter Gerry of Rhode Island. He was directly descended from the eighteenth-century governor of Massachusetts who was made famous by his invention of the gerrymander, the arranging of voting districts for political advantage. In 1941, Senator Gerry, a pretty awful man by any standard—he used, for example, to collect very unpleasant, often scatological, and always imaginary poison-pen stories about Mrs. Franklin Roosevelt—was rebuked by a gushing female interventionist for being a violent isolationist. "How can someone with your background feel as you do about this war, Senator Gerry, when Britain is in such danger?" the lady asked.

To this Senator Gerry acidly replied, "Well, madame, *you* perhaps won't understand; but in families *like mine* we still remember the lobsterbacks"—by which he meant the red-uniformed British troops in the Revolutionary War!

Along with these few still very rich survivors from the ultimate beginnings, the WASP Ascendancy, of course, included great numbers of people who had made fortunes just a little further down the road, like the Astors and du Ponts. Above all, the ascendancy of my time included great numbers of other families who had made huge fortunes in the later nineteenth and early twentieth centuries. The point about them all is that although these fortunes differed in their dates of conception, it was often difficult to tell the families enjoying them apart, except by their degrees of extravagance. It was easy enough, however, to spot a family of the ascendancy whose fortune had seriously contracted—and, of course, the older the family, the more likely they were to have declined in fortune a little.

The reasons for this rule of decline are only too obvious. First comes the luck of the draw. Stupidity or bad luck or both are a better-than-even bet to engulf any family in two or three hundred years. Just as dangerous, too, were the terrible temptations of fashion and show. When I was young, for instance, I remember one Boston family divided into three clans: "long-tailed," "bang-tailed," and "dock-tailed." These adjectives referred to the carriage horses formerly kept by the three clans. "Dock-tailed" horses (with tails chopped off to resemble elegant shaving brushes) were the most fashionable, but the dock-tailed clan of the family had long since spent itself into oblivion for fashion's devouring sake. The family's "bang-tailed" clan (meaning those who more humanely cut off their horses' tails just where the horsetails become only hair) were still surviving respectably and fairly comfortably—but hardly more. Meanwhile, however, their cousins of the "long-tailed clan," defiantly unfashionable about everything from horses' tails to summertime brown sneakers, were enormously rich and, I am told, still are.

It must be noted, too, that old families of the WASP Ascendancy who still retained large fortunes were often quite extraordinarily mean about money—which was, of course, another reason why they lasted. I remember when Mr. Frederick Winthrop, the Bostonian member of the clan already mentioned, was said to be the richest man in New England. His second wife, who had also brought him a considerable fortune, used to wear black cotton stockings, which she bought by the bundle from a bargain department store called Raymond's. There was another incident I remember, too. The father of a friend of mine at Harvard, who was then head of the biggest bank in Boston, was going down by train to the North Shore with his friend Mr. Winthrop. Mr. Winthrop was carrying a large brown paper parcel, and my father's friend said, "What's that, Fred, that you're carrying all the way down to the Shore?"

Mr. Winthrop replied laconically, "Melon. The Italian in the Faneuil Hall market has the cheapest melons in Boston and very good, too."

On Monday, they both found themselves sitting next to each other again on the return to Boston from the weekend. Mr. Winthrop still had the brown paper parcel, now more than a little bit damp in places and generally the worse for wear. My friend's father said, "What's that, Fred, that you're taking back to Boston?"

"Melon!" Mr. Winthrop replied. "It was overripe. I'm taking it back to the Italian to show it to him and get my money back."

This is a true story, and it still makes me laugh every time I think of it. Here was a man with $40 million, the equivalent of something close to $400 million nowadays, and he was going to great trouble to save no more than a few dimes—for melons were then unknown out of season and very cheap in season. This extreme carefulness no doubt helps to explain why he was exceptionally well off; and his descendants are not suffering either. It must be added in fairness, however, that the capacity for survival among the more fortunate WASP clans of today has by no means always depended on a knack for sustained economy and a carelessness of fashion. However careful about cash, stupid families did not long survive, in truth. Finally, I can name at least three families famous for their hereditary beauty, and beauty, as a general rule, attracts wealth.

The tendency of some to defy fashion or ceremony should by no means be taken to imply that the members of the WASP Ascendancy were incapable of conspicuous display, particularly in New York and on the North Shore of Long Island, which was the favorite rural stamping ground of the very richest New Yorkers. The whole North Shore, from Manhasset eastward to Huntington, near the middle of the Island, was formerly a curious mosaic of very big country places with very big houses occupying all the empty land between the towns, which were rather small and countrified. Next to polo, the favorite diversion of the owners of these large places was fox hunting, about which there was no difficulty because they owned so much empty countryside and Robert Moses had not yet divided the region with his vast highways.

On the North Shore, the real moment of display was just before the hunting season began in early autumn, when the "Long Island dances" took place. If the owner of one of the big Long Island places along the North Shore also had an about-to-be-marriageable daughter, he would then have been thought very eccentric indeed if he did not "bring her out" at a dance in late September or very early October, when these festivals always occurred. The expense of doing this was dazzling, for seven-, eight-, nine-hundred people—even a thousand or more—might be invited. All of that year's more respectable debutantes automatically had places on the list; for every girl, three dancing men had to be supplied; and all the family's contemporaries had to be asked, too.

Champagne was illegal because of prohibition; nonetheless, champagne had to flow like water. There had to be at least the main orchestra, usually that of Meyer Davis, plus the very elegant Hungarians of Mr. Alexander Haas in their red coats who played Viennese waltzes at intervals during the dance, to give Meyer Davis and his men needed breathing spells. There was nothing to stop a host and hostess, either, from having two orchestras plus the Hungarians plus an entertainer or two like Helen Morgan, a singer now largely forgotten but very popular in those days despite her habit of drinking a good deal. I have seen her sitting on a piano disposing successively of no less than seven glasses of champagne while her mournful songs—"My Man" was the best—brought tears to every eye.

In addition to these expenses, it was, of course, necessary to put up an enormous tent in the garden with a special dance floor, which I believe migrated from great house to great house as the dance season proceeded. Then there was the expense for decorators, who were turned loose with lavish hands to transform the tent into a pleasure dome. And finally there was the very considerable outlay for a large supper—both hot food and cold—after midnight, plus the wages of the less fortunate young men who were not invited to dance, but were instead paid to park guests' cars in the huge, paddocklike enclosures that always had to be set aside for this purpose.

It was not at all unusual to hear the rumor (and there were always rumors on these subjects) that one of these dances on the North Shore had cost $50,000, and I remember one or two particularly splendid parties that people whispered had cost $100,000 or more. I look back on it all with a certain horror now, for a dollar then had ten times its present value; and all this still went on after the stock-market crash of '29, when people could, and did, feel very lucky to be employed at $20 a week. Yet I have to confess that my present horror by no means dilutes the memory of past enjoyment.

Best of all, however, I fear I remember the only one of these parties that I can think of that went really comically wrong. It was at the very end of the Hoover administration, when Ogden L. Mills had replaced Andrew Mellon as secretary of the treasury. At the treasury, of course, Mr. Mills had official responsibility for enforcing the Prohibition amendment. I don't remember which Mills daughter the party was given for, but for sheer physical loveliness the party took the prize among all the gatherings of my remote youth. Instead of a tent, the Mills's had built a huge Palladian pavilion with high, arched openings overlooking the garden. The interior of the pavilion was brilliantly silvered, and this enormous silver room had been further provided with a frieze worthy of Inigo Jones himself. It was in the form of long strings of balloons made to look like huge silver and gold fruit, threaded in swags on silver-wrapped wire and interspersed with fronds of silvered canvas leaves. The effect of the enormous silver space with this sole decoration of the silver and gold frieze was something to remember for a long time—as I have indeed remembered it.

Unfortunately, in order to do what is nowadays called "distance himself" from any direct violation of the Prohibition amendment, Mr. Mills had entrusted a huge sum—$10,000 to $15,000, I would guess—to his butler to buy the champagne, with no questions asked. The result was that the butler had pocketed nine-tenths of the money and had provided the only champagne I ever saw Prohibition-era young men and women refuse to drink. Even though there was more than enough alcohol in the nasty brew, the party began to show fatal signs of dwindling to an end not long before 1:00 A.M.

Memories of these festivals of the past make me rather uncomfortable, however. I prefer to recall the less glossy bits and pieces of this long-gone world that were more redolent of its beginnings and depended less on enormous riches. Here, I think first of my own place in this strange, widespread group. It was dictated by my father's decision to "get away from the rat race," as they say nowadays. But although he did not want to compete in New York, he certainly did not wish to take refuge, as was fashionable among the young not so long ago, in the then-remote countryside of Vermont, New Hampshire, or even Maine. He was deeply rooted in Connecticut, so he bought a farm south of Hartford in the middle part of the state. Since land there then cost $10 an acre, he was able to afford nearly 700 acres in the Farmington river valley, the center of what used to be the Connecticut Gold Coast, which was very different from the present Gold Coast in the northwestern corner of the state. The totally rural Farmington valley extended, as I recall it, from Talcott Mountain in the east, which divided it from Hartford, to the hills to the west, which cut off central Connecticut from the Housatonic river valley. It had extensions northward to Simsbury and beyond and southward to Middletown, where my father came from. I am still proud of the fact that this was the only part of the United States to meet with the unalloyed approval of Henry James, when the Master made the return journey to his native land that resulted in *The American Scene.*

I recall that portion of Connecticut as it used to be, with its fertile farms and little towns, as a golden and beautiful place. To understand it, one has to understand that life in those days was still entirely local. Few people had cars, and when my mother was first married, before she got her car, her excellent team of ponies, Brandy and Soda, needed two hours to get her from our farm over the Talcott Mountain to Hartford. In 1914, when Mother bought a car—an asthmatic Ford Model T cabriolet, strongly resembling a moderate-sized black box on wheels with a small black tea kettle on top—it was the 162nd car in Connecticut. Connecticut license numbers were issued sequentially, and my father, who already had a much grander Pierce Arrow, then changed his number (the Arrow had been number 78) to get license 163. Since license numbers are for some reason hereditary in Connecticut as well, my brother and his wife's cars are still 162 and 163. But the real point is that rural life could flourish untouched in a state that still counted its automobiles in the hundreds.

In our part of Connecticut, there were many better-than-well-off families willing to live on the incomes their forebears had provided for them in the same region where their forebears had made their fortunes. Sometimes they were not content with their family houses and embarked on new ones, like my very eccentric cousin Clarence Wadsworth. Clarence dwelt in a half-completed French palace and was reputed to keep his clothes, of which he had many, on a special catalogue system and to ask his valet not for "the blue suit today," but for "number XYZ-110 today." His wife, Cousin Catherine Wadsworth, was the object of general sympathy, but the sympathy would have been less if Cousin Clarence's inherited fortune had not been substantial by those day's standards.

Perhaps the fact that many of the families in the towns of this bygone Connecticut Gold Coast had been there for generations explained the high tolerance for eccentricity. My great-aunt, Theodore Roosevelt's sister, Mrs. William Sheffield Cowles, who was a central figure in this bygone bit of world I grew up in, was an exceedingly eccentric person by any modern standard. She had a splendid face, like a successful Roman emperor, but she had a small, misshapen body. In fact, she had been a hunchback from her childhood. Her father, the first Theodore Roosevelt, gave great sums for the New York Orthopedic Dispensary and Hospital so that she could have a place to be treated. These treatments had at least given her comfort, although, to being a hunchback, Mrs. Cowles had added progressively crippling arthritis in her middle age. She had married her president-brother's naval aide for the sole purpose of begetting a son. Despite her physical handicaps and despite the fact that she had reached the age of forty, she had managed to raise a son who turned out brilliantly well. Furthermore, as soon as my great-aunt was married to Admiral Cowles, she persuaded him to retire to Farmington, which was a kind of capital of the old Connecticut Gold Coast.

As I remember Auntie Bye, as we called my great-aunt, arthritis had immobilized her in her wheelchair, and she seldom appeared except at tea or dinnertime. The house she, her admiral, and, rather soon, her son occupied was called Oldgate because it had a superbly handsome Chinese Chippendale front gate. It was designed by an eighteenth-century architect who had directly imitated the Thames-side water gate of some great London house. The architect was a Revolutionary prisoner of war, as were the workmen who labored under him; and all were rented cheaply from one of the Revolutionary wartime POW camps in Connecticut. The house, by eighteenth-century standards, was huge and grandly designed. Indeed, Oldgate is in all the illustrated books of fine American houses of the eighteenth century. However, it by no means satisfied Auntie Bye. She promptly added a very fine garden designed by the younger Olmsted (the son of Frederick Law Olmsted, designer of New York City's Central Park), and she put a big wing on the house to accommodate what she considered a reasonable household.

One can see what this meant when I say that until the death of Admiral Cowles, my great-aunt always maintained a butler, Hopkinson; a Scotch maid of her own, MacDonald; for the admiral, a chauffeur by the name of Scott; and every so often she would add a footman on a less permanent basis than the three great pillars of the household. In addition, of course, there were the cook and kitchen maid, plus numbers of other maids to take care of the big house and to produce the nearly continuous luncheons, teas, and dinners for a fairly constant flow of guests.

By the time I recall Auntie Bye really clearly, she rarely left her bed except to bathe, dress, and get into her wheelchair; and her cruel arthritis also prevented her from leaving her house. So the world came to her. She had invented an extraordinary costume for herself—a hairdo of puffs and piled-up protuberances that must have taken her maid three-quarters of an hour to construct, plus a curious dress, combining a great deal of lace with a great deal of fine white woolen cloth, which vaguely suggested what a Roman toga might have looked like if women had only been admitted to the Roman senate. All of this was put on most often after luncheon. She had installed a kind of giant dumbwaiter in which she traveled between the two main floors of the house, and in this she came down for tea, went up to prepare for dinner, and came down again for dinner.

A continuous stream of distinguished or even famous friends and visitors from Connecticut and from the outside world poured through the house. I can recall one extraordinary occasion when my great-aunt had staying with her both Franklin Roosevelt, then governor of New York, and one of the founders of Groton School, Mr. William Amory Gardner, who was by then a very old and ill man. I stayed very late at tea that day and saw them preparing to go upstairs. Mr. Gardner would not use the dumbwaiter but protected his weak heart on the very long staircase by loudly declaiming a line from the *Iliad* in the original Greek from each new step he reached. This performance was watched with fascination by Auntie Bye and the governor of New York, who was also in a wheelchair. Only when Mr. Gardner had safely reached both the second floor and the end of Homer's "Catalogue of Ships" did the two wheelchairs head for the dumbwaiter together. Once upstairs, various diamonds were attached to this and that part of my great-aunt's costume, for diamonds were her way of dressing for dinner. Meanwhile, both Mr. Gardner and Franklin Roosevelt got into their dinner jackets, as was to be expected in those days.

Auntie Bye had a tongue that could take the paint off a barn, while sounding unusually syrupy and cooing. The harsher the sentiment, the sweeter the tone seemed to be her recipe, which was regularly borrowed by her niece Eleanor Roosevelt, whom she helped to bring up. For example, when Auntie Bye summed up a foolish woman, she would almost coo, as she said commiseratingly, "Poor little irrelevant Mary." She could also be what now seems very harsh and hard despite the cooing. The admiral had a stroke rather early and, until he died, could usually be seen in the corner of the living room playing a very complicated form of solitaire. One day he had done something to annoy Auntie Bye, and she suddenly looked up from her bridge game, observed the admiral at his solitaire, and remarked in an offhand way, "There sits darling Bearo—like a great rag doll."

I cannot resist adding a brief portrait of one more Farmington eccentric of my childhood: Mrs. Dunham Barney, who lived not far from my great-aunt and was an almost equal personage on the Connecticut Gold Coast of the day. She came from a very old Connecticut family that had kept its money, and her husband, Colonel Barney, made a good deal more money as the head of a large enterprise in Hartford. Consequently, the Barneys had a very big place in Farmington, which is now a "think tank," I believe.

Mrs. Barney's two passions were gardening and bridge, and she was more than a little unconventional about both. I discovered her unconventional approach to gardening when I was about nine. My mother took my sister and me on some mission or other that required settlement of a point of charities policy with Mrs. Barney. At a rather early hour, we reached the Barney place, which had the best-kept and greenest lawns I have ever seen in the United States. We advanced across an acre or so of sward to the flower garden in search of Mrs. Barney, and there among the flowers we found an ample lady of about sixty in what was considered to be a ladylike nightgown of that period, made of a material that I think was called lawn. At any rate, the material was, basically, rather thin handkerchief linen, and a single water spot made it almost completely transparent. Mrs. Barney had been working hard in strong sun for some time, and large areas of her nightgown clung to her damply, transparently, and (to us children) most surprisingly.

In addition to the nightgown, she wore a large beflowered hat and sturdy gum boots. This costume was completed by a trowel, already dirt-infested from severe use, which she waved at us in a friendly way, greeting my mother with the remark, "Oh, Corinne, I *do* hope you won't mind how I look. I can't *bear* taking *two* baths in the morning, so I get my weeding done first, and then I wash off all the dirt in one go." Whereupon the charitable business was rapidly but calmly disposed of, while my sister and I gaped, fascinated, at the large expanse of Mrs. Barney in her nightgown until farewells were said.

Mrs. Barney's other diversion was bridge, at which she could not resist an occasional attempt to cheat, usually by failing to follow suit when it was inconvenient. Her habit was to make a joke—usually historical, for she was both a great wit and a tireless reader of English and American history—to cover her revokes, which quite often went unnoticed while everyone laughed. Her triumph in this line was at my great-aunt's house, when she put a club from dummy on a spade from her own hand. As she did so, she looked dreamily up to the ceiling, and remarked, "Were I ever to have a had an illegitimate child, I should like it to have been *by Charles James Fox.*" Since she had a rather high and penetrating voice, everyone in the room burst into laughter not only because the thought of Mrs. Barney seriously contemplating the production of an illegitimate child was downright bizarre in itself, but also because a kind of bizarre extreme was reached when she added to the combination Charles James Fox. Large-bodied, ebullient, capable of losing three fortunes at the gambling table in the course of one night, Fox was the hero of Devonshire House and the old-fashioned English Whigs, and (one supposes this was his recommendation to Mrs. Barney) the most eloquent defender, with Edmund Burke, of America's desire for independence.

It took more than a surreal joke to make Auntie Bye miss tricks, however. She said coldly, "That's all very well, my dear; it's very funny, but that's a club and that's a spade, and you've revoked again."

To which Mrs. Barney replied with evident disappointment, "Ohh, Bye, darling, you are *too* unkind!"

Although one could go on telling improbable stories about the WASP Ascendancy of the past, it is important not to romanticize this group of people. To begin with, they were decidedly snobbish in their own peculiar way. I once described them in print as the "who was she?" group. This was the automatic response when the name of a newly married couple was introduced into the conversation. The name would not have come up at all unless the male member of the married couple had a more or less recognizable and acceptable label. Even if he was only barely placeable by name, it was assumed that his wife also must be placeable. So the ladies in the room would turn their eyes to the ceiling and almost simultaneously say, "Now let me see, who was *she?*"

My mother was never very good at this game, but my great-aunt was one of the all-time winners. And the champion in my mother's generation was Mrs. Herman Kinnicutt, the mother of the great decorator Sister Parish. Mrs. Kinnicutt was a specialist in unlikely identifications, such as "I don't believe you know them, Corinne, but she was one of those Hazards from Providence, the ones that tend to go a little bit mad." Or again, "She was an Albany Pruyn, but one of the poor Pruyns, you know." Once these identifications were made, everyone could then be easy and settle down to discuss what the husband of the married couple did, whether to have them to tea or to dinner, and suchlike.

The prevailing snobbery of the WASP Ascendancy manifested itself in other ways, too. It is enough to say that they could be hard when it came to persons they considered undesirable outsiders or when their offspring chose an undesirable outsider for a mate. There is no use pretending, either, that the WASP Ascendancy was not anti-Semitic in a mild, old-fashioned manner. The viewpoint is expressed in Mrs. Franklin Roosevelt's First World Wartime letters to her formidable mother-in-law Mrs. James Roosevelt. Eleanor Roosevelt in those days was not only mildly anti-Semitic, which she later honorably overcame, but also exhibited more than a fair share of anti-Catholicism. To be fair, her early biases were no more than was fashionable among WASPs of the day.

On balance, if one thinks about the weaknesses of this WASP Ascendancy of the past, one must also add a certain provincialism and an all-too-common hostility to the intellectual life. With respect to both literature and art, the WASP Ascendancy tended to be intensely conservative. Unless I am mistaken, I owned the only copy of Joyce's *Ulysses* in Harvard's class of 1932. For the great majority, too, the word "modern" was pejorative, particularly when applied to "modern art," although several members of the ascendancy were among the great pioneer collectors of the Impressionists and Post-impressionists.

I suspect that the beginnings of the decline of the ascendancy were traceable to both the corruptingly vast amounts of money that could be made after the Civil War and to often very silly attempts to use this money to ape European ways and to add the United States to the cultural sphere of Europe, or at least England. One of the most sedulous apes was Ward McAllister, the favorite toady of the famous late nineteenth-century Mrs. William Waldorf Astor, who was thought to rule New York society. McAllister's line was always to be more English than the English and more European than the Europeans. I remember him here because I want to commemorate the "Ward McAllister Cheer," which was devised by Nicholas Longworth and Rodolphe Agassiz when they were undergraduates at Harvard. The cheer (which I heard from Alice Longworth) was "Ward McAllister—Wow! Wow! Wow! Were hit not for that vulgar hupstart, George Washington, we might still be livin' under the rine of 'er grycious majesty Queen Victoria! Ward McAllister— Wow! Wow! Wow!" I still like to remember that mocking cheer because I hate to think of the shamefully widespread acceptance of the gilded foolishness that inspired it.

I have dwelt too long on the superficialities of the WASP Ascendancy, however. It is important, in concluding, to explain how the WASP phenomenon arose. First, the leaders of the ascendancy got to the United States and staked out the best land—a very helpful beginning. Second—and I doubt very much if the ascendancy would have survived as long as it did without this early achievement—the early members of the ascendancy provided the leaders of the American Revolution and the writers of our Constitution.

The founders' boldness in these achievements has been underestimated, it seems to me. Not all of them were very rich men, but most of them were at least richer than their contemporary Americans. George Washington and Charles Carroll of Carrollton, in Maryland, were reputed to be two of the richest men in the country. By doing what they did, they stood to lose every nickel and every acre they had if the revolution had gone against them, as it might well have done if King George III and Lord North had not chosen the worst war minister on record—Lord George Germain.

For two or three decades after the official founding of the United States, the WASP Ascendancy remained highly political. But when Thomas Jefferson was elected, the Federalist party's goose was cooked, and in most parts of the country the members of the ascendancy were Federalists. After that, their political activities were usually local and sometimes fairly odd, but one can make no rules. For example, the ascendancy produced both Theodore and Franklin Roosevelt, the two most conspicuous American presidents of this century. And I believe that Franklin Roosevelt was one of the three greatest we have had, in a special group with the father of our country, George Washington, and Abraham Lincoln, our unique saint.

Although it is not commonly realized, there are still ancient political WASP families in several states who are far from played-out. In an obscure and trivial way, my own family was one of the oldest political clans of Connecticut. To date, we have had a member of the state legislature or Senate in every generation since the beginning of the eighteenth century. The recent governor of New Jersey, Thomas Kean, belongs to one of the WASP Ascendancy's more ancient political families. Judging by his activity, the Keans are still very much alive. Then, too, one of his neighbors is former Congressman Peter Frelinghuysen, who comes from another ancient ascendancy political family. A Senator Frelinghuysen was President Harding's favorite golf partner, and a still earlier Frelinghuysen was a vice-presidential candidate in one of Henry Clay's campaigns, with the wonderful campaign song "Hooray, Hooray, the country's risin'/For Henry Clay and Frelinghuysen."

A less conventional example of a WASP in politics was the immensely disreputable Philadelphia boss Boies Penrose. He would have been an eminent member of the Philadelphia branch of the ascendancy if he had not vastly preferred the company of prostitutes to the company of ladies belonging to the Philadelphia assembly. On his deathbed he gave the orders that put Harding in the White House, and earlier he generated a political story that is one of my favorites.

He had made a particularly raw appointment in Pennsylvania, and clerical and female deputations came to his office, where they found him lying back in his big chair—he was enormously heavy—smoking a huge cigar and reading Ovid's *Ars Amatoria* in the original. They made their protest about the dreadful appointment, and Senator Penrose, looking up from his book, took a pull on his cigar and said, "Ladies and Reverends, I am sorry you don't like my old friend Bill. I've just got a telegram to tell us that he has unfortunately died, and I shall have to find someone to replace him."

The ladies and reverends burst into the usual chorus of protests that, despite his other defects, Bill was terribly kind to his dear old mother, nice to children, and so on.

Penrose took another long pull on his cigar and said, "Ladies and Reverends, you remind me of the last time I went to Lucy's, where I take my pleasure. I rang the bell, Lucy came to the door and asked me, 'Senator, who would you like to see tonight?' I said I'd like to see Sally. Lucy said that Sally had just passed on. I said, 'I'm sorry to hear that, Lucy, because she was a good girl, a nice girl, and good to be with.' And Lucy said to me, 'Ain't it the truth, Senator, you never hear the best of anyone until they are in the cemetery.' "

It would be foolish to pretend, however, that politics preoccupied the WASP Ascendancy more than intermittently after the first few decades of American independence. Money was the true preoccupation. Money was the source of the ascendancy's authority. From the Revolution onward, in fact, the ascendancy retained a strong grip not so much on industry itself, but on the banking and financial system on which industry depended for credit. The centers of power in the banking system were in the East; and these centers were ascendancy citadels. The WASP Ascendancy must be understood in these hard terms, for they are the real reasons New York and, to a lesser degree, Boston and Philadelphia felt a right—even a duty—in my youth to set the tune for the rest of the country. These were the real reasons, too, for the ascendancy's decline; for it was the grossly selfish mismanagement of the nation's credit structure in the 1920s that finally brought down the WASP Ascendancy with the crash of 1929 and the ensuing Depression.

I am often asked whether I regret this decline. My answer is that it was delightful to live as I lived when I was a young man, before I went to work. The delights were many-sided, going far beyond the pleasure of participating in the conspicuous display of others. The WASP Ascendancy had its own peculiar culture, its own peculiar cookery (much better than what is now called "the new American cuisine"), its own peculiar certainties, and its own particular advantages.

The greatest advantage, to my mind, was that the young had their careers laid out for them in advance so there was no foolish waffling and wavering about what to do. If you had special talents in science or architecture or scholarship or some other respectable pursuit, you sought very hard to get to the top of the tree you had chosen for yourself. If you had no such inclinations, you could then choose among the various ladders that led to a respectable or even a high place in the WASP Ascendancy of your time. The ladders were essentially the various professions, headed by the law, plus businesses of the kind then held to be respectable, with finance and banking at the head of the list.

It's too easily forgotten now—or at any rate it used to be too easily forgotten by the young people who complained this or that "doesn't turn me on"—that any healthy man is turned on by the mere act of putting his foot on the lowest rung of the ladder. If he is a serious and ambitious young man, he will then wish to climb to the top of the ladder, whatever his profession. For these reasons, young men of the WASP Ascendancy did not suffer from the inner anguish and self-questioning that is all too common today. Guilt was an almost unknown quality in the WASP Ascendancy, although its members had plenty to be guilty about. Certainly, the young people whose parents and grandparents formed the WASP Ascendancy seem today to be extraordinarily guilt-ridden.

Above all—and I speak from a doubly privileged perspective, for, by the social standards of today, the ascendancy was very much a man's world—one knew pretty well who one was. I have never to this day understood the phrase "identity crisis" or, indeed, understood why people have identity crises. But this may be a sign of the narrowness and provincialism that too often marked the ascendancy in the old days.

I must add emphatically, however, that I am glad every day that the WASP Ascendancy collapsed when it did—essentially at the beginning of the 1930s, when the Great Depression totally demoralized most of its members—and that Franklin Roosevelt and those who believed in him seized the leadership of this country with almost no opposition. If the ascendancy had hung on to anything like its old leverage, I cannot imagine this country achieving what seems to me to have been its greatest single feat in the twentieth century. It is almost unknown for any other country to include as citizens with an equal share the members of excluded minorities. In fact, almost every European country today has an excluded minority suffering in greater or lesser degree from discrimination; the Soviet Union has too many excluded minorities for me to count, although the ruling Russians are beginning to be a minority themselves. In most of the significant nations of the Far East, the same rule holds to an even more extreme degree.

In America, when I was young, no efforts were being made to end the exclusion of *any* American minority suffering from discrimination. Instead, we had an enormous array of more or less excluded minorities. The best off of these was probably the Jewish-American minority, who suffered from social anti-Semitism, were subject to an admissions quota from universities like Harvard and Yale, but otherwise did very well indeed. Then there were all the so-called ethnic minorities belonging to the Catholic Church and to other exotic Eastern European churches. Of them, it is enough to say that finding an Italian or Polish or Irish name linked to a position of high government responsibility, or even in any serious university, would have been quite astonishing when I was a young man. Careers were not simply open to talent; careers were open to talent with the right kind of origin and the right kind of name. Thank God the criteria for success and achievement in this country has broadened dramatically in my lifetime.

The question of race remains an issue, of course, and, to be sure, the last great task facing the United States is to extend equality to the black minority. Even so, many of the men and women who were excluded from participating in the full life of this country when I was young are included today. Their families have been raised not just as Italians or Poles or Jews, but as Americans, and this strikes me as a truly staggering national achievement. It is certainly an achievement no other major modern country can match and one that makes me proud to be an American.

On the other hand, a question I am often asked in my old age suggests that we have paid a price for the collapse of the old WASP Ascendancy. Our culture was a WASP culture, our history a WASP history. In the course of assuring an equal share for so many other peoples of so many other different origins, it is understandable that, like a lizard losing its tail, we lost most of our old culture and forgot a great deal of our old history. We have lost, at least for the time being, a crucial human resource. The best men in the old WASP Ascendancy, generation after generation, made great contributions to American life. It is hard for me to imagine Americans of later generations making the kinds of contributions that the two Roosevelts made as presidents without the almost excessive self-confidence that they enjoyed as conspicuous members of the old ascendancy.

More important, Franklin Roosevelt collected a truly remarkable group of men at the time, when, as he put it, "Dr. Win the War" replaced "Dr. New Deal." At that time, the president, in fact, had only to crook a finger and an army of public servants, as selfless as men can be, as trustworthy as men ever were, all totally dedicated to the American future, reported to Washington. The older ones, Colonel Henry Stimson, who was secretary of war, and Frank Knox, who was secretary of the navy, are forgotten nowadays. Both were Republicans, appointed to their posts to lend a bipartisan flavor to Roosevelt's war effort; but they were big men in their time, and Stimson was a very great man.

Their "juniors" recruited by Stimson and Knox are now rightly remembered as "the Wise Men." They were the men who ran the war for Roosevelt and his two elderly war and navy secretaries. After the war, moreover, those who stayed on in government designed the permanent structure of American foreign policy and remained on through most of the Truman administration to make sure that this structure was solid and beyond attack. One of them, Robert A. Lovett, was so much admired by President Kennedy that, after the 1960 election, Kennedy offered Lovett his choice of State, Defense, or Treasury Department. Lovett had to refuse because he was already suffering fearfully from the ulcers that the strains of wartime government had given him.

Many others of Lovett's stature came into the government after the war: Dean Acheson, John J. McCloy, Ellsworth Bunker (usually unfairly forgotten), Paul Nitze, who is still contributing, Charles ("Chip") Bohlen, who was my contemporary and dear friend, and many more who would be tedious for me to name. These men were public servants without compare anywhere else in my experience. The question I am often asked is where we are to get other men like these. The answer, I am afraid, is that the whole view of the world and of history, the personal culture and the private manners that produced these men, have all gone by the board.

I do not for one moment mean that everyone in the WASP Ascendancy resembled Bob Lovett and Dean Acheson. In any large group, the very best men are always a very small minority, and the very worst of the WASP Ascendancy were pretty awful. But the fact is that without the ascendancy's view of American history and its peculiar culture, really good men of this kind could not be produced at all in however small a minority. So we must somewhere along the line find a new American culture and a new American view of history before we produce new "wise men" more representative of the mixed America that gives me such pride. Thank God I am confident that this will happen.

2

Avon

Although we were certainly not poor, it was universally agreed that the Alsops were "not at all well off." This meant we were much less well off than my mother's family, although not my father's, and much, much less well off than the majority of my mother's and father's friends. It must be understood that in the small, peculiar world I was born into, being "well off" commonly entailed having a house in New York or Boston with a staff of five or six, usually including a butler; another similar establishment for the summer in Maine or somewhere else along the coast; a chauffeur who appeared early and went home late if the senior members of the family were dining out; younger children at the most expensive schools, daughters coming out at eighteen in the old-fashioned way, and sons going on to Harvard, Yale, or Princeton with allowances permitting something close to undergraduate luxury; memberships in half a dozen clubs in town and country; and enough money left over to indulge in any favored sports and to patronize all the best suppliers of everything from clothes to marmalade.

It is hard to believe nowadays, but until the Second World War it was possible for a couple to live in this way with hardly more than

$50,000 a year, provided they were satisfied with a reasonable number of children. For this simple reason, a great gulf was fixed between being well off and being rich. As an adolescent, I once stayed with a friend from one of the really rich clans who then inhabited the North Shore of Long Island, and I still remember the chilly consciousness of downright indigence that came over me because of an anecdote told by the lady of the house with no sign of shock or much amusement. It seemed that at lunch that day with Secretary of the Treasury Ogden L. Mills, someone had raised the question of how much one could live on comfortably. Someone else had timidly suggested $50,000 a year, whereupon Mills replied with open scorn, "On $50,000 a year you can't even keep clean."

In the large, rambling house I was born in, on the 700-acre Woodford farm in Avon, Connecticut, we certainly managed to keep clean. Indeed, it took a Japanese internment camp to cure me of the Avon-learned habits of bathing at least twice a day and sending all personal linen to the laundry after it had been worn just once. But we had far less than $50,000 a year, so there was no butler or chauffeur; we could not afford a second place for the summer; and there were other necessary economies that set our way of life apart from that of most of my mother's and father's friends. On the other hand, we had a superlative German cook, Emma Schunck, who called me "Lambie" (I was the oldest of my generation of Alsops) and was largely responsible for making me a fat boy and thus, alas, a fat youth and a fat young man. We also had two maids and a nurse, Agnes Guthrie, a wonderful, strong-willed woman who came to us straight off the boat from Scotland when I was six months old and stayed until she died well over fifty years later. And finally we had an "odd man" who cleaned shoes, polished floors and brass, laid fires, and helped with the garden, as well as a laundress who lived down the road and weekly washed and ironed countless female undergarments, even more numerous sheets, pillowcases, towels, tablecloths, and napkins, and, when my father and his three sons were all at home, approximately two score shirts, two score sets of male undergarments, socks in mountains, and pajamas and handkerchiefs on the same scale.

As for food and drink, I still miss our farm table. The young in the family were allowed no alcohol until they had reached eighteen, a rule that, in those remote days, was not thought a hardship. The things I miss most are the heavy cream and fresh butter from the farm dairy, our own chickens (which meant full-grown roosters and tiny broilers, both now all but unknown), the ripe summer berries from the berry patches of early and late strawberries and red, black, and "white" (really yellow) raspberries, our own melons, vine-ripened and still warm from the sun, and, above all, the fresh vegetables from the enormous vegetable garden.

My father was a vegetable snob, so peas were picked when they were hardly larger than big pinheads and also at their sweetest; lettuce, string beans, lima beans, and brussels sprouts were culled when they were barely more than gleams in the eye of Mother Nature; and the asparagus bed began to be ravaged when the first spears were still in adolescence. Even eggplant, squash, and okra were harvested as young as possible; tomatoes were the only vegetable Father considered better when fully mature.

Moreover, the "corn relay" was an almost daily ceremony throughout the season for sweet corn through all the years when we children were still fairly young. The corn relay began after sundown, or about forty-five minutes before dinnertime—7:00 P.M., when the family had no guests. My sister Corinne and I and my two brothers Stewart and John would proceed to the corn patch, bearing baskets suited to our sizes. The best ears would be pulled from the corn stalks until a basket was full. Taking turns in order of seniority, each of us would then run (no mere walking was tolerated) to the back door of our farmhouse to deliver the full baskets to the kitchen, where the ears would be rapidly shucked. The water already would be boiling in a large kettle, and four full baskets would provide enough Golden Bantam or Country Gentleman to give each member of the family, young or old, four or five ears apiece for our first course at supper. In all my life, I have never had anything better than that young sweet corn, newly snatched from the stalk, downright sugary, and slathered with fresh butter from our own dairy. All the fashionable luxury foods seem seedy by comparison.

By the standards of our Connecticut neighborhood and by modern culinary standards, too, ours was an odd table. Many of our neighbors were bewildered by our unanimous preference for all red meat on the rare side; for those were still the days when most Americans considered meat not properly cooked—and perhaps even dreadfully unhealthy—if it were not brown to its innermost depths. For modern culinary critics, meanwhile, the enormity of our breakfasts, the peculiarity of some of our favorite dishes, and our habit of eating jellies and pickles with meats of all sorts would all have caused raised eyebrows.

Breakfast was early, a habit formed when my father was still actively managing a big farming enterprise. The standard menu began with fruit, with cream and sugar for berries and peaches, plus porridge, with more heavy cream and sugar. Next came the main course, comprised of toast and muffins or thin, round cornbread cooked in pie pans, all of which were consumed with butter or jam or marmalade (always Dundee), eggs, bacon or sausage, and grilled or deviled kidneys, if there was a guest in the house. On Sundays, even if we were alone, there was always creamed liver with creamed potatoes, a horribly fattening but deliciously rustic combination if made with farm cream; and at least once a week we had poached eggs on toast buttered with anchovy paste. This last was one of several culinary oddities in the Alsop house—a Victorian hangover cure, I think—but my father loved it and passed on the taste to all his offspring. Other oddities were steamed marrow bones, to be excavated at table onto warm pieces of toast, then heavily sprinkled with paprika; a flavorsome dish known as marinated lamb, which we all preferred to the leg of lamb it came from, although the marinade made the meat as black as boot polish and highly spicy; boiled mutton with caper sauce, excellent if well cooked; boiled chicken doused in egg sauce with strips of crisp bacon, which went with rice; and other favorites of a couple of generations ago such as kedgeree, again with bacon, for lunch.

Yet even this list does not convey the full eccentricity of the customary Alsop menus; for Emma Schunck, a tiny woman but a giant in the kitchen, made a specialty of jams, jellies, and pickles, and filled whole cupboards full of strawberry and raspberry jam, grape jelly, currant jelly, green-tomato pickles, peach pickles, and other such delights. Barring the strawberry and raspberry jam (for use at the breakfast and the tea tables), each of these special preserves had a dish it went with—currant jelly with broilers, grape jelly along with mint sauce and leg of lamb, green-tomato pickles with steak and sometimes roast beef, and peach pickles (best of all) with roast ham. I suppose this mixing of sweet tastes with meat tastes was distinctly Germanic, but I should do it today if I could get the kinds of jellies and pickles our cupboards used to yield all year 'round.

In addition to the huge breakfast and a good but light lunch, there was always an afternoon tea table, including a curate's assistant containing buttered toast, cookies, or paper-thin sandwiches (the latter provided only for grand guests), and a cake made by Emma; and this ample tea was followed by dinner a couple of hours later. My parents dressed for dinner until the end of their lives, so that when my mother grew old, hers was the only house in the United States to which I always took a black tie for evening wear. Except in summer, we children did not "come down" until we reached the age of seven or eight; and when there were guests, we only "came down" after the age of thirteen, at which time we were successively provided with evening clothes of our own. The thought of those dinners bewilders me nowadays, for we nightly sat down to a first course of such things as smelts with tartar sauce or marrow bones, or else a good, cream-heavy mushroom or tomato soup or oyster stew or clam chowder. In summer, we had corn or asparagus with a roast or game (my father loved shooting), with vegetables coming next, followed by salad and cheese, and topped off with a dessert that tended to be rich and full of chocolate.

If nourishment seems to bulk large in my memories, this reflects a reality, for I have always enjoyed food, thank God, and we ate a lot at Avon. What we ate had no relation whatever to the fancier, more foreign-style food Americans have now been driven to because they can no longer get the wonderful raw materials that were the glory of good American cookery in my youth.

It can be seen, at any rate, that being "not at all well off" scarcely implied a life haunted by hunger pangs or a need for any of us to contribute to our own well-fed well-being. We were neither trained nor required to take care of ourselves in any way, except to help sometimes with fruit and vegetable harvests. This I now bitterly regret, but there is no remedy. I have made experiments; and in the kitchen I either burn myself or someone else or spill in a devastating way, and elsewhere I break whatever I touch. So I have concluded there is no substitute for early training for persons as unhandy as I am.

It must not be imagined, however, that life on the farm was grand or imposing, even though a life so amply nourished and so self-indulgently effortless seems exceptionally luxurious nowadays. The house was big and rambling, but only because the original late eighteenth-century farmhouse had been inexpensively added to by my father as the size of his family increased. The furnishings would have given severe indigestion to any modern interior decorator, for both my father and mother believed that a chair was a chair and a table was a table, with little to choose between one chair or table and another except that both had a prejudice in favor of what they called "family furniture." My father had a good deal of this, from the eighteenth and even the late seventeenth century; some of it was very fine, although all of it had been cruelly treated over the years.

There were many family portraits, too, almost all hideous works by bad artists. Some of the other family-descended objects were romantically pleasing, but there were just as many ugly things as good things in our big, oddly shaped living room, made by throwing together three smaller rooms, including the old farm kitchen. We mainly sat around the huge late eighteenth-century fireplace of the former kitchen. It was lined with slabs of red sandstone, still had its basting hook and other internal apparatus, and was flanked by intact baking ovens we used as wood boxes.

The main staircase of the house was steep and confining. Emma Schunck, who had cooked for my father before his marriage and was jealous of my mother until they got used to one another, had a way of standing at the foot of the stairs when I was on the way, murmuring gloomily in my mother's hearing, "Stairs too narrow for a coffin, too!" Similarly, the bathrooms, such as they were, were only reachable after long walks down the narrow corridor, and even the guest bedrooms were distinctly poky. None of this deterred my mother from hospitality, which she loved to dispense, but it was anything but grand hospitality by the standards of that period.

The Woodford farm was large by the standards of the day, and in that unmechanized era of American farming a good many hands were needed to work it properly. What with the cow barn, calf barn, bull barn, dairy, large tobacco fields, and big tobacco barns for drying the leaf, and several teams of cart horses, the men working for my father totaled no less than twelve and sometimes fourteen when I was a little boy, before the first tractor was acquired. Almost all of them lived on the place, in houses or apartments provided by my father; for the farm had a good many subordinate dwellings, including two big eighteenth-century roadside inns, which had been divided into apartments. Most of the men were from the northern part of Italy, where they had been recruited by my father on his wedding trip with the help of my mother, who spoke a little Italian. Their children, mostly near my own age, were my regular companions until I began going away to school. They were also splendid people, handsome, hardworking, shrewd, and given to saving money, which they invested in land in the customary way of Italian country folk with a little cash to spare.

As a result, I am proud to record, several of my childhood friends now have rather more money than I do; for their families bought land at $10 an acre, and they have sold at suburban land prices. Avon, which began as a Yankee village, became mainly an Italian village, for the friends of our men in their home villages around Lake Garda, in the mountains west of Verona, heard this was a good place and came to Avon on their own. Now it is a mixed suburban town with not one working farm left.

In its Yankee and then its Italian phases, the Avon of my youth, although only seven miles from Hartford across Talcott Mountain, was still a country village. My mother, when talking to her New York friends, referred to the town as "that distant spot." She was always full of tales of Avon's pure Yankee period. By the time I went off to Harvard, in truth, the Yankee families of Avon had largely died out, except for the Thompsons, who owned another big farm at the other end of town, and the nearly immortal Woodfords, original settlers from whose large holdings my father had acquired our farm. I can still remember being taken to call on the white-bearded Woodford patriarch, who was said to have been born not long after the War of 1812 and was proud to have voted for Abraham Lincoln. One of his descendants, Scott Woodford, a slender, wiry, leathery man with a superb, humorous Yankee twang, also lived to be nearly one hundred, having easily survived being run over by a tractor when he was close to ninety. But the Woodfords and Thompsons were exceptional. Perhaps the other Yankees of Avon did not like what they had seen of the twentieth century. At any rate, they all but ceased to reproduce themselves, like the Polynesians when the modern world abruptly entangled them.

One of my mother's tales concerned precisely this point. When I was about to be born and she was conspicuously pregnant, she once walked the mile or so to the village center. A senior Yankee matron met her on the bridge crossing the Farmington River, which divided our farm from the more populous area. Thin-lipped with disapproval, the matron took note of Mother's conspicuous pregnancy and asked whether there was any errand in the village that she could do so that Mother would not have to expose herself and her "condition" to all those curious eyes. Mother thanked her, and to change the conversation asked for news of the matron's only child, a daughter who had married about a year earlier and gone to live in New York State. "I suppose Milly must also have a baby on the way by now," said Mother brightly.

"No, Mrs. Alsop," said the matron, more thin-lipped than ever. "Why, she and her husband aren't nearly well enough acquainted for that."

Mother thought it best not to ask what "that" meant.

It always amused me to see the altogether different strategies Mother and Father used in their roles as Avon's leading citizens. Mother, being a New York girl, rumored to have fancy ways, was at first greeted with some suspicion and finally given a warm welcome because she cared greatly about other people and had a way with them. To earn the welcome, however, she made no concessions of any sort, either in dress or speech. My father, in contrast, had the odd knack of assuming a second persona. In his own circle and at our dinner table, he was a good talker, solidly educated, interested in many things, and lacking any trace of Yankee twang, although he often used some very old-fashioned turns of speech, such as "it

don't" instead of "it doesn't." Among his country neighbors, however, and when he was out and about our farm, "it ain't" was added
to "it don't," his twang resounded, and he managed a fair imperson-
ation of the true Yankee farmer with no evidence of the advantages
he had been lucky enough to have.

In part, these two were Avon's leading citizens because of their
education (my father must have been one of only two or three men
with college degrees among the Avon voters in my boyhood); because they were, if "not at all well off," at least distinctly better off
than anyone else in the Avon of those days; and because their big
house, their household, their easy hospitality, their habit of dressing
in the evening, and other such features differed sharply from the
customary ways of Avon. The differences did not create a gulf,
however, because Mother and Father cared deeply about the community that harbored them and knew how to make themselves liked
and trusted.

In the latter part of his life, when Father had dropped all other
political activities, he served as first selectman of the town. (Even the
smallest village is a town in Connecticut, providing it is self-govern-
ing; and in the old, unregenerate days of rural control of the state,
every town, however tiny, had a representative in the state legislature.) His policies were not always what is now thought of as progressive. He clung to balanced budgets with real ferocity, and he
insisted upon giving absolute priority to adequate teachers' salaries
instead of spending on grander school buildings and other less-than-
direct investments in education. As a result, the Avon school system
had one of the best records among rural communities in Connecticut—for good teachers, after all, are what chiefly matter. Furthermore, he plainly gave satisfaction to the majority of voters, for the
Democrats soon stopped running candidates against him when election time came. The loyal Italian block customarily referred to him
as "the Padrone," and he ran without opposition for his last twenty
years in office.

As for my mother, she joined the movement for women's suf-
frage somewhat reluctantly, but she was elected town chairman of
the Republicans of Avon in no time after the women got the vote,
and thereafter she, rather than my father, had the task of cultivating
our small political vineyard. Roads, schools, poor relief, and the like,
and presiding over town meetings were my father's sphere. My
mother's sphere was keeping in constant touch with the voters and
getting out the largest vote she could every Election Day. Mother
was one of the few absolutely hardheaded female political realists I
have met in the course of a long life.

Two of the others were Mother's two very different close

friends and first cousins—Mrs. Franklin Roosevelt, whose rather ostentatious high-mindedness merely masked her realism, and Alice Roosevelt Longworth, who positively disliked high-mindedness. Until the day she died, Mother could call the Avon vote within 10 either way and the Connecticut vote in any statewide election within less than 3,000 either way.

Mother's greatest triumph as a realist perhaps deserves recounting here, since it is a story that casts a curious light on both persons principally concerned. As a young newspaperman on election night of 1936, I covered the events at the Roosevelt home in Hyde Park, New York. Although the senior Mrs. Roosevelt was most reluctant to do anything of the sort, the president's mother was persuaded to invite all those accompanying the president—all the president's staff members, advisers, and Secret Service guards, plus all the newspapermen, radio correspondents, and even photographers, roughly fifty people, if you can imagine a presidential party so small—to have supper at the big house and wait there for the election returns.

I have described this curious and nostalgic scene elsewhere, so it will be enough to set down what happened when all of us were invited into the rather small dining room at about 9:30 P.M. to congratulate the president on his smashing victory. Three press tickers still clattered away in a corner; the whole floor was deep in discarded ticker copy; and the president, Stephen Early, and Marvin McIntyre had big piles of particularly significant slips of ticker copy before their places at the fully extended dining-room table. As the line moved toward the president's place at the head of the table, I happened to notice a mere sliver of ticker copy placed separately, next to his own big pile. I offered my congratulations with the joy I felt, and the president accepted them delightedly, but he delayed me until he had reached over for the sliver of ticker copy and handed it to me. "How will Corinne like that?" he asked in a tone of triumph.

I glanced at the slip with great surprise and found it announced that formerly Republican Avon had changed its politics to give the president a comfortable majority. Hence, I had to reply in all honesty that my mother, the Corinne in question, would certainly not like it a bit. But still the president had not done savoring his victory, for he greatly minded the plain, inescapable fact that almost all his Roosevelt relations and friends of his youth—my mother was both—remained aggressively loyal Republicans despite his own presence in the White House. He told me there was a telephone in the hall and instructed me to call my mother at once and find out for him how "Corinne is taking it." So I went to the pay telephone booth, which Mrs. James Roosevelt had installed because she was convinced her son's presidential staff members were making long-distance calls charged to her own number.

Within a few seconds, I was speaking to Mother only to discover, to my complete bewilderment, that she sounded a bit tipsy. (Unlike her two cousins Alice Longworth and Eleanor Roosevelt, Mother was not a teetotaler, but she never had more than a single drink before dinner, an old-fashioned, which she liked very sweet. Furthermore, all three cousins shared the same horror of alcoholism, born of the fact that almost all their male relations, except Mother's father and the two Roosevelt presidents, ended as alcoholics—before my own generation came along.) When I repeated to her the president's message, she replied belligerently, "Joe, you can hear I'm drunk; don't pretend you can't because I know you can—and no wonder! I've spent two whole weeks going to every Italian house in Avon, showing how to vote a split ticket. I knew what was coming, and there wasn't any other way. Furthermore, you know how hospitable they always are, and how it's thought rude if you don't have something to eat and a whole glass of red wine in each house. So I've been overfed and drunk for a fortnight. But you can tell Franklin that all the Italians did split their tickets, so we still sent Mr. Woodford to the state legislature by just as good a majority as Franklin got for the presidency."

Later, I duly reported my mother's message to the president, who roared with laughter and commented, "I knew Corinne was a professional," as indeed she was.

When I was a boy, Avon, as I have said, was really a country and farming village. By then, to be sure, the future was already in preparation, although no one foresaw that the internal combustion engine would make Connecticut into a land of cities and suburbs and superhighways with second- and third-growth forest filling up all the chinks. This happened because so many Connecticut farms were abandoned to the wild when there were no more horses in New York, Providence, and Boston to consume the hay that had been a main Connecticut farm crop. Yet soon after Mother got her asthmatic Model T in 1914, the first change began. The old rocky, winding, barely motorable road over Talcott Mountain was much improved so that the drive to Hartford, seven miles away over the mountain, took no more than half an hour instead of two hours; and our ritual isolation began to fade.

This did not happen all at once, however, so I remember the old ways very well indeed. Oddly enough, this helped me greatly to understand President Johnson more than half a century later. I had long since observed that Lyndon B. Johnson was the last frontiersman in American politics. (In fact, he was our very last frontier president as well as the first we had since Abraham Lincoln and Andrew Johnson.) Hence, I did not tremble when President Johnson first inherited the White House and everyone else trembled with shock and horror because the new president regularly took his male luncheon guests for a swim in the White House indoor pool without bathing suits and was rumored to have chatted at length with members of his staff while seated on the presidential toilet. I assumed that sociability in backhouses and everyone plunging naked into the swimming hole reserved for men were both perfectly natural along the Pedernales River. Certainly they were both natural along the Farmington River until I was ten or twelve. In my boyhood, several of our neighbors still had backhouses instead of indoor plumbing, and Avon had a particularly fine men's swimming hole about a hundred yards above the bridge across the river, where all went in naked without regard to age.

Throughout the hot weather—and it can be oven hot in the beautiful Farmington river valley at any time from early June until late in September—most of the male population of Avon went to the swimming hole every fine evening when the day's work was done. The swimmers ranged from five years old to upward of eighty. There might be three score of them on a good evening; and all left their clothes in heaps under the wide-branched willows on the bank and went in together where the river had a long patch of sandy bottom. The sand was a bit slimy since the Farmington River was then a light coffee color from pollution, but no one gave a thought to that.

On our farm, one of the farm wagons waited for swimmers after work every hot summer afternoon unless it was raining, and as soon as I, at seven, had learned to swim, I climbed aboard the wagon with the rest. I loved this type of casual swimming. I loved the coolness at the end of the afternoon and enjoyed swimming in company, a habit reinforced during the long summers spent at Henderson, my mother's family's estate near the town of Herkimer on the lip of the Mohawk valley in upstate New York.

The "pond" there had been built at great cost in the 1840s by an eccentric uncle who wished, as he put it, "an eye in the landscape." He therefore built an enormously high dam straight across a wooded ravine. The resulting pool was forty feet deep and fed by cold mountain springs, with a raft on one shore for entering and another in mid-pond for resting. Every morning before luncheon, Grandmother Robinson, wearing a large garden-party hat, a voluminous black silk dress and black silk stockings that covered both her legs and arms, would set off in a stately breaststroke and swim the length of the pond twice. In stark contrast to Avon, I would be made to wear one of the all-covering bathing suits men used at the time and was taught to swim by Courtney the chauffeur, who tied a rope around my waist and sat on the bank playing me like a salmon at the end of the line.

Such were the limits of my swimming instruction, and for all their odd ingenuity one of the things I regret about my boyhood was that I never learned how to swim or do anything else of that sort really well. I suppose my mother and father felt that omitting expenditures for children's riding lessons, tennis lessons, swimming lessons, and the like was sensible for those "not at all well off." The young could be expected to learn these things without paid instruction. This was no doubt true in my mother's and father's youth, when horses were the only means of transportation except for walking or taking a train. And swimming, tennis, golf, and other sports were all in fairly primitive stages of development. I never learned to be secure on a horse or to progress beyond Courtney's preferred technique in swimming—or to perform respectably in any other sport, for that matter.

This was another reason that I not only started as a plump, unathletic child, but soon became a fat and even less athletic boy. And although I often went out and about the farm and up onto Talcott Mountain with my brothers and sister and Italian friends, my preferred refuge after I learned to read was a large chair in our living room, the walls of which were lined with a richly but eccentrically stocked library.

My first favorite, improbably enough, was Bret Harte, a late nineteenth-century American to whom I had been originally attracted, I suspect, by the handsome red-leather binding of my parents' wedding-present edition. By the time I was much past eight, I must have read my favorite Bret Harte story "Maruja" often enough to quote the text almost by heart. But I glanced at it again the other day—for I now own that wedding-present edition—and I found "Maruja" all but unreadable. My family never seemed to care much what I read, even if my choices from our many books were of a character then usually thought unsuitable for the very young. Both Father and Mother cared greatly, however, about introducing us to all the books they regarded as classics for boys and girls.

My father read to his children every evening for half an hour or more before dressing for dinner—and with surprising dramatic emphasis for so unstagy a man. With Father, we successively got through *The Wind in the Willows*, Lewis Carroll's *Alice* books, and

The Hunting of the Snark (from which I can still quote), followed by large doses of Kipling. A good deal more followed, including several former classics now in obscurity, like Lucretia Hale's *The Peterkin Papers*, which ought not to be forgotten, and Thackeray's *The Rose and the Ring*, which bored us all a little even then. Thus my father had the principal responsibility for making reading the main private refuge for all his children.

With Mother, meanwhile, we also read a lot on a more random pattern, and she gave us a long Bible lesson every Sunday afternoon. She concentrated on the Old Testament, which she knew backward and forward, on the theory that we would all be exposed to the New Testament in school. She was dead right, and all four of us enjoyed her Bible lessons because she had a wonderful knack for making us feel the glory of the prose and for bringing to life the Old Testament's often-bloodstained stories. The blood did not bother Mother in the least; and I can still recite by heart the terrible chapter in Kings about the death of Jezebel and how she was eaten by the dogs in the streets of Jezreel, save only "the skull, and the feet, and the palms of her hands."

I am further convinced that one of the many true shames of modern American education is the simple fact that most people now grow up without so much as a nodding acquaintance with the King James Bible, which I have long thought of as the most beautiful and rewarding single book in the English language. As I have approached eighty, I have wanted to begin going to church regularly once more because I now find church moving and rewarding (my brother John says, "It's really for insurance at over seventy"); but I cannot do so because there seems to be no church in Washington that regularly uses the King James version of the Bible or the magnificently lovely old Episcopal prayer book. I commit the sin of anger and am out of temper for the rest of the day if I hear the language of the Bible—which, in fact, is the prose of the incomparable Lancelot Andrewes—castrated by trendy revisions.

As for the rest of my education, I got most of it at home, just as I learned at home to read and to love reading. Part was acquired in the library in the way I have described. Some was also picked up from an Edwardian compendium called *The Book of Knowledge*, a perfect hodgepodge of information about everything from Assyrian and Egyptian history to astronomy and geography, which I wish I could buy today for my godchildren. I found the entire compendium (many volumes long) unfailingly fascinating, perhaps because there are few subjects I have not enjoyed learning about.

Another part of my education came from listening to adults, for we children were almost always at the luncheon table, always in the circle around the tea table, and, after the age of eight, always at our parents' dinner table except on party nights; as I have said, we were not thought acceptable for dinner parties until we were equipped to dress for dinner. Mother and Father had innumerable friends, most of whom were amusing or interesting or both, and both my sister and I became close to a whole series of aunts and uncles; for Corinne and I were more often quartered with relatives than the younger boys, when their turn came.

Finally, I went to school, of course, first to a one-room school-house then still in use for the Avon children on our side of the Farmington River. Then, when I was eight, I was sent to Kingwood School in Hartford (to which I was transported each morning on our farm's milk truck). Finally, at thirteen, I was sent to Groton, where my father had also gone. But although I was a good scholar and got through my schoolwork with unvarying ease, I remember little of those early school days, for the center of my sheltered little world was my family and that long-ago farmhouse in Avon, Connecticut.

3

Schooling

A s I look back on myself at the age of thirteen, when I went off to Groton School, I can't help but feel an instant revulsion. I was overweight, physically timid, and had not the dimmest idea of how to get on with my contemporaries. Because my father and mother were rather vague about those matters, I was even dressed in a way that caused shock among the other boys I first met at Groton. To encourage native industries, for example, my father had bought a bolt of Connecticut homespun, a grey, rasping, woolen material, very close indeed to what was then worn by the less pretentious liveried chauffeurs; and from this came my best suit.

I had been brought up until the age of thirteen in a way that was almost insanely unconventional by the standards of the boys I went to Groton with. I had gone to a good day school in Hartford—on my father's milk truck. For base, I had my family's farm, and I cannot recollect a single other Groton boy in those early days who really lived in the country. They might live in the pseudo-country inhabited by the rich and very rich; but the real country, where farmers actually worked their own farms, was unknown to them. The families of the sort of people who sent their sons to Groton

were headed by bankers and lawyers and other professional men—
or indeed by people who were just very rich—but in general by men
in situations of leverage in the economic world of the United States.

Then, on top of that, my mother's family place, Henderson, in
northern New York, on a high rock shelf looking north over the
glorious Mohawk valley, was about as eccentric a summer resort as
you could find by taking a complete census of Groton School. I
could tell a hundred stories about Henderson, for I loved the house
very much and often think about it to this day. Essentially, it was an
imitation of an English country place, housed in a pseudo-Scottish
baronial castle. The interior was late Regency—and I mean late
English Regency, for that was its approximate date. There was
nothing lonely about it because my wonderful and extraordinarily
hospitable grandmother kept the huge old house and its several de-
pendencies full from the start of summer to Labor Day. Only a mile
and a half away from Henderson, too, was the big house of my
uncle, my mother's eldest brother, Theodore Douglas Robinson,
which was called Mahaqua—and it, too, was full of guests.

From my standpoint, life at Henderson had only one flaw. It
made me feel like a poor relation, which in fact I was in those days.
Later, with the exception of my remarkable cousin Dorothy Kidder,
my mother's family came pretty close to total shipwreck mainly on
account of the fatal gene that caused a high percentage of them to
become drunkards. But they were remarkably glossy and successful-
seeming, as I remember them in my pre-Groton years, and their
haughtiness—or at least the haughtiness of my cousin Douglas—
caused me a good deal of anguish each summer.

I still remember two symbols of Mahaqua from that time. One
is the vision of my slightly older first cousin Douglas Robinson,
lithe, handsome, patronizing, and superior, mounted on a splendid
and spirited horse, looking down upon me with an understandable
sneer. The other is of Mahaqua "Sunday Stables," as it was called.
After the crash of 1929, this exhibition had to be given up, but to me
it now seems so odd that it begs a brief description.

Mahaqua had a huge stable lined with shining yellow wood,
with all the horses—and there must have been sixteen or so—in
separate loose boxes. Before Sunday Stables came lunch at Mahaqua—always the same lunch, which appeared on I-don't-know-
how-many Sunday luncheon tables of the WASP rich in those days.
Because we were too far from the shore to have oyster stew, first
came cream of mushroom soup, made with real cream and a proper
duxelle of mushrooms. This was followed by a huge roast of beef
with Yorkshire pudding, roast potatoes, mustard pickles, and small

green peas or string beans; and that course was invariably followed with homemade vanilla ice cream, again made with thick country cream, with a chocolate sauce that all but congealed into fudge when it was poured on the ice cream. I loved the lunch, but I didn't much like Stables, which followed, because I was afraid of horses, as I was of a great many other things.

All the same, the Mahaqua stables were something to see. Barker, my uncle's short, jolly, rotund English head groom, was very proud of his horses and his stables, and used to spend the winter, when he had little work except exercising the horses, making yard upon yard upon yard of an extraordinarily pretty, decorative garland composed of golden-ripe wheat ears woven together with woolen ribbons—blue and yellow, since these were my uncle's racing colors. Every loose box was decorated with many yards of this extraordinary garland, with extra sheafs of golden wheat in the ear at intervals. Each horse—and they were very fine, alarmingly spirited horses—was also got ready for the occasion the way English nannies used to get children ready to bring down for tea. They were brushed and curry-combed until every one positively shone with beauty and health, and in addition to this and solely for this brief occasion, each horse had its hooves shined with a substance known as dubbin.

The object of Stables was to praise Barker, admire the general scene, be impressed by the horses, and feed the favorites lumps of sugar. I was far too fearful that the horse would take my hand off instead of accepting the lump of sugar, and it always took a dreadful effort of courage to give the sugar to whichever horse my uncle Teddy chose for my patronage. At any rate, this was not the kind of occasion that persuaded a fattish little boy from a working farm in Avon, Connecticut, where there were no horses except farm horses, that we were quite on a par with my uncle's family or that I was fit to compete with my cousin Douglas, who was so outstandingly good at everything I could not do well, if at all.

Even in his youth, Douglas was not a particularly nice fellow, containing more than a grain of the man of the future, whose life, to my knowledge, never really touched another life without bringing some form of destruction to it. But in those days, the tragedies that overtook my uncle Teddy and aunt Helen and their family were far in the future. What was in the present was that my cousin Douglas Robinson was a gilded young man whom I could only envy without imitating; that Avon and our working farm had none of the gilding of Mahaqua; that, in short, I and mine would be poor relations forever.

There were other odd rituals from that Henderson of long ago worth remembering here. It was, for example, the only big American house I know of where Sunday-night prayers were held. My grandmother, in order to continue the prayers that had been the rule at Henderson since 1835 or so, had had to make a sort of concordat with the Catholic bishop of Herkimer because the household staff, which had been Scotch Presbyterian, had become Irish Catholic by force of changing immigration patterns. Every Sunday after a very jolly dinner, chairs were carted into the big hall, and prayers were duly held with sixty or more people in attendance. Guests and family sat at one end of the room, and "people in the house and people on the place" sat facing them, like two antiphonal choirs of sheep and goats. Because most of the farm workers had been Methodists in earlier days, the Moody and Sankey hymnal was used; and there were special hymns for special days and special persons—"Yield Not to Temptation for Yielding Is Sin" was always archly sung, for instance, for the most perfectly blameless of all Grandmother Robinson's male friends. As the eldest male grandchild, I pumped the large, creaky organ, and after Grandfather died, our uncle Teddy Robinson, as "head of the family," had the job of reading a selection from a particularly bleak book of sermons that had been used for Henderson prayers since the mid-nineteenth century.

Since Henderson prayers were always followed by two vast simultaneous and especially riotous parties, one above stairs and one below, they probably did not contribute very greatly to our moral welfare. But to this day, when I chance to hear the old hymn "God Be with Us till We Meet Again," which was always sung on the last Sunday evening of the Henderson summer, I cannot repress a choky feeling.

One more such reminiscence is all I dare allow myself. In brief, whoever was the parlor-maid-in-chief at Henderson was always required to learn to play two tunes on a xylophonelike arrangement of brass bells that hung on a frame in the pantry. The first tune was "The Bonnets of Bonny Dundee." This served to warn people that they had better go upstairs, take their baths, and dress for dinner— for even at Henderson, a thousand miles from nowhere, we wore dinner jackets in the evening. As for the second tune, it was "The Campbells Are Coming," and this one was the announcement that cocktail hour had ended and that dinner was ready to serve. Mary Delaney, the wonderful parlor-maid-in-chief for all the years that I remember Henderson, used to be a master hand at both tunes and was also a genius with a large conch shell, which, for some lunatic reason, was always blown at the front door when guests were leaving Henderson.

As I think about it now, Henderson, despite the dark patches,

still seems a wonderfully rich and rare passage in my past. I loved it.
But when I went to Groton, it became a handicap—first, to feel I
was a poor relation; second, to feel I was somehow inferior because
horses inspired me with terror; and, third, to feel, above all, that we
Alsops were sadly different from everyone else because the sort of
people who went to Groton in those days either spent their summers abroad in Europe or went to the half-dozen well-known East
Coast summer resorts.

All of this, in retrospect, seems to me comically illustrative of
the foolish lengths to which the young can carry the desire to be like
everybody else. After all, Henderson was a huge old house, larger by
far than the houses inhabited by all but the richest of my Groton
contemporaries. Its interiors, if they had survived, would also cause
any one of the new breed of fashionable New York decorators to
come close to apoplexy with excitement, for my mother's clan favored family portraits as a form of wallpaper and had an enormous
accumulation of very good old family furniture. Indeed, the place
bulged with oddities, like President Monroe's White House waffle
iron with the president's seal carved into it. All the bedrooms and
halls had tartan carpeting first imported a century earlier from a tiny
mill in Scotland, which fortunately went on and on turning out this
peculiar material. In all, Henderson was pretty as well as romantic
and rather grand—as my Groton contemporaries found it later,
when I asked one or two of them there. The trouble was that it was
utterly unlike anything that the families of any of my contemporaries had in the year 1923, and both Henderson and my father's
farm were also far, far distant from the usual playgrounds where
other boys at Groton had formed their friendships with one another.

In consequence, I went to Groton in 1923 with only a single
friend, Richard M. Bissell, whose father ran a big insurance company in Hartford. The Bissells had only recently left Hartford for
the Farmington valley. Mrs. Bissell, a most wonderful woman, was a
close friend of my mother; and before I went to Groton, I used to see
a great deal of Dick when transport permitted (we lived about six
miles apart). Dick was and is one of the truly remarkable people I
have known, but when he was young he was also one of the most
domineering people I have ever known. His friendship provided a
sufficient refuge for me during my first year at Groton. But I date
my own real independent existence from October 1924, the autumn
of my year as a Groton third-former, when I declared my independence of Dick—or anyone else.

This was a bold thing to do, given the character of Groton in
those days. Although the Massachusetts school was still among the

newest of its kind in the country, the atmosphere, which purposely followed the proper Anglican pattern of such English public schools as Harrow and Eton, was both rigid and rarified to an almost stifling degree. In my father's day—and he belonged to one of the very first troops of Groton boys—Groton School drew a very large proportion of its students from the wealthiest families of New England and, to a lesser degree, New York. By my time, this trend toward a proper kind of money and a proper kind of style was even more pronounced, although the school's awe-inspiring founder, Dr. Endicott Peabody, did his level best to drill his boys in the gentlemen's values of sport, religion, and learning. The result was a fiercely rarified and homogeneous environment in which obedience and conformity were commended by one's teachers as well as by one's peers. Independence, in almost any form, was punished.

It is easy to forget that the young often are much more snobbish than their parents. At any rate, the young at Groton were snobbish to a particularly nasty degree, and their judgments were chiefly based on the outward aspects of their contemporaries. It was a general rule at the Groton of those days (and may still be so today, for all I know) that boys who were badly overweight, had spots, were totally unathletic, and ridiculously ill-turned-out were unlikely to win any school popularity contests. I, therefore, had done the opposite of winning a popularity contest in my first year at boarding school.

Indeed, the only asset I had—and this was no social asset at all—was to be good at my studies and a passionate devourer of the books in the large school library. How little this helped my standing not just among the other boys but in the school as a whole can be guessed from a story told by my mother. When she delivered me to the school campus in the autumn of my first year, Mother sought for her son a personal introduction to Dr. Peabody, who had been fond of my father when he was at Groton and was an old family friend. However, when she at last found the headmaster, she went on, in the embarrassing way proud mothers do, about the precocity of my reading habits. Dr. Peabody, whom everyone referred to as "the Rector," apparently was suspicious of precocious reading habits. After my mother had discoursed too long about my bookishness, the Rector, who, on the day all the new boys arrived, was regularly besieged by concerned parents, said firmly: "That's all right, Corinne, we'll soon knock all that out of him."

I am not conscious that any effort was ever made to "knock all that out of me" at Groton. Clearly, though, my independent reading habits were of little social value in the clannish, brittle world I was entering. Since the only friend I had at Groton was Dick Bissell, my declaration of absolute independence from him was, therefore, a serious step. This meant that I abandoned any form of human company except semihostile human company throughout the autumn and winter terms of my second year there. A Groton winter term is grim under the best of circumstances. A Groton winter term without human company was grim beyond imagining. So those few months were a desolate and lonely period; indeed, it was the only time I'd ever thought seriously of taking my own life. I decided in the end, however, that it would be better to try to remedy the basic cause of my despair, which was, quite simply, friendlessness. I, therefore, set out to make friends—at first simply by making jokes, which, for understandable reasons, is always easier for those who are fat or physically awkward.

The sequel illustrated a rule that ought to be hammered into the heads of all shy or fearful young people. It is that those other young people like to make friends, although friendship, on the whole, requires effort. By the end of that spring at Groton, I had learned this lesson, and consequently I had exchanged my formerly solitary life for a happy new condition in which I was beginning to make all sorts of new friends. It was a lesson I would carry with me to college and on into my adult life. In the main, sociability is a knack; but it is also partly a skill, to be learned and cultivated like any other. Therefore, friendship returned is almost invariably equal to friendship given. Over the years, assiduous attention to this rule has been one of the happy constants of my life. It has provided me with a long and rich vein of sustenance and security, not to mention, in my later years, close to thirty godchildren.

I don't know that I got the best out of my years at Groton. I managed to elude anything dimly resembling an athletic program through five continuous years, although athletics were put on a par with studies by the school. I also managed to add five additional years to the four years I had already given to the study of Latin, but without learning to read Latin one-tenth as well as I could read French after four years of Groton's quite admirable French teaching. Barring the classical languages, in fact, the school had a splendid academic program, and I was a good student. The school never interfered with my independent reading either, just as long as I didn't talk about it to anyone; so I went ahead, perfectly cheerfully, with my private program of reading everything I could and making all the friends I could.

From the very beginning at Groton, I did well academically. Term after term, the future mayor of Albany Erastus Corning and I

would divide first place in our form. All the same, when it came time
to choose a university, my success at making friends proved the
deciding factor. Yale was my family university. Both my father and
grandfather had gone there, and although it was unsaid, I was expected to follow them to New Haven. But the majority of my most
admired friends at Groton decided on Harvard. So I asked Father
and Mother for permission to go with my classmates, and permission was readily granted.

I am glad my parents let me go to Harvard, but I cannot say
that I think my formal college education did an enormous amount
for me. Partly by fluke and partly because of my insatiable reading, I
had achieved a perfect score of 100 on my English college entrance
examination. This was a feat so without precedent in those days that
it caused the Rector to declare, in my honor, a half holiday for the
boys at Groton School. My perfect English score was not without
its damaging side, however. In the first place, it caused the English
Department at Harvard to expect much too much of me. This expectation no doubt also had something to do with my worst decision
upon entering Harvard, which was to take English as my major
subject.

With one or two exceptions, especially the late Bernard De
Voto's course in creative writing, I am afraid I don't think that my
Harvard English courses taught me a great deal. It was valuable to
read the texts that the courses required with the care that they demanded. But I was already a genuinely serious reader and the texts I
was assigned to read in my English courses at Harvard were, with
rare exception, already on the curious mental list I had brought with
me to Cambridge—a mental list of everything I had convinced myself a man must be familiar with in order to be able to claim to be an
"educated gentleman."

The very phrase "educated gentleman" makes my flesh crawl
today, for it shows how callow I was and how snobbish was the little
world I came from. All the same, the mental list was not a bad thing.
French was my only other language; and, in addition to all the
English texts, I solemnly read my way through all the great French
texts, except Rabelais and, of course, parts of Balzac. I found Rabelais boring, probably because I was too young to understand it, and
reading *all* of Balzac is not an undergraduate's assignment. Nevertheless, for example, I read all Montaigne's essays with delight and
with a benefit I hope endures to this day; and I even read an enchanting pornographic novelist, Crébillon fils, who got away with publishing *Le Sopha, La Nuit et le moment,* and *Le Hazard du coin du feu*
because he was in the happy situation of official literary censor to

Louis XV and could, therefore, give himself the needed licenses to print his own frothy (and profitable) pornography.

I believe I would have completed my reading program at Harvard whether or not I had concentrated in English. The amount of French I plowed through—all of Corneille, Racine, and Molière, and all of Proust twice over, for instance—suggests that I would not have given up the great Englishmen any more than I gave up the great Frenchmen. I was helped by being a natural speed reader. Therefore, I wish I had chosen history instead of English. The kind of history taught at Harvard in those days is no longer fashionable, although I must say I grow nostalgic about it when I see what passes for rigorous intellectual standard in the history departments at too many modern American universities. Concentrating in history would have forced me to give serious study to a whole series of vital historical texts that I have now read only in bits and pieces and in a disorderly manner. History would have served, too, as a strict intellectual discipline in a way that studying English could not.

However, the choice of history as an undergraduate major probably would not have made any immediate difference to my overall intellectual makeup, for I do not think, as I look back, that reading was my most important activity at Harvard. Startling as this may seem, I would put eating, drinking, and chatting higher than other, more studious pursuits. This is partly because I believe strongly that undergraduates ought to seize their chance at university to have the last relatively unfettered good time that their lives are likely to provide.

In my case, however, this unfettered pursuit of pleasure went a good deal further than usual. Even after the anxieties of my Groton days, the consciousness of being a poor relation and the sense of somehow being out of step had by no means been overcome. All these crippling doubts and petty inferiorities still afflicted me in what now seems to me a ridiculous and grossly disproportionate degree throughout my first year at Harvard. It was the beginning of my second liberation when the undergraduate club I wished to join, the Porcellian, offered to take me in at the end of the first semester of my sophomore year.

I no longer approve of what the undergraduate clubs were and stood for at Harvard in my time, although it seems to me social blue-nosery to blame the clubs for not being egalitarian. The trouble with the Porcellian Club was not that it was far from egalitarian or even that it was capable of being extremely snobbish. (The snobbishness was at least picturesquely old-fashioned. Franklin Roosevelt, as history knows, was not asked to join the club, a blow that cut him deeply. I believe I was put on the list-for-consideration because my several-times great-grandfather was the first undergraduate marshal of the club—although how anyone discovered this fact, wholly unknown to me at the time, I cannot imagine.) My club's trouble, rather, was that as a social institution it was in danger of becoming wholly out of date without knowing it. Indeed, the Porcellian, in those days, was *the* undergraduate citadel of what I have called the WASP Ascendancy at Harvard, and the first crack of doom for the WASP Ascendancy had already sounded before the huge February dinner at which I was taken into the P.C.

This dinner took place in February 1930, only a few months after the great stock-market crash. In my callow, protected state, I was only dimly aware of the crash and of its gloomy economic ramifications. On that particular evening, I was more horrified by the fact that new members of the club were required to attend the February dinner in a special costume—dressed as riding jockeys. I nearly burst out of the ridiculous turnout I had been given because it was much too small for me. Add to the physical discomfort the total strangeness of the occasion; then add further that because I was remotely connected to him by marriage, I was told off to look after my very grand cousin Nicholas Longworth, who was then Speaker of the House of Representatives.

Nick Longworth was a brilliantly witty and worldly man with a talent for conviviality and the constitution of a horse. I remember him buying no less than nine bottles of champagne to drink and share with friends between the time of my assignment to him, early that evening, and his departure in a sleeping car on the old Federal to Washington, after sitting through the interminable Sunday lunch the next day, which was (and is) called the "February Breakfast." I was astonished when I finally opened my eyes at about four o'clock on Monday afternoon and read in the papers that the Speaker of the House had gotten off the Federal in time to report to President Hoover for a White House breakfast discussion of the farm problem.

That Porcellian dinner and the breakfast that followed it were unforgettable scenes partly because I never saw anything like them again. To begin with, what made them essentially different from the many later February dinners and breakfasts I attended was the clear evidence it provided of the WASP Ascendancy's still dominant role in American life. In attendance at that 1930 Porcellian gathering were the Speaker of the House, the governor of Massachusetts Leverett Saltonstall, one or two others prominent in national politics, and a gathering of men who were among the leaders of the financial world—the Whitney brothers, for example. Mr. George Whitney was then the best-known active senior partner at J. P. Morgan, at the time the most powerful bank in the world. For Mr. Richard Whitney, of course, Sing Sing prison still lay far in the future; instead, in 1930, he was the powerful president of the New York Stock Exchange and had just made the famous bid for the United States Steel Corporation, a bid that was wrongly supposed to have stopped the Depression in its tracks.

There were a great many other, older graduate members at the dinner, too. All of them appeared distinguished, and a number actually were. As impressive as the assemblage of humanity was the simple sight of the dinner itself. The Porcellian Club had a reputation of being very expensive for its young members, although the reputation was utterly false. The club carried a substantial endowment; undergraduates paid no dues, and there was no subscription except fifty dollars for books for the library, which was enormous though unread. All through the nineteenth and early twentieth centuries, moreover, the club's innumerable better-than-well-off members had a habit of giving the club presents of all kinds, some quite startlingly lavish.

However, anyone witnessing the February dinner of those days would have come away with the impression that the Porcellian was a high-priced club indeed. To start with, the club maintained its own very pretty porcelain from Paris, plain white with a green band around it and the club's boar's-head crest in the middle, for slightly more than four hundred people; and, for the same number, a matching set of agreeably plain flat silver, again with the club's crest. Then the huge gridiron of tables in the banqueting hall must have carried several tons of ornamental silver—nearly life-sized silver pigs, vast candelabra, punch bowls, and the like. I later discovered that Harry Meyers, the club's ageless steward, always got in four or five extra men about a week before each February dinner for the sole purpose of silver polishing. And then the food itself, though not elaborate, was delicious, and the tables seemed nearly to sag under the weight of illegal (and, therefore, expensive) champagne bottles, which all the older members ordered in large numbers.

Breakfast the next day was even better than the dinner. Sunday was bright and sunny; the rooms in which the breakfast was held were far more pleasant than the big dinner room; there were well over a hundred present out of the original four hundred odd; and those who came to breakfast were obviously those who were especially determined to have a good time. At neither meal, moreover, did that good time consist of drunken conversation. Instead, dinner was organized as big men's dinners are organized in early nine-

teenth-century English novels, with the equivalent of a "Mr. Chairman" to keep order as the proceedings unfolded. For through the
meal and beyond, club members either asked, or were called upon,
to voice a repertoire of songs and recitations reaching back over the
years, very nearly from the P.C.'s founding in 1691. These odd
performances seemed more and more wonderful as one glass of
champagne followed the next.

There were sea chanteys from the clipper-ship years and eighteenth-century drinking songs; there was what must have been the
earliest version of the best song of our early Wild West, "The
Streets of Laredo," which to my vast surprise had been sung in the
Porcellian by a certain Mr. Mudge in 1870. There were other bal-
lads, redolent of the American past, like the one—said to have originated in Appalachia—that effectively belonged to Chip Bohlen and
his family, with its pretty refrain: "For to see the waters glistening,
hear the nightingales sing." There were wonderfully funny pre–
First World War music-hall songs, of which I best remember my
great friend Bill Patten's favorite offering, "Petticoats for Women."
The tune was strongly pro-petticoat and contained the immortal
lines concerning the happy period when women wore numerous,
voluminous, lacy petticoats: "They could get on top of buses looking lovely from beneath—just like something bubbly frothing over
upside down!"

There were also old prose recitations, which used to be a peculiarly American comic specialty, as the writer and historian Bernard
De Voto once told me. They tended either to be highly stylized
accounts of the more acutely dangerous trades of the early nineteenth century, such as whaling, or old political satires that may
have been heavy-handed in their own time but had gained a special
patina with age. The one I remember best seems to have dated from
before the Civil War. The theme was the corrupting influence of
luxury, compared with the invigorating effects of the hard life. The
form used was that of a very flossily ornate speech in the Arkansas
House of Representatives, and I have never forgotten one rhetorical
question and its answer: "I ask you, Sir, *where was Andrew Jackson* at
the Battle of New Orleens? *Up to his ass in blood,* Sir, that's where he
was." Nor have I forgotten the grand finale: "Change the name of
Arkansaw to Arkansas! No, goddamit, Sirs, not while red blood
flows in the men of Arkansaw!"

There was much else about the Porcellian Club that brought
back the American past besides these curious dinners. In the 1860
catalogue, the very year Abraham Lincoln was elected president, the
last of the rich southern planters to attend Harvard, Charles Alston

Pringle of Charleston, South Carolina, appears cheek by jowl with Robert Gould Shaw, leader of the Massachusetts Fifty-fourth, the famous black regiment that fought for the North in the Civil War. Then, in the class of 1861, a member of the Hallowell clan who served as an officer under Shaw appears also, along with the future justice Oliver Wendell Holmes, who was the most famous of all the Civil War heroes from the WASP Ascendancy. (The ascendancy was, as a matter of fact, far from universally in favor of the war because many of its members had important business interests in the South.) The catalogue of Porcellian members includes many who made the big money during and after the Civil War alongside the sons of families from the earliest times who were still keeping their noses above water. A grandson of a signer of the Declaration of Independence, the third and last of the Charles Carrolls of Carrollton, for instance, was in the class of 1887.

Not all my classmates responded in this sentimental way to the Porcellian Club's evocation of the American past. At any rate, these were not the club's major pleasures. Friendship obviously was paramount. Indeed, this was the time in my life when I began to make friends easily—not as a feat to prove to myself that I *could* make friends, but simply because I cared about and admired the friends I made.

I suppose Franz Colloredo-Mansfeld, half Austrian, half American, and one of the two or three men I have thought most highly of in my whole life, was the friend from the Porcellian I cherished most. Franz was both exceedingly intelligent and dashing. He volunteered for the RAF as soon as the Hitler war began. After a tour as a fighter pilot, he was made captain of a Spitfire squadron operating over the English Channel; and without regard to the RAF rule that one tour leading a squadron was duty enough and duty well done, he stayed with his squadron through three tours. He was brought down over the channel on his last scheduled flight just before the Normandy landing. Soon after the war, Bill Patten and his wife Susan Mary—my own future wife—found Colly's grave in a village cemetery on the French channel coast.

The other aspect of my Harvard experience I look back on with delight I can only describe as a sort of special WASP chic (it sounds remarkably silly, but I can think of no other word). Even if one was not an usher at a spring wedding, for instance, it was de rigueur to wear a white linen waistcoat with one's blue suit. And to this day, my idea of heaven is to dress in my best garments for a wedding, sit at a table of pleasant friends, and drink champagne in an apple orchard under a New England June sun. It sounds materialistic, but perhaps it is slightly less so than the definition of heaven written by Sydney Smith, my hero of the early nineteenth century who was, after all, a clergyman and a canon of St. Paul's Cathedral. He said that his idea of heaven was "eating foie gras to the sound of trumpets."

It would be misleading, however, to describe my Harvard experience as entirely focused on social amenities. To begin with, there were two drawbacks to be overcome. One was my indoctrination in the snobbery of the WASP Ascendancy. The other was drinking too much and learning to take pleasure in it. Too many of the men I knew at Harvard became drunkards because of the fashion for drink, which arose directly from the foolish constraints of Prohibition. After Prohibition was repealed by the Twenty-first Amendment in December 1933, alcohol soon became a far less serious problem at Harvard. It was, however, an appalling problem in my young days there. And no wonder, for we thought nothing of having two or three light martinis before lunch and three or four martinis (the drink was a lighter one in those days, although the accumulated impact was considerable) before dinner, as well as assorted other drinks that might be available.

Indeed, the Porcellian encouraged drinking. On the top floor of the club building on Massachusetts Avenue, set in a closet, was a great copper still that consisted of a tank so large that a walkway had to be built around it. This contraption, carefully constructed and maintained, was used for the sole purpose of manufacturing the club gin. Three times a year, in ritual fashion, the steward, Mr. Meyers, would pour the required three months' supply of alcohol, distilled water, and drops—his own secret recipe—into the still and, with an enormous paddle, walk around the walkway, stirring the mixture in order to make it smooth. The process took an entire day, during the course of which the fumes would make Meyers a little drunk—the only time of the year we ever saw him in such a reduced state. No doubt Meyers considered this momentary infirmity worthwhile, for the club gin sold at near to two dollars a bottle and, aside from benefiting the club finances, provided the fuel for many an undergraduate career.

For example, Chip Bohlen, at the height of his brilliant career as a public servant, had to have a routine medical examination and thoughtlessly told the State Department doctor the truth about how much he was accustomed to drinking. I do not think it was an extraordinary amount, although the horrified but respectful doctor said, "All I can say is, Mr. Bohlen, you must be one of those rare persons for whom alcohol is a food." Yet Chip was certainly no drunkard—the very opposite in fact. As for myself, I am sure that I still drink just a bit more than I ought to at the age of seventy-eight, although I have been lucky in having what we used to call a "hard head" and, for a very long time, could drink a good amount of alcohol without feeling ill effects.

Aside from these social points, there are only two further features of my Harvard days worth commemorating. The first was the comparative cheapness of undergraduate life. With two hundred dollars a month, then the standard rich boy's allowance, I paid all my school bills—tuition, the house plan in the years I spent in the college dormitories, my club bills, my bills from tailors and such like, and my room bills in the two years when I did not live under roofs provided by Harvard. Even so, I had about a thousand beautiful Hoover dollars left over every year with which to buy books, take trips to New York, and enjoy myself in one way or another.

As for the other aspect of my Harvard life that strikes me now, it was its relatively uninventive monotony. I ate with friends, drank with friends, went to the theater and to dances with friends, and then spent the rest of the time reading. On the whole, I enjoyed myself enormously, but I did not learn as much as I ought to have done. About this, I am deeply regretful even today. As I look back, I clearly had a better mind when I was young than I do today or, indeed, than I did forty years ago. If the mind I had when I was younger had been stretched to its utmost by rigorous and demanding training, I like to think I should have accomplished a great deal more than I have. In the American educational system, however, rigorous, demanding training is not easy to come by unless it is self-administered—in the manner of the ambitious new group now deservedly soaring upward in this country, the Asian Americans. As it was, I did what the institution expected of me in the way of academics, which was no more nor less than I felt moved to do on any particular undergraduate afternoon.

I have let myself wander on about my time at Harvard and Groton because I believe these years constituted important stages in my development. It always strikes me as laughable to contemplate the total unpredictability of what will be good and what will be bad for the young. If I had been advising my father and mother, for instance, I should certainly have told them that they ought to consider pulling me out of Groton instead of risking my committing suicide there in the winter term of my third-form year. In point of fact, that term of utmost misery was one of the best things that ever happened to me because it drove me to decide that I must make friends—and, therefore, to learn how to make friends. By the same token, a great deal of wasted time and, above all, innumerable opportunities for serious learning were missed during my years in the Porcellian. But at least I came out of the experience with no remains of the timidity that goes with thinking of yourself as a poor relation.

Since I'd lost my timidity and learned how to make friends, I had had the best preparation I can think of for plunging, cold turkey, into an entirely foreign environment, which was just what I needed. The truth is that when I finished Harvard, my mind needed to be given the kind of thorough airing required by beds that have been slept in too long. Although I had no notion of it at the time, the thorough airing I required would come to me because of my mother's family's tendency toward alcoholism. Later, the results of this tendency were awful, but at the time I am speaking of they merely made my father, mother, and grandmother apprehensive.

My mother had been raised in an atmosphere of convivial drink and knew that such youthful habits, no matter how gay, rendered weak men useless in later age. Her uncle Elliott (President Theodore's older brother) was a hopeless drunk, and his son Rosy was much the same by early middle age. Of her three brothers, the eldest, Stewart, died intoxicated at age twenty-one. Stewart and a group of friends were attempting to re-create Pierre's opening drinking scene in *War and Peace* on the top cornice of the AD club at Harvard, when he slipped and fell, breaking his neck on the pavement below. Another brother, Teddy Robinson, was less overt in his addiction but ended a confirmed dipsomaniac all the same, as did his son Douglas.

The third brother, my uncle Mose, was said to have been an enchanting and very brave man in all respects save one: when he began to drink in earnest, the only predictable result was that he would not stop until he was in the hands of a doctor. Uncle Mose fought in the First World War with distinction. He was at Belleau Wood, one of the worst battles Americans were involved in, and this led, indirectly, to his most memorable outrage. He had picked up in the shell-torn wood an abandoned and truly savage German police dog known as Bella. Bella repaid Mose's act of kindness by giving him ferocious loyalty. If his master went to sleep with the final words "Bella, en garde!" Bella would stay on guard with her fearful teeth bared until Mose woke up. As his bed one evening, Mose chose the lobby sofa of a small New York men's club, extremely popular and much envied in that period. The club's founder was very much alive and, within the confines of that small world, still a man to be reckoned with. But Bella had not been warned about the importance of the club president or any of its members when, at about five in the morning, my uncle Mose fell into a drunken sleep in the club's front hall after saying, "Bella, en garde." In consequence, neither the club's founder nor any of the members were able to pass the front door until late that morning, when Mose finally woke up. This made a dreadful scandal, and in the upshot Mose had to resign from the club.

By the same token, there were other less entertaining episodes, which made my family worry constantly for fear that Mose's affliction was going to turn up among the males of the next generation. Nor do I blame my family particularly for feeling this kind of fear about me. By the time of my graduation in 1932, my intention for my future, as far as I could be said to have one, was to go on from Harvard College to Harvard Law School, which would have meant another three jolly years in the Porcellian Club, as well as some hard work, and then taking my luck among the big New York law firms. I thank God I was rescued from my own intention; and, if I am to be brutally honest, this rescue really occurred because my entire family thought it unwise for me to stay another three years in the same dangerously alcoholic vicinity. I suspect they were right.

By May 1932, Governor Franklin D. Roosevelt was frantically gathering delegates for the Democratic convention that June in Chicago; Adolf Hitler in eight months would assume the chancellorship of the Weimar Republic; and the United States had long since become, in the words of the humorist Will Rogers, "the first nation in history to go to the poorhouse in an automobile." With the possible exception of the fate of the Prohibition amendment, which undergraduates followed with keen interest, few of these public events, their ramifications, or progress had penetrated my stuffy little college world. Nor were personal or professional futures much discussed among my friends in the senior class. It was the established view that one had one's place in the outside world, and in due course, with a certain amount of family help, one would be appropriately fitted in.

So it happened, in mid-spring of 1932, that a special family council was convened, without consulting me and without my knowledge or presence, in my grandmother Robinson's house in Manhattan. The purpose of this meeting, as it was later put to me, was to decide the perplexing question of "what to do about Joe?" Scholastically, I had done what in those days was considered unusually well at Harvard. I received a magna cum laude and would have gotten a summa and been chosen for Phi Beta Kappa had I not incautiously taken an appalling calculus course freshman year. This class had begun at a very early hour and had involved an enormous amount of very complicated mathematics, which, due to a combination of innate inability and poor study habits, I got very wrong.

The family council was by no means impressed with this record, however. My father, as he told me later, was convinced that I would make a hopeless failure in business. With both law and business ruled out, the meeting was at a loss for a moment, until my grandmother remarked that my letters sent to her from Harvard had demonstrated a talent for writing and that she was sure she could persuade "dear Helen Reid" to give me a job on the *New York Herald Tribune*, which the Ogden Reids then owned. This was a much more original proposal than it would now seem, for there were very few reporters in those days who had been to universities, and neither my grandmother nor any other member of my family nor I, for that matter, had ever known anyone at all who had gone into the newspaper business except, of course, the Reids.

All the same, my grandmother's suggestion was eagerly agreed to at the council table; a promise was secured from Mrs. Reid; and I learned my future in a letter from my grandmother later that spring. The letter instructed me to report to New York on a given date for interviews with the city editor of the *Herald Tribune*, Stanley Walker, and the managing editor, Grafton Wilcox. I duly presented myself, and, since I was fat, soft, wholly untrained, and had an odd accent, I naturally evoked emotions of pessimism and horror. Stanley, a great man and usually a great judge of human material, described me as a dreadful result of "Republican inbreeding"; and he and Grafton Wilcox, both soon to be good friends of mine, joined in begging Helen Reid to welsh on her promise to my grandmother. Mrs. Reid said she could not welsh, and so I was grudgingly directed to report for duty at the *Herald Tribune* on the first working day following the long Fourth of July weekend, 1932.

During my first days on the job, I did not do a damn thing except try to learn how to type. Toward the end of the week, I was sent out on a nonjob of some sort or other, most likely just to get me out of Stanley's sight. Not much later on, one of the makework projects that my editors suggested to me was an obituary of Mrs. Benjamin Harrison, wife of the former president, then living in some style on Park Avenue. Papers in those days, as now, kept a running bank of obituaries on the living, ready for quick use when their subject was gathered. I knew nothing about this practice but was aware, by that time, that the *Herald Tribune* had an obituary page for the purpose of announcing and eulogizing the deceased. I studied the style and, after appropriate research, wrote an actual obituary of Mrs. Benjamin Harrison, killing the poor woman off well within the ten o'clock deadline. Just before putting my story into the paper, Lessing Lanham Engleking, the night editor, smelled a rat and called me up to the desk. "Is Mrs. Harrison really dead?" Engleking asked with a tone of elaborately kind restraint.

I replied, "No, of course she is not."

After Mr. Engleking had gotten over being enraged, he congratulated me warmly on how well written the story was.

Editors like Walker and Engleking placed a premium on stylish writing, regarding it as one of the hallmarks of the *Tribune* and their edge over the stolid and well-staffed *Times.* Reporters at the paper who were able to energize the mundane were given a very long leash, no matter how odd their habits and dress. When I came on staff, Walter ("Red") Smith and the legendary Stanley Woodward inhabited the sports bullpen in the far corner of the city room. Walter Lippmann would soon come from the *New York World,* bringing the country's most erudite political voice. And critics like Virgil Thomson (the arts) and Clementine Paddleford (food) had long been in residence, helping contribute to the *Tribune*'s reputation as "The Paper," a sheet of highest moral and intellectual standard.

On the *Tribune,* it did not take long for me to discover, and above all for Stanley Walker to observe, that I had a knack for what were called "feature stories." Walker was the premier newspaper editor of his day, a thin, short, sardonic man who always wore blue suits. He was a Texan and frightfully shrewd and tough. He was interested in the city and anything about the city, and as a newspaper editor he wanted to catch its oddities, its excitements, its small crimes and large dramas. So a feature could be anything from an interview with a celebrity to a description of a folk festival, with all sorts of stops in between.

I am glad, as I look back, that this is the way I started newspaper writing. On the one hand, I learned so much about the variety of the world we live in and about its many patches of wretchedness and its few patches of splendor that I lost (or think I lost) the narrowness of viewpoint instilled by the kind of experience I'd had at Groton and Harvard. One could not fail to lose one's narrowness of viewpoint if one was sent one day to talk with the denizens of the wretched shack colonies—called "Hoovervilles"—which existed for two whole years in the middle of Central Park, and then sent the next day to interview Tallulah Bankhead, staying at the Waldorf Astoria. (I was ushered into the room to find the great actress half invisible on the other side of a table behind an enormous ice-sculptured fish whose flank was filled with caviar, to accompany the still-illegal champagne also on the table in copious quantities.)

There were other such profiles of well-known persons, including Henri Matisse, who informed me, in between my attempts at conversation in heavily accented French, that the black panther in the Central Park Zoo was the most beautiful thing in all of New York. I remember with admiration and heartbreak a ghetto mediation court that very poor Jewish immigrants had organized for themselves on Manhattan's Lower East Side. I remember with delight being extremely unkind, though only by being perfectly exact in what I wrote, when I interviewed the all-powerful, incomparably self-important Hearst movie critic of those days, Louella Parsons, the terror of all Hollywood, whose face exactly resembled a suet pudding into which were set two raisins.

Being a practical man, I remember that turning out these feature stories for the *Herald Tribune* had two major rewards. In the first place, Walker and Engelking often thought my work good enough to put my byline above it, which was a tremendous privilege. In the second place, because my features so often carried my byline and also perhaps because they had a certain individual flavor, I began to make a reputation of sorts and to be asked to attempt writing outside the *Tribune.* Harold Ross, the great editor of the *New Yorker*, commissioned a piece on the small but vibrant Japanese immigrant colony in New York. I was not as yet well enough trained to write for the *New Yorker*, so I never got the story done; but it was a valuable experience.

Harold Ross I came to know only slightly, and he seemed to me a curious and enigmatic man. He was a great, big raw-boned fellow with a shock of black hair. In appearance and manner, he acted every part the ebullient, somewhat frantic midwestern farm boy, although I always thought he pretended to be much more of a hick than he was. The last Mrs. Ross, however, was no hick at all. Before marrying Harold, she had been a $100 girl at 21—very expensive in those days. During the height of this nighttime career, her services were monopolized by a syndicate of rather powerful bankers, including a prominent partner in J. P. Morgan's firm. What I chiefly remember about Mrs. Ross was the extraordinary and very arousing way in which she shook one's hand. Her hand would go to nothing, like bird bones and silk in one's grasp. For the briefest time, she would let it lie fluttering, and one would feel perhaps one might just keep it there and put it in one's pocket as a souvenir.

At any rate, although the bulk of my work was still, of course, with the *Tribune*, I began to take on potboiling jobs for various magazines in the city. I was still getting $18 a week on the *Tribune*, and initially, my father, in his old-fashioned way, also gave me an allowance of $100 a month. But soon the potboiling jobs began to bring in more than my allowance, and I was able to tell my father that I could stand on my own. This was in 1933, in the depths of the Depression, and I remember with acute pleasure Father's expression of astonishment, mingled with delight and a new respect, when this news was given him.

In one book or another about the newspaper business of those days, a great many silly stories have been told about my early years on the *Herald Tribune.* Very few of them are true except that Bill Patten and I took a flat together in New York, and I found a wonderful old Japanese manservant named Buto to look after us. We both liked to be hospitable, and Bill enjoyed my new friends from the *Herald Tribune* as much as I did, so we often had people in after we had found accommodations big enough. (Our second flat, on Eighty-fourth Street, had three bedrooms, three baths, a large kitchen, a dining room, and a living room, and cost $85 a month.)

Initially, I was pretty well enclosed in my strictly *Herald Tribune* life, for, at first, my day off was on Thursday, and my hours were such that I could never have dinner with anyone other than members of the *Herald Tribune* staff. There, thank God, I made a few very good friends. John Lardner, a great reporter and most admirable writer in his own right and the son of the great Ring Lardner, was chief among my new friends, and I cannot think of him to this day without growing sad because he died so young. But there were many others, and I can remember few parties that I have enjoyed more than the late-evening whiskey and crap-shooting parties Bill Patten and I used to give at our apartment. In the last year I was in New York, Bill and I were joined by his extremely proper, almost constipated sister Nancy, not for nothing the stepdaughter of a bishop. All the same, she used to serve the drinks, and every so often she would even shoot craps with irritatingly good luck.

Eventually, as my work made me something of a reputation, the *Tribune* authorities allowed me more reasonable hours, and I had a more normal life. Curiously enough, New York in those days, when the economy was still in disastrous condition, was an infinitely more pleasant place than New York is today. I remember trips I took up to Harlem, usually with John Lardner, who liked smoking what were then called "reefers." The marijuana cigarettes could usually be purchased from bartenders in some of the better establishments uptown, although I preferred a scotch and soda or gin and tonic in those days—and, for that matter, still do. Sometimes, with my more worldly friends, I would dine downtown before traveling up to Small's Paradise, a splendid ballroom with a largely black clientele. "Dinner somewhere" then meant in evening clothes, and I still remember the dancing at Small's as the most wonderful I have ever seen.

Nor can I remember a moment of tension on my many uptown excursions with John. I went all over the city by subway and can remember no single incident that was in the least threatening any more than I can remember ruined streets or rows of abandoned housing. Hence, the New York of today always seems to me a tragically melancholy place—rushed, harried, and dirty, like a grand old woman gone majestically to seed. To be sure, when I first went to work in 1932, New York had a horrible side that we were never allowed to forget. The unemployment was fearful; there were no adequate institutional means for aiding the unemployed; and despite the stoical good temper that most people displayed, one felt the misery that was so prevalent as a kind of personal affliction that one could do nothing about.

From the New York of those days, two sharply contrasting pictures remain with me. One is of the huge municipal dumps, seventy and more feet high, that lined East End Avenue from about Eightieth Street down through the mid-Seventies, where immensely expensive apartment houses now stand. In the first year I was in New York, if one took a taxi in the morning down East End Avenue, one invariably saw scores of mostly respectable older-looking men and women clambering precariously over the horrible dumps in order to find something that might possibly be eaten or sold for enough to purchase a meal.

The other picture is the view from the first apartment that Bill Patten and I inhabited. Ours was a railroad flat in a cleaned-up slum that had a wonderful view of the East River. In the little park just across the street stood the enchanting but half-ruined Gracie Mansion, and just above Gracie Mansion there was a half-ruined old dock on the East River. All summer, this dock was used as a swimming hole by all the men in the neighborhood in just the way the men's swimming hole was used in my own home village of Avon, Connecticut. All ages went in without a stitch, leaving their clothes and, presumably at least in some cases, their money, in charge of an old man who made his living by getting two or three cents per person for looking after clothes and other belongings.

In all the long summer while Bill Patten and I had that first apartment of ours overlooking Gracie Mansion, the East River, and the swimming hole, there was not a single case of anyone trying to snitch the clothes or the money of the innumerable bathers. I know this because I asked the policeman on the block—there really were policemen on the block in those days—and he told me that because of the widespread unemployment and hunger he had feared just what I asked him about but had discovered no case of it. It was an altogether rural and neighborly scene, and I remember it as though it were yesterday mainly because I myself was surprised to find anything in the least resembling Avon, Connecticut, in the city of New York.

There are many memories of that lost New York: for example, the marvelous bar/restaurant Bleeck's, on West Fortieth Street between Fifth and Sixth Avenues, which served as an unofficial clubhouse for reporters and editors on the *Tribune*. Bleeck's was a noisy establishment with a dark wood décor and a menu that was mildly German in flavor. After a day's work, I would retreat there for dinner—usually veal cutlet garnished with egg and anchovies or another old-fashioned dish called deviled bone—and play an arcane house favorite called the match game with John Lardner and other friends. It was at Bleeck's that I once rescued my proprietor, Ogden Reid, from imminent drowning when he had gone to sleep, very drunk, with his face in his soup. There were other reporters present senior to me who might have effected the rescue of the publisher if they had not feared what Mr. Reid would say when he discovered that he was being dragged from an early death in his soup by one of his own employees. I took a more pragmatic view, and Mr. Reid thanked me like the gentleman he always was.

I recall a great many other friends of those days: Emma Bugbee, the *Herald Tribune*'s indomitable woman reporter whose heroine was Eleanor Roosevelt; Dick Watts, who was the paper's movie critic and a wonderfully good companion; and Dick Tobin, John Lardner's cousin and my friend. Some of these people would later be present during the one night I spent on a picket line during the winter of 1936. This produced the odd sight—for it was a chillingly cold night—of an Alsop (the first in the family, no doubt, for I was one of the founding members of Heywood Broun's American Newspaper Guild) agitating for workers' rights (I believe the paper in question was the *Newark Star-Ledger*) while dressed in a formidably large raccoon coat. At any rate, I could go on with memories that please me from that time long ago, but it is enough to say that I greatly enjoyed those earliest years of my professional life. All in all, it was an exciting and liberating time, for I was making my own wage, making new friends, and, most importantly, getting my first genuine taste of the world outside the narrowly prescribed boundaries of Avon and Cambridge.

I suppose this New York style of life could have gone on indefinitely, for I was well suited to it. But professional prospects have a way of changing life drastically, especially for the young. So it was that the next turning point in my career took place in Flemington, New Jersey. The kidnaping and death of the Lindbergh baby in March 1932 had deeply moved the entire country. I cannot think of another trial in the whole of American history that received anything like the national coverage of the trial in Flemington of the baby's alleged kidnaper and murderer Bruno Hauptmann, whom I still believe to have been guilty as hell. I do not approve of murder trials being thought of as good fun in any normal circumstances, but the circumstances of the Hauptmann trial, which began in early January of 1935, were entirely abnormal. So many newspapermen flooded into the then-modest county town of Flemington that two of the churches (the Methodist and the Presbyterian, as I recall) made small fortunes by serving lunchtime church suppers in their basements every day. The housing situation was so horrible that the *Herald Tribune* contingent, led by a wonderful senior reporter, Joe Driscoll, took a small private house that the owners had gladly rented for an exorbitant sum.

Snobbishly, the contingents from the *Herald Tribune*, the *New York Times*, and the *New York Daily News* formed a kind of permanent mess. I half fell in love with Grace Robinson, the star reporter of the *Daily News* and a woman who would track a bloodstained murderer into a dark cellar still wearing all the outer manners of her convent training. It always amuses me to hear the women's liberation movement of the 1960s credited with women's progress in the newspaper business. I do not believe that New York has a woman reporter today in the preeminent situation of Grace Robinson or of Anne O'Hare McCormick, the perambulating foreign correspondent of the *New York Times* and one of the most admired reporters of her time, or even of Ishbel Ross, who was a star of the *Herald Tribune* city room until she retired in 1931. Furthermore, Grace Robinson, small, quiet-seeming, grey-haired, and, above all, ladylike, was romantically loved by Bob Conway, the second star reporter of the *New York Daily News* in those days. Bob, a splendid, burly, jolly fellow, was also at Flemington, and he served Grace almost like a copyboy.

The *Times* representation in Flemington was strong and genial. Since I was the junior man in this much-envied *Times-News-Tribune* mess, I used to have the task of finding a decent place for us to eat at least four nights a week. My best success in this line was a genuine old country inn of the kind that used to serve the national road system when people traveled in horse-drawn vehicles. The very old people who ran this dying inn on what had been the turn-pike crossing New Jersey to Philadelphia produced marvelous old-fashioned dinners for us—with the whole table covered with their specialties, like roast, partridge (highly illegal), fresh ham, and suc-cotash cooked with a slice of salt pork. They also served a thor-oughly lethal drink made with applejack, which they called a "Stone Fence." The Stone Fences seemed much less dangerous than they really were, but they did cause my heroine, Grace Robinson, to become a bit tiddly—the only occasion that I saw her in this condi-tion.

Mainly, however, my time in Flemington was spent sitting on top of a radiator—thank God not a working radiator—in the un-bearably overcrowded courtroom. From this unlikely position, I would watch and take notes on the proceedings, and finally I would find an angle plus the needed factual material for a respectable "side-bar." A sidebar was the feature run on the front page in the shelter of the lead story, in this case always one of Joe Driscoll's splendid pieces.

"Bruno Richard Hauptmann's fight for his life offers a spec-tacle in which the ridiculous, the sordid and the emotionally moving are curiously mixed," began one early and fairly representative ex-ample of my work from the trial. "Elmer Hahn, court crier, a bald-headed man with a long face who is, in private life, addicted to smoking large cigars in a pipe, advances to a post before the bench. Justice Trenchard, a pink-faced man in dignified black robes, enters from his chambers and takes his seat on the elevated platform as-signed to him. Hauptmann, grey-faced and expressionless, shambles in from the jail behind the courthouse with his guards. The jury arrives from the hotel escorted by two woman bailiffs and two men. Elmer Hahn mumbles something about 'the honorable court of Oyer and Terminer' being in session, and the trial has begun for the day."

I suppose that if I exhumed other samples of my sidebars from Flemington, I should be much embarrassed, but they were success-ful at the time, which is what counts. Indeed, my reporting of the Lindbergh trial, which ended in February of that year, attracted a good deal of attention among those who counted in the *Tribune* newsroom, and this eventually caused the Reids to send me to Washington as a new kind of political correspondent.

4

Dining-Out
Washington

I suspect the Reids' idea in sending me to Washington was, for the
long run, to have a leading Washington correspondent fully
sympathetic to the *Tribune*'s moderate Republican views. I was
young, impressionable, and possessed the appropriate family background. I would grow into the job. They were, however, taking my
rather unformed politics for granted, and, as it happened, they were
wrong, for I was a nascent Franklin Roosevelt sympathizer.

Such partisan leanings may have been rooted in my tribal past,
for in going to Washington, I was lucky in one very obvious way.
Since my grandmother was Theodore Roosevelt's sister, Mrs.
Franklin Roosevelt was my mother's first cousin, as well as her dear
friend. So was another of the most famous Washington figures of
those days—Alice Longworth. In the way that was then usual, we
young Alsops were brought up to call Mrs. Franklin Roosevelt
"Cousin Eleanor," Mrs. Nicholas Longworth (wife of the House
Speaker and TR's eldest daughter) "Cousin Alice," and so on
through the elder generation. As governor of New York, Franklin
Roosevelt had been only a dim figure in my early years, and, of
course, once elected president, he instantly became "Mr. President"

for all of us. These connections were suitable enough to win me a New Year's Eve invitation to the White House shortly after my arrival in Washington. This, I suppose, was a privileged beginning, although I remember little of the evening, save seeing the president at his desk in the upstairs Oval Room, jovially mixing the long, tawny cocktails for all and sundry in the way he liked to.

Washington has been my base, my home, and the place that shaped my viewpoint for considerably more than half a century. The old prewar Washington was the backdrop of everything that happened to me in my young professional life and had its influence on my every idea as it developed until my faintly comic departure for the Far East as an amateur intelligence officer a few short months before Pearl Harbor. This noble, congenial, curious old world became a kind of personal benchmark for all that came after it, so I will attempt to describe it here.

I am not at all sure that anyone fifty years old or under would be able to survive a full year of life in the Washington of the second half of the 1930s, the first year I lived there. Despite its standing in the nation, despite the monuments and the lumpish federal architecture that had come up in Hoover's time, prewar Washington was not like a city at all. Downtown, instead of street upon street of identical façades and the avenues of storage warehouses for government clerks so prominent today, there were just the ancient centers: the White House, the Treasury, and the endearing old State, War, and Navy Building—now known as the Old Executive Office Building—at one end of Pennsylvania Avenue, and the Capitol, the House and Senate office buildings, and the Congressional Library and Supreme Court at the other.

Air-conditioning was, of course, totally unknown except in a small number of especially luxurious movie theaters, where a cruelly dank cold was maintained all summer to draw in gasping customers. The absence of air-conditioning had its advantages, however. First, because all but the very rich senators and congressmen lived in small, desperately hot apartments, it made it almost impossible for Congress to stay in Washington through much of the summer. The lack of air-conditioning also gave the city a special look in summertime because by mid-May, when the heat began to set in, wardrobes changed dramatically. Women wore large, shade-giving hats and dresses of brightly colored cotton. The more respectable men favored white linen suits or even cream-colored silk suits or, if they were economical about it, cotton suits made from seersucker. The men also wore straw hats, generally Panama.

In that old summer Washington, before the days of daylight

saving time, it was possible to dine outdoors coolly and comfortably when the night air came down into the Potomac river valley after sundown. The river, itself, was so free of pollution that people quite regularly swam in it. Radio was a curiosity and television unknown, so one could think, talk, and, indeed, work in relative serenity. Only the very rich owned motor cars, but trolleys were plentiful, and, if one was in a hurry, there were also plenty of taxis. Nor were there any suburbs to speak of, so that a trip to the country was still, in those days, a bona fide and welcome event.

Normal Washington life proceeded in neighborhoods, the rhythms of which were seasonal and decidedly southern. Indeed, after the bustle of Manhattan, the pace of the place was very engaging and pleasant, for no one hurried and few ever worked later than 5:00 P.M. There were more jokes in those days; and there was less pretense in the daily routine of the capital and decidedly less show. The great security apparatus so common today had never been heard of or imagined anywhere in government, and almost everybody could know everyone else if they just made the effort. Cultural diversions were few, and there was no really great restaurant in Washington, nor was it missed, although I suppose the forerunners of that grey mass of lobbyists who now inhabit Duke Zeibert's on Connecticut Avenue may have pined for one.

Beneath this easy, pleasant exterior, however, Washington was a deceptively complicated place, for the town was endlessly divided by a series of tall, unseen barriers. The most important of these was the barrier that separated white Washington from black Washington. As is still the case today, the wealthier, white neighborhoods were located in the northwestern section of the city, although when I first moved there, Georgetown—now among the very wealthiest and most exclusive sections of town—was home to many middle- and lower-middle-class black families. The larger black community, however, occupied the neighborhoods that spread south and east of the Capitol building, and, much as today, there was very little cross-over between the residents of the black community and the white men and women who made their lives on the opposite side of the city.

On the professional side, too, the small world of newspapermen I entered was only one Washington among many. The Senate Washington, which I also inhabited when I first arrived in town as a reporter, was paralleled by congressional Washington; and there was an army Washington, navy Washington, and business Washington. Then, as government grew larger and more powerful under Franklin Roosevelt, there was an embryo lobbyists' Washington, which now has grown into a monstrously large, monstrously rich, and monstrously sleazy community. These professional barriers were far more pronounced than today, for the government moved along at a slower, more regional pace. The great government agencies were not the giant competing institutions they are now, and there was no need, especially among the small troops of civil servants, to know how fiefdoms in other areas of the kingdom were operating.

However, the most curious divisions in the city (and in many ways the most rigid) were to be found in the realm of society and entertainment. In nineteenth-century novels and in reminiscences of perfectly intelligent persons a generation older than I, one finds regular mention of an unexplained body named "society." Even a person as careless of worldly opinion as Eleanor Roosevelt admits in her informative autobiography that it was a long while before she ceased to worry over the approval of what she called "New York Society." "Society" is a word that had already all but gone out of use in Eleanor Roosevelt's day, and we, in our time, were brought up not to use it. However, we also were brought up to be aware of a large, recognizable, semiorganized body of style and etiquette to the fringes of which, at least, it was important to cling.

Dining-Out Washington, as I will call it, was the remnant of this organized body called "society" that had enjoyed itself and made fools of many of its members ever since Washington became a city in the early 1800s. Its members were connected to one another not by their proximity to power (as is the case in what passes for social fashion in the capital today) or by fantastic wealth, but by a certain longevity, a modicum of breeding, and a decidedly southern sense of grand style. Their world contained an astonishing number of large houses through which revolved the same three or four hundred full members of Dining-Out Washington all autumn, winter, and spring. Dinners usually seated no less than forty of these three or four hundred, an arrangement that insured that everyone in the group saw everyone else in the group about once a fortnight. In consequence, each member came to know the others only too well, and if the company was not always invigorating, the ritual of dinner, dance, and bridge offered to each member a certain comforting permanence. The permanence proved an illusion, however, for this world vanished soon after the second war, and I am not so sure this was a bad thing.

I arrived in Washington just after Christmas 1935, and although my income did not justify it, my family connections and friends launched me immediately into the Dining-Out Washington of the rich. A Harvard friend had asked his mother to put me up for a week or two until I could find my feet in the city. As a result, the first house I stayed in was that of Mrs. Dwight Davis, the former Mrs. Charles Sabin, whose successful contribution to the repeal of the Prohibition amendment I have already mentioned. The house she occupied when I came to Washington was in Georgetown and had been rented to her by Mrs. Ruth Hanna McCormick, a considerable Republican personality in her own right and the widow of Joseph Medill McCormick, the former senator from Illinois. This was the only Georgetown house Mrs. Davis ever occupied, although until the end of her life she had the odd and expensive habit of moving from one enormous Washington residence to another, each time making the new house ravishingly pretty at what must have been very substantial cost, and each time moving on again in a year or so to repeat the process.

I learned soon enough that in coming to Washington I had made a step back into the American past, for Mrs. Davis's first rather stern instruction to me was that after attending a dinner, I must leave a calling card with my hostess on the morning following the event. I told Mrs. Davis I could not possibly leave calling cards, that, to begin with, I had none and, moreover, I would have no time to tour the city, dropping squares of cardboard at people's houses instead of covering the Senate, which was to be my beat for the *Tribune*. Mrs. Davis suggested that whenever I went to dinner at a new house, I write a little letter that explained my working situation, gave the hostess my warmest thanks for her hospitality and said in passing that I hoped she would accept this explanation of my situation as a substitute for possible calling cards in the future.

The first of these letters went to Mrs. Henry Keep, who invited me to dinner as soon as she heard I was coming to the city. Mrs. Keep was an old family friend—my father had very nearly married her sister, Mrs. Winthrop Murray Crane, long before my mother came along, in the dim, dark, distant past, during the time of Theodore Roosevelt. Mrs. Keep's invitation filled me with considerable uneasiness—first of all, because guests to the gathering were instructed in no uncertain terms to wear white tie and tails. In New York and Boston, dining out in white tie was unknown for anyone under the age of forty and considered rare even among the aged. Possessing only the dinner jacket customary for those of my age, I, therefore, had to rent a white tie, tails, and evening coat, with all the proper accessories. I dutifully did so, but because of my unusual heft the whole getup fitted very badly, although Mrs. Davis was polite enough not to offer any comment on my appearance.

This odd costume, plus the fact that the city was completely unfamiliar, filled me with trepidation as I made my way at the appointed hour to Mrs. Keep's large, pseudo-Adams house on Sheridan Circle. When I rang the bell and the door opened, the first thing I discovered was a table covered with small envelopes, one of which had my name on it. When I opened it, I discovered the instruction "Please take in Lady Rumbold." I had no notion of who Lady Rumbold was; worse still, I had no notion of what "take in" meant; nor did I have time to inquire because Mrs. Keep greeted me warmly and led me into a huge, rather ornate living room, the interior of which was all late eighteenth-century pastiche, except for a cavernous pseudo-medieval fireplace. From the fireplace, where he had been warming himself, an immensely elegant old gentleman promptly advanced on me in an alarmingly purposeful way and said in crisp and almost accusing tones: "You Joseph Wright Alsop?!" I replied in the affirmative. "Well, Alsop, your great-grandfather was my godfather." It turned out that this indeed was true; for the elegant old gentleman was the son of General George Brinton McClellan. McClellan, of course, had commanded the Army of the Potomac with no great distinction during the first years of the Civil War. Prior to battle, as his son happily explained to me, the general had served as the engineer for the Illinois Central Railroad, which my grandfather, on the Alsop side, had controlled.

For a young, overly impressionable man, this was a disconcerting beginning. It was even more disconcerting when I learned, first, that it was just as well that I had come early and, second, what "take in" meant. Both these important facts were imparted to me by Felicity Rumbold, who turned out to be an enchanting girl, younger than I and married to the third secretary of the British embassy, Sir Anthony Rumbold. Felicity began by congratulating me on my promptness and warning me, as a newcomer to Washington, that no drinks were served in most of the big houses until the last dinner guest had arrived. This meant, of course—and it happened to me more than once because of an unfaithful taxi—that if a guest arrived even so much as ten minutes late, he or she could expect to be met with looks of blackest hatred from the rest of the assembled party. The unfortunate miscreant would also come close to being trampled by the rush of footmen bearing silver trays of delayed cocktails, which consisted in those days, when no choices were offered, of rather weak, tawny-looking martinis and even more awful Manhattans (a drink that tasted to me like sweet varnish and is happily now nearly extinct).

As for the matter of being "taken in," Felicity informed me that in most big Washington houses guests still went into the dining room like the animals going into the ark—two by two. Invariably, the procession, which, for obscure reasons, was called a crocodile, proceeded in strict order of rank, with the exception of the hostess, who brought up the rear with the male guest of honor. As Felicity and I were the lowest ranking persons present, our place in the procession was directly in front of Mrs. Keep and her principal guest, the impossibly grand and imposing chief justice of the United States Charles Evans Hughes. As befitted his position, Chief Justice Hughes wore a splendid thatch of white whiskers. So it was an odd sensation for me, all of twenty-five years old, straight off the train from New York, and wedged into my elaborate costume, to march in to dinner as if on parade, just ahead of a man who looked remarkably like an early Renaissance painter's portrayal of God Almighty.

The dinner table itself was also a considerable surprise to me simply because of the fact already underlined by my ill-fitting white tie—that pre–Second World War Washington maintained much more of the old pre–First World War style than was the case in New York. As our procession wound into the dining room, I heard Mrs. Keep explaining to the chief justice, "I always like a simple dinner." Our "simple dinner" consisted of a consommé that must have cost the lives of innumerable chickens and perhaps some animals, too, followed by two impressively large salmon, accompanied by a generous vat of hollandaise sauce, and a cucumber-and-tomato salad on the side. These delights, in turn, were followed by roast guinea hens with fried bread crumbs and bread sauce, served with hot vegetables. Then came two mousses of foie gras with green salad, and, at long last, an ice-cream bombe wreathed in the peculiar spun-sugar hay that I remembered from children's parties. This plus three wines were enough to send one away comfortably full. But it was nothing, I must add, to Washington's grander dinners (for Mrs. Keep's table was thought to be simple by the city's standards), of which I shall describe shortly.

Mrs. Keep's table was seated in rigid accordance with protocol, with the most important man placed to the right of the hostess and the most important woman to the right of the host. Guests of uncertain rank like myself were always "bout de table," set fast in the middle ground. While the identity of those guests at the tops of table tended to vary, few young people were asked to big dinners, so those of us who had passed the unwritten tests for admission tended to sit next to one another over and over again at the grand houses. So it was that I sat next to Felicity that evening and would do so for many evenings after that, or at least until Mrs. Davis and her friends decided to expose me to Mrs. Davis's stepdaughter, young Helen Davis.

Helen was the youngest of three beautiful Davis daughters. During one summer abroad, in Germany, she had fallen deeply in love with a German officer of uncertain origin who was rumored by the ladies of Washington to be handsome in a tiresome Germanic sort of way. Young Helen came sadly back to Washington, where she remained very attached to her lover, so much so, all the ladies agreed, that drastic measures had to be taken. By this time, I was thought to be a coming young man, hard-working to be sure, and, at 240 pounds, looking not at all like a member of the Prussian military aristocracy. I soon found myself seated next to poor, bereaved Helen at dinner after dinner over the course of several weeks. She, I think, was equally shocked at this development, although we both carried on politely as best we could. However, our topics of conversation were exhausted after the first few seatings to the point where I finally turned to her and said: "You know, Helen, I am just as aware as you are as to why we are sitting together. You don't have to worry. You don't have to marry me. I don't intend to marry you. So let us both just keep up appearances until these tactics are recognized as futile." Helen agreed with evident relief, and so we finished the remainder of our dinners together in peace.

At any rate, Felicity Rumbold and I passed our first seating together in great good spirits, enjoying the marvelous food and convivial conversation. When the last course had been cleared, however, the group rose as one, whereupon the men, led by the venerable chief justice, separated from the ladies for about half an hour of talk. Later on in my Washington life, I, too, would adopt this odd custom of separation, although I was persuaded to end it finally by my great friend Katharine Graham, publisher of the *Washington Post*. By the late 1960s, Kay had suffered the experience called "having your consciousness raised." She let my wife, Susan Mary, and me know that if we persisted in separating after dinner, she would leave our dinner as soon as the last woman left the room after supper. Since Kay's friendship meant a great deal to both of us and since the almost nightly separations had begun to seem irrational anyway, we agreed to her request. However, there were others, like Averell Harriman, who insisted on this ritual until the day they died.

Separated from the ladies after dinner, the gentlemen would talk of politics and sundry topics of the day over cigars and brandy. In grand houses, one sometimes was served scotch and soda, after which time—usually between 10:30 and 11:00—the servants arrived bearing pitchers of orange juice and trays of boiled eggs. The eggs were already peeled, in silver platters, resting on beds of crushed ice, ready to be dipped into little dishes of mixed salt and pepper. The guest of honor was required to leave the party promptly at 11:00 P.M., and if he or she overstayed, it was very much resented by the rest of the party. Those grand guests who played bridge and loved sitting around and drinking the champagne that flowed freely later on in the night would sometimes feign departure. Following elaborate farewells, they would walk around the block once or twice only to return, with a wink to the hostess, to the bridge table, thereby releasing the other guests to go home to bed.

I do not remember how the chief justice departed that first dinner at Mrs. Keep's, although I am inclined to think a bridge game never materialized in deference to such an august and formal guest. I myself ended the evening feeling giddy and somewhat dazed, happy to have witnessed such an archaic gathering but glad, all the same, to have survived the event without precipitating some sort of social disaster.

Perhaps I should not have been so surprised to find the old ways—and leaving calling cards after dinner really was one of the old ways—still preserved in the city I had come to live in. The truth is that Dining-Out Washington had existed for a very long time without any break except on the celebrated occasion when the British put the torch to the White House in 1814. Within my own business, I should add, there was not much crossover into Dining-Out Washington, for, as I have said, newspaper Washington was again a semiseparate community within the city and had its own order of precedence based, in those days, on seniority of membership in the Gridiron Club. Besides a few columnists, I was the only reporter I can recall who frequented Dining-Out Washington. The first time I ever met *New York Times* Washington Bureau chief Arthur Krock, he said to me, "You know, Alsop, the first thing you have to realize is that in Washington newspapermen have no place at table." Arthur was absolutely dead right. Newspapermen in Washington now have a great deal of leverage, but in those days they had no place in society. Then the high seats belonged, as they still do, to members of the cabinet, ambassadors, Supreme Court justices, and members of the Senate.

Even in my day, admission to this world was subject to the city's ancient and peculiar snobberies. If one reads the papers and diaries of Henry Adams, one finds that he saw very few people socially who were not foreigners, a tendency, I am sorry to say, that can be laid to straight old-fashioned snobbery. However, it was not so much that Adams admired foreigners as he disparaged the dubious locals who failed to pass his unwritten social tests. These tests, although greatly diminished and diluted, still had some importance in the Dining-Out Washington that I knew, although the accepted group was still thought by some society-minded outsiders to be decidedly mixed. Often, old-fashioned New Yorkers, like my friends Martha and Ducky Harrison, came down from Manhattan, spent a year on the Potomac, and crossed so many people off their lists that they ended up living in a very reduced city.

At any rate, among those who ruled this odd little world, there were two broad divisions. The first were those who were strictly Washingtonians who controlled the organizations of this part of the city, like the Dancing Class, a ball to which everyone went three times a year in white tie. Then there were those in a somewhat higher group—if that is the way it ought to be phrased—who had connections with the larger world outside Washington—in Boston, New York, and even Europe. Mrs. William Eustis, Mildred and Robert Bliss at the famous Dumbarton Oaks mansion, Mrs. Truxtun Beale at Decatur House in Lafayette Square just across from the White House, Mrs. Robert Bacon, Mrs. Dwight Davis, and, above all, Alice Longworth, were the most conspicuous members of this special group.

It seemed to me, as an innocent perhaps, that all these formidable persons, who were so kind to me, were also, at base, rather eccentric. The great patrons of Dumbarton Court, Mildred and Robert Bliss, for example, came close to being brother and sister although they were married. The mother of Mrs. Bliss had begun as Mrs. Barnes, with a huge West Coast fortune made from Fletcher's Castoria, a major laxative of the day ("Children cry for it!" was its advertising slogan). When Mr. Barnes died, Mrs. Barnes came east to find a second husband. She found Colonel Bliss, a handsome bridge player in the city's oldest men's club, the Metropolitan. Mr. Bliss had a little son named Robert, and he and Mrs. Bliss's daughter Mildred were brought up together from a very early age. The attachment was to prove more than sibling in nature, and in the upshot, Mildred Bliss, who was a woman of extremely strong character, firmly married Robert Bliss at the first suitable opportunity.

After their marriage, Robert and Mildred, encouraged by their huge fortune, decided on diplomacy as a vocation. This permitted them to give to both the Republicans and the Democrats at each presidential election—a practice invented long before the Blisses were born and followed long after they had dropped it, by Averell Harriman among others. As for the Blisses, political generosity secured for them postings to the embassies in Sweden and, later, in

Argentina (their Dumbarton Oaks home in Georgetown would also be the venue for the famous Allied meeting that laid the foundations for the formation of the United Nations shortly after the Second World War). I always wondered whether they might not have done better to forget about diplomacy and become full-time scholarly amateurs. Indeed, when they were both over eighty, their enthusiasm for their main subject, Byzantine art, was so great that they made the very arduous trip across the Egyptian desert to visit the monastery of St. Catherine of Sinai. They were, in fact, pioneers of serious Byzantine studies. Bob Bliss was also one of the first serious collectors of pre-Columbian art. I always suspected him of choosing to collect pre-Columbian objects in order to have a room of his own into which Mildred could not enter. Whether or not that was his motive, he chose his collection, which is now on display at their old home, with an almost unerring eye.

As citizens, the Blisses were strictly law-abiding, but they could not imagine a dinner without wine. So, when the horrors of Prohibition loomed before them in 1918, they bought a cellar of great French wines that Bob Bliss believed would last his time. Indeed, the cellar did last his time, but as decade followed decade, the Lanson 1911 champagne turned a delicate brown and began to have the aroma of Russia leather. The clarets, if they were particularly good and had been especially well kept, lasted longer than the champagne, but were on their last legs when I knew them; and all the white wines had followed the champagne. Still, the Blisses, who did not seem to have good palates, simply went on drinking up their wine. Nobody ever made a remark about the oddity of the wine at Dumbarton Oaks, I suppose partly because this was one of *the* leading Washington tables and partly because everyone had learned to accept the Bliss's peculiarities long before. I myself got rather to like the taste of the over-age Lanson, for it was the first champagne I ever drank in quantity.

The comic side did not matter, however. Later on, the Blisses created a great institution of scholarship in Dumbarton Oaks, and by building their splendid gardens they added materially to the beauty of Washington. My favorite among all the Bliss gardens is the one Mildred designed and built to keep herself busy after Robert died. I used to love to go to see her at work on it. Very soon after Robert's death, she adopted pale lavender mourning and always carried a pale lavender parasol to match. Her hair had remained a rather unobtrusive and artful red until she was over eighty, and she was very slender and quick in her gestures.

The garden she had designed was like none I have ever seen: a complex and delightful pattern of pebbles set in cement, with water playing over the pebbles and giving life to the whole. Mildred would go there every day, shaded by her parasol, to have a talk about the work in progress with the aged and gnarled Italian who laid the pebbles. Rheumatism in the man's knees prevented him from squatting, but that did not matter. Since he was able to bend over at the waist and since he had the longest arms I have ever seen, he was able to insert the pebbles in the cement like a deft chimpanzee. He spoke a very coarse Italian dialect, Mildred spoke a mellifluous and rather ostentatious learned Italian, but they found plenty to talk about, and I have always been convinced that it was not limited to pebbles. In fact, it was a very funny spectacle to see these two old people, so different in every respect yet genuinely fond of one another, enjoying their jokes in the intervals between their arguments about the pebble design.

Then there was Mildred Bliss's staunch ally, Marie Beale at Decatur House. That building, designed by the great architect Benjamin Latrobe for Stephen Decatur, a naval hero of the early 1800s, was a busy center of hospitality when I first knew it. It was the only place in Washington where one saw General Pershing, who then lived in nearly total seclusion at the army's Walter Reed Hospital in the northern part of the capital. The old general loved going to see Mrs. Beale, however, and she very properly made a great fuss over him when he came.

The best of all the Decatur House stories concerned the historic evening when President Wilson appeared in the President's Box at the National Theater for the first time accompanied by the future second Mrs. Wilson, Mrs. Edith Bolling Galt. The Widow Galt was amply formed, and she had decorated her bosom with about three-quarters of the orchids in the presidential greenhouses. After the play, there was a posttheater supper party at Decatur House. The president and the Widow Galt were not present, and there was a good deal of rather cynical speculation about where else they might have gone and what they might be doing in bed or elsewhere. This was put an end to by the Russian ambassadress of those days, Madame Bakhmeteff, who was in fact the sister of the owner of Decatur House, Mr. Truxtun Beale. Said Madame Bakhmeteff in a mock sincere voice, "I'm sure you're all *much* too unkind and have *unpleasantly* wicked minds. As for me, I feel sure Mrs. Galt has just eaten her orchids and gone to bed."

Another of the grand group of Washington hostesses was Mrs. William C. Eustis. No minor figure, she was the daughter of Vice-President Levi P. Morton, who, before joining Benjamin Harrison on the Republican ticket in 1888, had also been ambassador to

France. This experience had conferred on Mrs. Eustis a half French accent with a trilled *rrrrr;* God had conferred on her a genial and entertaining nature. Unlike her more staid contemporaries, Mrs. Eustis genuinely enjoyed making trouble, but her malice was always funny and the trouble, when it came, was always well worth watching. She had provided refuge at her country place, Oatlands, for the second President Roosevelt when he was assistant secretary of the navy during the first war and for his beloved of those days, Miss Lucy Mercer. For this, Mrs. Eustis was never forgiven by Mrs. Franklin Roosevelt in the same way Alice Longworth was never quite forgiven for her knowledge of the FDR-Mercer love affair, although the suitable gestures of cousinhood had to be made by Eleanor Roosevelt to Alice Longworth.

I was connected to these ladies and their world—and, to some extent, the greater world of political Washington—by Alice Longworth, whom I used to call "Mrs. L" in order to avoid the family rules requiring familiar names for elderly relatives. Possibly the luckiest thing that happened to me in Washington was that Mrs. Longworth took a liking to me—as she would later to my brother Stewart—enough so that I saw her fairly constantly during those early years. Mrs. L's admirer when I came to Washington at the end of 1935 was the *Baltimore Sun*'s then-famous, extremely conservative, and sharp-tongued columnist Frank Kent. After I was liberated from the Senate (which, as I have said, was my first assignment in Washington for the *Tribune*), I was invited to lunch with Frank and Mrs. L at least once a week at the F Street Club, sometimes with the addition of one or two other regular guests. The object of these lunches was the destruction of political characters and political pretenses. I used to call the lunchers "the scorpions," but I enjoyed myself enormously, and, given my age, I was lucky to be there.

At any rate, Alice Longworth was one of those rare people who bulk large in their own time but leave no record and so are easily forgotten. To convey the flavor of her vanished presence, one must begin with the fact that she was very beautiful in a fine-boned way, although in her later years she made no effort whatever to look younger than her age. An aggressive atheist, she came close to disliking simple human goodness as a boring quality, but she had courage, which is the quality that always saves. She was witty, intelligent, and tough-minded, and she had a mortal horror of anything or anyone with the least savor of gush or sentimentality, earnest dullness, or overly ostentatious virtue. Such persons she enjoyed shocking, sometimes profoundly, as she had done to Eleanor Roosevelt since they were children together.

In appearance, Alice Longworth was unique, having invented

her own style of dressing that had nothing whatever to do with current fashions. In daytime, she always wore versions of the same wide-brimmed hat and a suit with a special jacket; and in the evenings, she wore dresses with rather plain lines, always floor-length, and, once again, always made in the same way and with very rich materials, which she had in enormous store. She dined out nonstop, but after she reached the age of seventy-five, she began to be insulted if she were asked with her contemporaries.

Yet I often wondered whether Alice Longworth did not go out so much because she feared loneliness. She was well known to read until nearly 6:00 A.M. after she had arrived home from dinner. For reading, moreover, she preferred serious works—above all, the Greek philosophers—and I am quite certain that if her mind had ever been disciplined in any way, she would have made her mark as a scholar or a thinker. She always managed to keep her body supple through yoga exercises, and she was the only woman I have ever known who was able to place her foot behind her head without apparent discomfort.

In her old age, the Kennedy administration added a new high point to her career. She was by then eighty, but the young president and his still younger wife and brother Bobby all adored "Mrs. L," as they, too, called her. In these Kennedy years, she was better company than ever; and it always used to entertain me, watching all the young beauties grow green with envy because this woman of eighty managed to be surrounded by all the most admired men in the city.

Alice Longworth had a thousand stories about the Washington past, most of them very funny. One concerned the love affair that her husband, Nick Longworth, had with Cissy Patterson, the eventual publisher of the *Washington Times Herald*. Mrs. Patterson had left her bag on the sofa in the Longworth house and gone upstairs with the then-Speaker to sit in the library after dinner. The next day, Alice Longworth sent Mrs. Patterson her bag with an acid note, and Mrs. Patterson sent back a short letter thanking her warmly but enquiring for her silk stockings, which she said had been stuffed down the sofa, and her chewing gum, which she claimed to have parked under the mantle.

Mrs. L's imitation of Eleanor Roosevelt was viciously accurate and hysterically funny. I am afraid she made a specialty of first ladies, for her other great turn was Mrs. William Howard Taft. She could transform her face and her voice entirely when she did these imitations. No one I have ever known had a wit like hers. It depended on extreme precision of language combined with the wildest fancy, which produced the most astonishing combinations. When

Wendell Willkie was nominated as the Republican presidential candidate at Philadelphia in 1940, I remember foolishly saying that the movement for Willkie came from the grass roots. Mrs. L gave a loud snort and said, "Yes, from the grass roots of 10,000 country clubs."

In spite of—and perhaps because—she was Theodore Roosevelt's eldest daughter, her childhood had not been an easy one. The president's first wife died giving birth to her, and she was brought up by the second Mrs. Theodore Roosevelt. I always thought something of her own basic unhappiness was explained in a story that she used to tell of leaving her family and the White House following her marriage to Nick Longworth. According to Mrs. L, her stepmother accompanied her to her room after the wedding ceremony. She watched as her stepchild dressed for going away, and after all the packing was done she said, "Well, good-bye, Alice. I'm not sorry to see you go; you have never been anything but a trouble to me."

By the time I came to live permanently in Washington, the Longworth house on Massachusetts Avenue was a large, hospitable, remarkably ill-kept establishment. The long, dark rooms had lost some of the high gloss exhibited when I first knew them in the 1920s, when there were a couple of footmen at the door and the goose hung very high indeed. However, in entertainment, as in her dress and her politics, Mrs. L stuck to the old ways as though this were the privilege of people who mattered. On her placecards at table, every man was plain "Mr."—including members of the cabinet, senators, and congressmen—the only American exceptions being those with legal titles like the president and the chief justice.

The food Mrs. L offered was a marvelous demonstration of how delicious, although nowadays impossibly expensive, a good plain American dinner used to be. A standard dinner in springtime at the Longworth house began with the best creamed crab soup I have ever had or else a consommé so strong one felt one could skate on it. If the start was consommé, this was followed by soft-shell crabs, perfectly sautéed, without any of the carapace of crumbs that deviant chefs in those days had begun to give them. The accompanying salad contained tomatoes sliced paper thin and skinned, and cucumbers properly soaked in salt and, therefore, limp and less bitter to taste. The main course was usually a saddle of lamb—enough so that guests could eat as many slices as wanted—with glorious fresh vegetables. All this was followed by crème brulée, which her cook knew how to make better than any other in my experience.

The quality of Mrs. L's table, however, was neither lesser nor greater than that of the other grand hostesses I have mentioned. The great Washington houses in those days were the last to preserve grand, old-style American cookery. They depended, first of all, on the possession of farms near the city or acquaintanceships with nearby farmers. The results were marvelous milk, real cream that hardly poured, butter with little relationship to the sad substance that now carries that name, and mountains of fresh vegetables and fresh fruit in season. The vegetables were always picked when they were still tiny, and I am bewildered to this day as to how those ladies managed to persuade their cooks to shell peas hardly bigger than pinheads in quantities sufficient for forty people.

To these basics were added delicacies: shad in season, not boned but so slowly cooked in a sealed container that the bones melted, giving it ten times the taste of the flannellike fish we get today; shad roe in mountains; soft-shell crabs; oyster crabs, which are tiny parasite crabs that inhabit oysters and have the tastes of both animals, not exactly in mountains because they were too expensive, but as a recurrent prize dish; in the autumn, turkey broilers (meaning specially fed, very young turkeys that were literally small enough to split and broil); reed birds, the pride of southern houses; all sorts of game as well as guinea hen; then, too, there were the game birds one sees no more like plovers and wild turkey; and there was, above all, terrapin in season.

This creature—halfway between a sea turtle and a land tortoise—was, to me, the greatest of American delicacies, and since it had inhabited the Maryland estuaries in great numbers, it became a staple of grand Washington dinners. Properly made (without cream sauce), terrapin appeared on the dinner table as an unctuous, even gelatinous stewlike dish, with the tenderest bits of the terrapin's meat plus its liver and the female terrapin's eggs all floating gently in an enormously rich sauce made by endlessly boiling down the broth derived from the rest of the terrapin, plus fresh butter in huge quantities, sherry and cayenne pepper. I don't know how to describe the taste except to say that although its aroma reminded one a bit of the way feet sometimes smell, it was absolutely delicious.

Terrapin had been a principal American delicacy for so long, however, that it had come close to extermination. As it grew harder to get, the price had soared. Hence, only a few very rich houses still offered terrapin by the time I arrived in Washington. The best known of all of these rich houses was that of the old chief of the Southern Railroad, Mr. Henry B. Spencer, who had a terrapin pen in his cellar, where the beasts that would eventually be consumed on his table were fed to happy repletion on a diet of cornmeal. About half-a-dozen terrapin cooks used to perambulate rather profitably from one house to another when terrapin was in season, their services being much in demand.

Properly cooked and aged Virginia ham, now just as unobtainable as terrapin, was not then such a rarity as terrapin had already become, but it was not easy to find, and no wonder. Ideally, the finest Virginia ham was four years old when eaten, and the haunch was as hard and dry as a board when initially taken in hand for the dinner to come. The first step was to set aside a guest-room bathroom or a large tub in which the ham was soaked in water that had to be changed twice a day. The person charged with the duty of soaking the ham had to watch the ham carefully, too, for the haunch would begin by floating with the heavier bone side down, but would prove its readiness for consumption by turning over of its own volition when the meat side had absorbed enough moisture.

After this preliminary, which might take four days, the ham was removed from the bath and boiled, quite often in wine. After boiling, the surface of the ham—the fat, of course—was skinned, rubbed with brown sugar and spices, carefully scored in a diamond pattern, and decorated with a clove in each diamond. After that, finally, the ham was baked and was then ready to be cut into very thin slices and offered cold at the dinner table, accompanied by salad. The fat, which was eaten, was sherry-colored and rather sweet, while the flesh was mahogany-colored, moist, and astonishingly rich-tasting. Some foreigners found our Virginia hams a bit salty, but for me they had a flavor I have never experienced before or since. If offered a Virginia ham of the old sort today, I think I could go on eating nothing else for a week.

By now, it will be clear how important food and society were in Washington. As for me, I have always enjoyed company, and, as a curious, amply fed young man, I soon developed a taste for my new Washington life. But the truth is, in the almost primeval Washington to which I was transferred, my life, as I have said, was in effect cut in half. One half was this dining-out life I have described, with all sorts of friends, both younger and older. The other half was of more consequence. It was my life as a young *Tribune* reporter in Washington. And here, I think, is where I should turn now, for these are, after all, the memoirs of a newspaperman.

5

Working Life: The Senate

I was not elated by what I found when I reported for work at the *Herald Tribune*'s Washington Bureau shortly after that new year of 1936. Whereas the *Times* had a whole suite of offices downtown, the *Tribune* operated from a poky room and a half in the old National Press Building. It was also quite evident that the exceedingly kind and hardworking head of the *Tribune* bureau, Al Warner, had no more faith in my qualifications as a reporter than Stanley Walker had the first day I walked into the *Tribune* office in New York, and for exactly the same reasons. No doubt the reasons were even stronger, for whereas I had weighed about 215 pounds in 1932 when I reported to Stanley Walker, I was pushing 245 when I reported to Al Warner three years later.

The New York office had in fact thrust me on Warner unceremoniously and had further ordered my assignment to the Senate press gallery, a great journalistic plum then and now. Even so, Warner tried to get permission to put someone else on the first big Senate story that came up, which was the second installment of the so-called "Nye hearings," chaired by Senator Gerald P. Nye, a Republican from North Dakota. Nye, who had a reputation as a progressive, was, in fact, an old-fashioned American populist, and far from a nice one. He was an athletic man with a leathery face, greasy reddish-brown hair, and a knack for the kind of eloquence that used to do well on the stump back in the Great Plains. However, he had no principles whatsoever, and this lack led him to take up a cause of which he may or may not have had a full understanding but which was surely fashionable, given the standards of the day.

The underlying theory of the Nye hearings, cloaked, as the legislation bearing the senator's name later came to be known, under the broad label of "neutrality," was popularized much earlier in England by a leading member of the British Labour party, George Lansbury. Lansbury was the archetype of the kind of man old Doctor Johnson had in mind when he said, "Hell is paved with good intentions." Although it has no historical basis, Lansbury's proposition that arms races cause wars became popular in the 1920s and 1930s.

Lansbury's theories drew enough political support in Britain to make him chairman of his party. By giving the British public something silly to believe, he became one of those responsible for the fact that his country faced Adolf Hitler inadequately armed. Lansbury not only committed the Labour party to a ludicrously inadequate defense policy, he also encouraged a similar policy among many of the Tories who did not wish to pay the taxes that a serious defense policy involves. Only after the infamous Munich Agreement in the summer of 1938 did Clement Attlee and Ernest Bevin, in my opinion two great men, all but drive Lansbury out of the Labour party. He wept self-pityingly as he went—but the old man should have wept for his country, not himself, for he had served his country ill.

None of this, of course, was foreseen when Lansbury's ideas were imported by American liberals in the late 1920s with the addition of two special American twists. First, it was argued that the "merchants of death"—the arms manufacturers—promoted wars to secure more business. Then, the additional argument was made that international bankers, by lending money to belligerent powers to pay for arms, also tended to involve their countries in wars in order to make sure they got their money back. This last notion was the true theme of the Nye hearings when they first convened in 1934. The house of Morgan was deeply involved because it had been the leader among the international banks that financed Britain and France in the First World War. Some initial "neutrality" legislation had also resulted from the first Nye hearings, but I shall limit myself to the second hearings, which I still remember vividly.

When I came to Washington to take up my new duties with the

Tribune, I had given no thought to worldly matters like the above. Life at Harvard had been all books and good times, and there was nothing I experienced in my New York years to make me look outward toward events in the rest of the world. In short, I was a tabula rasa. So when I began to cover the second Nye hearings, I found myself intimidated by my colleagues in the press gallery, the best of whom were clever, progressive-minded reporters.

My position was inadvertently improved by Arthur Krock, the Washington Bureau chief of the *New York Times.* Arthur had avoided trouble for the *Times* among the higher echelons of the New York business community as well as elsewhere by assigning to the hearings a kindly senior reporter whose mind appeared to have been pickled by drink. This man was almost incapable of writing a coherent story. I, meanwhile, became fascinated with the proceedings and began turning out copy in vast quantities at high speed. As a result, the *Herald Tribune* was generally read by everyone in New York interested in the Nye hearings, while the *Times* was not.

Each working day followed a similar routine. I would sit through the hearings until they ended. I would then speed to the *Tribune* office in the press building, clutching the documents that I wished to have printed. Sitting down at the typewriter, I would then dash off an average of 4,000 words, a frightening volume to think about, but in those days the average newspaper reader had a far longer attention span than is common now. Reporters typed their stories onto "books" comprised of cheap paper backed up by three or four flimsies interleaved with very tired carbons. Triple-spaced, each of these books contained up to a paragraph and a half of text before it was ripped off and given to the copy editor. I never got through writing until half an hour before the last deadline, which was 9:30, and, as a rule, I never saw the whole of my story until it was printed on the front page of next morning's paper.

The Nye hearings were of intense interest in New York because they involved the house of Morgan. Reigning over Wall Street, Morgan was regarded among conservative New Yorkers—the majority of whom were *Herald Tribune* subscribers—as a kind of club for archangels. Conscious of being the new man on the block, I wrote copy that at least avoided my colleagues' disapproval. I must have been successful in this at least, for during the hearings, Mr. Thomas W. Lamont, who, after George Whitney, was the most active Morgan partner, went to the *Tribune* and asked to have me taken off the story. To his credit, Ogden Reid, to whom the matter was referred, told Mr. Lamont to go to hell.

In several ways those long weeks of work on the Nye hearings were an important episode in my early Washington years. They dissolved any doubts Al Warner still had about my professional abilities and squared my reputation among colleagues in the press gallery. In those days, very few Washington newspapermen came from New York, and almost none had gone to university. Certainly, no working newspaperman that I knew of had been drawn from the more fortunate group of WASPs except Henry Cabot Lodge, who had done a brief stint with the *Tribune* some years earlier. By now, I had outlasted Cabot and, in the process, proved myself at least not to be a worthless parasite. No doubt I was still viewed as an eccentric in some journalistic quarters, but at least I was thought to be a competent eccentric.

Any eccentricities I had were to serve me well in my job. With the Nye hearings over, I was free, over the next year and a half, to cover one of the great idiosyncratic institutions of the day: the United States Senate. In those years before the war (I covered Capitol Hill in 1936 and 1937), the Senate still reflected something of the parish-pump character of pretelevision American politics. It was a more local place, by which I mean the members were of distinguishable local origin and, because they generally stayed in office longer, had no cause to be anything other than themselves. Television had not yet arrived to make all American politicians go to the same hairdressers and try to sound alike. Nor did most senators then care very much about national newspaper publicity, for, in the main, they regarded themselves as representatives of their local states. It had been a long time, also, since one of them had been a candidate for the presidency. Governorships were where the public looked in those days when they wanted to find presidents.

On the whole, therefore, the politicians I encountered when I first settled into the old Senate press gallery were honest, independent, and marvelously varied, whether in appearance, costume, character, or viewpoint. The Senate's members ranged from James Couzens of Michigan, who wore impeccable, unvarying, pinstriped black suits and was rumored to send his marvelously fine white shirts to Paris to be laundered, to the always rumpled and moderately grimy Spessard Holland of Florida, who kept no apartment in Washington, slept on his office sofa, and did such washing as he cared to do in his office lavatory.

Jim Ham Lewis, a grandiloquent Democrat from Illinois, successively wore three wigs—one short, one medium, one long— to give the impression his hair was growing. For heightened effect, when the middle-length or the long wig was in use, he would sprinkle over his shoulders what I think was sawdust, finely ground, to suggest dandruff. And when Senator Lewis wore his long wig, nothing pleased him more than to be told that he was in need of a haircut.

The celebrated Tom Connally of Texas had genuine long, silver hair, always wore black clothes, and when he indulged in one of his flowery orations, the general effect was to make you wonder whether the Senate floor had suddenly gained a visitor from the nineteenth century. Hiram Johnson of California, one of the toughest of the Republican progressives, looked as though he might bite one of his colleagues at any time. Senator Hugo Black, a kinder, more engaging man, was one of the few senatorial progressives among the southern Democrats and the only member of the entire Senate whom I knew of who owned a translation of Marx's *Das Kapital*—although he was frank about never having bothered to read the volume through.

Then there was Key Pittman of Nevada, chairman of the Senate Foreign Relations Committee from 1933 until his retirement from the Senate in 1941. Pittman drank heavily and, as he was getting along in years, had difficulty with bladder control when he drank. Unfortunately, the senator's weak bladder in no way weakened his appetite for social entertainment. Indeed, Pittman liked very much to dine at the Washington embassies, and since he was Senate Foreign Relations Committee chairman, protocol dictated he be asked at least once a year to almost every foreign legation. (In the Washington of those days, the embassies numbered, I should guess, no more than one-fourth of the present total.) One or two of the ambassadresses became so impatient of the inevitable result of having Pittman as a guest that they used to put special rubber seat covers on the chairs they assigned to the right honorable senator from Nevada.

For a reporter, moreover, these curious and wonderful men were both a known and knowable quantity. Nowhere in Washington, including even the White House, was there anything vaguely resembling the vast security apparatus that pervades the city today. Anyone invited to dine with the president and Mrs. Roosevelt simply drew up to the front door of the White House and rang the bell. So it was with the Senate. If guests invited to dine in official Washington in 1936 had been asked, as they are nowadays at the White House, to supply their birth dates and Social Security numbers and to carry with them identification papers and, finally, to walk through a detection gate to reveal whether they were carrying concealed weapons, I suspect that a fair proportion would have turned on their heels and gone home.

At the White House there was nothing even vaguely resembling the present White House staff, and on Capitol Hill there was nothing like the present senatorial and congressional staffs. The president had advisers, but they did not all, as a rule, congregate in the offices in the White House. Indeed, the mere mention of a "White House chief of staff" would have caused a nationwide attack of apoplexy. The permanent staff consisted of an astonishingly efficient corps of lady secretaries, an establishment of telephone operators who could have gotten you the devil in hell within five minutes, and two or three officials like Steve Early and Marvin McIntyre who tended both to the president's daily schedule and to the newspapermen who needed anything beyond what was provided by the president's twice-weekly press conferences. This whole group was comfortably housed in the West Wing, and the present ridiculous but deadly competition for offices as status symbols was decades in the future.

The air of casual familiarity prevailed to an even greater degree in the Senate. Unless I am mistaken, the swollen congressional and senatorial staffs of today are an outgrowth of Senator Robert La Follette, Jr.'s Legislative Reform act of 1946, of which the Wisconsin senator was justly proud. If he could see what this portion of his act finally let loose, however, I do not think the great senator would be so proud. The constituents of today vote for their senators in the confident belief that they, as citizens, are going to be fairly represented by the man that wins the majority; instead, they get faceless administrative assistants who provide the senator with his ideas and programs. This system, which now prevails in the House, too, strikes me as questionably democratic, and I regard it as certainly the greatest and most pernicious organizational change that has overtaken the American government in my lifetime.

To picture the Senate that I covered as a young political reporter, one must bear in mind that a senator's staff usually consisted of one $6,000-a-year patronage appointee—someone whom the senator had to take care of and could usually expect little work from— plus a couple of hard-working stenographers. Because their staffs were smaller, the entire Senate could be accommodated in the first and handsomest of the now numerous Senate office buildings, which was built in 1909. There was little more in the standard member's office than an ample desk and chairs, along with the occasional couch on which a senator might sleep when he felt dozy. The Senate press gallery of those days led into the Senate gallery itself, where reporters listened to the day's debates, if they wanted to. But this was uncommon; for the key to successful political reporting then

was to know the senators—before television, no politician was required to resist the appalling temptation, which politicians apparently never can resist, to make a fool of himself before a television
camera—and in those days, office doors were always open, their
occupants usually affable and, if one took the initiative, willing to
discuss and explain the issues of the day.

The politics of these men were as various as their costumes.
The dominant legislative group, the so-called southern "conservatives," were less conservative than is now imagined. To begin with,
they detested the financial power then concentrated in New York,
loathing with all possible malice the northern bankers who still held
the South quite largely in pawn. Although socially conservative in
the strictest southern sense, these senators were generally discontented with the workings of the existing economic system, which
had put the South squarely on its back in the Depression, and they
were ready to experiment in a limited way with alternatives.

However, this group presented two limitations that Franklin
Roosevelt could overcome only with difficulty. The leading southerners feared an excessively unbalanced budget and the spending
that produced it, and they were hostile to the rising power of the
labor unions. There was also one more all-too-obstinate view that
Franklin Roosevelt never dared tackle: the southern senators' views
on racial questions. Although deeply wrong by present standards,
these were the views about race that were all but universal among
white southerners of those days. Nevertheless, with the exception of
two or three men like Senator Walter George of Georgia, the southern senators were passionately partisan men who had hated the
Republicans since birth and, furthermore, remembered with disgust
the Republican decades that had preceded Roosevelt. As partisans,
they were prepared to follow their party and its president wherever
he led them, as long as this did not lead to any tampering with the
social mores of their native states.

This was certainly the view of the Senate majority leader Joseph T. Robinson of Arkansas, who exerted far greater power and
enforced far sterner discipline than any subsequent Senate leader,
including Lyndon B. Johnson. Indeed, one can hardly imagine such
a man as Robinson today. I always thought of him as a huge aurochs
left over from the primeval time, when the great-muscled oxen
roamed the forests. In physical stature, he was a large man and as
near to menacing as any politician I have seen. He always kept his
word and indulged in a minimum of oratory on the Senate floor, but
his aspect, even in repose, was that of a particularly dangerous bull
in a stiff white collar.

Robinson dealt in the old currency of American politics—"pork," meaning government projects that created patronage and jobs for the faithful. During the Depression era, the ability to produce government jobs for the home voters was a main source of success: inability to produce such jobs caused the ruin of many a career in politics. In return for his unwavering support on the floor, President Roosevelt had the good sense to let Senator Robinson be the main dispenser of patronage and pork. In consequence, the majority leader's pockets bulged with senatorial IOUs, and these, in turn, permitted him to call the tune in terms of Senate legislative policy whenever it pleased him.

The best patronage story I know concerns Senator Pat Harrison of Mississippi, who was a strong supporter of Robinson's, chairman of the Senate Finance Committee and, in his own way, one of the most powerful members of the Senate. George N. Peek, who was a friend of Harrison's, was head of one of the earliest of the New Deal agencies, the Agricultural Adjustment Administration or AAA. At the time, Harrison lived in deadly fear of one of his constituents, Theodore "The Man" Bilbo, a particularly unappetizing Mississippi version of the kind of neopopulist demagogue the South then sometimes produced. At all costs, Harrison wanted to prevent Bilbo, then in an interlude between a disgraceful governorship of the state and a later term in the Senate, from running against him in the next election. His method was to neutralize Bilbo by procuring for him a soft spot on the payroll of George Peek's AAA.

Senator Harrison called on his old friend and explained to him the circumstances of his predicament, giving Bilbo a big buildup as an able, patriotic fellow, while delicately insisting that the job he was asking Peek to provide for Bilbo would have to carry a substantial salary. Peek, who understood practical politics, immediately granted Harrison's request. Harrison thanked him profusely and began to leave the room. When he was halfway across the room, however, the senator stopped and turned around to say, "Now, George, I don't want you to get me wrong. This man Bilbo will do a great job for you and the government, I've no doubt about that. But he comes from our piney-woods district; the people are kind of rough there. So I just don't believe I'd put him in any job where he'd have to do any speaking for you. Maybe he'd embarrass you."

Peek thanked Harrison for the tip. Harrison thanked Peek for the favor, said good-bye, and this time got halfway through the door. Then he turned and began a second time. He repeated the statement with the warning that since Bilbo was from the piney-woods country, it might be unwise to let him handle large sums of money. Peek again said he quite understood, and he was glad to have the warning.

The third time, Harrison got clean out of the room, but reopened the door and put his head around it. "Now, George," he said, "please don't misunderstand me. I promise you this man Bilbo will make a great public servant. But they're not just rough people in our piney-woods country; they've got rough ways, too. So I don't believe I'd let Bilbo be around any pretty girls for very long."

This third time Peek said, "I quite understand, Pat. Your man Bilbo will make a great public servant if I just gag him, bind him, and geld him. He's got the job!"

So for the next two years, Bilbo, who later became a U.S. senator despite Pat Harrison, drew a salary of $6,000 per annum and, by order of George Peek, occupied a kind of closet on a corridor in the AAA's office building along with a woman with whom only a madman could have dared to tamper. She and Bilbo were assigned to make "significant" clippings from newspapers, and this she did incessantly. Bilbo did so intermittently, whenever it was necessary to return to the office to get his paycheck. In this odd way and at the government's expense, "The Man" was neutralized, at least for the time being, for he did not run against Pat Harrison in the next election.

Using such ammunition, it was Robinson who, with his partners Harrison and James F. Byrnes of South Carolina, the Democratic whip, pushed through Congress the bulk of President Roosevelt's first New Deal legislation. This trio had in fact solidly supported Roosevelt throughout his first three years. They were still solidly supporting him when I reached the Senate press gallery just after the New Year, 1936; but by then, they were beginning, as I have said, to show disquiet over Rooseveltian spending and Rooseveltian support for the growth of labor power.

One who did not go so easily with the crowd was old Carter Glass of Virginia, who had been showing disquiet about these issues for some time. I often think of Glass and did so with nostalgia after seeing the seven candidates for the 1988 Democratic presidential nomination debate one another on television. The politicians in this strange group all appeared to have acquired their faces and their hair from the same fashionable supplier, except, of course, for the Reverend Jesse Jackson. With the same exception, the candidates' views on so-called issues of substance were even harder to differentiate. It makes me wonder how such a man as Glass could have lasted as long and had the kind of impact upon politics that he did, while still commanding universal respect from those who agreed with him and those who did not.

Carter Glass was a tiny man, barely five feet tall, with an enormous nose and, when angered, a very curious habit of talking out of the side of his mouth. He was capable of bitter hatred, although he hated seldom. He rather liked FDR, for example, but I cannot think of an issue on which he and the president fully agreed. His most bitter hates were reserved for the past—specifically the Wilson administration, when he managed to create the Federal Reserve Bank almost singlehandedly. Among these, his chief hate was Wilson's secretary of state William Jennings Bryan. I remember visiting Senator Glass once and watching the side of his mouth drop nearly to his chin as he told me: "Can you imagine, Alsop—*just can you imagine*—that goddamned nincompoop once said to me that *any man with real goodness of heart* could write a banking act!"

President Roosevelt referred to Glass rather sourly as "the unreconstructed rebel," for the Virginia senator was one of the few members of the Senate who withstood Robinson's often-rough political brand of medicine. Robinson, too, as an old colleague, knew Glass's recalcitrant side and was wary of it. According to Senate legend, Senator Robinson visited Glass privately during the 1936 session in an attempt to bring him around on some bill or other. The Arkansan, as Glass later related the story, declared that many of the New Deal measures that he had sent through Congress wounded his finer sensibilities and explained dolefully that only party loyalty had kept him regular.

"I've admired you, Carter," Senator Robinson said, "and I want you to know it. But I've just had to go along. I've done it for the party, and I want you to know, Carter, that I've been through hell."

"Well," drawled Glass in reply, "anyway it's nice to know, Joe, that the road through hell is paved with postmasterships."

More often than not, however, Robinson, with his solid Democratic majority, got his way, and this was thanks in large part to a small group of progressive senators whom I have elsewhere called the "lawmakers." In the real left wing of the Senate, and in part of the House, too, these were the men whom one old Republican leader once tactlessly called "the sons of the wild jackass." Among them, in fact, were a good many Republican progressives—veterans of the progressive ferment started by Theodore Roosevelt—and, as I look back on them, they were remarkable men.

Until the Second World War, the liberals and progressives in Congress were by no means content simply to make noble speeches, strike noble attitudes, and cast noble votes. Since 1945, with the possible exception of Senator Bill Bradley's 1986 tax-reform bill, few single major pieces of forward-looking legislation that finally reached the statute books has been the work, individually, of one of the Democratic senators or representatives from the left—or, for that matter, from the right—side of the political spectrum. In the earlier time, however, the able men in Congress—particularly senators, and most particularly those from the left—used to focus on one great problem or other, develop their own solutions, and fight for these year after year until their solutions became the law of the land.

These men could, as I have said, be Democrats or Republicans. Couzens, Robert Wagner, and even Senator Arthur Vandenberg of Michigan, the real author of Federal Deposit Insurance for banks, were among those who had great enactments to their credit. These were the bills, like Wagner's Labor Act, which could never have been passed during the more right-wing Republican heyday of the 1920s. However, these men bided their time and made themselves experts in their chosen fields. Because they knew more than any other members of the Senate on their specific issues, they could be deflected but never argued with. When Franklin Roosevelt took over the White House, he signed their long-preserved bills in one form or another, and he made sure that the progressive Republicans got their share of postmasterships and other patronage and pork—and also that they got full public credit for their achievement.

My own particular favorite and the man in the old Senate whose memory I cherish most, possibly because he seemed to like me, was always ready to see me, and never failed to enlighten and entertain me, was Charles McNary of Oregon. As the minority leader, the senator gave constant offense to his more partisan Republican colleagues because, despite his office, he had an extremely soft spot for Franklin Roosevelt and was in some sense a captive of the president's charm. In appearance, McNary was a very curious man—tall and lanky, with a tiny head and a round face that flushed ruby red when he was angry. His long neck was always encircled by a high stiff collar—an unblemished tube of starched linen of a kind hardly seen since about 1910. The collar must have measured about four inches top to bottom, it held a very small bow tie, and it was complemented by a pair of very long starched cuffs, which Senator McNary would shoot repeatedly—dragging them down over the backs of his hands as though to show them off better—when he was angry.

I last saw Senator McNary in 1940 in his almost prehistoric suite at the Bellevue-Stratford Hotel in Philadelphia. The senator had arrived there with the purpose of presiding at his party's national convention as an anti-Willkie leader. By the time I reached him, however, Willkie had already won the Republican nomination, and the disappointed McNary was being pressured by party leaders to accept the second spot on the ticket, a job he wanted no part of. I remember the scene as if it were yesterday. I knocked politely on the door, and after a brief time Senator McNary himself let me in. Before I had time even to sit and make myself comfortable, the senator produced a bottle of bourbon, poured himself three full fingers, took a strong restoring draft, and began cursing roundly into his drink. Party loyalty counted for a great deal more in those days than it does now; and if the Republicans agreed that McNary's candidacy would give them the best chance at the election, then he had no choice but to accept. He called Willkie—as Roosevelt's secretary of the interior Harold Ickes had earlier described him—that "damn barefoot boy from Wall Street," which was indeed largely accurate, and he said the vice-presidency, even under the best of circumstances, was "no better than a goddamned spare tire." I muttered my assent to this tirade, which lasted more than a few minutes, and then begged good-bye, for although I hated to leave the senator cursing by himself, a second bourbon was out of the question since I had other work to do. In the end, of course, McNary resigned himself to his fate, and although his misgivings about Willkie were borne out from the general campaign's very first day, he never showed it in public.

As I look back, it seems to me that 1936 and much of 1937—it was hardly more than that—when I was covering the Senate and getting to know old-fashioned Washington, was about as enjoyable as any time in my professional life. It was not easy for a single reporter to cover the whole Senate, but in those days a young and active man could do it if he took the trouble to learn the maze of connections—and the parallel maze of favors exchanged—that tied most of the Senate together. The people one dealt with might be eccentric, but most of them were immensely likable. My journalistic colleagues were much older, on average, than my colleagues in the *Herald Tribune* city room, but they were by and large just as interesting and just as pleasant as the men they covered.

The truth is that the Senate's all-too-human atmosphere of the older America of little government was a paradise for political reporters. And as the rest of Washington was undergoing drastic and inexorable change thanks to Franklin Roosevelt and his young crowd of New Dealers, the Congress, as a whole, continued to provide the old reporters with a familiar point of reference. As survivors from the Wilson-Harding-Coolidge-Hoover era, these newspapermen still clung to such men as Robinson, Harrison, McNary, and Vandenberg because these American political types were easily identifiable by past experience. By the same token, most senior political reporters of those days regarded the New Dealers as eerie and unconversible. Later on, I would find that this ingrown aversion would give considerable competitive advantage to younger newspapermen who were willing to seek out and question Roosevelt's bright young officials. During my time at the Senate, however, it was a unique pleasure for me to bask in the easy congeniality of the place and to learn from my colleagues the old ways of doing business, while these old ways lasted.

The most elaborately painted of all the Senate rooms was the President's Room, which led through a side entrance to the Senate chamber. Standing guard there was a young, rather fat, very virtuous seventeen-year-old page named Richard, a hard-shelled Baptist who aimed, it was fairly obvious, to form some kind of connection with his church when he grew up. Between his many errands, Richard would often lecture me about my evil ways, adjuring me to forswear the demon drink and cast away my vile cigarettes. I would weather these attacks before asking Richard if a certain senator were available for questions. He would then disappear with a nod and sometimes return with the news that he couldn't find the senator on the floor. More often than not, however, the senator would come and sit with me for several minutes in the Presidents' Room under the portraits of George Washington's cabinet, or I would be directed to appear at the senator's office at an appointed time.

The press gallery itself is worth describing, for it was where the journalist's daily routine began and where much of the business of newspapering was conducted. The room itself was a softly lit, comfortable place that looked as though time had stopped while TR was president or perhaps a little earlier. The floor was composed of English Minton tiles that had been imported in the mid-nineteenth century, and between the big windows on the north side there was a huge fireplace that burned brightly all winter. Above the fireplace hung a large gilded mirror, its frame a splendid explosion of Victorian Baroque. Some of the typewriters, which were laid out in rows for our use, must have been purchased before the first war, and the large, deep sofas and chairs were made of a very special type of buttoned black leather that plainly dated from the McKinley era.

Today, when I attend what now passes for grand entertainment in this city and hear the pompously discussed concerns of Washington in the 1980s, I like to think of the times in the old Senate press gallery when news was scarce and there was not much work to do. The beat reporters would draw lots to see whose duty it would be to sit in the gallery proper and keep watch over that day's

Senate proceedings. One or two of the older men would nod off to sleep in one of the ample sofas, and the rest of us would draw the huge leather chairs up around the fire and trade tales and gossip about the old Senate. These sessions produced countless stories, some of them lengthy and involved, like the one I have told about Pat Harrison, and others more pithy and peculiar, dealing with the private travails or personal oddities of the lawmakers of the day.

My favorite of the countless ancient tales told and retold during these cozy sessions was the story of the famous "Million-Dollar Spit," which relates how a very randy governor from North Carolina had his career temporarily blighted in a most vile and amusing way by the engines of progress. The incident took place at Biltmore, the enormous Vanderbilt family château in Asheville, North Carolina, when the house and grounds were still inhabited by that great family instead of being used as a tourist sight, as it is today. Mr. George Washington Vanderbilt had just been gathered to his maker, and the Widow Vanderbilt, after a decent interval, had begun to entertain suitors. The governor in question was a bachelor and, therefore, an obvious candidate; and, by all accounts, the Widow Vanderbilt was initially impressed enough with his credentials—he had also served as senator from that state—to offer him an audience.

The governor was a gregarious and effervescent man, and the two saw a good deal of one another, enough so that observers within the family were predicting further developments. Unluckily, at this critical point, Mrs. Vanderbilt invited the governor out for a drive around the Biltmore land in her splendid new Rolls-Royce. At this juncture, it must be explained that in that long-ago era (Vanderbilt died in 1914), only the most luxurious American cars came equipped with plate-glass windows. Many automobiles had no windows at all, especially the secondhand ones common in the more depressed states. The governor had the habit of chewing tobacco, and on this day, as was his wont, he was discreetly working away on a rather large quid. Presumably he was too engrossed, either with his tobacco or with the charms of the Widow Vanderbilt, to notice that the invisible Rolls-Royce window had been rolled up. During a lull in the conversation, therefore, the governor, seeing nothing blocking passage to the great outdoors, sent a discreet line of spit in the direction of the window. The results, however, were not discreet at all, for the governor's brown quid splattered all over the shining new glass and, one must imagine, all over Mrs. Vanderbilt as well. Thereupon Mrs. Vanderbilt decided she had better look elsewhere for a successor to Mr. Vanderbilt, and the unfortunate governor departed the grounds, in prospects at least, a poorer man.

During other hours of inactivity at the Senate, when I was not trading tales with my fellow newspapermen, one of my favorite amusements was to wander the Capitol itself, which I gradually discovered to be an immensely endearing building, as it was before Congress began tampering with it. Among the spectacles it afforded was the two-story lobby on the Senate side, which today is known as the small Senate rotunda. This smallish, circular space was encircled by a balcony, and George Washington's tomb would have been on the lower level, if his family had not so obstinately preferred Mount Vernon. Because of the uses that balcony was later put to, this lobby on the Senate side used to be called "America's Spittoon," a name given it, unless I am mistaken, by Mark Twain.

The quickest way to get from the Senate to the House was through the simply hewed granite of the Capitol's supporting undervault. In its plain, solid way, that walk always struck me as being wonderfully beautiful. Much of the simplicity of the old Capitol building is gone now, especially in the interior spaces. But if we could get rid of the monstrous pieces of sculpture in what is now called Statuary Hall—this was the old chamber of the House of Representatives, where John Quincy Adams died while speaking up for the right of petition—this would stand forth again as one of the most beautiful and powerfully designed rooms in America.

Oddly enough, however, the feature of the Capitol that I have always remembered the best was Thomas Moran's vast painting of Yellowstone Park that hung in the old press gallery. This portrayed Yellowstone in detail, with many a geyser gushing away. Its history also seemed to me worth the price of admission, for Moran went West to do this picture—and later another painting, equally vast, of the Grand Canyon—because the post–Civil War report of the U.S. Geological Survey about the wonders of the American West seemed simply too lurid to be believed in the East. For most easterners, in fact, Moran's pictures were meant to—and did—play the role played nowadays of photographs taken on an expedition into unknown wild country. What I liked to do was search through their vast expanses—for I sometimes visited the House press gallery just to have a look at the Grand Canyon—for animal or human life. Alas, there were no Indians, but I found a grizzly bear in the Senate press gallery's picture and a dead deer, too.

I delighted in my work in the Senate during that remote era, and I think I did it well. The *Herald Tribune* beat the *Times* on several major Senate stories—something that mattered more in those days than it does now—and often I would receive congratulations from my bureau chief as well as from New York. Looking back, it seems improbable to me today that in the course of a year and a half a fat near-boy with an odd accent came to know and be accepted by just about everybody in that grand institution.

I suppose the answer to my success lay in the three reportorial rules I made for myself very early. One was always do your best to learn your subject so that you don't ask foolish questions; two, always do your best to avoid wasting time during an interview, even when your line of questioning follows a tortuous and difficult trail; and, third, no matter how big a bastard you have to talk business with, never be rude unless the bastard is rude first. There have been a few, very few, people in public life—the late Senator Joseph R. McCarthy was one—with whom I felt justified in never talking at all. And even in the extreme case of McCarthy, my refusal to talk or shake hands would be made necessary by a shambling McCarthy attempt at self-ingratiation.

Per contra, I have seldom been more proud than when called in by Hugo Black after FDR had named him to the Supreme Court in 1937. President Roosevelt had in fact chosen Black as the man the conservative senators would hate most to vote for but for whom, because of senatorial courtesy, they would be forced to vote. This turned out to be the case. However, almost immediately after his confirmation, the Alabama senator's appointment was called into question over some public allegations of an old membership in the Ku Klux Klan. Black and his wife Josephine thought well enough of me to ask my advice on the matter. Josephine, who was one of the finest and most agreeable women I have ever known in Washington, was visibly worried—not just for Hugo, whom she loved, but also because she longed for a refuge from the rough and tumble of politics, and she saw the Supreme Court as an ideal way out. Hugo's outlook on the matter, meanwhile, verged on the belligerent. It seemed to me that all that mattered was the justice's real public record (he had in fact joined the Klan but had quickly resigned); hence, I suggested Hugo state his case in public as crisply and as briefly as possible and let the chips fall where they may. I was sure that the current row would prove to be a two-day wonder, and, after Justice Black addressed the issue over national radio, so it was.

Long before receiving Justice Black's confidence, however, I had been voted a success in the Senate in another and most satisfactory way. In the 1930s, with television all but unheard of, the immense prosperity of the mass-circulation magazines was still on an upward course. The great magazines offered their writers and their subjects exposure comparable to the top television news shows of today. Writing, say, for the *Saturday Evening Post* in that time was almost the equivalent of being a highly visible anchorperson on a television network in the 1980s. Writers for the *Post*, however, were not attended by armies of gofers and flacks, nor was their hair elegantly arranged and possibly artificially improved before work could begin.

The *Post* then counted its circulation in the several millions and was the leading mass-circulation magazine in the United States. One reached an immense audience by writing for the *Post*, and, what was much nicer, one was very generously rewarded by the standards of the day. For my purposes, the most important editor of the *Saturday Evening Post* was Martin Sommers, an old friend from my New York reporting days. When he first offered me a writing assignment with the magazine, the price named was $1,500, which is not far from the worth of $15,000 now. After a very short interval, my price rose to $2,500, and it had reached $3,000 an article before the beginning of the second big war. Added together, these numbers were several times the wages the *Tribune* was paying, and so I did my best to make my magazine stints a success.

To my alarm, Marty Sommers first suggested I write a profile of Joe Robinson. I thought I was too much a greenhorn and too little acquainted with the real sources of Senator Robinson's extraordinary authority to do him justice. Although less sure of my political reporting skills, I had confidence in myself as a writer, and, consequently, I invited the political reporter I admired most in those days, Turner Catledge of the *New York Times*, to join me as a partner. A tall, moon-faced man with a small, upturned nose, Turner was immensely jolly and companionable. Although his native Mississippi drawl had begun to soften by the time we met, Turner retained an enormous knack for making friends, particularly among the southern politicians he covered. Pat Harrison adored him, and I believe Huey Long also liked him. With humor and deference—and, I must say, a good deal of shrewdness—Turner played the role of Junior to their wise Grandpa and in such a way learned the particulars of old-fashioned American politics better than any man I knew.

Turner had never attempted magazine writing but was willing, for the sums mentioned, to give the new form a try. So we formed the partnership of Alsop and Catledge, and signed our stories in that order, although this enraged Turner's Gridiron Club colleagues, who thought me an upstart and felt (not without justification) a man of Turner's stature and qualifications should get the top billing.

In fact, although I had brought Turner the initial assignment and the actual prose that went on paper was mainly my work, our partnership would be wholly equal. In those days, as I have already tried to show, the Senate floor was like an enormously varied but prosperous vegetable garden, offering every delicacy, like asparagus and baby peas for easy picking, if the *Post* wanted that sort of article, as well as ample supplies of cabbages, potatoes, and kohlrabi, if the editors desired heavier fare. Turner and I did a creditable job on the Robinson piece and found we enjoyed working together. More importantly, Martin Sommers liked our work, and so Turner and I soon became regular contributors to the *Saturday Evening Post.*

In time, our work together followed a steady routine. Reporting for any particular magazine piece was done in and around our regular duties as daily newspapermen. When we had our facts in hand and had made a rough outline of the story, we would then meet for several evenings in succession in the study of Turner's small suburban house. Laboriously, we would work out orally what we wanted to say, paragraph by paragraph. I would then begin to dictate my notion of the phrasing of each paragraph to Turner, who would be sitting over his old rattletrap typewriter.

By established precedent, Turner had a right either to offer a suggestion or to make me rephrase the language before each new paragraph was undertaken. In this way, each paragraph was crafted and polished singularly before moving along to the next. As a general rule, we would stick to the typewriter and to the work connected with the typewriter for no less than one hour before we allowed ourselves even one small drink. After two hours of labor, we would allow ourselves one large drink, and so on, until the general thread of the article became too muddled to continue with. Turner would then drive me home to the small men's club I inhabited downtown when I first moved to Washington.

Turner and I prospered together, both as professional partners and as friends. Before very long, our editors at the *Post* had stopped asking us to write solely on subjects dealing with the Senate. We happily obliged, and the resulting article on the politics of the Roosevelt relief programs enhanced our small reputations around the capital. In this congenial way, I was able to broaden my professional sphere from the more local routines of Capitol Hill out into the larger world of FDR's Washington.

6

The Column

In the spring and summer of 1937, three things happened to change my life dramatically. The first event was historical and decidedly beyond my control, for that was the year of President Roosevelt's attempt to pack the Supreme Court. The Court fight, as it came to be called, was the greatest national debate to take place in the Congress during my short career there (nor has there been any congressional debate to compare with it since). It was the biggest story of Turner's and my young journalistic lives, and from an early date, we were both captivated by it. The second event was of a very different nature and frightening as hell, for the stress brought on by the combination of steady overeating and a hectic work schedule gave rise to a crisis in health that very nearly cost me my life. The third happening was directly related to the first, for my work with Turner in covering the Court battle eventually resulted in the offer to write my own political column. It was an offer that I eventually accepted, although not without a measure of trepidation.

These developments, by turns jarring and invigorating, took place within the space of six months and left my young world radically altered. But they cannot be adequately explained without first giving some attention to the Court fight itself, for the story occupied Turner and me day in and day out for more than half a year. It is still the greatest single political drama I have witnessed in Washington in over half a century of reporting and, as such, one of the great journalistic adventures of my life. Turner and I were lucky, too, for the dramatic debate, although encompassing the entire government, was focused in the U.S. Senate, where we were both well connected as reporters and welcomed as friends in a way that would be unimaginable in journalistic circles today.

The president's announced intention, in early February of 1937, to expand the Court from nine justices to as many as fifteen came as a complete bombshell, for literally no one in either party expected Roosevelt to take such a gamble. During the election year of 1936, the Supreme Court had reached the arrogant stage of vetoing just about every item of the New Deal program that came before it even though these items of the New Deal program enjoyed powerful popular support, passed Congress by huge majorities in most cases, and had been jubilantly signed by the president. In a negative way, the Court had assumed legislative powers on a gigantic scale, for it is really an exercise in legislative power to say, as the Court had said, that the antiquated wage-and-hour laws of the day might be unattractive but were still untouchable because of the Constitution.

The liberals of those days asked only that the Court, in effect, stop legislating and limit itself to sympathetic and sane examination of legislation produced by the branches of the government that were charged with making law. The liberal argument then was in fact not very different from the one that, in more recent history, caused such outrage when it was enunciated by the right-wing supporters of Judge Robert Bork. If principles matter at all, the way the liberal principles of 1937 have now been stood on their head by just the kind of people who supported them most vociferously in the old Court fight still offers a good deal of sardonic amusement for those who enjoy such amusement.

The ins and outs of the ensuing political struggle were made more dramatic because the president started with such an apparently unchallengeable lead and then saw his lead erode month by month by the departure of Senate supporters who thought he had gone too far. It was a tremendous horse race right down to the wire, and the eyes of the whole country were glued to it. Each time a legislator crossed over to the opposition, he would explain his reasons for doing so on the Senate floor. The debate lasted for months, pitting the powerful Senate majority leader Joe Robinson of Arkansas, on whom President Roosevelt depended absolutely to carry a Senate majority, against another Democrat, Burton K. Wheeler of Montana, a very shrewd, very vain man who had high political ambitions of his own and had come to dislike FDR because the president was stealing some of Wheeler's own thunder.

Very early on in the fight, Roosevelt took the position of a monarch who believes a campaign so important that he supersedes his generals and takes the field himself. One by one, the president lost supporters whom he had counted upon and found himself successfully outmaneuvered by people he thought were incapable of it. Chief among these was my old dinner partner Charles Evans Hughes, the chief justice who looked like a Renaissance portrait of God Almighty but was, in fact, much closer to a judicial version of Machiavelli. For his own reasons, Chief Justice Hughes had, on several occasions, voted with the majority of the Court on some of its most extreme anti-Roosevelt decisions. In the end, he delivered the most important death blow to the Court bill by persuading the large, amiable, but always malleable Justice Owen J. Roberts to join him and then go over to the other side, thereby astonishing Roosevelt and his strategists in the White House with a spate of Court approvals of New Deal measures (upholding, specifically, Wagner's National Labor Relations Act and, later, the Social Security Act) that they had counted upon to be disapproved and thus to increase public fury against the Court.

The president's cause was further weakened by a clever trick of the opposition that somehow persuaded Justice Willis Van Devanter to resign, thus leaving Roosevelt face to face with his own commitment to Senate Majority Leader Robinson to give the latter first place on the Court in exchange for the majority leader's unbending support on the Senate floor. The liberal community set up a characteristic clamor over Robinson's conservative southern record, and this alarmed Roosevelt, especially because his advisers were just as worried about the prospect of Robinson sitting on the high court as were the liberals in their New York strongholds. Nonetheless, the commitment to Robinson finally forced the president, after weeks of delay, to send his son James Roosevelt to the majority leader as an emissary for the purpose of begging Robinson to pay a call on the White House. In the course of the call, Roosevelt began by assuring the Senate leader that he (Roosevelt) had never for a moment considered welshing on his promise of a Court seat for Senator Robinson, and having so cleared the air, he ended by giving Robinson carte blanche to get the best bill he could.

Robinson accordingly settled for a compromise bill that would have added two or three new justices to the Court. With the tenacious leader's backing, this measure would certainly have passed except for a final, dramatic dictate of fate. That July, in his lonely and dreary apartment at the Methodist Building just across the park from the Capitol, Joe Robinson suffered a massive heart attack that seemed to have killed him instantly. The old politician was found dead the next morning by the cleaning woman, and with him died every last IOU from other senators that he still had in his pocket. In short, when Joe Robinson died, so did Roosevelt's chance for the kind of Court bill the great senator had promised his president only two weeks before.

I thought then, as I do today, that the instinct governing Roosevelt's attempt to enlarge the Supreme Court in order to alter its opinions was justified, although the route was ill chosen. The implementation was foolishly planned, not surprisingly, because the judgment of a president who has just achieved a landslide is always suspect, and Roosevelt's 1936 landslide was the biggest ever. Turner and I followed the story from the beginning, and we ended by writing a series of three articles for the *Saturday Evening Post* and turning those three articles into a book. I am proud that our book is still accepted over half a century later as the only authoritative account of this great episode in recent American history.

This labor took its toll, however. During those first six months of 1937, I had been dining out more than ever, and I had also been working harder than ever because of the Court fight. In consequence, I began to wake up every second dawn or so with my heart behaving in a most peculiar manner—sounding, in fact, like the random banging of a loose shutter on a very windy night. Concerned, I consulted my doctor, who, in turn, put me through a severe examination. When the results of the various tests and procedures were known, my doctor blankly informed me I had only two choices: I could either lose a good portion of my present body weight, or I could expect to die within about twelve months. I relayed this information to my family, and they at once volunteered to pay for a serious course of dietary treatment.

I was lucky because John Eager Howard, a great man and doctor, had just taken the lead at the Johns Hopkins Hospital in working out the details of what the calorie theory really meant in practical terms. The Johns Hopkins Diet, as it was then called, begat the classic thinning diet everyone eats nowadays unless they have taken to the current fad for liquid diets or gone to one of the innumerable diet quacks. However, Howard's regime was a novelty then, so the hospital had begun searching for volunteers on which to test what came to be called "calorie counting." Gratefully, therefore, I traveled by train to Baltimore and installed myself at the hospital in a well-lit corner room with an enormous borrowed library to pass the time.

I have always thought of myself as a lucky man, and John Howard was one proof of this. Another proof of my luck was John's decision to send me to Mr. and Mrs. Kendall, who had devised the special exercises that were then given to the child victims of poliomyelitis. Upon my arrival in Baltimore, I was nearly in the same shape as one of these sad children since I had done almost no exercise during most of my life and quite literally had no muscles to speak of—except in my legs, which were always in fairly good training because they had been weight lifters all my life. Mr. and Mrs. Kendall, unsung geniuses whom I still profoundly admire, took me in hand and, quite literally, muscle by muscle rebuilt my entire musculature from my pelvis upward with their exercises.

The task took three months plus an extra month's dieting after I returned to Washington; but at the end, I had been magically transformed so that, at long last, at the age of twenty-six, I could claim to look just about like everyone else of my age. In retrospect, I have always felt that I paid for being very fat with my youth, for it is impossible to have a youth in the normal way when one is horribly overweight. From the age of seventeen, I had lived, in effect, like a middle-aged man. On the other hand—and here was the advantage to me when I started out in Washington—one is accepted as a middle-aged man, provided one is reasonably intelligent and can maintain the kind of discussion that middle-aged men are expected to maintain. In that way, indeed, I think that being dangerously fat was downright helpful when I was thrown at very short notice into an entirely new milieu, where I was expected to engage in a novel and grown-up kind of competition.

But I have never counseled young, ambitious newspaperpersons to grow bellies. On the contrary, I count my real youth as having begun that spring and summer of 1937. Altogether, I lost more than 12 inches of waistline and over 65 pounds—nearly one-third of my entire body weight. The effect was astonishing, for with my extra foot of waistline gone, I actually felt younger—not merely lighter on my feet, but lighter-hearted and lighter-headed. Not to mention the sudden psychological burden lifted of always thinking oneself somehow sodden and out-of-tune. I could now dance, if I wished (I didn't); but, above all, I gained everyday pleasures such as breathing deeply and crossing my legs, for when one is fat every breath comes hard and crossing the legs is about as easy as it would be for a penguin. Once thin, this latter maneuver especially is ac-

complished with easy grace, and I spent days crossing and uncross-
ing my legs just for fun after I made the discovery.

Ironically, this newfound youth of spirit coincided with the
beginning of my real adult life as a professional newspaperman.
When Turner and I undertook our articles for the *Post*, the characters of the Court battle, its back-room debates, and narrow balances
were not hidden, as they would be today, under vast thickets of
bureaucracy. We cared a good deal about being dependable and so
were able to interview everyone involved in the drama with the
exception of the president himself, Chief Justice Hughes, and Joe
Robinson. I alone compiled some 1,500 pages of single-spaced type-
written notes in the process, and Turner's attention to detail was
equally arduous.

While I was at Johns Hopkins, Turner used to come over on
the train, and together we would write our chronicle of the Court
fight and send it up by installments to the *Saturday Evening Post.* In
writing, we attempted to re-create the drama as it unfolded, scene by
scene. The result was an odd form of living history, an analysis of
the facts through a dramatic retelling of the story. Published under
the title "The 168 Days," it made a much greater impression than
any other magazine article I have had anything to do with. Because
of it, Jack Wheeler, the head of the North American Newspaper
Alliance, offered Turner and me a shot as syndicated political
columnists—the third life-altering development of that year.

I should explain that Wheeler specified a two-man team because he wished to re-create a partnership along the lines of Drew
Pearson and Robert Allen, specialists in a kind of urgently personalized political gossip who were then at the height of their success as
columnists. My half of the contract offered by Wheeler was, I think,
three times what I was earning from the *Herald Tribune,* and
Turner's half was substantially more than his salary from the *New
York Times.* The *Times,* however, promptly outbid NANA, and
Turner chose to stay with his old paper. The *Tribune* was not as
generous when I presented them with news of Wheeler's offer, and
so I decided to take the gamble. I could, I reasoned, always return to
some form of daily newspaper work, should this adventure as boy-
columnist fail. To get the second man that Wheeler wanted, I, therefore, made an offer of half a share in the column to Robert Kintner,
whom I had watched with admiration as the *Herald Tribune* man at
the treasury.

Bob was the only newspaperman in Washington who was close
to the more important members of the New Deal crowd, which was
then headed by the president's young advisers Tom Corcoran and

Ben Cohen. He was a first-rate financial reporter. He knew a great deal more than I did about the ins and outs of the executive branch, whereas I knew the ins and outs of practical politics and the goings-on of Capitol Hill, which to Bob was unfamiliar territory. It was a good partnership—although we were strictly collaborators rather than friends at the outset and only became real friends when Bob acquired a wonderful second wife, Jean Rodney. Jean went out of her way to bring all three of us into a friendly combination, and I was glad that she did. Kintner and I were thirty and twenty-seven years of age, respectively, when we began our work together. Even though newspaper columnists came in a much wider variety in those days than they do now, our age was precocious by any standard, although Bob and I proved, after more than our share of pratfalls, to be ready for the challenge.

The 1930s were the real heyday of the nationally syndicated political columnist. The form ranged from the truly vigorous to the very pallid and tended to be much more personalized than today. More importantly, political columnists in those days were far more widely read than they are now, although I am not at all sure this was an entirely good thing.

When Bob and I were starting out, I considered my dear older friend Frank Kent by far the best of the vigorous political columnists in Washington. Frank's early reputation was based in part on his ability to express contempt for Calvin Coolidge in highly colorful language. Frank, like the equally forgotten columnist Mark Sullivan, was among those impressed by Herbert Hoover, "the Great Engineer." For a stern Wilsonian Democrat, moreover, Franklin Roosevelt was far too much for Frank to swallow, and he went from founding the anonymous "TRB" column at the *New Republic* to joining the fairly extreme conservative faction in politics.

Besides pure political columns like Frank's, there were nearly pure foreign-policy columns like that of Dorothy Thompson, of whom Alice Longworth remarked acidly—for she disliked Thompson heartily—"Dear Dorothy is the only woman in history who ever got paid for having the menopause in public." Walter Lippmann wrote pure "think" columns that were based, in fact, on very solid and assiduous reporting. Then there were reportorial-analytical columns like that of *New York Times* bureau chief Arthur Krock, as well as straight gossip columns like the one Drew Pearson and Bob Allen wrote until they began to be serious about the Second World War.

In retrospect, I suppose the model Bob and I used in starting out was Arthur Krock. It was Arthur who quoted FDR's chief ad-

My father
shortly before
his marriage.

My mother
in her twenties.

Above: Rear and side lineup for the four Alsops, aged four to eight. *Left to right:* John, Stewart, Corinne, me.

Right: My brothers Stewart and John on Shetland ponies at Henderson.

Opposite top: My grandfather Douglas Robinson and my great-uncle Theodore Roosevelt on horseback.

Opposite bottom: Henderson, as it stood during my great-grandmother's time (1880).

JOSEPH WRIGHT ALSOP, JR.
b. October 11, 1910

Assistant Crew Manager '28
Grotonian Board
Dramatic Association '27, '28
Captain of Ciceros, Junior Debating '26
Debating Team '28
Civics Club '28

"Woodford Farm"   YALE
Avon, Conn.

Groton yearbook, 1928. (Courtsey Groton Library)

Myself *(far right)* with members of the Porcellian Club at Harvard.

Our family house at Woodford Farm in Avon, Connecticut, as it looked in the 1970s.

My mother with her cousin Eleanor Roosevelt on a trip together in Connecticut.

Nicholas Longworth and my cousin Alice early in their marriage.

Stanley Walker *(center)*, city editor of the *New York Herald Tribune,* in 1934 with fellow newspaper editors Paul Bellamy of the *Cleveland Plain Dealer (left)* and Grove Patterson of the *Toledo* (Ohio) *Blade (right).* (AP/Wide World Photos, Inc.)

Senator Hugo Black before his
nomination to the high court in
1937. (National Archives)

Senator Charles McNary in
1940. (AP/Wide World Photos,
Inc.)

Senator Joseph T. Robinson.
(National Archives)

Robert Kintner, my partner in
the 1930s, as chairman of the
board of NBC (1965).
(AP/Wide World Photos, Inc.)

viser Harry Hopkins during a lull at the race track as cheerfully saying, "We're going to spend and spend, and tax and tax, and elect and elect!" At his best, Arthur caught such phrases, phrases that struck every ear in Washington. Bob and I wanted to attain the same kind of rattling, newsworthy effect. We hoped also to shed some light on the political process, to make the government come alive in print in its serious, comic, or merely puzzling aspects. And we reasoned that an emphasis on straight reporting, a trade that combined drab routine and public responsibility, offered the best chance for success.

The rules that obtained in those primeval days of newspapering clearly have changed today, but as a columnist, I regarded myself as a reporter first and foremost. I believed then, and believe still, that if a columnist bases his material solely on personal conviction, within six months the problem of becoming repetitious raises its ugly head in an inflamed way. Walter Lippmann was a very brilliant man, but even Walter's column was saved from constant repetition only by the simple fact that he changed his views roughly once every eight months.

Lacking views in general, Bob and I had no such problems in those early days of our partnership together. We took an office in the old Bar Building downtown, where the ceilings were high and the open, work-style elevators grated and creaked. I occupied the smaller room, Bob the larger. Our secretary, a very blonde, very efficient woman married to a very respectable academic, occupied a small common room dominated by an aged and comfortable leather lawyer's couch. In this familiar, somewhat dilapidated environment, we set about finding our way.

Bob Kintner considered himself an ungainly writer. I agreed with him; so I did the bulk of the writing for our column, much in the same way I had done with Turner. Bob and I had to produce five columns a week, however, and, therefore, were under stricter deadlines and tended to argue more. It was, nonetheless, a fully equal partnership. First of all, Bob had a first-rate mind and was an accomplished newspaperman. It was he who really taught me how to be a Washington reporter, which was far more complicated and demanding than being a Capitol Hill reporter. Second, although I sat at the typewriter doing the writing, we generally composed the columns together, and, as a rule, I never wrote a sentence of which he did not fully approve.

The political issues with which Bob Kintner and I struggled as beginning columnists were usually matters of straight practical politics, such as who was trying to get what from whom politically and officially. In time, we expanded into the realm of legislative policy, which was Bob's specialty since he had been at the treasury and knew the young Roosevelt men there better than anyone in town. We spent much of our time tracking the boringly recurrent rows between the budget balancers, meaning Henry Morgenthau and the president himself—who was never in the least converted by John Maynard Keynes—and those young New Dealers, with the astute and manipulative Tom Corcoran in the lead, who were in favor of a more radical fiscal policy.

Tom Corcoran was a dominant figure in the Washington of those days and one of the more fascinating public servants the town has produced. Amiably cherubic and fantastically energetic, Tom looked like a Jesuit altar boy grown up, which, of course, he was, having been raised a staunch Irish Catholic in Rhode Island. A protégé of Felix Frankfurter's at Harvard Law School, Corcoran was sent to Washington to serve as private secretary to Justice Oliver Wendell Holmes. No doubt this was a difficult experience for a pink-cheeked young man who was full of ideals, both good and bad, for Holmes had few ideals. The justice believed in the United States of America, to be sure. He believed in courage on the battlefield, of which he had a vast store, and in simple human qualities like style and generosity. On most subjects, however, Justice Holmes was a corrosive skeptic. There was no room in his lacunae for the Blessed Mother or the Sacred Heart and no earthly room for eternal verities.

For poor Tom, this jolt of rigorous skepticism must have been like being put in a bath of acid. Once purged of basic ideals by Justice Holmes, he resembled a spinning top: just get him spinning, push him in the desired direction, and he spun interminably. Under the directions of President Roosevelt, Tom Corcoran spun furiously through the government, where, in time, his smiling, irrepressible brand of back-room politics earned him the nickname "Tommy the Cork." Later, as war came on and his Irish isolationist tendencies rose, his new wife Peggy would pick Tom up and send him spinning off toward the private sector, where the same endless fund of energy brought Tom a sizable fortune as a hired lobbyist and private fixer.

During those first early years in Roosevelt's government, Tom's spin was generally leftward, generally world-improving. Badgering old colleagues, recruiting new ones, Corcoran served as a major catalyst for the New Deal. He brought together a group of brilliant and dedicated legal intellectuals who, as believers in aggressive liberalism and pleaders for a policy of no surrender on any front, possessed a community of purpose rare in the political experience of this country.

Corcoran's great collaborator was Ben Cohen, a brilliant

scholar from Muncie, Indiana, by way of the University of Chicago and legal practice in New York. To me he looked exactly like a kind, somewhat stooped Talmudic ascetic. Corcoran, by an odd trait, needed to work with someone he admired, and Cohen, afflicted with a peculiar inertia, needed someone like Corcoran to galvanize him into action. Corcoran was the team's front man, Cohen the slightly preponderant intellectual; and together they were probably the best draftsmen of great and complex pieces of legislation Washington has ever seen (see the Securities Exchange Act of 1934, which spawned the Securities and Exchange Commission).

Concerning such issues as the budget, Ben Cohen did the basic thinking, after which he retired to the sidelines and wrung his hands almost constantly, for he was a pessimist. Tom Corcoran, in contrast, had a vast web of appointees, cronies, and semidependents running straight through all the critical departments of government and centering chiefly in the departmental legal offices. For each fight between the budget balancers and the Keynesians, Tom mobilized all his men with their legal foolscap waving and their pens threatening destruction to the enemy.

The fights were exciting but would have been more so had not Tom Corcoran's side, which had the support of Harry Hopkins at the Works Progress Administration (WPA), always triumphed, even though the president, as I have said, was genuinely apprehensive about unbalanced budgets. (If one goes back and looks at the relatively minor deficits then considered excessive—an exercise that I recommend—one will see how the world and our currency have changed.)

Bob Kintner's early connection to Corcoran and his men was one of the keys to the early success of our column, for in those days in Washington, journalists still clung to the old centers of power like the Senate and the White House and more or less ignored the kind of legislative policy that Corcoran and Cohen were constructing. Bob and I fell on our faces heavily with the first two or three columns we published, but after that we got the knack of what we wanted to do. Before long, we were causing a lot of talk in town, which naturally pleased the members of the North American Newspaper Alliance, who alone had the right to publish what we wrote. Over time, our column also impressed the authorities at the *Herald Tribune,* who had been miffed when two of the paper's better young reporters left to make more money. Consequently, it was not long before I was encouraged by the owner, Mrs. Reid, and by the director of the paper's editorial page, Geoffrey Parsons, to see if I could not make peace for Alsop and Kintner with Mr. Reid, who was the one who most resented being abandoned by his employees.

Peace with Mr. Reid finally was made at the Chicago Democratic convention in 1940, when Franklin Roosevelt won his party's nomination for a third term. The scene of the peacemaking was a striptease joint of a clean and altogether extraordinary innocence, save for the size of the ladies' bosoms and the ingenuity of the things that they were able to do with them. Ogden Reid had sensibly taken a prominent box at this establishment for the duration of the convention. It was not easy to conduct negotiations about a new contract while a rather ample lady was counterrotating her tasseled bosoms—a trick that still mystifies me—but Mr. Reid and I did so negotiate and did it well. As a result, Bob and I returned to the *Herald Tribune* as syndicated columnists and happily resumed a relationship that lasted, save for a break during the second war and a change of partners, until the paper sadly folded in 1966.

I was encouraged by the early success of the column to take a step I had been contemplating for some time and rented a house in the 2700 block of Dumbarton Avenue in Georgetown. My house, though far from pretentious, was extremely generous for a rent of $125 a month. I could have twelve or, at a pinch, fourteen people for dinner. I had a permanent manservant, a wonderful Filipino named Nicholas Reyes, whom I recruited straight from a Washington taxicab and paid $25 a week to cook, clean, wash, press linen, and wait at table. Add to this a beautiful garden, a big living room, a large library, a decent dining room, and a big bedroom-dressing room and bath, and I had all—and possibly more than all—that a single man could ask for.

Then there was the block itself. On one corner of Dumbarton Avenue lived an undertaker; on the other corner stood what was reputed to be the local whorehouse, although I never investigated this charge. Just beyond the whorehouse stood a black Baptist church, where the singing was so beautiful I used to stand listening at my windows on Sundays. Across from my rented house was a second church, this one Catholic, belonging to the Oblates of Saint Charles, a missionary order founded by the first American archbishop, John Carroll, to convert "the Negroes and the Red Indians." With the exception of my landlord, who lived next door, all the rest of my neighbors were black, save for the abandoned mistress of the famous Senator Reed Smoot of Utah, who was chairman, during President Hoover's time, of the Senate Finance Committee. After Senator Smoot's return to Utah, the abandoned lady in the tiny house lived in a permanent condition of melancholy verging on tears. The kind black matriarchs of the block would pay her visits occasionally to try and cheer her up by claiming that Senator Smoot was a well-known son of a bitch and that a girl so pretty ought really to move on with her life and get a new man.

Georgetown was not yet the glossy fortress of the rich it would become, and the atmosphere along Dumbarton Avenue in those days was that of a street in a relatively prosperous farming town. Everybody knew everybody else by sight, and a constant current of gossip kept all of the residents of the 2700 block well informed about each other's affairs. To my astonishment, when I came down with flu one winter, I was all but drowned by my neighbors in delicious and nourishing soups; so I had to establish a counterrule of sending something good and nourishing whenever I heard that one of my neighbors had taken ill. There was a good deal of street life, too, most of it highly entertaining. In summer, everyone had barbecue picnics in their backyards, and I can still, more than fifty years later, take delight from the memory of the smell of the good food in the soft evening air and the sound of rich laughter.

We never locked our doors and never so much as thought of the horrible word "security." Crime was nonexistent. When I walked out to dinner in evening clothes, the young men on the block, whom I knew by name, would make friendly jokes about my silk shirts and evening pumps, both of which they considered too close to women's garb. These jokes were not the least bit malicious. Indeed, the amusement for the boys was such that I came to expect a good-natured chorus every time I ventured out for the evening in my pumps. None of this caused the slightest tension, and I dealt with it the only way I knew how—by smiling good-naturedly and laughing along.

By the time I settled into my new home, I had become something of a personage in Washington as, alas, a boy columnist. The chief result at first was that I saw more and more people and was more and more active in a social way. Indeed, with my newfound shape, I had a fund of energy in those days that astonishes me still. One of my principal memories was being invited to use the Dumbarton Oaks swimming pool, then one of the two or three pools in all of Washington. The pool, which was a heaven-sent privilege during the Washington summers before air-conditioning, was a deep-blue in color and situated on a terrace overlooking the fabulous gardens of the house. Most of those invited to swim were diplomats. All the men were required to wear tops as well as shorts, and most of them had woolen tops from Brooks Brothers with broad blue and white stripes, standard issue in those days. The guests would cluster around the pool, talking what I can only call light "cambric tea" politics.

Such invitations, of course, made me privy to the odd little scandals of the town. None was odder in those years just before the war than the scandal caused by *Times* columnist Arthur Krock's young son Thomas. Thomas P. Krock was the son from Arthur's first marriage to a woman from a dilapidated but distinguished family in Arthur's home state of Kentucky. Young Krock grew up with a history of erratic behavior—at least according to John Lardner, who was a neighbor of the Krocks. Whether the son was driven mad or not by Arthur I do not know. If this story is to be believed, however, Franklin Roosevelt used him to coopt Arthur and, through Arthur, the entire *New York Times* Washington Bureau.

Not wanting any criticism from the *New York Times* during the Court fight, the president had arranged for Arthur to have young Krock shipped off to Ireland as an honorary attaché at the U.S. legation in Dublin. The Dublin legation had been used in this way before. Indeed, during those years, it served as home and base to a supposedly scandalous aunt of Cousin Eleanor's, who had a tendency to overspend her income and to fall in love in an indiscreet manner. These were two very shocking traits, especially in her earlier years, when they earned Aunt Pussie, as the lady was called, a certain anonymous distinction as the original model for Lily Bart, the heroine of Edith Wharton's *House of Mirth.*

Thomas P. Krock did not fare well in Dublin, however. Indeed, his behavior became so lunatic that Aunt Pussie's husband, a very conventional gent named David Gray, petitioned the president to have the boy sent home. Back in Washington, Thomas Krock gained further notoriety by sending out invitations—one of which I received—to a dinner at the then very fashionable F Street Club, to which he did not belong. Adolf Hitler was beginning to be noticed at the time, and the card, which went out to all of Arthur's friends, was noticed, too, for it was embossed with the name of one "Baron Thomas von Pollykrock." Needless to say, when Arthur got wind of these invitations, the dinner was hastily canceled. I doubt that Arthur held the president responsible for his son's odd behavior. It is true, however, that Arthur, who had been one of the few staunch journalistic supporters of the president's Court plan, turned on his old hero like a viper at about this time and rigorously followed Joe Kennedy's isolationist line up to wartime.

This tale is, I grant, malicious gossip. My interest in it at the time—and, indeed, my interest in retelling it here—is evidence of one lamentable fact: by the time Bob and I got our column up and running successfully, my personal outlook, social habits, and political interest were thoroughly and enjoyably ingrained into the life of the capital. It had not taken long—only three years—for the transition from Avon and New York to be complete. I had become that sad and rootless thing: a "Washingtonian."

7

"Dr. Win the War"

Unless a great disaster forces this country to build from zero once again, we shall never see anything like Roosevelt's Washington. Its best symbols were probably the White House and its fence, so different from the modern-day fortification that is around nine feet high and reinforced in various elaborate ways. Erected by Theodore Roosevelt to protect the house lawns and grounds, the fence, during those prewar days, could still easily be vaulted by a reasonably athletic ten year old. Likewise, the state rooms under Franklin Roosevelt were very nearly, if not exactly, the way they had been when Theodore Roosevelt persuaded Stanford White to restore the White House to its pre-Pullman-era condition.

I was never on intimate terms with my distant relative in the White House. I have written that Franklin Roosevelt, along with Washington and Lincoln, was one of our three greatest presidents. The qualities of greatness, however, were never readily apparent in the man's mysterious personality. President Roosevelt's advisers—themselves so clever—all began by underestimating the man, with the lone probable exception of Harry Hopkins. The president impressed John Maynard Keynes not at all during their famous meeting, and earlier on in his political career, Roosevelt had earned the contempt of Edmund Wilson and the rest of the New York intellectuals.

In these narrow judgments of Franklin Roosevelt's character and style, I must say, I concurred. Although I supported FDR politically, the president was not attractive to me in his early days as president for the same snobbish reasons he had not been attractive to the same sort of people in his class at Harvard. Franklin Roosevelt was too damned affable, always ready to slap one on the back and call him Charlie in tones that sounded smashing over the radio and worked like a charm with members of the House and Senate but in person had a slightly counterfeit ring. Of course, I later learned to judge the president on results rather than style and soon came to revere Roosevelt both as a leader and as a man.

In those prewar years, my only real firsthand views of the workings of the Roosevelt White House came at the small Sunday-night suppers to which my cousin Eleanor would invite me every two months or so. Scrambled eggs are not an easy dish to cook in such a manner that hungry men turn away in discouragement, yet even I found the eggs Cousin Eleanor made in a chafing dish for Sunday suppers discouraging. The White House menu was in general notoriously bad, although I thought the salads especially deplorable, for they tended to be complicated and decorative and might even conceal bits of marshmallow in their dreadful depths. Even still, although the company at these affairs was often miscellaneous (the Roosevelts enjoyed having the odd family friend for supper as well as members of the staff), the food decidedly flawed, and the president's table stories sometimes stale, the simple, generous hospitality of an old-fashioned American gentleman's house was always the note.

President Roosevelt's press conferences were downright cozy too, on a purely professional level. Even during the most extreme crises, these sessions were held in the Oval Office. Instead of the preening media personalities of today, those present were only the most seasoned professional reporters, all of whom knew one another and did not wish to make asses of themselves either in front of their colleagues or in front of a president they much liked and admired. Before this intimate congregation, President Roosevelt would sit behind his desk, perpetual cigarette in its holder tilted at the accustomed angle, full of confidence and jokes, giving the reporters substantive information of value to them and to the country.

These presidential press conferences, in turn, set a general tone. Newspaper work in the Washington I knew before the war had not

vastly advanced from the early stage best represented by the successful enterprise of the lady reporter who got an interview with John
Quincy Adams by the simple expedient of catching the president in
the Potomac River during one of his habitual before-breakfast swims
and sitting on his clothes on the bank until he promised to talk to
her. As a reasonably reputable newspaperman, one was known to
everyone and all one had to do was walk into the presidential office
wing, which in those days housed the entire staff, hang up one's hat
in the press room, and ask friends, "What's new?"

In general, Bob Kintner and I did not spend much of our working time at the White House, although the focus of the column
during those first years was very much on the domestic aspects of
the executive branch. After the signing of the Munich Pact in September 1938, however, Bob and I had a brief disagreement. My
partner felt no one would be interested in any writing about foreign
and defense policy. In those days, not a single Washington correspondent covered these subjects with any regularity, and few
columnists concentrated on them. I disagreed with Bob, however,
because I have always believed that any column that gets too far
from the headlines is bound to be disregarded. I was certain that
after Munich the headlines would have more and more to do with
foreign policy and defense. So, for a time, I took up the task of covering these two subjects for our column, leaving the rest of Washington to Bob. Since I have always found it difficult to make a beginning on any subject on which I was totally unprepared, I set myself
firm days in each week that were to be devoted entirely to reporting at the State Department and the Navy and War departments.

On Thursdays, I followed a routine of going to see people at
the State Department. The department then occupied what is now
called the Old Executive Office Building, across the street from the
White House. The building—then, as today, an elaborate Victorian
structure—had no guards; there was no visible security; and there
was an altogether refreshing absence of self-important staff people
charging up and down the halls wearing ugly security lavalieres
hanging on chains. There was a single doorman, a very nice old man
called Charlie, whom I knew because he often moonlighted as a
waiter at dinners in some of the grander Washington houses. I
would mount the steps to be greeted by Charlie, who invariably said,
"That was a nice dinner, Mr. Alsop, at Mrs. X's or Mrs. Y's." I
would then ascend to the second floor, walk down the long corridor
to the secretary of state's southeast corner office, and stick my head
in the door.

There, I would always find Blanche Hallé, a most remarkable

woman who had the double duty of serving Secretary of State Cordell Hull as the head of his office and of vetting and, if need be, revising all (and I repeat all) outgoing State Department telegrams and letters for their "stylistic correctness." I would ask Blanche whether there was any chance of seeing the secretary that afternoon, and she would generally reply, "It's a busy day, Joe, but he likes talking to you, so if you come back in an hour I think I can fit you in." With that half promise, I would retreat to the so-called "Executive Corridor," where the second echelon of bureaucrats—the assistant secretaries and their support personnel—were housed. There, I could always find one or another of the more important people on the second level of the department willing to talk for three-quarters of an hour. At the appointed hour, I would then return to Secretary Hull's suite—he had a front office, a personal office, and I suppose some sort of bathroom—and Mrs. Hallé would show me in.

With his silver hair and fine features, the old Tennessee mountaineer was a distinguished presence in those days; and in the grand scheme of Roosevelt's men, I am still inclined to think of him as an underrated figure. Hull, who had served in the Congress for nearly three decades before moving to the Senate in 1930, was a lawmaker of the old school. The author of a number of important pieces of legislation while still in the House, he made it his business, after moving to the executive branch, to further the cause of free trade. During a time of fierce economic nationalism, Hull was a conspicuous advocate of the president's "good neighbor" policy and played a large role in seeing the all-important Trade Agreements Act through the Congress in 1934.

It is true the president dealt with the State Department mainly through the under secretary of state Sumner Welles, whom he had known at Groton. However, the views on the necessity of maintaining free and open markets championed by Hull still deeply affect the trade policy of the executive branch, whether it is in Republican or Democratic hands. Even if seeing Secretary Hull was seldom politically informative, it was always enjoyable to hear him talk about the Japanese, to whom he famously referred, after Pearl Harbor, as "them goddamn pissants."

In comparison to Cordell Hull, the leaders of the various branches of our armed services seemed downright eccentric. Roosevelt's first secretary of the navy was a very intelligent and cynical old Virginia politician, Claude Swanson, always worth talking to even if not about naval affairs. Swanson was the originator of the immortal rule for politicians "When the water reaches the upper deck, follow the rats." His successor was a far less interesting and engaging man, and the navy was something of a closed preserve until the period just before the United States entered the war, when President Roosevelt took his scattered defense departments in hand.

The way the War Department was run was truly shocking. The secretary was Harry Woodring, a peanut-sized Kansas politician distinguished only by the meanness of his nature. The under secretary, Louis A. Johnson, who came to the War Department from a lucrative business career, was even meaner than Woodring, however. I would have extensive dealings with Johnson later on and came to regard him as one of the two or three truly evil men I have encountered in American public life. He was savagely ambitious, and since his ambition during those prewar years was to supplant Woodring and Woodring was determined not to be supplanted, they were not on speaking terms. I could always see either of these men at length, provided I invited the one I was calling on to recite the sins of the other.

This odd, crackpot atmosphere at the War Department was further enhanced by what I found at the G-2, or intelligence section, which quickly became one of my favorite haunts. I have never understood why all the military services regard assignment to intelligence as somehow demeaning. It is a fact, however, and in the case of the G-2 of the U.S. War Department in 1938 and 1939 the results were bizarre. The head of the department was a nice, decent, but slightly worry-prone Virginian, Colonel Warner McCabe, whom I am afraid I used to call "the old Virginia Gentlewoman." McCabe was thoroughly at home among the other leaders of his section—or, I should say, the real leaders of his section, for the G-2 of the War Department was actually run by a series of formidable ladies in silk shirtwaists who had been left over from World War I. These ladies made the assignments to intelligence posts abroad, and, it was rumored, they even rewrote intelligence estimates that they thought too lurid or not up to the standards of their section.

Perhaps the oddest member of the army's G-2 intelligence department was Colonel Truman Smith, who had been military attaché in Germany. To his credit, Colonel Smith knew more about Hitler's army than anybody else in Washington, and he was dead right in warning everyone that Hitler's army was very much more formidable than anyone else supposed. He had his debits, however. He openly admired Hitler; he was quite anti-Semitic; and he had serious diabetes, which caused him to fall into diabetic rages closely resembling fits, as he once did in my presence. None of these traits were calculated to inspire confidence in his impeccably correct military data.

If the conditions of our great cabinet departments on the eve of war seem both ridiculous and perilous, the condition of the U.S. Congress was even worse. At this time, the Congress was riven by the problem of the Nye Neutrality acts (an earlier result of the first Nye hearings) which forbade the sale of weapons to our allies abroad in the event of war. The isolationist sentiment that produced these foolish but fashionable pieces of legislation during the early 1930s was still strong, although President Roosevelt, Secretary Hull, and the executive branch in general were desperate to secure their early repeal.

Roosevelt would never have signed the Neutrality acts if he had not feared incurring the displeasure of the American liberal left, which, of course, supported neutrality. Even after Munich, when this group began slowly to change its collective mind on the issue, Roosevelt still had to deal with a fundamentally right-wing group— the isolationists—who sought to keep the U.S. government from exercising any undue influence overseas. The Senate Foreign Relations Committee was narrowly divided on the issue, and so, after long thrashing about, the president decided to bring the issue to a head at a meeting at the White House on which Bob Kintner and I had a clean scoop for once. The people called together in the evening by President Roosevelt were my friend the Senate minority leader Charles McNary; the Senate majority leader Alben Barkley; the principal members of the Senate Foreign Relations Committee, including republican senator William Borah of Idaho; and Secretary of State Hull, with two or three of his ablest people from the State Department.

The thrust of the argument presented by the president at this meeting was that the sole chance of averting conflict was to give the executive branch a lot more hard bargaining power and even some threatening power. The only way to accomplish this, as both the president and Secretary Hull pointed out in the strongest possible terms, was to repeal the Neutrality acts—or at least the clause making an arms embargo mandatory against all belligerents—and to make it known at once that if Hitler chose war, he and the Germans would have to face the English and French nations provided with great quantities of the best arms then available from the United States of America.

To my mind, at the time, this was a reasonable proposition that established a precedent for support but did not commit us to war. Senator Borah, however, argued that a war was unlikely, and should Hitler threaten one, the British particularly would sell out once again to the Germans in a repetition of what happened at Munich.

Secretary Hull answered, with all the considerable eloquence at his command and with all the facts before him, that the British were not going to stand for another Munich, that another war was in fact imminent, and that Senator Borah was in error. To which Borah, who lost his temper, replied with inconceivable arrogance that he knew he was right, that he had better information than the State Department, and, furthermore, that he had paid for it.

The next morning, vague word of a White House meeting was in the newspapers, but the reports offered no more than hints of what had actually transpired at the meeting. Consequently, I went straight to Senator McNary's office to see what information I could gather. I found the senator angrier than I had ever seen him, and he was a man who was capable of extreme anger. Shooting his cuffs at great speed, McNary gave me a complete account of the meeting. I do not think that he had ever liked Borah, but I am quite sure that Borah's show of arrogance, self-centeredness, and complete absence of any national feeling had brought my friend Senator McNary to the point of being entirely willing to cut the throat of his own party's chief expert on foreign affairs.

Having heard the startling story of what had passed at the White House, I hurried along to Senator Borah's office, where I found him complacently willing to discuss what he had done. There was only one question to which I wanted the answer. So I waited through some minutes of conversation until I could slip my question in casually. "Senator," I said, "there's a story going around that you told the secretary of state that your information was better than his and, furthermore, that you'd paid for it. What did you mean by saying that you had paid for it?" Without hesitation, Borah reached into the top drawer of his desk and pulled out a copy of an extremely suspect English political tip sheet called the *Week*, edited by Claud Cockburn, a leading British communist in those days. Cockburn was also on the staff of the *Daily Worker*, although the *Week* was in no way affiliated with the party. Senator Borah told me that his subscription to the *Week* cost him £5 a year. It was on the *Week*'s information that whatever chance the United States had of reminding Hitler that he might be running a bit of a risk was thrown down the drain of history.

It was this same issue, I am afraid, that caused me to lose an old friendship with the devout and kindly Senator Guy Gillette of Iowa. Gillette held a key swing vote on the Foreign Relations Committee for or against the Nye acts. If Borah had been for repeal, Gillette would have agreed to repeal. As it was, both the committee and Senator Gillette trembled in the balance; and, since I knew the senator had the swing vote, I went to see him every day. Gillette would talk to me about how hard he had prayed for an answer to his doubts, but he would insist that his doubts persisted. Finally, one day I went to see him and found him looking pale and exhausted. He told me that he had been on his knees all night, praying to be told the right thing to do. And he wound up by saying, "And, Joe, in the end, God told me to vote against repeal."

To which I replied, "Senator, I am afraid I think God told you wrong." It was an impertinent remark for a young reporter to make, however justified; and remembering the incident makes me blush with shame.

These whisps of memory from the past give some idea of the congressional atmosphere that made it so very difficult for Franklin Roosevelt to remodel his government in the radical way the coming crisis demanded. I have always been dead sure that the president would have liked to clean out his private Augean stable in the War and Navy departments as soon as possible after Munich. Yet the president's sole step toward this end that I knew of before the all-out German offensive in the spring of 1940 was to bring back from exile the one American of my time to whom none can be quite compared—General George C. Marshall.

General Marshall, who was made chief of staff of the army in 1939, considered the future of the institution to lie in the higher school system that General Pershing had established in order to provide us with intelligent, educated generals. All armies have elites, although I am not quite sure why. As usually happens, the elites of the moment gang up to make the important high-level appointments. As late as the mid-1930s, the elite group of the U.S. Army was still the U.S. cavalry, and thus the cavalrymen, with their always-shiny boots and usually tiny minds, tended to make the important appointments. Marshall's emphasis on a new intellectually based military meritocracy was designed to surmount this control of the cavalry elite. The result—a true change of elites—was brilliant and profound, yet its significance was little recognized at the time.

There was other business that needed doing as well, such as sending both Woodring and Johnson to the fate they deserved. Unfortunately, this was one eventuality that would unite Johnson and Woodring. If they were both shown the way to the trash can, they would hurry in tandem to Capitol Hill to make a fearful row before Congress. So Roosevelt left the two men in charge of the U.S. Army and the Army Air Corps until the fall of France in the late spring of 1940. Then his incomparable political judgment told him that the time had come when the country would support a strong move toward intervention. He asked for the immediate resignations of his secretary and under secretary of war and his secretary of the navy and, at long last, got them.

In June 1940, President Roosevelt named as his new secretary of the navy the old Rough Rider and Theodore Roosevelt–adherent, publisher of the *Chicago Daily News,* and a considerable power in the Republican party, Colonel Frank Knox. As secretary of war, Roosevelt named that astonishing statesman Colonel Henry L. Stimson, who, aside from holding the very same post between 1911 and 1913 during President Taft's time, had been secretary of state during President Hoover's administration. In matters of style, the white-whiskered, straight-backed Stimson was as impossibly grand a figure as there was in Washington; and in matters of substance, he was as great a public servant as this country has ever seen. I held the great statesman in awe, and on the few impersonal occasions when we did meet, I could manage little more than a muted and respectful greeting.

President Roosevelt gave Stimson the flat promise that the White House would in no way interfere with his appointments of subordinate civilian personnel from the highest subcabinet level down to the bottom of the department. What followed amounted to a total transformation in Washington, which Roosevelt described as the replacement of "Dr. New Deal by Dr. Win the War," for Stimson brought with him from the great private banking houses on Wall Street a corps of young men like Robert Lovett, James Forrestal, and Bob Patterson who would change the face of Washington forever. This transformation was also a sharp blow to the solar plexus of the Republican party, for Roosevelt's choices of these two very eminent Republicans for the highest imaginable jobs in government left the Republican convention of 1940 (which followed immediately after these major appointments) all but gasping for breath.

This was also the period when the "Wise Men," as they are now called, came to Washington with Stimson and Knox or, in the case of Dean G. Acheson, who had been practicing law in Washington, returned to government to become again part of the action. I suppose it reflects the narrowness of my world that I had some sort of family connection with an actual majority of these men and their wives. Jim Forrestal and his wife Jo were great friends of my cousin Sheff Cowles; and during their stays with Sheff at Oldgate, they had met my mother, whom Jim particularly admired. Dean Acheson was born in Middletown, Connecticut, and had gone to school at Groton on the advice of my father and my two uncles, a decision that he may have regretted. Archie MacLeish, who came down from

New York with this group and was a friend of all of them, was also a friend of my family's; and his wife Ada was the daughter of the president of the Farmington Savings Bank.

The group had other members, of course. Justice and Mrs. Frankfurter were highly respected members, even after Felix was appointed to the high court in 1939. I myself recruited a foreign member when I lunched one day with Mr. Arthur Purvis, head of the British Purchasing Commission, and found at table as another guest that truly extraordinary French economist and statesman, Jean Monnet, who would later be instrumental in building a new economic order for postwar Europe. Monnet had just arrived in Washington as a member of what would later be called the British Supply Council, where he would play a large role in coordinating the Allied economic effort. He was a short, ebullient man with flashing eyes and mesmerizing intelligence, and I took such a liking to him that I asked him to a dinner I was giving that evening to which the Frankfurters were also coming. As happens often, Jean and his charming wife Sylvie soon became closer to the Frankfurters and all their highly placed friends than to me, although I am proud to say that the French couple remained my friends through the postwar years.

The war brought many other able foreigners to Washington. The new British ambassador Lord Lothian performed remarkably until his early death from an intestinal infection. The British air attaché Sir John Slessor had insisted on flying in combat although he had only one leg. He would later end as marshal of the Royal Air Force and, after that, chairman of the British Chiefs of Staff. Chiang Kai-shek's chief representative in Washington T. V. Soong, whom it is now fashionable to denigrate, was in fact a most serious person whose organization, China Defense Supplies, did a superior job gathering economic and military support for China's Nationalist government.

Then, too, the historian and philosopher Isaiah Berlin, detailed from his college at Oxford to the British embassy in Washington, suddenly fetched up in my house on Dumbarton Avenue, where he instantly enjoyed a most enormous and resounding social success. Marion Frankfurter, a bit jealous, accused him of "swimming too easily in rancid butter" because he had half of Washington's dining-out world pursuing him, including Alice Longworth, who proclaimed his intelligence and virtue on every street corner. Isaiah, then as always was as extraordinary a man as I have known, brilliantly able and intelligent and brilliantly funny. His keen intellect was leavened with a delightful dose of the absurd and a comic and unending propensity for worry. Although a superb conversationalist, Isaiah was sometimes prone to mumble, and it quickly became fashionable to say that one could not understand a word of his brilliant discourse.

It was a curious period, that late spring and early summer of 1940. All the men I have named—and usually their wives—had fun in one another's houses, and I am proud to say they came often to my house. All sorts of matters were discussed that, as a newspaperman, I should not normally have heard. It is a dreadful thing to say, but before nuclear weapons had to be worried about, wars tended to quicken the pulse, heighten the interest, and intensify the pleasures of Washington life. I should explain, too, that we were all what are now called "activists" to an extreme degree. All the officials in the "Win the War" group I have been speaking of—descending from the sublime to the very minor, myself as well—were passionately committed to defeating Hitler, and we all foresaw that in the end the United States would have to go to war to do so.

This made us impatient with the slow pace set by President Roosevelt, who was, of course, better informed and more politically astute than we were. Take, for instance, the famous deal in which 50 overaged American destroyers were swapped for wartime antisubmarine bases on English islands in the Caribbean, which took place in the early fall of 1940. By the spring of 1940, Hitler's armies had moved into Western Europe with fierce resolve, causing the quick capitulation of France and threatening all of England with direct attack. The Neutrality acts had not been completely repealed, and restrictions still remained on the ability of the United States to supply weapons to the threatened countries of Europe. Few of us in the "Win the War" camp thought the British forces—in particular, the British navy—would be capable of sustaining a prolonged fight without a substantial amount of direct aid from the United States.

Winston Churchill, as it turned out, had the very same worry, and so the British leader had begun that spring, as disaster was unfolding along the beach at Dunkirk, to beg President Roosevelt for a few of the scores of destroyers in the American navy's mothball fleet. Roosevelt's response to Churchill's private request had been less than encouraging, for 1940 was an election year and the president was loath to give Wendell Willkie and the Republicans any more political ammunition about America's sliding into an unwanted war. The exchange between Churchill and Roosevelt, meanwhile, was being watched with agonizing apprehension by John Foster, another astute and unconventional Englishman who had been cast up on the wartime beach of the British embassy in Washington.

Without authorization from his superiors in the embassy, John rather improperly imparted to me the substance of the despairing telegrams from Churchill to Roosevelt, begging the president for the destroyers. John and I had our talk in my garden after dinner the day before I went to the Democratic convention in Chicago. After further researching the issue, I presented what information I could later that July to the so-called Century Group, many of whose members had come together that spring when William Allen White had founded the Committee to Defend America by Aiding the Allies, known more simply as the William Allen White Committee.

Although smaller and less formal than White's committee, the Century Group was no less effective in its efforts, both public as well as private, to agitate for American involvement in Europe. Among the group's members were Dean Acheson, New York lawyer Allen Dulles, and, for a time, *Time* publisher Henry Luce, although Henry soon clashed with members of the group and resigned. I have a horror of committee meetings, and so I went to only one session of the Century Group in New York. My sole contribution was to point out that we should not make propaganda for transferring the overage destroyers if, first, the administration did not want the deal done and if, second, the transfer was in any way against American military interests. I further argued that the easiest way to override any legal objections—and, indeed, to prevent any one side from making political hay of the issue—was to see to it that both President Roosevelt and his adversary Wendell Willkie endorsed the transfer together.

Roosevelt finally acted on the destroyer deal in September 1940. Willkie behaved very well about this, and after a brief pause he ended by supporting the transfer under the caveat that the issue never be put before the Congress. In the end, the deal was brokered through the executive branch alone, and the destroyers were delivered in exchange for long-term leases of British submarine bases in the Caribbean.

The barrage of propaganda organized by both the Century Group and by White's committee helped Roosevelt to act, and one of the features of that propaganda—an idea of mine—helped Roosevelt after he had acted. I undertook, in brief, to organize commitments from all the leading columnists—not difficult in those days since a majority were interventionists and many were my friends—to support Roosevelt when the destroyer deal was announced. From the most anti-Roosevelt people like Frank Kent and Mark Sullivan all the way to the members of what then passed for the liberal left, I got firm commitments from all the major columnists save one. Although Walter Lippmann supported the movement to the hilt early on, even drafting a major speech on the subject for General Pershing, in the end he became alarmed about the extreme use of executive prerogative and chose, as Walter sometimes did, to write on both sides of the issue.

There was one episode of this period I must recall in some detail because it would have a profound effect on my future. It was my first meeting with a former U.S. Air Force captain named Claire L. Chennault. Late in the fall of 1940, Chiang Kai-shek's Washington lobbyist T. V. Soong asked me and the famous foreign correspondent Edgar Ansel Mowrer of the *Chicago Daily News* to dine at his lavish Washington home. The honored guest was Captain Chennault, who had been hired some years earlier by the Nationalist government to revamp and train their air corps. Over dinner, Colonel Chennault (he had been given the new rank by Mme. Chiang Kai-shek) explained his job to us, which was to train and equip a fighting air corps under the command of Chiang Kai-shek to be used against Japanese forces already operating in China. Chennault envisioned this force as ultimately being more than just a defensive one, and to this end he had come to Washington to try to drum up as much logistical support as possible. I believe he had in mind somewhere between 500 and 1,000 American aircraft, including long-range bombers.

Japan's full-scale invasion of the Chinese mainland had begun in July of 1937. By December, Chiang Kai-shek's government had been forced to abandon its capital in Nanking and move inland to Chungking, the largest city in Szechwan, China's central and most populous province. Although relatively free from enemy ground attack, the remaining cities of "Free China," as the Nationalist stronghold was by then called, were under constant pressure from bombing raids by the Japanese air force. Colonel Chennault spoke at length about the vulnerability of the Japanese in the air, about the virtues of Japanese bombers and fighters, but also about their extremely light construction, which made it easy to shoot them down, and about the rigidity of Japanese plans and tactics, which made it easier (much easier, as subsequent events showed) to develop successful counterplans and tactics.

T. V. Soong gave us a marvelous Chinese dinner. Chennault, who was a charismatic man and physically impressive, made a profound impression. Indeed, it was an altogether satisfying and exciting evening until T. V. Soong asked my opinion of the colonel's project. I said it would be well received at the White House, for I had understood Colonel Chennault to mean that the Japanese weaknesses he stressed would make it possible to use outdated American equipment. When the colonel understood that he might not get the quantity of top-line equipment he sought, he grew angry. Chennault angry was an intimidating force. I hastily pointed out that every aircraft, ordnance, and ammunition factory in the United States was already being used to build the big, modern American air force that President Roosevelt wanted and simultaneously to supply the British generously because they were by now alone in the war against Hitler. Colonel Chennault quite plainly had no great liking for the British, and in any case he had no liking whatever for out-of-date equipment that could not do the job he envisioned. He said so in crisp language; and on that uneasy note, the evening came to an end.

Shortly after our dinner meeting, although I did not get wind of this until much later, Colonel Chennault adopted a less ambitious and, given the circumstances, far more practical plan for the air defense of China. He proposed to raise what was essentially an American mercenary air unit, the American Volunteer Group (later to be called, by others, the Flying Tigers). This outfit would use American equipment and would receive from the Chinese—or, rather, from the funds provided by the United States for aid to China—salaries substantially greater than those then available in the U.S. armed services. The Chinese were to provide the housing, rations, and all other necessary services, including a large part of the engineering personnel. In this way, a force with the fighting impact of a full air group could be put into action with no more than one-third the number of Americans an air group normally required.

Perhaps my warning about the overcommitment of the American air industry was useful in the sense that finding the airplanes he wanted was where Chennault began. He had long-standing business and personal connections, with the Curtiss Wright aircraft company, who told him of 100 P-40Cs, originally contracted for Britain with British modifications (the planes had already been fitted with British .303-caliber machine guns instead of American .30-caliber guns, and they lacked radios). They also said that the British might agree to taking a second batch of newly minted P-40 fighters in return for letting Colonel Chennault have the modified, remodified, and out-of-date P-40Cs.

Since it was the best deal Chennault could get under the circumstances, he took it. As I predicted during our dinner at T. V. Soong's, the whole concept of a friendly fighter group in China went down like jam at the White House; and Roosevelt, much against the will of his armed services, issued an executive order permitting any reserve officer wishing to do so—up to specified numbers—to transfer to Colonel Chennault's American Volunteer Group. The White House also cleared the way for the delivery of the P-40Cs to China, along with a general loan of $100 million to the Kuomintang government in Chungking.

Prewar Washington gave me, I fear, two of the things that I enjoyed most in my professional life: plenty to write about and causes in which I believed passionately. Bob Kintner and I were the ones who gave national publicity to the extreme isolationist propaganda that our former ambassador to London, Joe Kennedy, was disseminating throughout the country. Bob got the story (we were told that Kennedy was telling his Hollywood friends that the English were more anti-Semitic than Hitler), Kennedy complained of it to Arthur Krock, and Arthur, in turn, convinced Kennedy that we had gotten our information from Felix Frankfurter, whom Arthur disliked heartily and whom Bob did not know. For their own reasons, Felix Frankfurter and Arthur were implacable social enemies in Washington. Felix, who was by far the more gregarious man, habitually snubbed Arthur in public. Krock, in turn, did his utmost to discredit the justice among his own highly placed allies, of whom the ambassador was one. Nothing ever came of old Joe Kennedy's outrage, save for a general dislike, I fear on both sides, which I managed to repress much later on when I became close to the ambassador's son.

By the winter of 1941, the situation in Europe seemed so desperate that Bob and I decided to suspend the column and enlist in the armed forces for duty overseas. I had a high number in the draft but turned out to have an arrhythmic heartbeat of a kind common in my family (it forced my brother John to appeal his 4-F—unfit for duty—draft classification no less than thirteen times). I did not worry about this condition particularly, for I rather soon got the offer of a waiver to join the U.S. Navy from Admiral Alan Kirk. The waiver went through at once, but I began to sense something was amiss when I learned I was to be made an intelligence officer and stationed, of all unlikely places, in the Indian city of Bombay. For this assignment, I was to receive no training whatever except for three full days of lectures on "the philosophy of naval accounting," a necessary course, I was informed, for officers like myself who would be heading their own stations.

A frantic inquiry revealed that I had been recruited for the navy purely for publicity purposes. (To boost the image of their service, the navy was then seeking noted recruits like myself whose names would get dimly into the newspapers.) My duties in India were, therefore, nebulous at best. The west Indian port city of Bombay

had never been a hotbed of naval intrigue; and as I further re-
searched the topic, it began to look like the majority of my time
there would be devoted to dining out in competition with the State
Department's local representative. On the whole, this seemed to me
a poor way to do what I conceived to be my wartime duty; and so,
after reflection, I applied to Jim Forrestal for advice. Jim was then
under secretary of the navy, and Bob Lovett was in charge of the air
corps for Colonel Stimson at the War Department. Both men offered me similar counsel: they told me the story of a strange former
air-force man named Chennault who was forming a volunteer air
group with which to defend China. If I could somehow manage a
transfer to the air group's preliminary training base of operation in
Burma, both Bob and Jim assured me that I would see as much
wartime duty as anyone could want.

And that was how the greatest single adventure of my life
began.

8

Early
Maneuvers

O f all the ridiculous beginnings I have ever engaged in, my departure for the war in the summer of 1941 was without doubt the most ridiculous. Although my future duties as a "naval observer" in Bombay remained vague, the sartorial requirements for the post were most specific. Since I was to represent the navy, I was required to buy what must have been the last ceremonial costume naval outfitters ever sold—a fore-and-aft hat, not far from the kind worn by Admiral Nelson during his famous victory at the Battle of Trafalgar, a sword belt, a sword, and a few other expensive trifles of the sort not seen in serious naval circles from that day to this. I saved some money by borrowing the sword from an old friend, Assistant Secretary of State James Clement Dunn. In addition to my ceremonial costume, I was given a huge Colt .45 pistol, terrifying to look at and a full 8 pounds in weight.

I was to cross the Pacific by Pan American clipper, the grand but ponderous propeller aircraft of that era, and so my baggage-weight allowance was limited. Since the navy gave me no money to pay for overweight, I wore my ceremonial naval finery, including sword and pistol, onto the plane, where they could be stored in my berth. We left very early in the morning from San Francisco. A heavy mist had come off the bay, making the rubber matting of the walkway to the clipper extremely slippery. As I strode off to war, I slipped, causing extensive traces of the fine black rubber to come off on my formerly crisp dress-white trousers, making them unpresentable.

The flight itself—I was to stop at Pearl Harbor to call on the commanding admiral and then go on to Manila—proved to be a ludicrous experience. On board the clipper was the maharaja of Indore, the last descendant of the ruling family of one of the great Maratha warriors who gave the British such trouble in the eighteenth century. The maharaja was a long, thin man with a long, thin face centered around a long, thin nose. His body tapered down through a tiny waist, through long legs, to two interminably thin sandal-shod feet. His toenails, which showed at the open end of his sandals, were painted a bright crimson, and he wore bright green trousers and a crimson sport shirt.

The maharaja was a brilliant bridge player, and in those days I used to play bridge very well. After my official costume was safely stowed, we organized a game with an amiable young couple from Brooklyn who were going out to work in an insurance office in Calcutta. The Brooklyn couple were also first-rate bridge players but so careful about money that they would not play for more than one-tenth of a cent per point. We had a splendid running game, and play lagged only when the maharaja, who ingested small pellets of opium, retired to his berth for periodic naps. To the table would then come his aide-de-camp, a young Indian officer who possessed the most extraordinary combination of personal beauty and total mindlessness I have ever seen. He did not add brilliance to the bridge game.

The comedy of my journey to battle continued in Honolulu, where the clipper stopped long enough for me to call on the navy's area commander at Pearl Harbor, Admiral Husband E. Kimmel. I was still dressed in my soiled whites and hat, and must have seemed a ridiculous sight to the admiral's aide, who arrived to fetch me from my hotel. On the way to the meeting, I managed to expose my complete ignorance of all matters related to the navy and the sea. We drove past Pearl Harbor, unfortunately all too full of great American battleships. Still under the impression that all navy ships were the size of the *Queen Mary*, I remember gazing out over the harbor and commenting on the sleek lines of a particular group of destroyers. "Those are battleships, sir," came the aide's reply, quick as a shot and not without a hint of horror.

The undoubted climax of the journey came in Manila, where I found a very old friend, Warwick Scott from Philadelphia, also a pre–Pearl Harbor navy volunteer. Being a volunteer reserve officer, Warwick was more rule-bound than the regulars. In consequence, he was horrified to discover I had no idea at all about how to use my Colt .45. Unfortunately, Warwick also was senior to me and, therefore, could give me orders. So after a lame protest on my part, he ordered me to sequester myself in a nearby Nissen hut—a prefabricated bungalow made from corrugated iron and concrete, favored by the military in those days—with a very tough marine sergeant, who was to instruct me in the use of my pistol.

The galvanized iron shooting range under the tropical sun must have had an interior temperature of 140 degrees. It had no provisions against ricochet either, and consequently the lethal bullets of my dreadful pistol bounced about the infernally hot shooting space in a dangerously random manner every time I missed the target, which I invariably did. At the end of twenty minutes' firing, both the sergeant and I looked as though we had fallen into a swimming pool. Moreover, the sergeant was showing signs of serious nervous strain, as any sensible man would who is continuously exposed to ricocheting Colt .45 bullets.

I felt equally apprehensive and uncomfortable, and so I suggested to him that there was no chance at all that he would be able to teach me to use my weapon within any reasonable period of time. It was much more likely, I thought, that I would manage to kill myself or the sergeant, or at least wound one of us gravely, so I suggested that we agree to tell Warwick that I had passed my test and let it go at that. The sergeant, with visible and delighted relief, at once agreed. My first and last experience with firearms ended then and there.

I chose to travel to Bombay via the rather circuitous route of Manila and, later, Hong Kong and China because both Jim Forrestal and Bob Lovett had suggested that I locate Colonel Chennault, who was probably in Chungking, in order to escape my ludicrous and unwarlike assignment to Bombay. The admirals in charge of me immediately agreed with the idea that I go to Chungking en route to Bombay in order to gain a wider understanding of the situation in Asia. I fear the truth was that they did not care where I went, whom I saw, or, for that matter, what I did as long as I remained in navy uniform.

My next stop was the South China seaport of Hong Kong, an enchanting place in those days. The waterfront of Hong Kong island proper was a mixed Chinese and English business city, with its centerpiece the Hong Kong and Shanghai Bank and the British courts of justice. There was an open cricket ground in the middle of town; and an Anglican cathedral, which looked like an exercise in Victorian Gothic transported from a village in the south of England, stood a short way up the hill. At what the locals called "the mid-level," there were low, roomy houses and apartment buildings, and then there was a substantial gap in man's progress until one reached "the Peak"—the top of the volcanic island—where fog tended to prevail and the large houses of the rulers of the British businesses were located. The only two Chinese houses permitted on this eminence belonged to the compradors of the two great English trading houses Jardine, Matheson and Company and Butterfield and Swire.

The commercial center downtown was bisected by a series of long streets that ran parallel to the harbor. These thoroughfares were tightly webbed together by a maze of alleyways, each one of which was filled to the brim with the bustle of everyday Asian life. Rickshaws moved incessantly through the crowds. The Chinese men wore long gowns, old Chinese ladies with bound feet peddled God-knows-what on the sidewalks, and British ladies strode purposefully along from one British-supplied shop to the next. No matter what the climate, their faces were healthy and red, their clothes ruthlessly British. Watching them, I could not help feeling that their limitations were their principal source of strength. Steadfastly, they preferred canned kippers to the very excellent fresh fish of the China coast and snubbed the best produce from Chinese looms in favor of Liberty silks. All the while, they managed to carry with them their own healthy, right-little, tight-little atmosphere, no matter how exotic their surroundings.

I was not nearly so immune to the charms of the town, and spent my two days there in a state of delighted commotion. The first of my two "evenings out" was a Chinese dinner given to me by a young Chinese businessman to whom I had introductions. The food was superb. Since I was the guest of honor, two singsong girls, neither of whom spoke English, sat next to me at all times. After dinner, we visited a long round of Hong Kong nightclubs, which, to my tame view, were pale imitations of nightclubs at home. I had a difficult time. First of all, my hosts tried to make me drunk, which is polite on the China coast, extremely difficult to forestall, and rather embarrassing. Second, there were the girls, both pretty, both dressed in black-and-gold lace Chinese costumes, and both anxious to please. I should have liked to find out the ins and outs of the life of a singsong girl—a rather specialized profession—but since we had no means of communication, we had to converse in smiles and little gestures, which becomes exhausting after a time unless the gestures grow from small to large.

My plight may be imagined, my being poorly talented as a dancer and stone sober from my determination to resist excessive hospitality, solemnly jigging about with my partner, all the time conversing in smiles and little gestures as I jigged. This was what the Chinese call a "Western-style" evening. I very soon learned that one of the minor tragedies of travel in the Far East was that foreigners were always supposed to like only "Western style."

On my second evening out in Hong Kong, I had better luck. Emily Hahn, who had been warned of my arrival by mutual friends on the *New Yorker,* telephoned to invite me for dinner with an unexplained third party she described simply as "Charles." This turned out to be Charles Boxer, her lover and future husband. He was also the G-2 of the British garrison and a most agreeable and intelligent man who later made a considerable academic reputation among English and European scholars as the leading authority on the Portuguese Empire.

"Mickey" Hahn, as she was called, appeared at my hotel looking very handsome but very ample, as I had been warned she would look by her friends on the *New Yorker.* She took me to Charles's pleasant apartment on the midlevel, where we all made friends promptly and, after a suitable number of cocktails, ate a delicious dinner. Unfortunately, just as the coffee was being served, the party was interrupted by a call for Charles to go to the border in his capacity as intelligence officer. According to Charles, "There had been a bit of a bother about the Japanese."

At any rate, he left with apologies, whereupon Mickey turned to me and said, "Do you smoke?"

I had a perfectly good cigarette in my hand and said, "Of course, I smoke."

"I don't mean tobacco," she said. "I mean opium."

I replied that I had never done so but was willing to try. So we found ourselves an acceptable mode of transportation—rickshaws, as I remember—and set out.

The place, a rather dreary brothel in a Chinese tenement, was far from resembling the opium dens of fiction. In the first place, neither the den's décor nor the character of its inhabitants seemed sinister in any way. We walked in to find a hard-faced madame, her two bouncers, and a group of young ladies gossiping cheerily in the front hall. We explained that we would have a smoke but would not go upstairs and were promptly ushered into a cubbyhole furnished with two rickety couches, both covered in dreadful cheap cretonne, plus a number of cane chairs. Two naked electric light bulbs hung on wires from the ceiling.

The young girl who had been assigned to light our pipes, a cheerful, plump creature with a broad peasant's face, motioned us to the couches, which were excruciatingly lumpy, and took our shoes off. The smoking apparatus was then brought in. Opium was a government monopoly that paid a large part of the tax bill in Hong Kong, so the drug itself came from little tin tubes, like tubes for oil paints, with government seals on them. The girl cooked it over a lamp until it grew soft and bubbled, then skillfully molded half a saltspoonful into a large, rounded bamboo pipe and handed the pipe over to be smoked.

Emily and I smoked by turns, passing the pipe back and forth between us as the girl ministered to it. At first, the drug tasted like a corn-silk cigarette—hot, burny, and brown-papery—and had no appreciable effect that I could notice. Then, after a time, the opium began to take hold. It was not a jarring feeling, for the senses were not affected nor the head made light nor the body awkward. But conversation became very easy, time contracted and expanded in an odd way, and everything seemed somehow simpler and more pleasant. While Emily and I talked, the Chinese girl hovered over us, arranging pillows, lighting cigarettes, and occasionally filling another pipe. We must have stayed in the den for well over two hours, for at the end, as we rose to go, our hostess rather embarrassingly massaged our legs to bring back the circulation.

I suppose we smoked ten pipes between us, which was a lot for a beginner. I paid the bill—three U.S. dollars—feeling that I had had a splendid bargain evening. The truth is that good opium, correctly prepared, has the delightful and extremely surprising effect of making one believe that not only one's own words, but even the words of one's companions, are as worth hearing as the wisdom of the ages in the language of the sages. As I remember, Mickey Hahn and I took turns regaling one another on a number of topics, from the quality of food in President Roosevelt's White House to the state of Generalissimo Chiang Kai-shek's marriage. She saw me back to the hotel, elated, at 4:00 A.M.; and, as we traveled through the empty streets, we shouted to one another from rickshaw to rickshaw, convinced of our obvious brilliance. It was not until the next morning that I discovered the real drawback of opium, however well prepared: it gives one a hangover—or, at any rate, it gave me a hangover—of proportions so staggering as to make the consequences of too much alcohol seem trifling by comparison.

Despite my reduced state, I found that I recalled everything said during the opium high, all of which turned out to be more sophomoric than brilliant. Thus, I was doubly in agony when the telephone rang. When I picked it up, Charles Boxer instantly roared, "What do you mean by taking the mother of my child smoking opium?!" I did not think his rage would be soothed if I told Charles the truth: that Mickey had taken me and that I merely supposed her to be overweight rather than a prospective mother. Incoherence seemed to me to be the only wise, not to say gentlemanly, course, and so I took it.

Perhaps luckily, I had my plane ticket for Chungking early the next day. Indeed, I still felt the effects of the drug as I boarded the China Airways plane for the hair-raising flight to Chungking. The Japanese already held a wide strip of territory between Hong Kong and the Chinese wartime capital in the interior province of Szechwan. In order to avoid Japanese ack-ack, the China Airways C-47 passenger plane flew out of Hong Kong's Kai Tak airport in the early-morning darkness. We droned on for hours in complete blackout until, at first light, the deep gorge of the Yangtze River was revealed far below.

Colonel Chennault, whom I had yet to meet in China, had in fact helped devise the system by which this apparently magical feat of aviation was accomplished. It was not done by instruments. Although the Hong Kong airfield is two-thirds surrounded by mountains, the CAAC aircraft adhered rigidly to a carefully time-measured and direction-controlled flight plan, requiring a spiraled rise from the airfield as soon as the plane was airborne, a flight on a compass course thereafter, and a similarly controlled descent when the plane's time to Chungking was reached.

This strange flight plan, within which pilots had to allow for the vagaries of the weather, worked perfectly to get planes in darkness from Hong Kong to Chungking and back again. The worst part of the flight was, curiously enough, not the spinning night takeoff from Kowloon, but the arrival in Chungking, usually shortly after dawn. As soon as the gorge of the Yangtze River was revealed far below, the plane began to search for a tear in the mist that covered the land. When the tear was found, the plane plunged downward, flew to the lip of the gorge, and sideslipped into it—a sensation I have never experienced before or since on an airplane. It then flew breathlessly onward between the high cliffs of the gorge and just above the turbid river before finally landing on a tiny, stone-paved island in midstream. Years later, after enduring a similar landing, General Henry "Hap" Arnold, the great chief of the U.S. Army Air Force, emerged from his plane and, in forceful and highly colored language, condemned the island airport and its runway as both dangerous and unusable. His orders to that effect were, of course, ignored, and landings continued in the gorge throughout the war without incident.

Chungking, as I found it, had been subject to Japanese bombings at all hours of the day since the fall of Nanking in 1937 and was, in effect, a city under siege. Later, during my tour with Chennault's American Volunteer Group (AVG), I would spend long stretches of time there and become well acquainted with the soupy climate, endlessly precipitous rock-cut staircases, and Yangtze mud. The internecine squabbles of Chinese politics would become second nature to me as, surprisingly soon after my arrival, would the bombings. But I encountered during those first days in Chungking two things—one physical, the other largely psychological—for which I had not been prepared and which took some adjustment.

The first, so explicit a contrast after my faintly carnival journey to the battle zone, was the jolt of arriving in a nation at war. Nothing in Hong Kong, Manila, and certainly Pearl Harbor prepared me for the physical conditions prevalent in the Chinese capital. The city itself, now one of the largest in the world, was then a medieval town built on a long, high, narrow bluff at the convergence of the Yangtze and Chialing rivers. Dirty and bomb-scarred, it resembled at first blush a series of muddy anthills. The only roads that were fairly flat and usable were those running along the top of the long bluff. Traverses from place to place were, therefore, accomplished by climbing and descending countless staircases cut in the rock.

The city's buildings were a jumble of elegant old styles and blocky new ones, although rubble was the most prevalent architectural motif since a large portion of the city was always in ruins or being built up again as a result of the bombing. The hideous modern offices built to house the Nationalist government dominated what there was of a skyline, commingling with the miles of bamboo and matting huts hastily constructed to replace buildings destroyed by bombing. Both town and inhabitants were covered with a thin, grey film of plaster dust, making cleanliness of any kind nearly impossible. Baths were possible only when one could find a water coolie to carry water up from the river far below. Because electricity was limited and unreliable, peanut-oil lamps were the main source of illumination.

The city was protected by an air warning system that Chennault himself had installed. I never fully understood how the system worked, although I would benefit from it for most of the four years I was in China. The system was wholly improvised and made consid-

erable use of secret advance spotters, who set up near the enemy
bases and communicated, via field telephone, back to Chungking the
whereabouts and number of Japanese bombers as they took off.
When I was at Chennault's Kunming headquarters, as I was later for
many months at a time, our force would be informed within ten
minutes of any Japanese airplanes that had taken off from their nearest air base, White Cloud at Canton, and we would also be given the
numbers and types of planes and the direction in which they were
heading after takeoff. If they were coming our way, finally, we
would be periodically told of their progress and whether any additional airplanes had joined up with them.

It was this system that Chennault devised for the generalissimo
in 1937 that made it possible for "Free China," as it used to be
known, to keep going through the grim years between the flight of
the Nationalist government from Nanking in December 1937 until
the beginning of the Japanese-American war four years later. The
Chinese did not have the air power to protect their cities and other
centers, but they always had warning. The actual air warning system consisted of a series of balls suspended from poles on select
buildings in the city, the number of which relayed the force of incoming air power and the proximity of the aircraft. In this way, the
people of Chungking would be ordered to the air-raid shelters in
plenty of time to take cover, always bringing along their rudimentary possessions.

As it happened, I arrived in Chungking at the moment when
the Japanese were experimenting with the one approach that might
have defeated the air warning system. In the "48-hour bombing," as
it was called, they sent over their planes in small contingents. No
single contingent did much serious damage, but the round-the-clock
and apparently unending bombing kept most of the city of Chungking continuously in the shelters, bringing life to a nearly absolute
halt. Although the great distances traveled by the bombers made
surprise impossible and human casualties were few, the bombers'
constant presence overhead began to take its toll, disrupting the
routines of everyday life, making significant construction impossible, and visibly sapping the morale of the people.

During my three weeks in Chungking, I stayed at the Chialing
House, a rickety old government guesthouse that stood on a cliff
above the city proper. The roof of my room, blown off during a
bomb attack, had been replaced with bamboo matting and provided
fair shelter when the bombs were not falling. During air attacks, I
occupied a communal shelter nearby in a compound that had been
abandoned by a powerful official when his house was bombed. Even

the best of these structures were mere concrete tunnels, ventilated by downdrafts, with an opening at either end and benches along the sides. They were stuffy, uncomfortable, and lighted only by the peanut-oil lamps, so that no one wanted to spend more time in them than necessary. Consequently, we all waited until a coolie heard the planes and sounded the alarm, at which point everyone ran for the shelter. The more timid hurried inside. Bolder spirits waited at the entrance to see whether or not the bombers were heading in their direction.

I was exposed to this deadening round of scurry and shelter almost as soon as I set foot in Chungking. The shelter was invariably crowded and smelled it, as the cool of the rock began to give way to human warmth. No one talked; and if anyone even whispered, the others shouted to shut him up since they wanted to hear how near the planes were. As the bombers came closer, we heard a sort of heavy buzzing boom, and everyone in the shelter sat very still, some with their hands in their ears and all with mouths hanging wide open to meet the concussion produced by exploding bombs.

Then the bombs were dropped. First, we heard a sort of hissing sound, then a series of dull thuds and crashes; and if the bombing was nearby, the vibrations shook the rock into which the shelter was cut. The entire drama took on average about five or ten minutes. The noise, as the raid ran on, was incessant, although when it ceased—and one knew immediately—it ceased altogether. The very second the last bomb had exploded, people would begin to creep out into the open air; and by the time the noise of the aircraft was no longer audible, the shelter was nearly empty. After that we all simply sat down to wait for the alarm to end or the next batch to come.

I have never experienced greater boredom and impatience than I did in the Chialing House shelter for hours on end every day and during part of each night. Fortunately, the Japanese soon abandoned the 48-hour bombing possibly because this kind of unceasing operation put as much strain on them as it put on the Chinese. One wonders what the outcome might have been if this grim tactic had been sustained for a much longer period.

The resistance effort of the Chinese was unquestionably obstinate and tenacious, but it did not take me long to discover that the politics in Chungking was incessant, complex in a disagreeable way, and, in most cases, unpleasantly corrupt. The executive side of government was dominated by a highly conservative, even reactionary, bureaucracy. It was animated not so much by idealism as by a bureaucracy's more common motives and suffered from all the bureaucratic poisons I had known from Washington plus several more of a strictly Chinese invention. Extraordinarily, none of this had as yet been conveyed to the readers of the big American newspapers and newsmagazines that had correspondents in China. Indeed, on my first evening in the capital, I learned how completely I had been deceived about the real situation in China. I was asked to dine at the British embassy by the ambassador, Sir Archibald Clark-Kerr, to whom I had letters of introduction from Washington.

The embassy was located on a high cliff above the Chialing River, miles beyond the inner city of Chungking. Our small party dined outdoors in peace, for at that distance from the city it was unnecessary to worry about the bombing. Everyone there talked freely about the real political and governmental situation in Chungking, and I sat, mouth agape, comparing the enormous difference between everything I now was hearing and the optimistic, near-heroic reports of Chiang and his Nationalist government that I had read in Washington.

I still remember that evening long ago, the table under the stars, the marvelously adroit, white-gowned servants, ghostly in the heavy-scented nighttime garden, and the strained look of one tired guest who was known to be alarmed even when sheltered by a heavy overhang of rock. He correctly and gloomily forecast "a bad bombing day tomorrow." He got a puckish answering grin from Archie Clark-Kerr, who was one of those rare men who positively enjoy danger. As for myself, I was reaching a decision that I never changed: the decision never to write about serious overseas problems until I had at least gone overseas myself for long enough to smell the weather in the streets.

Like most in Washington, I had taken at face value the standard press dispatches from Chungking, all of which portrayed Free China as morally heroic and, generally, politically stable in every way. I soon found that heroism in the face of repeated Japanese bombing raids was common enough in Chungking. The stability of Chiang Kai-shek's government, however, was very much open to question. The generalissimo himself was undoubtedly a very brave man. His efforts were greatly complicated, however, by a patchwork arrangement of military commanders—some of whom were corrupt, others fiercely loyal—and by a web of political intrigue and alliance that appeared to have come straight from the court of one of the more feeble-willed Ming emperors.

At the center of this bizarre tangle were the three Soong sisters and their brother T. V. Soong. Taken separately, the four Soong siblings were remarkable individuals, each polished in appearance, impeccably educated, and highly intelligent. Taken as a group,

however, the Soongs were as competitive and as ferociously ambitious a family as I have known. Their father, Charles Soong, had
made a lucrative transition from Methodist missionary to Shanghai
banker. He raised his children in mandarin splendor and, since he
was a graduate of Vanderbilt University in Tennessee, insisted they
be educated in the West. The eldest son, T.V., was sent off to Harvard. The second daughter, Soong Ch'ing-ling, returned from Wes-
leyan College in Georgia to marry the father of the Chinese revolution, Dr. Sun Yat-sen. Not to be outdone, the youngest sister, Soong
Mei-ling, married Chiang Kai-shek two years after Dr. Sun's death
in 1925.

By the time I arrived in Chungking, Chinese politics was curiously divided into provinces, in each one of which a member of the
generalissimo's family by marriage played a leading, if not dominant, role. Mme. Chiang Kai-shek led the very considerable faction
that formed around the generalissimo and his Secretariat—what I
used to call the "Palace faction." Mme. Chiang was also allied with
her older sister Soong Ai-ling, Mme. H. H. Kung. Her husband,
whom Mme. Kung was rumored to cuckold with generous frequency, was a large, smooth, fat man with the exterior of a YMCA
secretary (which I think he had been) and the training of a Shansi
banker (for he came from a family of Shansi bankers, although they
claimed connection with the other Kung clan founded by Confucius). Later, I would learn in person that he further possessed a
degree of oily rapacity that I have seldom seen equaled.

Mme. Kung and Mme. Chiang were in part kept together as an
alliance by Mme. Kung's daughter Jeannette, whom the generalissimo's wife was devoted to, despite the younger girl's unexpected
habit of dressing like a man. More important, Mme. Kung was the
real head of the very large reactionary group in the Kuomintang
apparatus. The other two Soong siblings, T. V. Soong and Mme.
Sun Yat-sen, much disliked by these two allied sisters, also were
exceedingly fond of one another. T. V. Soong, whom I had gotten
to know well in Washington, had lost all favor with the generalissimo in an earlier period, and in 1941 he had only begun to rise again
because of the pressures exerted by the war. As the head of China
Defense Supplies Inc., T.V. was simply China's chief lobbyist in
Washington; and, as I have already said, he had done a remarkable
job there for China, both making valuable friends and acquiring
invaluable credits and supplies for the Nationalist war effort.

T. V. Soong was probably the most significant figure in the
small but important modern-minded faction within the Kuomintang. His closest friend in the army was General Ch'en Ch'eng, who

later became vice-president on Taiwan and even in 1941 was enormously admired by all Americans. T. V. Soong's closest civilian friend was Pei Tsu-yi, the father of architect I. M. Pei and, what was more important in 1941, the head of the Bank of China. The other men T. V. Soong was close to were of the same sort, although it should be understood that these associations greatly increased the generalissimo's suspicion of his brother-in-law. Furthermore, since westernized Chinese were still regarded as traitors by the Chinese majority, they were by no means popular leaders.

As for Mme. Sun Yat-sen, although she was still living in Hong Kong in 1941, I later came to know her well. As soon as she fled the Japanese from Hong Kong to Chungking, her charming sisters put her under house arrest in a small villa with a sewer running through the garden, over which one had to cross on a wooden bridge. When one reached the door, there was Mme. Sun to open it herself, all demureness, all sweetness, in a little sweater she always made sure her guests knew she had knitted for herself. She was in fact the chief propaganda agent for the Chinese Communist party in Chungking. Hence, this one family, the Soongs, had Mme. Chiang leading the palace faction, Mme. Kung at the head of the reactionary faction in the Kuomintang, T. V. Soong at the head of the much smaller, modern-minded faction in the Kuomintang, and Mme. Sun doing a highly effective job for the Communists. Furthermore, when I got to know them all, I thought they were exceptionally well equipped for the very important places that they occupied—for, as I have said, stupidity was one quality all of them lacked.

In all, I stayed three weeks in Chungking, enough time to make a few friends in the press hostel, among the diplomats, and among other civilians who would later be important to me when I returned to Chungking. Also during this time, I took my first ride in a wicker carrying chair, which I happily adopted as the quickest and most commodious way of travel about the shattered city. This was a split-bamboo contraption, like a piece of Chinese porch furniture, slung between two long bamboo poles and equipped with a footrest and a thing like a buggy top, made of canvas and intended to keep off the sun. Two poles protruded out each end of the chair to a length of about eight feet. At either end, these poles were joined by a crossbar, and the four chair men carried the entire machine by resting the crossbars on their shoulders and hands. Thus, one was carried at shoulder height, in a semireclining position. The chair men went at an astonishing pace, considerably faster than a fast walk, constantly shouting at people to get out of their way. The chair was not without its perils since most of the journeys were over steep and treacherous staircases. It is less than pleasant to be halfway up a flight of steps, almost high enough to reach the top of a high building, with the steps falling steeply away behind, reclining in a comparatively frail bamboo cage.

Just the same, this feudal form of travel was an intoxicating way to see the countryside. Indeed, the experience I remember more clearly than any other during that first visit to China was a six-mile trip I took by chair out to the villa belonging to a friend of T. V. Soong. The route lay first through the southern suburbs of Chungking, through little, narrow, old streets, stone-paved and fronted with row upon row of open shops in which Chinese families carried on their lives with complete freedom and indifference to publicity. The architecture looked oddly like English half-timber work, although no English village in the world could give such a sense of teeming life as a Chinese street does. After passing the suburbs, we struck out into the country, up and down over abrupt humpbacked little hills, still climbing and descending stairs, for the path, which was the Chinese equivalent of an important country road, was stone-paved throughout. We passed a brick factory with a big mud chimney cleverly camouflaged with palm branches; an abandoned temple; a mound covered with graves, built like stone pigeonholes.

Then, among the little hills, rice paddies began to appear. We had reached the farmland, and the journey became one long, breathtaking panorama, like a richly wrought Chinese scroll. Sometimes we passed through villages, where the women were weaving or dying the local cloth. Sometimes we were on the level, among the paddy fields, where the farmers and their children worked with water buffalo. Sometimes we were climbing those fantastic staircases through thick woods on a hillside or hurrying up a ravine with a torrent rushing beside the path. One sees much more going fairly slowly; and so there was more to see than on any other trip I can remember. At length, we reached the top of the small range of hills and crossing it, found a high valley with an immense, sweeping view. On a hilltop stood the small villa belonging to T.V.'s friend. The journey's conclusion was a little embarrassing, for the chair men, making a demonstration at the end of the journey, carried me straight into the villa garden, where my host, an important government official, was holding a meeting of some kind.

As week succeeded week in Chungking, I began to worry about concluding the real purpose of my going to the capital, which was, of course, to get in touch with Colonel Chennault. Luckily, though ludicrously, we finally met at a garden party given by Generalissimo and Mme. Chiang Kai-shek. It was a huge gathering set in a small wooded dell in the lovely western hills on the western bank of the Yangtze, far away from the rubble-strewn capital. The dell contained a lake, across which stretched a stone dam on which rows of tea tables had been set. From the tables, one could look down across the sweep of the valley, at the opposite end of which stood a small Confucian temple.

For once, the bombing had stopped; the weather was pleasant at last, the air crisp and breathtakingly clear. The dignitaries had come in legion up from the city, conveyed by sedan chair and limousine. In clusters of three and four, the guests mingled stiffly together, eating ices and stale tea cakes as the generalissimo and his wife circulated through the party. For pure social spectacle, the gathering was oddly reminiscent of garden parties I had attended at the Roosevelt White House in Washington. It had the same fantastic mixture of people, the same slightly suspicious food, the same curious atmosphere of graciousness mingled with constraint, even the same earnest, devoted, and slightly bossy female followers of the lady of the house to hand out the food and shepherd the customers.

Mme. Chiang, however, was infinitely prettier than her opposite number at home. Soong Mei-ling, as she had been called before her marriage, was just past her fortieth birthday then, although one could not find the least hint of middle age in her costume or bearing. Her hair was tied back in a smooth lacquer bun, and her complexion was startlingly light, although I would later learn this was something of an illusion. My initial impression was of a truly striking, rather sinister, polished woman, although we barely exchanged a word at that first meeting. As for the generalissimo, he wore an expression of constant, polite bemusement and smiled far less than President Roosevelt. Instead of calling everyone by first name, he contented himself with nodding to guests as they approached and emitting a dignified but noncommittal "Hao, hao," which translated literally from the Mandarin means "Good, good."

In the middle of all this, looking rather irritably at a tea cake, I found Colonel Chennault. The aviator was then fifty-one years old, a little deaf from years of air-circus flying, and outwardly, at first glance, every inch the tough, experienced soldier. His face was craggy and immensely picturesque, with something of the "gamecock of the wilderness" about it. The colonel had been in China since the spring of 1937, when he, at the request of the generalissimo, had taken over the job of advising the Chinese air force as it then existed. Italian advisers had preceded him and done a lamentable job. They were sent home or simply went home—I never knew which—when the Japanese war in China began in earnest. As adviser to the unhappy Italian-trained pilots, Chennault had formed an admiration for the Chinese, based on an appreciation for Chinese natural intelligence and the extraordinary capacity of the Chinese for hard work and for showing great courage if they were given a good lead.

By the time Chennault was called in, however, it was too late for much to be done with what remained of the Chinese air force. The Japanese, with their superior numbers and equipment, succeeded in destroying nearly all the Chinese combat pilots. During this bizarre interval in his career, Chennault himself became a combat pilot—bizarre because he was, after all, middle-aged and had been dismissed from the American service on grounds of ill health. As an American, furthermore, he had no business fighting on the side of the Chinese, and the U.S. embassy in China kept chivying and harassing him during those years. As a result, he had a phobia about any discussion of the subject, although he finally talked to me about it with some frankness. The truth—which I checked with Chinese friends—is worth setting down.

In brief, Chennault fitted for his own use an American Hawk-75 monoplane with special armor to protect his back and seat. It was a light, speedy plane and had to be used in a special way against the Japanese, but it was also a plane that the Japanese found very hard to damage. In this plane, Chennault knocked down a total of more than 40 Japanese aircraft at a bounty of $500 per plane. As Mme. Chiang and the generalissimo grew more pleased with the results—which they always carefully checked, the ante was raised to $1,000 per enemy plane destroyed. This was not at all sufficient, however, to deal with the deteriorating situation caused by the Japanese bombing. In time, members of T. V. Soong's staff at China Defense Supplies, with the advice and support of Roosevelt's men, put before Chennault the idea of the American Volunteer Group.

The AVG, as Chennault planned it, was to be a voluntary, mercenary fighting outfit. As I noted earlier, he sought to secure the basic essentials in the United States: planes, ammunition, pilots, and engineering personnel trained to keep the planes in the air. He further proposed to let the Chinese take care of everything noncombatant such as housing and feeding the group, and he wanted finally to use a very large element of Chinese on the engineering side, where they were to be trained by Americans. He believed, and he persuaded the generalissimo and Mme. Chiang, that with such an outfit aided by the air warning system, he could defeat the much more numerous Japanese forces in China. He also said he could protect the Burma Road, the critically important highway that ran from

Kunming in southwest China down across the vast Mekong and
Salween gorges and onward into Burma and the railhead at Lashio.
By the time of my arrival in Chungking, the Burma Road provided
the last tenuous ground link between Free China and the outside
world.

When I finally spoke with Colonel Chennault in Chungking,
he was still struggling to put together the AVG. He proposed to
take me on as a staff officer because the executive order by President
Roosevelt, which permitted him to recruit the AVG, covered only
reserve officers, most of whom lacked training in staff duties like
administration and equipment procurement. As it turned out, I
would be just about the only staff Chennault had except for a marvelous naval typist/secretary/office manager, Tom Trumble, who
had volunteered for the AVG "to see the world."

At the garden party, we agreed to meet later at Kunming,
where Chennault had his Chinese headquarters; and I then made
plans to leave Chungking for that city in the southwestern mountains of Yunnan province and to continue my strange journey, ostensibly to Bombay, by going down the Burma Road from there
with Tilman Durdin, a correspondent for the *New York Times*.
Kunming then was a lovely, very primitive, and very filthy Chinese
city that still retained something of its prewar character because it
had suffered fewer bomb scars. Upon my arrival, I was put up at the
Bank of China's huge and unbelievably hideous guesthouse—a large
bogus-modern villa, elaborately camouflaged in green and brown,
with a garden around it like the drab railroad-station gardens in
France. At the end of a long lunch there, the colonel asked me to
join the AVG as his aide and chief odd-job man.

I accepted Chennault's offer with alacrity for two reasons.
First, a job with the AVG seemed to me to be an opportunity to do
something real under a real leader. I wanted to get as near to the war
as I could and was not fool enough—at the age of thirty, unable
either to shoot a gun or drive a car—to see myself as a useful soldier.
Moreover, the alternative duty in Bombay seemed to offer the prospect of much food and little work; and since I had had much food
and plenty of work to do in Washington, I did not relish the exchange. Furthermore, I had been advised to make the exchange by
two officials in Washington whom I admired. Second, I was also
drawn to Chennault, for in our two short meetings he had impressed
me as a man of singular character. Obviously something of a military
genius, he possessed an old-fashioned American humor as well as a
peculiar, homemade learning of the kind one might have found in
one of Andrew Jackson's commanders. Jackson himself must have

been the same type of man—more flamboyant, less canny, but with the same saltiness and the same daring.

Chennault's father ran a large farm in Louisiana, and his grandfather, who had fought with distinction during the Civil War, had been killed by a jealous husband at the age of ninety-six! Similar wild qualities had not endeared Chennault to his military commanders. Many of them regarded as cockeyed his theories of air warfare, which he had adapted from General Billy Mitchell, the original advocate of strategic air power, during the late 1920s and promoted aggressively. Mitchell, of course, was court-martialed and drummed from the military for promoting his views. But Chennault's connection with Mitchell did not affect my judgment of the man. On the contrary, the echoes of the American past in Chennault's character and his mastery of the most modern of weapons—air power— seemed to me an appealing mixture. Chennault's record in China, moreover, had proved his critics wrong; this, and the promise he and his new outfit held for immediate action, made my choice to serve with him an easy one.

The decision reached, I wired my official resignation from the U.S. Navy directly to Secretary of the Navy Frank Knox in Washington. With my colleague from the *Times*, I then set out from Kunming in a battered, heavily overladen American sedan car, compliments of T. V. Soong and the Bank of China. As we departed, an air warning alert sounded with the result that the entire population of Kunming was suddenly out on the street milling about our little troop. I still remember the spectacle of that morning—mothers, fathers, grandfathers, and grandchildren streaming out into the country with all their worldly goods on their backs or in small carts. The roads were crowded, the canals full of boats, and every path among the rice paddies had its own procession, all bound for the hills an hour away, where they would wait out the alert. Traveling with a driver, a servant, and our guide, the obsequious Mr. Kao—all thanks, once again, to the good offices of the Bank of China—it took some time to fight through this throng.

We did not learn what the real Burma Road would be like until later that afternoon. The highway suddenly narrowed, and the springs of the sedan came down on the back axle with a crash that almost jarred my back teeth out. For the next five days, we traveled on the Burma Road, the spectacle of which was quite beyond imagination. This crucial strategic link was, at first inspection, no more than an ordinary dirt country road of the sort the people in Avon complained about to the first selectman (my father at the time). However, the entire length had been cut by hand in a matter of just a few years through some of the roughest country imaginable. Indeed, the Burma Road stretched some 712 miles through hills as big and more abrupt and twisted than the foothills of the Rockies, and across valleys that made me think of Shangri-la.

"Yunnan," the Chinese province through which the road travels into Burma, means "Southern Clouds," and the whole province is formed essentially of a high, bare limestone plateau. Cut into the limestone are endless potholes, and these ranged in size from nearly 100 miles across, like the valley that holds Kunming, to a few miles, no more than enough to cause a detour of the road. A journey south through Yunnan is a journey from one of these pothole valleys to another. Each of the valleys is entirely enclosed in its own ring of hills so that each day's trip was a climb over one or two sections of high, flat, treeless plateaus into the pothole valley that was the day's objective. This routine was varied by occasional descents into, and climbs out of, precipitous, swirling river gorges. Every time we descended into one of the river gorges, we broke one or another spring, so that after the first day we were one spring poorer every morning until the fifth day, when, at long last, we pulled into the town of Lung-ling past midnight in pouring rain and quite springless. Till and I finally abandoned our car and companions and made the last day of the journey by bus, an illegal cooperative enterprise that the local magistrate helped us to discover.

Although we were well cared for by Mr. Kao and the local representatives of the Bank of China during the trip, their attentions sometimes proved overbearing. Invariably, when we arrived in the evening at one of the small valley towns, we were ushered to the Bank of China headquarters, generally the most handsome old-style Chinese house in the town, set in a large compound. The beds consisted of a number of boards of varying thickness laid on a bedstead and covered with a blanket, and I never managed to sleep soundly on them regardless of how much Luminal (a sleeping medicine) I took.

Our sponsorship precluded meals at the many roadside restaurants, but when our hosts gave us a Chinese dinner, it was delicious. During most of the journey, however, Till and I survived on the dreaded "foreign style" cooking, of which our evening in the town of Pao-shan was, alas, characteristic. We arrived there at 7:00 P.M., having been on the road since 6:00 that morning. We were covered with dust and feeling the kind of dull, heavy hunger one feels when one is desperately tired. We were served Ovaltine and thick British biscuits (long past their prime) in a small room off the court filled with Western-style chairs of unbelievable hardness. There we conversed with our host, the submanager of the local bank branch—an intensely ambitious young man with an omnipresent autograph book full of flowery sentiments—until 8:30 P.M., at which point the cook produced the first course of our foreign-style dinner.

To not cut up the food is the first thing Chinese cooks learn about Western-style cooking. So we were served our meat dishes whole but given only chopsticks to eat with. Decidedly over-matched, feigning great enthusiasm, we wrestled with a succession of game and poultry dishes, the last of which was a plate of pigeons, roasted whole with their heads on and eyes still staring. Chatting to our host all the while with great politeness, Till and I would plunge in with our chopsticks only to get back the thinnest, most unsatisfying morsels of pigeon. This unhappy comedy continued until 10:30 P.M., when at last we were allowed to make our weary way up to the board beds.

In sum, this was one of the most uncomfortable journeys I have made. Most of the time, however, the sights and the scenery were indescribably beautiful. Everything was new to me; and if I kept my eyes open, I could draw great lessons just from the way the Chinese—far, far from any major center of China—gained their livelihood and carried on their lives. The most interesting aspect of the trip, from my perspective, was the countryside itself. I remember our stopping the sedan for lunch one afternoon on the lip of the Mekong gorge. We had spent the bulk of the morning creeping along the side of the gorge on a track some 13 feet wide, from which the gorge itself fell away in a hair-raising drop to the river 2,000 feet below. The region had been settled only four generations earlier, but in the interval the village on the plateau overlooking this particular sector of gorge had built terraces of rice paddies, which were the damnedest feat of capital creation I have ever seen. The paddies began at the river's edge, where they were not much wider than a large living room, and moved in steady progression all the way up the side of the gorge to just below where Till and I were picnicking, by which time the terraces were roughly 2 feet wide and 3 feet high.

When we at last reached Rangoon via a combination of bus and river steamer, Till and I put up at the Strand Hotel, the best public accommodation in Burma but horrifying to me because I had not gotten used to the old sort of British colonial hotels in which goat chops were always prominent features of the menu. In my innocence, I had supposed that the ten days or so that had elapsed between my first cable from Kunming and our arrival in Rangoon would be sufficient to let the U.S. Navy act on my request for transfer. Instead, I found not a word waiting for me. In time, Till departed, and so I hung about for ten more days in Rangoon, tasting the extremely limited delights of what was then probably the least interesting of all the large colonial cities in the Far East.

Eventually, a message arrived from Washington. It completely ignored my original request and without further comment ordered me to proceed to Bombay. I proceeded dutifully to India and upon arrival there presented my papers to the warrant officer of the naval observer's station. From Bombay, however, I again cabled the Navy Department, requesting a final decision on my status and pointing out that my job with Chennault would not wait forever. The admirals responded that I could not be let go until my naval accounts had been properly audited. As it happened, I had not yet disbursed so much as 50 cents of military money in India, and I had no official naval accounts from my China journey either since I had been living on my own traveler's checks. So I decided to risk court martial rather than risk losing my job with Chennault. I wired Jim Forrestal, then under secretary of the navy, begging him to sustain my financial credit with his much stronger credit. I thereupon wrote the orders—part of my prerogative as naval observer—to abandon my post. And, without further delay, I set off back to Rangoon to join Colonel Chennault.

9

The AVG

(September 1941–July 1942)

I reached Rangoon in September and stayed in the city long enough to pick up what seemed to me to be the two essentials: a sensible khaki uniform and a bearer to take care of me in Burma's unbearable prickly-heat–begetting climate. Perhaps it is a major failing, but throughout my long life I have always sought out people who, for either love or, more usually, for money, will care for my daily needs. The name of my servant in Burma was Paideyah, and as both friend and employee he went perhaps further in performing these duties than most. A slight, energetic man, he was a deeply devout Tamil Christian and one of the most honest, intelligent, and generally decent people I have known. Alas, Paideyah must have been killed by the Japanese or died from another cause because, although I searched for him after the war, he had altogether vanished from Rangoon.

The AVG had its main training base in an abandoned Royal Air Force facility north of Rangoon outside the shabby little town of Toungoo. Here, the outfit could be assembled and trained in relative safety before moving on to Kunming to face the enemy. When Paideyah and I found it, the base was in a state of frenzied dilapidation. The buildings were no more than large bamboo huts of various shapes and sizes—hardly cover at all, it seemed to me, in southern Burma's ferociously hot climate. The pilots were a motley bunch, largely untrained as fighter pilots and hardly disciplined as men. Their planes were overaged mongrel P-40s that had been passed from one owner to the next and stupidly modified with each new contract. They even lacked decent gunsights and, worse still as I soon found out, had almost no spare parts.

Our arrival at Toungoo caused a mild sensation. I suppose my accent and appearance seemed odd enough to the assembled fliers. However, the real sensation was caused by Paideyah, who, as a professional bearer in the oldest colonial tradition, thought it his duty to do everything—from laying out my clothes in the morning through scrubbing my back in the bath (if I had let him do so) all the way to making my every arrangement for an air or rail journey to any place on earth. Imagine the general consternation, then, on the morning after my midnight arrival at the base, when Paideyah drew the mosquito curtains of my cot in the officers' dormitory, helped me into my dressing gown and slippers, and then followed me with sponge bag and razor into the communal bathroom.

The young fliers recruited for the AVG were even less used to this sort of thing than I was, and their reaction was considerable and, at first, rather hostile. Within a few days, however, my fellow AVG members observed that Paideyah saved me all sorts of bother, including the fearful job of dealing with the local washerwomen, who were both bad-tempered and incompetent. Gradually, therefore, the use of body servants spread like a disease. I think I was the only one to have a bearer all to myself, but many of the others clubbed together or made larger groups so that by the time I left the outfit, a substantial population of Tamil Christians had been added to the AVG. All in all, the experience made me feel like the title character in the Mark Twain short story "The Man That Corrupted Hadleyburg."

Paideyah's services aside, the amenities of life at the base were few. The quarters were bare, the food inedible, and the weather brutally humid. However, nobody in the AVG had time to notice or complain. The young pilots listened for a couple of hours every day to the tactical lectures Colonel Chennault gave them, and this was followed by hours of flying. Since our P-40s had so many faults and many of the pilots were just learning to fly them, their flights too often ended in a semi-smashup on landing. These smashups kept the engineering contingent desperately busy.

For his part, Colonel Chennault, who was a natural leader, devoted all his energy to training and pulling his outfit together. I have never seen men respond better to leadership under difficult circumstances. I have never known quite what gave Chennault this quality, except that he possessed personal charisma and a high degree of confidence. In appearance, too, he looked every inch the dashing, battle-tested veteran commander, which, indeed, he was. Years later, at the Allied meeting in Cairo, Winston Churchill observed Chennault's craggy, angular features and said, "My God, that face; glad he's on our side." The colonel sounded like a leader, too—always clear and bold. He made decisions with clarity of mind, with speed, and, where needed, with great fairness.

Chennault's considerable skills were tested to the limit, for the outfit was scheduled to go into combat in China three months later, in December. Of the 100 or so fliers at Toungoo, roughly 60 percent had never flown the group's basic aircraft, the P-40. Furthermore, in order to enable the P-40 to outfight the more nimble Zero, Chennault had devised an entirely novel system of tactics, which had to be learned and drilled home. The Japanese Zero was a very light and well-armed plane that could turn on a dime. Our P-40s were heavy, and their only effective ordnance were the .50-caliber machine guns synchronized to shoot through the propeller and the four .30-caliber machine guns mounted along the wings.

With the Army Air Corp conventional "turning tactics," the P-40 could not possibly compete with the Zero, as would be proved completely and tragically at the beginning of the real war in the southwest Pacific. Chennault's tactics combined reliance on the efficiency of his own air warning net (the AVG was hired, it must be remembered, by the Nationalist government to fight the Japanese *in* China) with the power and weight of the P-40s. The essential defensive tactic involved taking a position in the eye of the sun (the air warning net would have provided the rough location and number of Japanese planes in the vicinity) and then flying from high altitude straight out of sunlight to dive onto the oncoming enemy with the .50-caliber machine guns blazing. Chennault taught his pilots to fight in groups of two and three and not to stay behind for a conventional dogfight, but to dive straight through the formation of Zeros. In that way, they concentrated their own fire (the .50-caliber guns were lighter than the Japanese 20-mm. cannon but had greater range and a higher rate of fire) and neutralized the Zeros' maneuverability. Being heavier and stronger, they could dive much faster. If the Japanese did not break off the encounter, the P-40s could use their superior acceleration to climb and dive again.

These tactics were to prove devastatingly successful. In December 1941, when the fighting began, Chennault's P-40s frequently obtained a kill rate of 10 to 1. They literally drove the Japanese air force, very much larger in numbers, out of China's air space within two weeks of the AVG's appearance in combat. With more difficulty because of the absence of an air warning net, the AVG P-40s also did very well in the defense of Rangoon, all of which happened while P-40s, using conventional tactics, were being knocked down with frightening frequency in the Pacific war.

In those hectic months before Pearl Harbor, however, it was uncertain as to whether our P-40s would be able to fly at all, let alone fight. As I have noted, the planes had arrived in the Far East with no spare parts, not even spare tires, although the Toungoo runway, on which one could have easily made an omlette at midday, was anything but good for the tires of P-40s, which were being landed much too fast. Shortly after my arrival, the engineering officer, a very capable man named Charles Sawyer, presented me with a ten-page single-spaced list of the spare parts he wanted sent out from Washington on a high priority. I did not know what any of these spare parts were, but I got Colonel Chennault to let me go down to Rangoon to get this monstrous list transmitted to the United States.

A good deal of my time in the ensuing months would be taken in trying to procure spare parts from various authorities. The task was made furiously difficult for two reasons. First, Colonel Chennault had no staff training himself, nor had the couple of old China coast friends, who claimed—quite falsely, as it turned out—to be able to do staff work. Second, the AVG had no central base of supply. As I discovered within a day after joining it, our outfit was communicating with about as many independent headquarters as the duke of Marlborough had to communicate with when he guided the Grand Coalition that destroyed the power of Louis XIV. To name them, we had Chungking and the generalissimo; Yunnan and the extraordinary old warlord there, Lung Yun, because our main base was to be there, in Kunming; the British civil government and the RAF in Rangoon; the highest echelon of the RAF down in Singapore; T. V. Soong and China Defense Supplies which was charged with our support in Washington; and, as courts of last appeal, Bob Lovett, who was head of the air force, the president's adviser Harry Hopkins, and, finally, President Roosevelt himself.

The task of readying for war was all very dramatic. As Chennault's chief staff aide (I had no official rank), I had wonderful help, especially from Tom Trumble. Throughout those early weeks of preparation, however, I felt the unremitting responsibility that any decent noncombatant would feel if he belonged to an outfit that was soon to go into combat with every kind of gap in its equipment and with the job of filling the gaps entirely his duty. By the end of my first months with the AVG, in fact, I had reached the stage of such frantic overwork and worry that I was taking double and even triple sleeping pills, and then only getting about four and a half hours of real sleep each night.

Much of this frenzied time was devoted to travel, for when regular communications failed to get the desired supplies, I was often dispatched by Colonel Chennault to plead our case in person. I remember one quite depressing visit to Singapore to see whether I could find tail wheel tires to fit the P-40s and a jeweler—the need was so desperate that we were quite ready to go to a jeweler—who could make a tiny but essential component of the .50-caliber machine-gun firing mechanism called an E1B Solenoid.

The flight to Singapore had been difficult, and I was feeling rather grim when we taxied to a stop in a driving rain. I was met by an RAF squadron leader with an enormous mustache who was standing just in front of an open hangar full of aircraft that seemed to have come out of a British boy's book on the First World War. They were biplanes with enormous engines, no cowlings, tiny machine guns, and a kind of wire tatting to bind their upper and lower wings together.

I asked the squadron leader what these planes were. He replied in a hopeful voice, "That's one of our fighter squadrons, you know. They're a little old-fashioned, but they're jolly maneuverable. I think they'll make a very good job of it with the Zeros." I could not help but feel that I was talking to a doomed man, for I believed, following Chennault's thinking of those days, that when the big Japanese move occurred—and I had no doubt that it would—Singapore would be among the first points of attack. I had already seen the Japanese air force in action over Chungking and knew, from Chennault's instruction, what the Zero was capable of doing in a fight. I suspected these rattletrap machines would be next to useless when the Japanese attacked, although I did not say so. Barring this melancholy memory—and a gold watchband of an RAF design guaranteed to prevent prickly heat (humidity rash)—nothing whatever came out of my trip to Singapore since the British were as strapped for supplies as the AVG.

My hectic prewar experience did have comic interludes, however. The most memorable of these took place aboard the British imperial train that bore Alfred Duff Cooper, Churchill's newly appointed minister of Far Eastern affairs, his wife Lady Diana, and his large staff on an inspection of Burma's defenses. Duff Cooper wished to consult with Colonel Chennault on the intentions of the Japanese, although the meeting, as it turned out, was poorly timed, for it took place in December 1941, just days before the attack on Pearl Harbor. Aside from holding a number of high-level posts during his illustrious career, Duff Cooper was also a charming man and wonderful company. He had arrived at his post a week or two before our meeting and would be recalled to London about a month later, shortly before the fall of Singapore.

Of course, our little party had no inkling of the tragic events to come, although the AVG by that time was set on a definite schedule for attack. The atmosphere in the British camp during those months before the war was, as a rule, formal and rather fuddled. I think Chennault's views on the situation were sought as an afterthought; at least the strange venue and timing of the visit made it seem that way to me. Since Duff Cooper's entourage was traveling by train, the hour of rendezvous was 5:15 A.M. at Toungoo railroad station. Nevertheless, the colonel and I were there in plenty of time to see the small, narrow-gauge imperial train—the carriage a spotless cream color, painted with purple British imperial crowns—make an impressive entrance into the station.

Unfortunately, 5:15 being 5:15 does not have a good effect on me. Consequently, when Chennault and I boarded the train, I stumbled straight into the bedroom car of Lady Diana Duff Cooper. I had first met Lady Diana in Washington in 1939 and had thought her then the most beautiful woman in the world. In 1939 and many times thereafter, the feature of Diana that struck me were her eyes, which were enormous and had a bright blueness like no other I have seen. Consequently, my horror at stumbling into Diana's bedroom was tripled, so to say, when I discovered that she slept with the pupils of her eyes rolled up into her head so that what was left of her glorious eyes, still open, looked like a pair of white marbles.

The fact was that Diana had begun having her face lifted rather early on in life, and the early cosmetic surgeons sometimes made it difficult for their patients to close their eyes. Later, Diana would become a dear friend, and I ceased to be disturbed by the memory of those white marbles. When circumstances required it, she was a woman of extraordinary self-discipline, and she was also brilliantly intelligent and down-to-earth. I am sure, therefore, that when she discovered her surgeon's error, she simply trained herself until she could turn the seeing part of her eyes up into her head and so get a good night's sleep. I must add that the surgeon's error was worth it. Diana went on being the most beautiful woman in the world until she was pushing sixty; and in the years between her sixtieth birthday and her death in her nineties, she was simply a woman of notable beauty and bearing who caused heads to turn.

After that hair-raising early-morning meeting, however, I blundered out of Diana's bedroom car much faster than I had blundered in and proceeded to my proper place, which was a lowly seat in the imperial dining and sitting car. Here, the official party was served a ghastly meal, known in the British Far East as "chota hazri," by barefoot Burmese servants in superb Burmese costume including little turbanlike headdresses with imperial cockades on the sides. It seemed almost ridiculous to use such people to provide a large group with tea and a banana apiece. The chota hazri was soon disposed of, however, and we settled down to a tactical and strategic discussion of the Japanese threat to Burma.

Colonel Chennault bluntly offered his view that a Japanese move southward was imminent, and, as such, Burma was threatened, most likely from the mountains to the north of Toungoo, which effectively would sever the British connection by land with China. One of Duff Cooper's staff, a splendid red-faced brigadier, objected to this analysis by Chennault on the ground that "those mountains are impassable." Whereupon our little council heard for the first time from an extraordinary figure. He was introduced as Mr. Ferguson and addressed as high commissioner. In appearance, Mr. Ferguson looked nothing at all like a highly ranked representative of His Majesty's Imperial Service. Indeed, I had been puzzling over him ever since finding the right part of the imperial train; for he was a very short, tubby man, astonishingly turned out in very loose, long shorts, a silk shirt, and a large pink Buster Brown bow tie. I learned later that people called him "high commissioner" because he was high commissioner of the Shan States, the most mountainous and dangerous part of Burma, which lies along the eastern border with China.

When the brigadier proclaimed the high commissioner's mountains—Mr. Ferguson was very possessive about them—to be "impassable," the high commissioner was outraged. He voiced his disturbance in a high falsetto: "Brigadier, don't talk to me about those mountains being 'impassable.' *I've* passed them over and over again. And if *I* can pass those mountains, the Japanese certainly can." No one seemed to have an answer to this, and so rather than meet the high commissioner's unsettling challenge, we ignored it entirely and moved on to other matters.

Our discussion of the more general tactical and strategic state of affairs in the theater was brief because it was obvious that the British did not have sufficient forces in the Far East to defeat a serious

Japanese attack. Duff Cooper pressed Colonel Chennault briefly on the state of preparation of the AVG as well as on the plans for battle. The colonel, who had no great liking for the British, gave rudimentary replies to these questions, which I then attempted to fill out as best I could. Soon, therefore, we returned, with some thankfulness, to the dining part of our luxurious car and sat down for our real breakfast, an astonishing meal of rather good fish, eggs, bacon, and mountains of marmalade and jam.

The real crisis of the meeting arrived after breakfast, for when we returned to the sitting part of the car, we still had several hours ahead of us before we were due to reach Rangoon. Conversation of a jolly kind was not easy, partly because Duff Cooper had not at all liked what he'd heard—although he was not surprised by it—partly because the brigadier was still very put out by what he called the "defeatism" that prevailed, and partly because Chennault, aside from his surly mood, was already nearly as deaf as a post from years of open flying and could not hear what anyone said across the car from him, where all the British dignitaries were arranged.

We were rescued once again by the high commissioner of the Shan States, who piped up in his splendid falsetto, "Chancellor of the Duchy [this was one of Duff Cooper's innumerable imperial titles], long study has persuaded me that alcohol before sundown is the curse of the Caucasian races in the Orient. For my part, however, I have scientifically ascertained that a gimlet does not come under the heading of alcohol."

Duff Cooper, who loved a drink, could not have heard a suggestion that was likely to delight him more. He clapped his hands—people did that sort of thing in those days—and barefooted, elegantly attired servants promptly appeared; the called for gimlets, and the first round of the largest gimlets I have ever seen were put in our hands in record time. A gimlet, I should explain for those who have not experienced one, consists of a strong splash of simple gin and an emollient drop of lime syrup. These two ingredients are mixed together in a pleasing manner, preferably with a helping of crushed ice, although deep in imperial Burma the old British rule of iceless cocktails was rigidly adhered to.

Certainly, these refreshments pleased the assembled company, for the barefooted servants reappeared with new gimlets approximately every half hour. I also observed that nearly everyone, possibly except for Chennault, who had a head like a rock, was showing signs of having taken drink by the time the imperial train reached Rangoon. Diana Duff Cooper saw these signs at once and said perfectly calmly, "Duffy, darling, what on earth have you all been doing?" As for the mountainous purple-faced brigadier who was standing on the platform waiting to meet us in Rangoon, in a solar topee about the size of a double-beehive, I thought he was going to fall under the train when he saw the chancellor of the duchy and his distinguished entourage come staggering from their car into the late morning sun.

The high commissioner's warning did not matter in the end. Not more than one month after this sad little train ride, the Japanese Fifteenth Army swarmed into Burma below the Shan States from the southeast. Crossing the Thai border, they pushed west toward Rangoon and then north through the mountains toward the Burma Road. The direction of the attack, however, was not important. Duff Cooper knew this, and so did Ferguson, although I was never able to ask him about it; he died when his plane crashed while trying to land in Kunming during the first months of the war.

This was all in the near future, however, when Colonel Chennault and I arrived drunkenly in Rangoon. Back in Toungoo, by this time, the news was really alarming. A new contingent of pilots had been damaging tail wheel tires at a rate that the engineers' repair facilities could not possibly handle. Furthermore, the mysterious E1B Solenoid, a sample of which I carried in my pocket but did not understand at all, was failing at a serious rate. Charlie Sawyer, our heroic engineering officer, later told me that in those days before the AVG went into combat, he was sure we would have to give up fighting after two weeks because our machine guns would not fire for want of replacements for this miserable little part of the firing mechanism.

I, therefore, planned to travel without delay to the U.S. military command in the Philippines to see whether I could not repair this deficiency. To my surprise, I was received amiably in Manila by General Douglas MacArthur, who was by that time commander of the U.S. forces in the Far East. It turned out that the great general admired Chennault, perhaps because he hated the air corps and he knew that Chennault's doctrines ran directly contrary to the air corps' doctrines of that day. To be honest, it also may have helped that MacArthur knew that I was a formerly prominent member of the press and vaguely connected to the Roosevelts.

At any rate, the general gave me a whole hour of this time, which was apparently unprecedented. As a rule, I am not usually nervous or intimidated when in the company of grand or impossibly imposing people. Nevertheless, my first interview with General MacArthur was a disquieting experience. His desk and chair were set on a sort of dais about 6 inches high. His visitors, in turn, were shown to low chairs facing the dais. Consequently, when having an audience with the general, one was forced to look upward to the man on the dais, who, further, was silhouetted against a brightly lit window directly behind him.

The general listened politely while I explained my mission, and he told me at once that his air officer would be told to do everything possible for me. He then asked for Chennault's opinion of future Japanese movements. I repeated what I had heard Chennault say to the British—that the Japanese (who were already in Indochina) would move much farther soon; that they would attack Malaya and Burma as well as Indonesia, with its riches in oil; and, since they were conventional military thinkers, they would attack the Philippines because they would be afraid to leave the islands unneutralized on their flank.

MacArthur agreed to the first part of this analysis, but he told me that I need not concern myself about the Philippines. He gave a rather extensive account of his contacts over the years with Japanese leaders; he did not hesitate to say that he was held in the highest admiration by the Japanese who counted; and, finally, in effect, he told me I need not worry about the Philippines because the Japanese would not touch those islands as long as he, Douglas MacArthur, was on them and in charge. I left our meeting mildly puzzled because Chennault had told me that MacArthur had one of the best minds in the U.S. Army; and although I did not necessarily disagree with MacArthur's strategic assessments, the vanity I observed in that profile, carefully turned to be viewed against the light, gave me pause.

I was given a different opinion that evening, when I was taken to dinner by Chennault's friend, the chief air officer on MacArthur's staff. He was a pleasant, fairly conventional Army Air Corps colonel, and he very strongly inclined to the Chennault assessment rather than the MacArthur assessment. We drank a good deal over dinner, and he gave me an exact description of his own cruelly exposed situation. The MacArthur staff had not only refused to organize any kind of air warning system in the Philippines, they had also refused to approve the needed expenditures to build additional airstrips on which the aircraft under the unfortunate colonel's command could be dispersed. "All my planes are sitting ducks at Clark Field," the colonel said, "but they won't listen to me at headquarters, they just won't listen."

In the end, the thought of his own woes led the colonel to the awful confession that he expected to lose most of his command within moments after a Japanese attack (as actually happened); and this confession then reduced the unhappy man to convulsive sobs. I knew no way of comforting him. After all, a man whose highest rank in the past has been lieutenant junior grade cannot pat a full colonel on the back and say, "There, there, sir." The terrible moment soon passed, however, and, in time, the colonel recovered his composure and wobbled out of the restaurant with myself in support.

I spent another day in Manila in a fruitless search for parts for Chennault's antiquated P-40s. After a long, raucous dinner at the large, rather luxurious Manila Officers Club with my old friend Warwick Scott, I returned to my hotel to find an urgent cable from Colonel Channault. The message instructed me to take the first available flight back to China, no matter what progress I might or might not be making in Manila, and ended with the words "Repeat, the first plane available stop this is an order." After a brief fit of gooseflesh, I got the bell captain of the Manila hotel to locate, and then to book me a seat on, the first plane available to Hong Kong, which was flying at 11:00 A.M., not the next day but the day after.

I then went up to my room to consider the situation that faced me. I knew by now that E1B Solenoids to keep our .50-caliber machine guns firing would not be made available to us anywhere in the Far East. I knew also that we were scheduled to go into combat imminently, for the move from Toungoo to Kunming was already being prepared when I left Toungoo for Manila. I was tempted, therefore, to telephone Washington there and then to ask Bob Lovett to take care of the problem of the E1B Solenoids. But this would be a highly irregular action in view of the emphasis that Chennault always put on maximum secrecy. I, therefore, decided I had better sleep on it.

The next day I awoke still undecided. I paid a last call on General MacArthur, who again received me at some length, and finally in the taxi going to the Manila hotel, I made up my mind. I could not see that secrecy mattered very much on the eve of combat. If one had an imminently incurable and fatal disease, I reasoned, it hardly mattered whether enemies knew of it or not. In consequence, I decided to disregard all the rules of secrecy, security, and chain of command and telephone Bob Lovett directly, in Washington. Since he was the man in charge of the air force, it seemed to me that he was the only hope for a solution to the damnable problem of the E1B Solenoids. My first step was to go to the chief operator of the Manila hotel and give her a large sum of money. Having found out from her where the chief overseas operator of the telephone company could be found, I also went to that kind lady and gave her an even larger sum. Having thus got the authorities on my side, I started trying to put my call through to Bob.

At that time, there were no transpacific telephone cables, and the operators, although working diligently, kept reporting that atmospheric disturbances had cut radio communications. While waiting, I made preparations to leave the hotel without an instant's delay. I called the operators roughly an hour after dinner on and got nowhere. After snatching a few hours' sleep, I answered an early wakeup call to try and get through to Washington, again with no result. I took my bag down to the front of the hotel and found a taxi driver who the bell captain assured me was honest. Knowing the Manila airfield was on the outskirts of the city, I asked the driver how long it might take to reach the field in time to make an eleven o'clock flight. The driver guessed I should start an hour before and no later, at which point I presented him with a large preliminary tip, told him to wait, and promised an additional $20—a vast sum by local standards—provided he could get me to my plane on time.

Returning to my room, I went back to jiggling the phones again until finally the operators reached Bob Lovett in Washington. Bob was completely bewildered by my call from Manila and took some time to feel sure who I was and then some further time to understand what it was I was so frantically trying to persuade him to do. However, he soon caught on, saw the problem all too clearly, and said that E1B Solenoids had been giving the air corps at home a lot of trouble also. But he promised to scratch up the number I needed (which could in fact be fitted into a reasonably large cigar box) and to send them immediately by air.

After ringing off, I pelted down the stairs of the hotel, gratefully scattering dollar bills as I went, located my dutiful driver, and started off at top speed for Manila airport. It was the kind of cab ride that is best passed with both eyes tightly closed. I know we killed several chickens as we sped through the barrios of the city because I heard them squawk, and whatever other damage may have been done I don't wish to speculate about. Finally, we reached the airfield, which in those primitive days had only one grass runway and, thank the eternal God, no form of security or obstruction surrounding it. As we screeched into view, I saw the terrible spectacle of my airplane—it was an elderly Ford trimotor with an exterior covered with washboardlike galvanized iron—at the opposite end of the field, taxiing toward us for an imminent takeoff.

To my even greater horror, my taxi driver's response to this sight was to drive headlong out onto the runway and continue toward the moving aircraft at top speed. The pilot, thus left with the fairly grim choice between bringing the trimotor to a halt or attempting to take off through a speeding Manila taxicab, sensibly applied the brakes. This elated my driver, who promptly brought his car to a stop under the wing of the airplane. The door of the trimotor opened, at which point volleys of the blackest kind of profanity surged out. Radiating a benign kind of ignorance, my taxi driver remained in his seat and simply nodded his head and smiled repeatedly toward the direction of the furiously apoplectic pilots. I hastily got out of the car and began humbly to explain to the still-shouting men that I had been unable to restrain the driver since I could not communicate with him in Tagalog.

Still apologizing profusely, I then pressed $40—twice what I had promised—into the taxi driver's hands, seized my bag, and clambered aboard the plane. Presently, the trimotor took off, and I spent the rest of the flight musing over my narrow escape and wondering how to make a quick connection from Hong Kong to Rangoon. It was only the next morning, after arriving in Hong Kong and making my way to the American Club that I discovered how narrow my escape had been. This was the morning of December 7, and the Seventh Fleet had been decimated at Honolulu. MacArthur's Philippines were already under attack, and the Japanese army had crossed the China border on their way toward Kowloon. The little trimotor had been the last commercial flight to reach Hong Kong before the city itself came under fire.

In Hong Kong, I had word from Colonel Chennault to wait at the airport until I could get on one of the Chinese aircraft that were still flying between Hong Kong and Chungking by night. These flights continued to be made for three nights. However, I had no priority or special recognition signal to give the China Aviation officials at the airport. So I waited there with the rest of the mob who were trying desperately to flee the island until, on the third night, I was told I would be put on the very last flight to Chungking. And so it seemed, until, at the very last instant, I was informed by the unfriendly officials that I would not be allowed aboard the flight. I complained bitterly, and the level of my bitterness increased when I was informed by a fellow traveler that I had been bumped from my seat in favor of Mme. H. H. Kung's very large, well-fed dog.

After that, I had nothing left to do except to report to my friend Colonel Mid Condon, who, at the time, was the U.S. military observer in Hong Kong. I thought I should at least try to fight the enemy and first got Condon to offer me to the Hong Kong Volunteers—the only unit in the battle for Hong Kong that might conceivably have a use for me. Even the overwhelmingly civilian

Volunteers, however, did not want an additional member who had never shot a gun in his life and had never seen combat with anything above the level of an insect. Consequently, I next tried the St. John's Ambulance Corps, which served in Hong Kong the role of the Red Cross's mobile units. It was a grim, difficult service, for soon the Japanese bombers were strafing the civilians lined up on the waterfront to receive rations of rice. Casualties in the town were heavy and had to be carried in great numbers to the big hospitals, which lay beyond the fringes of Hong Kong city.

On the first night of my service, the particular ambulance corps to which I had been assigned was stationed in an empty garage at the city's midlevel, halfway down from the Peak. The conditions inside the garage were primitive, although preferable to being outside since the midlevel was being sporadically bombed and, I think, shelled. I had lost my sleeping pills on the airport side of the harbor and had also nearly forgotten how to sleep during the weeks when I acted as the entire office staff of the AVG. The head of my ambulance-corps unit pointed to a stretcher made of pipe and chicken wire on which several blankets served as a mattress. I did not believe that I could get a single instant's sleep atop this contraption but remembered reading somewhere that resting was almost as reviving as sleeping. So I lay down glumly, whereupon, with shells exploding overhead and nothing to worry me except a mere war, I dropped off at once and slept solidly for fourteen hours.

The British resistance on Hong Kong was brief, and when the city was surrendered, on Christmas Day 1941, only a few days after the Japanese attack, I reported again to Colonel Condon. This time he told me that my only course was to forget that I was a member of the AVG—fortunately, I had traveled in civilian clothes—and to pretend that I had never left my old trade as a newspaperman. He warned, prophetically, that Japanese military internment would be a very hard business indeed, but that civilian internment would be less hard and might even offer opportunities for escape. And, finally, he believed the Japanese might well end up exchanging many of the civilian internees because of the burden they would impose.

As it turned out, this was an incomparably brave and, in many ways, magnanimous thing for Mid to do since I was, in fact, a U.S. military officer and, therefore, in no way eligible for the kind of treatment he proposed. I should not have been able to masquerade as a civilian prisoner at all had Mid not, in effect, ordered me to do so. What is more, I now ran the risk, as a military man out of uniform, of being considered a spy. This did not occur to me at the time, although I am sure Mid was aware of it and chose not to tell me for fear I might give away the game. As it was, I had little trouble slipping calmly back into my former role of newspaperman, and without a uniform I am sure I looked less like a soldier to the Japanese than the great majority of other foreign male civilians then milling about in occupied Hong Kong.

Once this decision had been taken, Mid Condon and I proceeded to the old Gloucester Hotel in Hong Kong, where almost all the English and Americans in the colony had gathered. I had a fair number of second-rate sapphires purchased in Burma, and I wanted to get them sewn into the collar of my coat. Mid suggested to me that his marvelously beautiful Eurasian mistress, being convent-trained, would be able to do the job for me. She was staying also at the Gloucester, and so later on that evening I felt my way through endless unlit corridors until I reached her room. The room was lit by one candle, by the light of which Mid's mistress appeared even more beautiful than I had remembered her being (I think she eventually established a close connection with one of the higher Japanese administrators of Hong Kong). With her in the room was her sixteen-year-old sister, who was also a startling beauty. I explained to this unlikely pair what I needed; Mid's mistress explained that she had forgotten how to sew but that her sister, who was fresh out of the convent, would certainly remember. And so, in these odd circumstances, the job of hiding my jewels began.

The ensuing scene illustrates how so many of the dramas in my life have turned into comedies. Here, in the flickering candlelight, were two dazzlingly beautiful girls helping a soon-to-be prisoner of war sew jewels into the collar of his tweed jacket. Although the windows were closed to keep out smoke from the flaming city, one could hear the heavy beat of Japanese military bands as they led the victorious Japanese forces into the city (the majority had landed by sea, on the backside of Hong Kong island). A more dramatic scene would be hard to imagine. My sapphires glowed in the dim light as the lovely sister bent intently to her work. The comic touch was added by Mid Condon's mistress, who, throughout the operation, kept scratching herself and saying repeatedly, "Goddamn that Mid! He's given me scabies [an unpleasant skin rash caused by mites] he caught on maneuvers. Goddamn that Condon. I wish I'd never met him! Goddamn these scabies he gave me!"

After my sapphires had been sewed safely into my coat collar, I thanked the ladies most warmly for their kindness and departed. The next morning, I went to the American Club in the Hong Kong and Shanghai Bank building, the place of temporary internment earmarked by the Japanese for the small number of Americans then in Hong Kong. Unlike the others, I occupied myself, in the days before the Japanese gave us our orders, with borrowing all the cash I could and with buying all the food supplies I could for what was bound to be a lengthy internment. By the end of my time in the American Club, I had accumulated a considerable store of very cheap food. But I had not solved the problem of carrying it, nor had I done anything about bedding, which I was sure the Japanese would not provide.

Solving the bedding problem was the purpose of my last foray into the city streets. For one Hong Kong dollar (then U.S. 25 cents), I managed to buy a coolie's carrying pole, two bamboo woven baskets, and the means of attaching the baskets to the ends of the pole. The next day, the Japanese ordered us all to the parade ground just above the city center. As we left the American Club that morning, I solved my future bedding problems by pulling down from one of the club's high dining-room windows a very heavy brown, ribbed, silk-interlined curtain. Hence, I appeared at the parade ground, which was the assembly point for Westerners who were going into internment, with my coolie's carrying pole over my shoulder and, balanced on each end, my baskets full of provisions and bedding.

The sight of me so encumbered caused one of the great English traders of Hong Kong, locally called "taipans"—I think the man may have been the head of Butterfield and Swire—to reproach me with an air of haughty rebuke. Our Japanese captors had already informed us that we would be marched down the city's main thoroughfare, Queens Road, to our next place of internment. This order was not without symbolic purpose, for the Chinese had been commanded to gather in mobs on either side of the road purely for the purpose of spectacle. The white rulers of the colony would be thus be marched off to jail in humiliating and public defeat.

For the great taipan, this feudal ceremony was tantamount to walking naked down Queens Road, and he was in a furious commotion. "Young man," he said icily, "you're not going to walk down Queens Road with a coolie's carrying pole and those two baskets of stuff, are you?" I replied that I thought I would. "But don't you see," he said, "we'll all lose face." Thereupon, I'm afraid I turned on the taipan and said, rather rudely, that if he reflected carefully upon it, the events of the past weeks had not left the foreign community in Hong Kong with enough face to be worth conserving anyway. At this, the taipan turned bright red and stalked away, and that was the end of our conversation.

So I made the walk down Queens Road (which was not in the least humiliating, after all) to the next scene of my life in internment, which was, in fact, a rather third-rate brothel similar to the one where Mickey Hahn and I had smoked opium. I quickly recognized the quarters for what they were, reserved for myself a nice crib that had obviously belonged to one of the ex-brothel's more successful girls, and set about giving some variety to the long, boring days by making friends with my fellow internees.

Maybe for this reason, I was named from our particular section of the brothel to the advance group of prisoners sent out by order of the Japanese to inspect our permanent quarters. The noncombatants, of which I was now one, were to be held in the immediate surroundings of Stanley Prison, which is located on the far side of Hong Kong island. The Japanese gendarmerie, who were administering the former colony, had for one reason or another chosen part of the prison itself for their headquarters while designating the surrounding housing that had been provided for the prison guards as the civilian prisoner-of-war camp. To these quarters were added those of Hong Kong's most prestigious boy's school, a pseudo-Eton of the kind the British established in all their older colonies to provide a proper British education for the sons of the local rich.

Our advance party went out by boat, and the first place we investigated was an enchanting small villa located above the rocks that looked out over the bay on one side of the small Stanley peninsula. An older man in the party told me that this house had belonged to a locally famous Chinese aesthete-intellectual and aggressive pacifist who had written articles arguing that conflict with Japan could be avoided if only the British authorities adopted a more friendly attitude. Be nice to the men from the north, the scholar had argued, and they will be nice to you. The man was a master at the local Eton and had refused to be evacuated from his home even after the Japanese landing on that side of the island had begun. True to his principles, he was waiting in his library–living room when the Japanese troops entered his house, evidently led by an officer equipped with the regulation samurai sword.

One must suppose the aesthete-intellectual attempted to put into practice his doctrine of niceness begetting niceness. Alas, however, the Japanese officer did not understand the schoolmaster's scholarly brand of pacifism and cut off the poor man's head, very probably in one stroke in the approved manner taught by the Japanese army. When our party arrived at the house, the man's head lay in one corner of the library and his body in the other. I still feel deeply ashamed that, instead of joining my co-members of the advance party in respectfully tidying up this frightful scene, I went as rapidly as I could through the dead man's large library and took as many books as I thought would fit into the bag I had brought out to Stanley expressly for the purpose. I still have the eighteenth-century edition of the *Analects of Confucius* that I acquired on that occasion but have lost the other volumes, which I read throughout the rest of my internment. Sometimes, when I tell this story, I am accused by my friends of hard-heartedness. Yet I cannot see why. After all, I could not bring back to life the unfortunate schoolmaster.

Only a few points remain to be made about the seven long months of internment that lay ahead. There are, in fact, two basic rules for prospective internees of a wartime prison camp: first, medicated toilet paper is undesirable because it cannot be used to make cigarettes; and, second, always take into internment as much money as possible because the guards, who invariably run a form of black market, make a point of never searching prisoners with any care. The reason for this is simple: any money found during shakedowns of prisoners arriving in camp must be handed on to the properly constituted authorities, whereas cash circulating on the black market will end eventually in the pockets of the prison guards. For this reason, I was greatly helped by having taken into the camp all the money that I could possibly raise in Hong Kong.

A third point is worth noting about the internment experience, although this is a reflection, perhaps less of the experience itself than on what one learns of human nature when forced to adapt one's life-style so dramatically. Curiously enough, I have never looked back on Stanley as a boring or even a particularly painful interlude in my life. Indeed, the experience answered a basic question about myself that had always bothered me. Although I had been taken care of by others in one way or another since babyhood, I found, quite suddenly, that I was now well able to take care of myself. After Stanley, I have always felt I could find a way to survive even the roughest of circumstances, and, on the whole, experience has confirmed this belief.

Shortly after we settled in at Stanley, I discovered a wonderful American professor, Dr. Charlotte Gower, with whom I read straight through the copy of the *Analects of Confucius* purloined from the pacifist's library. During a fairly steady course of morning study, I managed, under Charlotte's guidance, to learn four thousand Chinese characters, three thousand of which I was able to write. Unfortunately, it is not possible to remember a Chinese character for more than a month if one ceases to use it regularly. So, while the experience of memorizing that ancient system of scripture has stayed with me, the characters were forgotten within days of my departure from the prison.

I learned little else, really, from my time as a prisoner of war except that some people were very much more sordid and nasty than one might expect. At least one person among the acquaintances I had made in Hong Kong through Mickey Hahn and Mid Condon became an informer for the prison guards in exchange for extra rations. Others surprised me with their generosity, however. The uncle of novelist Louis Auchincloss, William Stanton, was in the camp with his much older but extremely jolly wife Elsa, who was reputed to be the richest Westerner on the China coast. Mrs. Stanton had broken a leg during the fight for the island and so wore a huge plaster cast, which had to be renewed from time to time. I first met her when she was helping with the wounded in the hospitals, a task she performed with great efficiency despite the broken leg. When I got to know Elsa better, it would amuse her to fish down into the leg cast and show me the enormous diamonds she was concealing from her captors.

Considering the brutality that was the norm for the Japanese during the second war, the civilian camp at Stanley was not an uncomfortable place. At first, the food was grossly insufficient because the Japanese had sold the concession to a local Hong Kong merchant of the nastiest sort who profited by providing as little food as possible. Fortunately, a very brave Englishwoman who had been brought up in Japan managed to get through to the commandant of the camp, who was a young member of the Japanese nobility. The commandant was apparently persuaded by her claim that the Chinese concessionaire was shaming Japan by starving women and children. The next day, we had the exquisite pleasure of seeing the thieving concessionaire carried away from the camp in heavy manacles and chains in the back of an open truck. After that, the diet we received improved by a few calories, although, if one wanted to avoid beriberi, it was essential still to be able to purchase goods on the black market, which was why money from the outside remained so important.

My average day at the camp started with a careful check of black-market sources and an attempt to find new ones. Following this, I would normally spend up to an hour and a half working with Charlotte Gower on the Confucian *Analects*. Near midday, the prisoners were served a lunch of half-cold rice, into which those who were lucky enough might mix some condensed milk or a small portion of bully beef (tinned beef). In the afternoon, I spent most of my time learning by heart the new characters I had covered in the *Analects* that morning.

On such a low-calorie diet, we prisoners usually went to sleep

very early, for we were growing weaker all the time. In all, I lost
more than thirty pounds during my six months at Stanley. I tried to
exercise during the day, and of course I had to wash my own clothes.
Every so often—when, for example, tins of biscuits became available
on the black market—we would hold rather pathetic little parties,
with everyone carefully rationed to two small sweet biscuits apiece
plus one cup of weak powdered coffee, which was considered a
great delicacy.

In the American bachelor's quarters to which I was assigned, I
am proud to say I joined a sort of a revolution. After great debate,
the other bachelors and I ousted two American oilmen who had
appointed themselves our bosses because we thought they were too
smarmy with the Japanese. We replaced the oilmen with a large and
jovial Englishman—a former chief warrant officer in the British
navy—who went by the wonderful name of "Jingles." Jingles was
the cook for our quarters, a man of infinite courage and patriotism
who flatly refused to believe any news the Japanese authorities gave
him even when, alas, it was true. Whenever our captors proudly
announced their emperor's latest triumph, we were invariably presented with a duck egg with which to celebrate. Jingles always insisted openly that the news was false propaganda of the lowest and
most malicious kind but recommended that we eat the eggs all the
same.

There were other comedies, too. In the British married quarters, for example, a fearful fight broke out between the childless
adult prisoners and those with children over the rationing of the
emperor's duck eggs. As the weeks wore on, the children in the
camp had suffered particularly from the diet in the internment
camp, causing their parents as well as those who had families back in
the West to ask that the duck eggs be used as supplements for the
diets of the more frail among the young. The meagerness of our
rations were such that the married couples without children almost
unanimously opposed this proposal. The British community cooks,
who were all sailors and sentimental about children, rallied quickly
to the parents' cause, and a kind of judgment of Solomon was made,
permitting those who wanted their duck eggs given to the children
to do so, while those who wanted them for themselves got them cold
and uncooked, sitting on their dreary rice rations.

This latter development was the decision of the cooks, secretly
taken; and, in the upshot, a second, very entertaining scandal developed as hard feelings broke out among those who had to take their
eggs raw. One of the leading British ladies in Hong Kong had been
antichildren. Her greatest treasure was a parasol with a jade handle.

An imposing female, she chose to rebuke one of the toughest sailor cooks. He was not, however, listening to any rebukes from "an old, fat, greedy hag like you," to quote his reported reply to the attempted haughty, upper-class reminder that he ought to watch his p's and q's. The lady was so infuriated with this remark that she bought her parasol down on the cook with great force, hitting his shoulder hard enough so that the jade handle shattered, ruining the parasol for purposes of future display.

With the reading matter that I had secured from the aesthete-pacifist's library, my Chinese lessons, a few friends like the Stantons, and clandestine preparations to escape with an Englishman in the Hong Kong police, I found that the months in camp passed fairly easily. Then suddenly, one day toward the end of June, the prisoners were told that American newspapermen were going to be exchanged. Since I had falsely written myself down as a newspaperman in Hong Kong and my family had the wit to do the same thing in Washington, I was classified by the Japanese authorities as a newspaperman of minor importance.

In the end, it proved extraordinarily lucky to have taken Mid Condon's advice. By their own loony logic, the Japanese exchanged the British civilians they were holding in Manila because they regarded the Philippines as an American imperialist area, and they exchanged the imprisoned American civilians—at least in Hong Kong—because they regarded this as a British imperialist area. Within days, therefore, to my deep relief, I was aboard the Japanese ship that carried us on the first half of our journey home. Later, my group would be transferred to the Swedish hospital ship *Gripsholm* for our final return to the United States. It was a wonderful journey, as I remember, for several old friends were also on board the *Gripsholm*. Among them was my old college friend Chip Bohlen, who was then a member of the U.S. legation in Japan and had been detained in Tokyo after the outbreak of the war. (Chip, myself, and others spent many jolly evenings on deck together and on shore, too. For the *Gripsholm* made several stops on its long journey to New York Harbor.)

I was asked then and have been asked since whether I was at all bitter over my experience at the hands of the Japanese in Hong Kong. It is a rule that one learns from adversity, provided the experience is not too severe. As I have said, I learned at Stanley that I could take care of myself in a most basic way. And, strangly, even the comradeship one experiences in periods of shared hardship was worth the seeming waste of very nearly two-thirds of a year of my life. Having come out of Stanley, I also had a small and perversely satisfying feeling that I was engaged, as I had not been before, during a time of public crisis. But this feeling did not last long. In truth, I count myself extraordinarily lucky to have come safely through the entire ordeal.

10

To China, Again

(Fall 1942)

My delight when I got home from the internment camp was accompanied by regret when I found that the thirty pounds I had lost in the camp came back in about three weeks and rapidly turned into forty. That summer of 1942 seemed particularly lovely and lush in Avon. The family was glad to see me, and I, naturally enough, was overjoyed to see them. Of my two brothers, however, Stew was already on his way from London to the African desert as a member of the King's Royal Rifle Corps, an outfit in the British army (Stew also had difficulty passing his U.S. Army physical) that accepted officer recruits from abroad. Johnny, after a prolonged and bitter stint as a member of the Military Police, eventually would follow Stewart to Europe as a member of the Office of Strategic Service. So it was natural enough for me, after a polite respite, to set about reentering the war as fast as I could.

My objective from the first weeks I reached the United States was to rejoin Colonel Chennault, who had become, in my absence, something of a national hero. Indeed, the AVG's action over Burma during the grim early days of the Pacific war had provided almost the only good news produced in either theater of war by Americans.

Thanks to the colonel's innovative tactics and extraordinary leadership, the outfit had performed admirably during the prolonged battle for Rangoon. Always outnumbered, frequently outgunned, the AVG's out-of-date P-40s had provided valuable air cover for the harassed defenders of the city and in large measure facilitated the ragtag Allied retreat out of Burma in the late winter and early spring of 1942.

In China, moreover, Chennault and his pilots had brought the Japanese bombing of the free cities to a grinding halt within little more than a fortnight after Pearl Harbor. Even before the Rangoon operation was undertaken, the Japanese in China outnumbered the elements of the AVG in China by 6 or 7 to 1. In all, during those first seven months of combat, the unit took down more than 300 enemy aircraft, while losing less than 20 of their own in the air—a combat ratio never equaled during the entire course of the war. Their sole physical advantage was the extraordinary air warning net that Chennault had devised in 1937.

The Japanese view of the matter can be deduced from the fact that in the first winter after the AVG had entered China, their air activity practically ceased. For a time, fake lathe-and-plaster mock-ups of squadrons of P-40s placed in rows on the local airfield were enough to provide the whole defense of Chungking—and this where the Japanese had been free to experiment with 48-hour, round-the-clock bombing only a year before. This had permanent importance, for the Chinese would always remember that Chennault had stopped the bombing, and it would be a significant thread in the tangled web I found when I finally returned to Chungking.

As a result of his work in Rangoon and southern China, Colonel Chennault was taken back into the U.S. military and given the rank of brigadier general. The Flying Tigers (shortly before Pearl Harbor, the pilots had taken to decorating the fronts of their aircraft with great numbers of teeth) were renamed the China Air Task Force and based in Kunming. Oddly enough (it was probably due to the fact that he had known more success out of the army than in), Chennault fought this move tooth and nail. His fliers did, too, for they had relished their independence (and, no doubt, their high level of pay). Indeed, when the incorporation of the AVG was announced officially, a good majority of the original Flying Tigers chose to go home rather than fly with their old commander as members of the U.S. Army Air Force.

The public recognition, though doubtless gratifying, also had its bitter side within the army, for my old chief had always been seen as an outsider and a renegade within the stodgy confines of the old air corps. His tactics had always been regarded as cockeyed and his character irregular (for many years, he had led the air forces flying acrobatic team). On a personal level, Chennault could be blunt and tactlessly forthright to those with whom he did not agree or did not respect. So his first trip up through the ranks (in twenty years of service, he had been promoted only to the rank of captain) made him many enemies.

With hindsight, I suppose conflict was also inevitable, given the odd structure of command in what was then being called the China-Burma-India (CBI) theater of operations. In February 1942, General Marshall had appointed General Joseph W. Stilwell to command U.S. Army forces in the theater, an area as vast and disjointed as the name implied. With the exception of Chennault's newly repatriated force, however, there were almost no U.S. troops in the area. Except for the British, who would soon be defeated, the bulk of the Allied force in fact was Chinese and, therefore, loyal to the generalissimo. Even Chennault, despite his conspicuous new rank, owed his original mandate to Chiang.

Stilwell, therefore, had been assigned to Chungking with the additional title of chief of staff to the supreme commander of the China theater, a post that put the American general—supposedly the top military commander in the theater and answerable to Allied command in Washington—squarely under the supervision of Chiang Kai-shek. Although General Stilwell retained a good deal of leverage as administrator of all U.S. lend-lease matériel supplied to Chinese forces, in time the inherent contradictions in this arrangement would become clear.

During those first months of the war, however, as the British troops were being rolled back toward India, the American commander's first duty, as he rightly saw it, was to keep the Burma Road open; and to this end, General Stilwell had gone into Burma that March to salvage the collapsing military situation. Brave, tough, utterly indifferent to hardship, and richly endowed with the personal charisma of the good leader of men in battle, General Stilwell had shown great hardihood and courage in the fight with the Japanese for Burma. When all was lost in the bitter battles around Rangoon, the general had, in an odd but characteristically stubborn decision, refused the offer, by two AVG fliers, of rescue and air transport away from the advancing Japanese. Instead, he had made himself a national reputation by leading a small group overland out of Burma through the most wicked and difficult mountain country, without losing a single man or woman.

We have forgotten it now, but at that point in the war, the

defeat in Burma seemed an episode comparable to the heroic evacuation of Dunkirk. General Stilwell, upon coming safely to the Indian border at Imphal, had the remarkable good sense to tell the truth about it: "I claim," he said, "we got a hell of a beating and it's darned humiliating." "Humiliating" is the key word here—and an ominous one for the future—for Stilwell seemed to take the beating personally. He was an intense and choleric man, and the memory of this defeat seemed to obsess him in the coming years, leaving him with the belief that the only thing to do was to go back into Burma and inflict the same kind of humiliation on the Japanese. In the end, it seemed to me, he would seek to accomplish this goal at all costs, with or without the consent of his allies in Chungking.

The outlines of potential command trouble between Stilwell, the generalissimo, and, to a lesser degree, Chennault were already dimly visible as I made my hurried rounds through wartime Washington in September 1942. As a former member of the AVG, I had a theoretical right to a commission and a place with General Chennault under the deal that had been made when the AVG was dissolved and its members either joined Chennault with automatic commissions as officers or went home. I hoped to exercise this theoretical right but was frustrated, I think, by forces in the War Department who knew of my allegiance to the AVG along with my supposed influence inside the White House, and who, thanks to Stilwell's reports, were already wary of Chennault. After a good deal of wrangling, I was refused an air force officer's commission, although I did manage to get my medical waiver with ease.

I do not know what my next step would have been if I had not happened to go see Harry Hopkins, an old friend from the prewar days but now near to the second most important civilian in the American government. Although I would not have said so at the time, Harry was the ablest of all the men around the president and the most indispensable to Roosevelt over the long term. He was a most curious man—on one side a passionate social worker, toiling tirelessly to relieve human suffering, and, on the other, fun-loving and raffishly disreputable. Harry was so fond of betting on horses that when he ran the WPA during the Depression years, he often held staff conferences in the car on the way to the Laurel racetrack in Maryland. Although he cared nothing about money and his clothes always seemed to have been purchased at a pawn shop, he had a great liking for worldly and glittering company, adored pretty women, and greatly enjoyed a social drink.

Brought into government by Mrs. Roosevelt, Hopkins alone among the crowd of presidential advisers had been chosen by Franklin Roosevelt as a friend. When he became seriously ill with a rare stomach ailment, the Roosevelts took Hopkins and his wife Louise into the White House, where, as soon as he was well enough to lead a sort of active invalid's life, he saw more of the president than any other man in government. And there Harry stayed, serving as FDR's chief civilian adviser on foreign and defense policy until the very end of the war. Harry remained gravely ill for most of this time. He finally died in 1946, less than one year after President Roosevelt. In the end, this puzzling and (as I came to believe) altogether memorable and admirable man literally gave his life for his country as a soldier might in war.

One must imagine Hopkins exercising his vast authority from his White House bedroom, sitting behind his only desk—which was a borrowed bridge table—wearing bedroom slippers and a well-used cardigan sweater. General Stilwell had met with Harry before taking up his post and privately called him a "queer gnome" and, more charitably, a "pleasant old farmer." But Harry's haphazard appearance belied a tenacious and canny intelligence, and when I came to solicit his advice, he was already fully informed of events in China and the rest of the CBI theater, and aware that the Allied effort there was not progressing as planned. After consulting with Roosevelt's secretary of state Cordell Hull, Harry offered to solve my predicament by sending me to China as a civilian lend-lease administrator. This was an absolute boondoggle because no U.S. funds were then being sent to Chungking through strictly civilian channels, but it was a post all the same. Harry added, with some prompting on my part, that if I thought I had anything to contribute, he would be pleased to hear from me in China. I said I would not disappoint him in this and took my leave.

With no delay at all, I got the necessary papers and arranged to fly out to Chungking in a new C-47 transport destined for service there. Because of the plane's limited range, the journey took nearly two weeks and involved a series of exotic stops down the eastern coast of South America, across the south Atlantic, and up through Africa to India. I shall never forget the relief of seeing Ascension Island as a speck in the ocean after flying across the Atlantic from the bulge of Brazil, for at the time our C-47 had only a few gallons of fuel left. I also shall never forget the sheer horror of a luncheon at the RAF mess in Aden (the temperature was near 110 degrees) consisting of a large helping of overcooked goat covered in mucilage-brown sauce. Military transports in those days were uncomfortable and cold, and I might have died along the way had I not brought a hammock, which I slung between two supports in the back of the plane. There, tucked snugly under several army-issue blankets, I happily ingested as many volumes as I could of Arnold Toynbee's monolithic work *A Study of History.*

But the real story of my wartime duty in China begins at the horrible airport in Karachi, where I ran into one of the real heroes of the AVG, David "Tex" Hill, an able flier who already had a number of enemy planes to his credit and was returning to the United States for service elsewhere. Tex, whom I had always thought one of the most intelligent of the AVG fighting men, was in what I can only describe as an eloquent rage over the conditions he had left behind at the old base in Kunming. He told me a very ugly tale of petty harassment, supply starvation, and general persecution of his chief, Chennault, by Stilwell's air officer Major General Clayton L. Bissell.

Although highly personal in nature, the details of this dispute, as was often the case in the CBI theater, were grounded in the politics of supply. Even before Pearl Harbor, the Burma Road, which stretched from Lashio in northern Burma to Kunming, was the major link between China and the outside world. This land link was broken when the Japanese won in Burma. The China National Aviation Corporation (CNAC), no longer flying into Hong Kong, now flew over the lower chain of the Himalayas—"the Hump"— from Kunming to Assam in northeastern India. Some U.S. transport planes had been added; but General Bissell, who was in direct command of the U.S. Tenth Air Force based in India, had done nothing to bolster the U.S. contribution to this only outside link with the world that China now possessed.

For a considerable period, the CNAC, in fact, flew more tonnage over the Hump than was flown by Bissell's American transport planes. These supplies, naturally, were the life blood of any Allied war effort in China. Chennault's outfit depended completely on the fuel, ammunition, and spare parts that it received over the Hump. In addition, Bissell had done very little to improve the appalling airport situation at Assam or to spur the British to improve the rail links between Assam and the rest of India. He had also persuaded General Stilwell that the CBI theater should give up over half the airplanes first allocated for the Hump by Washington in order to meet demands elsewhere. Not unexpectedly, this decision, which was made by Stilwell after Bissell's strong recommendation, caused extreme displeasure to Chennault and the fighting men under his command.

When I reached General Chennault's base in Kunming, I was able to verify Tex's complaints. My old chief, although glad to see me, was, in fact, in a simmering temper. The China Air Task Force (CATF) was not being given enough supplies to operate, and it seemed doubtful that supplies to make the CATF really operational would ever become available. Friction with Bissell in India and with Stilwell in Chungking was fairly constant. The former, Chennault complained, robbed his unit of supplies, while the latter paid little or no attention to Chennault or his men.

The Allied command strategy in the theater added to General Chennault's disgust with the course of events. By the end of 1942, Japanese forces surrounded Free China in a wide arc that stretched from Manchuria in the far north, down through Shanghai, to Kwangtung province, then around to the south and up again through what was then French Indochina, to Burma. Thus, the Allied theater of operations was effectively cut in half, with the distance between Delhi and Chungking measuring a full 2,000 miles. For the moment, the Japanese appeared content to rest and to consolidate their considerable gains in this theater while concentrating their efforts on more pressing developments in the Pacific. General Stilwell, meanwhile, had begun to develop plans for a campaign designed to win a new supply route overland through northern Burma to replace the old Burma Road.

It was Chennault's view—a view based on, and biased by, his own experience—that the main business of the theater should be done by air. The prohibitive distances and terrain involved, plus the potential use of China as a sally point for bombing the islands of Japan, made this imperative in his mind. If Allied command proved willing, he believed sufficient supply could be brought in over the Hump to make the difficult and costly work of opening a land route unnecessary. In retrospect, some of the strategic views on the offensive use of air power implicit in these plans seem absurdly overambitious. For instance, Chennault believed, for a time, that with a minimum of 105 fighter aircraft and 30 bombers he could "cause the collapse of Japan."

There was no doubt, however, that air power, given the proper support, could do considerable damage in a theater such as the CBI, where troop concentrations were scattered so unevenly over such a large area. Even at reduced capacity, the CATF had managed to do damage behind enemy lines—most recently in an engagement over Canton Harbor, where at least 24 enemy planes had been shot down and 3 ships sunk in a single day raid. Such results, it seemed to me, were evidence of what General Chennault had been saying all along—that given the overwhelming logistical and political problems of the Chinese ground forces, gains in the air were the chief hope.

From my short experience in China, I also knew the Kuomintang army to be hopelessly inconsistent—its troops generally exhausted and disorganized; its commanders competent in some regions, in others horribly corrupt; in all, subject equally to the shifting political winds in Chungking. It was clear that Stilwell's command, being subordinate to that of the generalissimo, would be a difficult one, demanding imagination, open-mindedness, patience, and cautious diplomacy, qualities, it turned out, the American commander was wholly without. Therefore, it was obvious even at that early date, that if our war effort was to have any success at all in the mind of Chiang Kai-shek, Chennault and his men would have to play a large part. The AVG had, after all, been the generalissimo's idea, and Chennault's fliers constituted the only foreign Allied force in all of Free China.

In Kunming, I discovered that I could not join Chennault in uniform, for my old chief did not, as I had hoped, have the power to grant an officer's commission without the approval of his command in Washington. With Chennault's assurance that he would continue to work for a commission on my behalf, I then went on to Chungking to see how things stood in China as a whole and to take up my half-empty duties as civilian lend-lease administrator. I was lucky enough to find a very happy personal refuge there that endured until I left China for good in 1945. With the help of an old friend at China Defense Supplies, Whiting Willauer, I found accommodations at No. 17, Kuo Fu Lu, a large, unobtrusive house built of dark grey brick and set in a garden on a hilltop on the outskirts of the city. My lodgings cost $6 in gold a day; and for that sum, besides room, coals for heat, and three excellent but far too copious meals, I received a ration of Chungking gin, the services of a valet, and the privilege of having guests whenever I pleased.

The house, which belonged to Jardine, Matheson and Company, the British South China coast trading house, was shared by a changeable and eclectic group of Englishmen. General Gordon Grimsdale, the British military attaché, was senior in the group. The general was a small, intensely conservative man, as rigid as only British officers can be. He was capable of the violence of a cornered ferret if he felt that his conventions were being undermined. Nevertheless, he was an agreeable man and would remain a friend for many years. Hugh Richardson was a quiet, cultivated Indian civil servant with a passion for Tibet. In later life, Hugh would become a distinguished scholarly authority on that country, but in those days he longed to head the crown's political agency of Sikkim (on the Tibetan border), considering it the best prize for his career in the British civil service.

There were others, like Bosanquet, the China Coast banker, a youngish man, intelligent, faded-blond in appearance, but with a trying vocabulary of bad British slang; and Eric Watts, a witty and earthy fellow who had managed coal mines on the Manchurian border. My greatest friend in the house would be Whiting Willauer, a former Princeton football player and New Dealer. In contrast to the others, Whitey was very American, hard-driving, and serious, but wonderful company as well.

With the help of these men, I reacquainted myself with the foreign community in wartime Chungking. Among my English friends were the astute ambassador Sir Horace Seymour and his enchanting wife Violet, who somehow had many ancient connections in the United States. (The true state of President Roosevelt's marriage was a strict secret at the time, and so I was somewhat taken aback when her first question to me was "Tell me about my friend Lucy Mercer. Does your president still see her?") The one-eyed, one-armed General Carton de Wiart was also a friend as well as being one of the more picturesque figures in the capital. A man with a talent for military trouble spots, he had been captured by the Germans in two wars and had escaped both times, although his wounds were such that he was said to have retained only one of everything (he had only one eye as well as a single arm) except the Victoria Cross, of which he had two. It was a delight to watch the general's pleasure in recounting these adventures. He always wore an eye patch, an empty sleeve, and a breastplate of ribbons; and, when discussing a particularly nasty situation, he took on the pleased expression of a French provincial gourmet sniffing a dish of truffled quail.

The city of Chungking was much as ever, although busier, dirtier, more oppressed by inflation, and somehow less embattled than I had remembered. Carrying chairs had been banned by the generalissimo except for use by the aged and infirm, and so I moved about on foot or in one of the absurdly large American automobiles supplied by the Lend-Lease Commission. Although these were a wholly unsafisfactory substitute for my old chair, General Chennault's planes had put an end to the bombing, which made for peaceful travel. (The Japanese now had a major global war on their hands and were less willing to mount a full aerial attack.) But on making my preliminary calls, I soon found that the politics of the capital were as tangled and squalid as ever. The principal feature of this web—indeed, the feature that would color policy throughout the entire theater—was the appallingly inflamed relationship between the generalissimo and General Stilwell.

These two men would play a very large role in the Chinese

story—and to some degree in my own story—over the next two and a half years. Although I never got to know him at close hand, General Stilwell was clearly an extraordinarily courageous, exceptionally self-denying, and curiously picturesque old-fashioned American infantry officer. He had the gift of commanding loyalty from those who were close to him. He also had a considerable knowledge of China, derived from previous service there as language student, garrison officer, and military attaché. As a soldier, Stilwell wanted to lead men in battle, specifically in Burma; his main fault as an officer was his complete contempt for serious staff work. His obvious courage plus his habit of freely denouncing almost anyone he disagreed with, from President Roosevelt and Chiang Kai-shek on down, endeared him to many in the foreign-press hostel. With all his splendid qualities, however, he was as narrow as life in an old-time army camp and as prone to feuds as a Kentucky mountaineer. I later came to suspect that General Stilwell positively enjoyed inflicting pain on those he disliked.

Chiang Kai-shek, in my opinion, had the stuff of greatness, but he also had more than the average conflicts of greatness. I have rarely met a man less like a "peanut," which is the way General Stilwell contemptuously used to describe him. He was slender, of medium height by Western standards, always polite (at any rate, when Westerners were present), and quite dignified. He never spoke English, although I suspect he could have but with difficulty. I am certain that he understood English well unless a speaker's vocabulary or accent were peculiar. He not only understood, but to indicate his understanding he had the curious habit, which I have already mentioned, of nodding his head two or three times and saying, "Hao, hao." I never heard him utter another syllable, for I did not see him very often. But on the one or two times I saw him when decisions had to be taken, he took them clearly and, it seemed to me, shrewdly.

Early on, before the Japanese intervention, Chiang had come much nearer to unifying China than anyone, including Sun Yat-sen, had since the fall of the Manchu dynasty in 1911. He had three counts against him. First were the Chinese Communists, who, aside from being active against the Japanese in the north, had begun to wage a subtle propaganda campaign against Chiang and his government by the time I returned to China in 1942. Second, he was jealous of his own power and, like so many leaders who are jealous of their power, was inordinately suspicious of any subordinate who showed independence. Third, and worse still, the subordinates he suspected most were precisely those he needed most.

Chiang Kai-shek had an extremely limited education, mainly in

Japanese military school and the Soviet Union, and he knew nothing whatever of the Western world, above all the United States, although help from the West in general, and the United States in particular, would be so vital to China during the war years. As late as 1942, Chinese with serious Western experience, who knew just what Chiang Kai-shek needed most to know, were regarded with active dislike not just by Chiang himself, but also by the majority of their contemporaries.

It is ironic that many of these modern-minded men, like the chief army figures from this group, General Ch'en Ch'eng and the West Point–trained general Sun Li-jen, were precisely those Nationalists who loyally followed the generalissimo to Taiwan in 1949. In fact, the suspect, Western-experienced Chinese leaders of 1942–1943 were Chiang Kai-shek's chief advisers when the foundations were laid for the success that Taiwan has since become. As it was, reactionaries such as Army Chief of Staff Ho Ying-chin and Chiang's money-loving brother-in-law H. H. Kung held the ancient view that position and power were not public trusts, but sources of perquisites and profit. These men, along with the notorious Chen brothers who managed the Kuomintang party, blocked their more modern-minded colleagues at every turn. Together they were the bane of China, and ultimately they would play a very large role in the destruction of their leader, their country, and themselves.

Chiang may, in the end, have been powerless to stop this process, for just as they do with dilapidated machinery, the Chinese have an extraordinary way of patching dilapidated political systems and keeping them going longer than any other people I can think of. Patching cannot go on forever, however, and thus the strange rhythm to China's majestic history. Somewhere on the order of every seven centuries or so, the accumulation of debris from the past grows unbearably great, at which point a renovating government takes over. This first happened in the third century B.C. and the head of this well-documented renovating government, the founder of the Chinese empire, Ch'in Shih Huang Ti, was in fact one of the personal heroes of the third great debris-clearer and renovator Mao Tse-tung.

Chiang Kai-shek's main problem, impossible to understand without understanding that long rhythm of Chinese history, was simply that he was a conservative man with neither the vision nor the temperament nor, once the Japanese invasion had begun, the needed economic or military strength to undertake any vast renovation of China's crumbling imperial system. In fact, Chiang's government, which, in itself, represented nothing so much as a secretive, plot-ridden Mandarin court, included a very large number of human symbols of the accumulated debris of the Chinese past. One such souvenir of imperial times may have been the commanding admiral of the nonexistent Chinese navy, widely thought around Chungking to be the last surviving palace eunuch. I myself thought that this rumor originated from the admiral's undoubtedly and incomparably masterful cook, who had received much of his considerable training in the emperor's Forbidden City in Peking.

Since Chiang Kai-shek's unification of China was, to some measure, an astute and bold balancing act, he could not effect a clearance of debris on even a small scale without disrupting, and perhaps fatally undermining, his own government. Much later, this came to be the opinion of General Stilwell's chief political adviser John Paton Davies. During the war years, however, John and, above all, General Stilwell believed that the U.S. representative could somehow reform the Chinese army by application of head-on pressure and by ruthless plain speaking. In fact, however, the generalissimo's confidence needed to be won first. The more useful Chinese leaders like Ch'en Ch'eng and the head of the Bank of China Pei Tsu-yi had to be supported, and the more pernicious had to be undermined. Pressure and persuasion had to be delicately alternated; the vast influence deriving from American aid had to be used continuously, but always as a lever, never as a club.

Even at that early date in Chungking, it was easy enough to see that General Stilwell was wielding a heavy diplomatic club. In fact, by the time I arrived back in China, the American general detested the generalissimo, and neither he nor his staff made any secret of it. According to the Chungking gossip mill, this detestation had developed during the disastrous time in Burma because the generalissimo would not give General Stilwell adequate support. I would find out much later that Stilwell, in fact, had developed a hearty dislike for Chiang even before the Second World War—during service, much earlier in his career at the U.S. legation in Peking.

Upon his return from Burma in June of 1942, General Stilwell had reported to the generalissimo, with Mme. Chiang present, on the sorry performance of the Chinese troops there. (The Nationalists had lost an entire motorized army, the Fifth, along with large amounts of artillery.) Anyone who took part in the China drama can imagine the scene that day in the generalissimo's bleak reception room: Chiang Kai-shek himself, slender and unpretentious, listening with quiet alertness; Mme. Chiang interpreting briskly, all gleaming efficiency and charm; long-gowned secretaries and upper servants coming and going with many low bows; and, at the center of the stage, Stilwell himself, wiry, white-haired, bespectacled, pouring out his complaints in an angry, resonant voice.

In his papers, General Stilwell all but boasts that he made no effort to be tactful and also that he recommended the immediate execution of two Chinese officers who, in his eyes, had faltered during the fight. (Imagine President Roosevelt's response if an English general, in FDR's presence, had suggested decapitating two American generals in North Africa.) Indeed, General Stilwell himself described the effect of his recommendations as being "like kicking an old woman in the stomach." In a memo to the generalissimo, the American general further demanded that a new Chinese army be organized, with a new officer corps, under his own unrestricted command. He ended by insisting that the generalissimo give the orders to mobilize at once in order to reinvade Burma and open a new Burma Road between China and India.

By the time I arrived in Chungking in the late fall of 1942, T. V. Soong was back from Washington, where he had been orchestrating the lobbying efforts of China Defense Supplies. His mission now was to see what he could do to patch up the Stilwell-Chiang relationship and to secure agreement between the two men on some sort of future plan of operations against the Japanese. Since Soong was a friend from Washington days and since I was even closer to Whitey Willauer, who was T.V.'s deputy, I saw the effort to patch up an agreement at fairly close hand although, in a measure, through Chinese eyes.

The curious truth about this episode is that the generalissimo and T. V. Soong, because they had very little knowledge of the practical aspects of the modern war in which they found themselves, were just as convinced as General Stilwell that the real remedy to the situation was to open a new route into China to replace the lost Burma Road. The proposed "Ledo Road" was the centerpiece of the general's offensive plan. It was Willauer who convinced me that the road remedy desired by the Chinese and General Stilwell was, to put it mildly, a bit simplistic. Only a few minutes' work with a slide rule were required (and Willauer showed me how to do this since I did not understand slide rules) to discover that the hundreds of miles of road, most of it through awesomely rough terrain, could not, in fact, deliver any worthwhile supply tonnage to China. The U.S. Army trucks of those days would have needed to carry just about their total cargo capacity in gasoline for themselves in order to make the long transit from Assam to Kunming. Having expended their gasoline by the time they reached Kunming, they would then have been useless hulks. Even the tiny Chinese truck fleet of those days could not get enough gasoline to keep it on the road, and many of the trucks had, therefore, been ingeniously converted to burn charcoal—not at all the kind of operation the U.S. Army would understand.

Consequently, as an addition to the Stilwell road plan, Willauer advocated a portable pipeline like that which the Chinese had designed a long time before for use on the now-lost Burma Road. The Chinese design, it may be added, was admired for its soundness by the U.S. Army engineers. The result was the portable pipeline that had already made a very useful addition to the North African campaign. With Soong's approval, Willauer, therefore, began to petition members of General Stilwell's Chungking staff and soon succeeded in making most of them enthusiastic supporters of the pipeline project.

Impulsively, I went with Whitey to Stilwell's headquarters. But common sense persuaded me at the last moment that I did not share Willauer's knack of salesmanship and that it would be better for me to remain in the outer office, where Stilwell's chief of staff Major General Tom Hearn, presided. A slow, kindly, and exceedingly pleasant man, General Hearn took us aback at the very outset of our mission by warning Whitey that "the thing you've got to understand about the general is that it is always easier for him to accept a new project if you explain it in terms of trench warfare."

With this introduction, Willauer went in to see General Stilwell, while I sat on a bench by the general's office door. I did not have to wait long before Whitey came out with something less than his usual air of optimistic ebullience. When we had said farewell to General Hearn and had left the headquarters, Whitey then explained to me what had happened. He had not, in fact, been given more than about five minutes to explain the pipeline project and, above all, the need for it. General Stilwell, clearly annoyed at having found his own staff already sold on the pipeline, suddenly burst out to Willauer, "Goddamnit, everybody's talking to me about pipelines, pipelines, pipelines! But all I want is bullets, just bullets!"

Though greatly astonished, Whitey tried to explain that if bullets had to be carried by trucks and trucks were fueled by gasoline, pipelines could also be very important in providing bullets. This only appeared to further annoy General Stilwell. In the end, which came soon, he made it apparent that he had wasted quite enough time on the subject and on his visitor, too.

T.V. Soong, however, finally ignored the logistical problems and secured the generalissimo's conditional approval of the Stilwell road plan. General Stilwell was to have the use and also the eventual command of the two Chinese divisions being retrained and equipped in India at a big camp at Ramgarh. The two prospective divisions were labeled the "X force"; in addition, a "Y force," composed of thirty divisions, was to be built in southern Yunnan on the Burma border. These troops in China were to get all the American weapons they were thought to need—but solely for General Stilwell's use in Burma. This rule governing the "Y force" weapons surfaced later, however. Meanwhile, to show good will and at General Stilwell's own request, the generalissimo promoted General Ch'en Ch'eng, the already-mentioned leader of the Western-minded officers in his army. After this, the Chiang-Stilwell relationship very briefly verged on cordiality.

However, I could see nothing but trouble coming in the months ahead. General Chennault's views were still my main reference here, and from my old chief's perspective, the Burma plan could come to no good. Chennault felt that a ground campaign in Burma would be costly, prolonged, and ineffective. This vast expenditure of manpower, he believed, would do little to address the fundamental problem of Japanese forces *in* occupied China. His early experience with the Chinese air force, moreover, had made him keenly aware of the difficulties in working with Chiang's armed forces. As an advocate of air power, therefore, Chennault felt questions of supply could be solved with greatest efficiency and least cost by emphasizing the air route over the Himalayas instead of reopening the land route to Burma. To be fair, my old chief realized also that an expansion in Hump tonnage could only benefit his command. He was wary of his position within the CBI command structure and concerned that Bissell and, by inference, Stilwell might continue to try to undercut him as a rival.

As Chennault's former subordinate, I naturally shared these concerns. I believed, like Chennault, that air power could be a potent weapon in the CBI theater, although I thought some of the general's strategic schemes overly ambitious. General Stilwell's cavalier treatment of the generalissimo, on the otherhand, seemed to me bound to create problems in the long run in Chungking. As I have already tried to show, the overall structure of the Nationalist government was desperately tenuous. It was already patently clear to me that Stilwell, by his behavior to date, risked, at best, alienating the generalissimo and, at worst, undermining Chiang's authority. Either way, I felt, the Allied war effort in the theater would suffer if General Stilwell was not made to reform in any number of ways— from basic military strategy to the more subtle area of personal diplomacy, where he was quite obviously at sea.

Thus began my career as the chief "back-room boy" on my side of the policy struggle that was soon to rend China. At face, this would be a struggle over the conduct of Allied military policy in the China theater, although the conflict would become political and, in essence, personal. When I describe my role as back-room boy, I mean that I advised General Chennault—and sometimes my friend T. V. Soong—on approaches to Washington, that I drafted for Chennault any paper having to do with politics, and that I did my best to bring Chennault's problems before the leading authorities in Washington. I did all this with the full knowledge of both Harry Hopkins and the president. They might have stopped me if they had not tended to agree with me.

Furthermore, what happened in China cannot be understood without knowing that the policy struggle there was largely a struggle of back-room boys. I was not alone on my side, for I had friends in China Defense Supplies, the Nationalist government's lobbying group in Washington, to help me. On the side of General Stilwell, meanwhile, were the young State Department officers John Paton Davies, John Service, and Raymond Ludden, whom Stilwell had borrowed from the Chungking embassy as his political advisers. These men went considerably further than political advisers usually do, for at almost all times after the first year of my return to China, General Stilwell had one of them in Washington trying to promote his own views.

John Davies and Jack Service became my friends, although we knew from the first that we disagreed with one another. Both men were sons of missionaries—Jack Service particularly tended to take a moralistic view in political matters—and one did have to have a natural tolerance for the peculiarities of foreigners not to judge the Chinese Nationalists of those days with a measure of horror. Like Stilwell, they were suitably horrified. And so their main theme, when I returned to China, was that the U.S. government ought to be tough with Chiang Kai-shek in order to make him introduce military reforms so that Nationalist troops would be of some use in the Allied effort against the Japanese.

In time, these views would encompass not just military matters, but politics as well. Stilwell and his men came to regard Chiang and his government as duplicitous and hopelessly inefficient. As far as I knew, they did not officially advocate Chiang's removal, but they did recommend measures that severely compromised the generalissimo's political position. Implicitly, they came to view the Communist government in Yenan, some 450 miles northeast of Chungking, with a good deal more charity than they did the generalissimo. For my part, I came to champion not just Chennault's policies, but also those of modern-minded men within the Kuomintang like T. V. Soong, whom Chiang, in the main, so distrusted. I at no time had any illusions about the Communists' willingness to support a truly Allied war effort against the Japanese or their long-term designs on power in China. In any case, I was aware that any hint of contact with Mao would severely limit Allied leverage in Chungking.

Our struggles rarely came into the open, for my letters to Harry Hopkins were private, as were General Chennault's later letters to President Roosevelt. By the same token, neither Davies nor Service nor Ludden worked in the open. They worked with General Stilwell himself and they worked with the State and War departments and sometimes with the press. The elaborate rules and formalities that now govern the behavior of Americans in situations similar to John Davies's and mine simply did not exist in 1942. The old freewheeling ways to be found in any good account of every war America had fought from the Revolution onward were still widely regarded as perfectly suitable. And so we were able to play a small but, I think, substantial part in the principal drama of wartime China, one that would culminate with President Roosevelt's recall of Joseph Stilwell from Chungking in the fall of 1944.

11

Palace
Politics

(1943)

By the late winter of 1943, my letters to Harry Hopkins in Washington had grown more frequent. The general theme of these was consistent although, as I look back through them now, the tone I struck was occasionally overwrought and verged on the didactic. I elaborated for Harry something he surely already knew: that the cordiality between Joe Stilwell and the generalissimo had not lasted. Indeed, in December of the previous year, on what the Stilwell supporters came to call "Black Friday," Chiang had called off the Burma campaign altogether. The generalissimo—I think rightly—took the position that the campaign to gain control of the needed area in north Burma would be dangerous and would certainly cost vastly too much unless it were accompanied by a British effort to establish complete naval control of the Bay of Bengal.

General Stilwell, meanwhile, was not a man to accept amiably suggestions that elements in any plan he had made were erroneous or impractical. Still, the truth is that the tangle of divergent human personalities and competing political interests that I found in China might have resulted in some sort of military success if the underlying practical situation had not been so unmanageable. What made it unmanageable was, quite simply, the Hump. If any military effort were to succeed in China, thousands of tons of supplies would have to be lifted from airfields in northeastern India and flown some 700 miles over the Himalayan Mountains to Kunming. Flying very large quantities of supplies across this vast range of mountains was a new and extremely hazardous kind of air operation in 1942. Nevertheless, the Chinese, who felt horribly cut off, and my old boss Chennault, reduced by supply problems to operating no more than four or five times a month, still believed this airway to be their best means of support. Both blamed General Stilwell and General Bissell for failure to go the limit to solve the Hump problem.

As I look back, I doubt this was an altogether fair charge against Stilwell. He was not a man to welcome military novelty in any form, and the idea that every month tens of thousands of tons of supplies could be flown across the Himalayan Mountains must have seemed doubtful to him. So he persevered in his plans for an all-out ground attack and, in so doing, ran up repeatedly against the Chinese. The general's manner toward them was so overbearing (I once described it to Harry as resembling a bluff and only moderately affectionate uncle dealing with a hopelessly wayward nephew) that the two sides found it increasingly difficult to communicate. To further his case, Stilwell marshaled the forces of the War Department in Washington. I found myself aligned more and more closely not just with my chief, General Chennault, but with T. V. Soong and his staff at China Defense Supplies. With my help, their case was set before Harry and, on occasion, President Roosevelt.

As the months went on, the Chinese sided increasingly with General Chennault, seeing his emphasis on offensive bombing, I think, as the way out of what was becoming, for them, an increasingly costly dilemma. They had been contemplating a request for Stilwell's recall for some time but were still desperate for American military supplies and saw the American commander, with his connection to General Marshall, as the primary hope for this aid. On the other hand, this same American general seemed fanatically bent on a plan that would commit their own meager military resources to a campaign that, in the minds of the Kuomintang leadership, would not lessen Japan's hold on occupied China.

On the other hand, Chennault's men were continuing their successful raids into occupied southern China. For all of Washington's bluster over Burma offensives and military reform, these air fighters still represented the only Allied force in all of Free China. Chennault's men had whipped the enemy before; they proposed to do so again and again. It was only natural for Chiang and his advisers to show an appreciation of the China Air Task Force's efforts, an appreciation that further complicated the now open rift between the two American commanders, Chennault and Stilwell.

The principal go-between in these roundabout policy maneuvers was T. V. Soong, who by this time had coopted me under the title of "air liaison" as a full-time member of his China Defense Supplies staff. By training and inclination, T.V. was above all a brilliant banker, as befitted the eldest son of the immensely successful Shanghai banker Charles Soong. Given an aggressively Western education by his father, T.V. often ate Western food even when he did not have to. This horrified his contemporaries, who all but regarded it as a symptom of moral decay. (Actually, he preferred Chinese food but thought Western food healthier.) Returned from China after his American education, T. V. Soong rallied very early to the movement founded by Dr. Sun Yat-sen, whose last wife was T.V.'s favorite sister. He further supported the generalissimo in many useful ways during the unification of China and the subsequent progress (though not reform) that was achieved before the Japanese intervention.

It was during this period, when the generalissimo began to risk serious inflation of his already weak currency, that he and Soong quarreled. Quarrels with the generalissimo were never a healthy activity, particularly in times of grave crisis. And so, in 1933, Soong resigned as minister of finance and fled to Hong Kong, where he proceeded to make a large fortune as a private citizen. In time, he patched up his relationship with the generalissimo and in the late 1930s departed China for Washington to see what aid he could secure for the Kuomintang government. It was during this dramatically successful phase of his career, as I have said, that we first met and became friends, although our friendship never went beyond the narrowly prescribed boundaries of professional confidant and adviser.

The accusations of financial corruption against T. V. Soong that surfaced after the war were, I have always thought, almost certainly misguided. In the first place, he was a man who had a knack for making enormous amounts of money when he was out of office, as he did during his early exile in Hong Kong and again when he lived in the United States after the war. In the second place, one cannot judge the Chinese of that period by the standards of the financial honesty or dishonesty that were so blithely given lip service in American society.

Chinese standards of ethics among public officeholders of those days remind me of eighteenth-century England, when even the great political families profited heavily from their high positions in government. Younger relations were freely provided with government sinecures, and many other such devices—all regarded as permissible—were commonly used to enrich one's standing. This was in fact the way the Chinese thought of T. V. Soong, and God knows there are few connoisseurs of misgovernment more knowledgeable or outspoken than the Chinese.

On the other hand, some in eighteenth-century England also went too far, like the father of Charles James Fox, who was bitterly disapproved of as a shocking money grabber in office when he made a vast fortune as paymaster for the British forces. A Chinese parallel can easily be found in H. H. Kung, T. V. Soong's brother-in-law and finance minister after Soong's own flight to Hong Kong in the 1930s.

In May 1943, T.V. returned to Washington to be present at the Trident Conference, the great inter-Allied policy meeting at which the competing strategies for the CBI theater were to be aired. I went with him, for General Chennault and General Stilwell had also been called back to Washington to make their competing arguments. For Chennault's sake, I wanted to see in person what Trident would produce. But more than that, I wanted to see if I could do something about joining, in uniform, my old chief. In February of that year, the general had been promoted to major general and given his own independent military command. The CATF was renamed the Fourteenth Air Force and given effective independence from Bissell's command in Delhi. The order, which had originated in the White House, had naturally greatly cheered Chennault. It gave me new hope, too, for reassignment to Kunming. And so, before leaving Chungking without the august permission of the Lend-Lease Administration, I resigned my post as civilian administrator and urged that the superfluous post be struck from the lend-lease table of organization. This gave no pleasure to the Lend-Lease Administration, but I knew enough of Washington to be neither bothered nor surprised by their reaction.

Although I was his friend, I had no idea yet of the fundamental "Chineseness" of T. V. Soong's character, so it is perhaps worth recording what happened in Delhi when T.V. stopped there on his way to Washington. By then, he was China's foreign minister and was, therefore, invited to dine with the viceroy. I remained in Soong's large suite at the old Hotel Cecil and was still working late that evening in the sitting room when Soong returned from his dinner. The foreign minister seemed to be in a mood to chat, for he sat down and requested a drink. Quite naturally, I asked him what dinner had been like, and he replied that it had been pleasant enough but extremely dull and unproductive. Then he burst out, "But I have learned one thing, Joe, *this country will never succeed!*"

I remarked mildly that I could not see how he could have arrived at such a final judgment since this was the first day he had ever spent in India, except in transit, and had not, to my knowledge, spent five minutes reading Indian history. T.V. replied, "All the same, this country will never succeed. No country that burns manure for fuel can ever succeed." I was astonished, although I had already seen firsthand the Chinese reverence for fertilizer of any kind. The memory came back to me of a fearful scene in a village street in Yunnan of two children, both armed with dustpans, quarreling fiercely over a dog dropping. From this quarrel, the trouble had progressed to a full-scale interclan fight, with both sides challenging one another in an almost murderous manner.

However, I had not expected Soong to share these rural biases, for he had been brought up very softly and very far from any village street. All the same, it turned out that he viewed manure in the same way as the most impoverished peasant and could not understand it being wasted for mere fuel. On the drive back from the viceroy's house, he had noticed a poor Indian house by the roadside covered, as these mud-built houses always were, with cowpats plastered on the walls to dry in the sun for later use as fuel. He had asked the British officer accompanying him what these extraordinary decorations might be. When the officer had told him, T.V. had been profoundly shocked.

The episode was revealing and helped me understand T. V. Soong in the ensuing years. Even at China's wartime low point, for example, he never doubted his country's total superiority over all the world's younger nations, including the United States. He carried this Sino-centrism, all but universal among his compatriots but little understood among foreigners, to extraordinary lengths when he was stirred by events. This was one of the reasons he turned so quickly against Stilwell when the American general, in the most ham-handed and undiplomatic manner possible, began to challenge the generalissimo. Despite his Western training and extreme intelligence, T. V. Soong remained entirely Chinese.

I kept in touch with what was going on at the Trident meetings (the British, with Winston Churchill at their head, were also present) through members of General Chennault's staff and by visiting the China Defense Supplies office at regular intervals. I saw President Roosevelt in his office because he wanted me to tell him firsthand what I had been telling Harry Hopkins in my occasional letters, of which FDR clearly was aware. The proof of his awareness was in the fact that he made me talk and questioned me curiously, too, instead of resorting to his favorite trick when he did not wish to be bothered with a visitors' views, which was quite simply to talk himself.

Trident can be summed up by three things. First, General Stilwell managed to make an extremely bad impression on the president and others. Judging by his comments in his private diaries (published after the war as *The Stilwell Papers*), he seems to have realized this failure. Second, and in contrast, Chennault's silent cragginess made a good impression as far as it went, although I do not think his overambitious plans for the conquest of Japan by air won many converts. Third, the meeting did not modify the bitter opposition of the leaders at the War Department, including General Marshall and the chief of U.S. Army Air Forces, General Henry Arnold, to the new priority for increased supplies for Chennault via the Hump that T. V. Soong demanded on behalf of Chiang Kai-shek.

These feelings in the War Department, in turn, left President Roosevelt with a clear choice between annoying General Marshall and General Arnold on the one hand or bitterly disappointing the generalissimo on the other; and this led to a drama to which I was a near-witness at the Trident meeting.

The method the president used as a way to avoid having to choose between General Marshall and the generalissimo was shrewd but fairly scandalous and not uncharacteristic of Roosevelt. Mme. Chiang Kai-shek had also come to Washington for the meeting, and the president had long since taken the measure of Mme. Chiang's vanity. He invited her to come see him, and when she arrived at the White House, he flattered her skillfully and sold her a gold brick that he hoped she, in turn, would sell to her husband in Chungking. Roosevelt's proposal included none of the help for Chennault or the increase in the airlift the generalissimo wanted. Instead—thinking it a convenient way of bypassing the conflict between Chennault and the War Department—the president offered planes for direct use by the Chinese air force, an outfit that both the generalissimo and General Chennault (and Stilwell, too, for that matter) had long since decided was beyond wartime reform.

From the beginning of Trident, Mme. Chiang had tried to persuade Hopkins, and through Hopkins the president, to communicate with her instead of with her brother, the foreign minister. She had the influence in Chungking, she kept saying, while her brother, T. V. Soong, could get nothing of any real value done for the generalissimo. The sibling feelings can, therefore, be imagined when Mme. Chiang appeared at the office of China Defense Supplies on V Street and, before she had passed the vestibule, cried triumphantly, "I have won for China; I have got the generalissimo everything he wants!" Here I speak as a direct witness, for I had been at the China Defense Supplies offices for some meeting or other, and I came out just as Mme. Chiang entered the room in triumph. Hence, I found some excuse for lingering because I wanted to see how the drama would turn out in the end.

Upon hearing his sister's triumphant cry, T.V. immediately beckoned Mme. Chiang into his office, where the two remained closeted for an hour to discuss the matter. When Mme. Chiang finally left her brother's office, the thunderclouds accompanying her were all but visible as she crossed the opulent lobby of the CDS offices. As soon as the staff members had been filled in on Roosevelt's new proposal—which they immediately recognized for the gold brick it was—and saw Mme. Chiang's heady infatuation with it, they unanimously begged T.V. to ask his brother-in-law, the generalissimo, of whom he was still very afraid, to repudiate his wife. Emotions ran high, and I learned later that T. V. Soong, at one point, had shed tears when he pointed out the dangers of asking the generalissimo to contradict his wife before the president.

It must be remembered that T.V., like all of the Soongs, was acutely aware of the enormous pressures under which the generalissimo labored. Chiang worshiped President Roosevelt and was desperately concerned about maintaining face with the American leader. Any perception in Washington of Chinese confusion or contradiction over matters of policy would be seen by Chiang as a great blow to his own prestige. Moreover, any outright repudiation of Mme. Chiang could, within the charged confines of the generalissimo's small circle, be perceived as an attempt by T.V. to advance his own standing at the expense of his sister's. At a minimum, even if he did succeed in persuading Chiang to reject Roosevelt's proposed bomber deal, T.V. knew he would incur the wrath of Mme. Chiang.

T.V. must have been successful, for shortly after this drama, the generalissimo stated in a private cable to President Roosevelt that Mme. Chiang had no right to negotiate on his behalf and that he had to insist on his first request of an increase in supply over the Hump as well as an additional 80 fighter planes and 40 bombers to operate under Chennault's command. Roosevelt, who saw the point and understood the virtue of the first Chinese request quite well, granted it and then braced himself to face the fury of the War Department. The department was, indeed, angry but unready to reject a direct order from the president. So the Chinese got the original program they wanted at Trident, and Chennault could count on supplies and the continued resentment of his commanders in Washington.

This peculiar incident had its almost unearthly sequel when I returned to China. I had hardly reached Chungking when I bewilderedly received an invitation to tea with Mme. Chiang and the generalissimo at their villa in the Western Hills. Arrangements had been made for my transportation, and I arrived for my appointment in good time. The villa itself was a pleasant and unostentatious house furnished, alas, with the usual horrors the Chinese fancy when they want "Western" furniture. The setting of the house, however, was enchanting. It stood in a mossy glade of tall trees, through which unfolded wonderful views of the valley and mountains beyond. (As I left, I discovered that one of the uses of the enormous trees was to conceal a member of the generalissimo's guard behind almost every trunk.)

To understand Mme. Chiang, whom I saw fairly often during the course of my time in China, one must begin with the fact that the Soong family came from Hainan island. Hainan lies off the far southern tip of mainland China, and so the Soongs were regarded by all other Chinese as having a strong strain of Hainan tribal blood. The reason for this belief, which was probably true, was that, with the exception of Mme. Sun Yat-sen, the Soongs were uniformly darker-skinned than the average Chinese. This relative darkness of skin, in turn, may have explained Mme. Chiang's habit, shared by Mme. H. H. Kung, of wearing what almost amounted to a mask of makeup with the consistency of enamel. This enamel mask may have had another purpose as well, for Mme. Chiang had some sort of skin trouble, which led to Eleanor Roosevelt's being horrified by the discovery that during one stay at the White House, Mme. Chiang always slept in silk sheets, which she had changed daily.

Except for this heavy makeup, there was nothing in the least ostentatious or showy in Mme. Chiang's outward appearance. Soong Mei-ling was a handsome woman but by no means beautiful. Like all Chinese women whose lives have not been too cruel to them, she looked a good many years younger than a Western woman of comparable age. She had a pretty figure and extremely pleasing company manners, and for public consumption she chose and wore dresses with no hint of flashiness. All this being said, I finally came to the conclusion that Mme. Chiang was one of the most coldhearted and self-centered women I have known. At base, she always struck me as artificial. I often had the impression that I was being purposely charmed, the purpose being to make later use of me.

This aspect of Mme. Chiang's character was very much on display when we met for tea with the generalissimo at Huang Shan. The social aspect of the event resembled a strained three-cornered tea party anywhere in the world, except for the silent menservants in their long white gowns. With swift efficiency, these men passed the tea and pressed upon me more different kinds of sweet dumplings and cakes than I ever wished to consume. Mme. Chiang, meanwhile, kept up a flow of social chatter, and from time to time the generalissimo, who was the only other person present, interjected one of his exclamations of "Hao, hao." I said nothing of consequence except to reply to Mme. Chiang when necessary. Then the trap was sprung.

Mme. Chiang began by reminding me that I had been at the Trident meetings in Washington and that everything that had transpired at these meetings was of great importance to China. I said I had, indeed, been at Trident and was familiar with most of what had transpired during the meetings. She went on, in tones that I can only describe as sweetly stern: "Then you must remember, Mr. Alsop, how I saved the day for China when the conference was going the other way. You remember how I got the generalissimo everything he wanted?"

It was obvious at once that saying this to me in the presence of the generalissimo had been Mme. Chiang's object in asking me to tea. As I have said, although Chiang always refused to speak the English language, he understood it quite well, and I had no doubt at all that he had understood what his wife had said to me. I was being asked, in effect, to say that T. V. Soong, her brother, had lied to the generalissimo in asking him to repudiate Mme. Chiang. The effect of such an admission was patently clear: T. V. Soong would soon find himself on the outs at the palace, a situation that neither he nor his country could afford. To make matters worse, I myself would now be linked to these intrigues and, even more ominously, linked in the eyes of her husband to the clique surrounding Mme. Chiang herself.

I cannot recall feeling so trapped socially on any other occasion in my life. Fortunately, I remembered one of my mother's richer contemporaries, Mrs. Leonard Elmhirst, who was born a member of the Whitney family. I had often heard Mrs. Elmhirst converse at great length without using a single word. Her method was to intone "Mmmmmmmm mmmmmmmm" emphatically or soothingly or with horror, as the conversation's course seemed to demand—but always noncommittally. So I borrowed this device and replied to Mme. Chiang's question with emphatic "Mmmmm . . . mmmmm . . . mmmmmmms," trying to put as much simulated conviction into my noncommittal coos as I possibly could. After that, I was able to make my escape, hoping for the best for the future. But I do not think Mme. Chiang ever forgave me, and I myself came away with a deep conviction that Mme. Chiang would do in her brother T. V. Soong whenever the opportunity arose.

So began my education in the strange family rivalry surrounding the generalissimo and in the uppermost recesses of the Nationalist government. That there was more to politics in Chungking than met the eye became clearer to me—and I can still remember the evening vividly—when I was asked, several months after my meeting with Mme. Chiang, to share a Mongolian "hot pot" with Mme. and H. H. Kung. The hot pot, a kind of elaborate fondue that uses water instead of boiling oil, was incomparably good. The work that eating a good hot pot involves, except the actual transfer of food into one's own mouth, was entirely done by four wonderfully adroit menservants in the usual long white gowns.

The real interest of the evening lay in the opportunity to study Mme. Kung, outwardly a plainer but tougher-looking Mme. Chiang and clearly the formidable elder sister of the Soong family. I am sure I floundered badly in the course of the evening, for she put me, always asking her questions in the sweetest tones, through the nearest thing to a third-degree cross-examination I have ever experienced. I came away from the dinner with the firm conviction—one that I hold to this day—that in that household, Mme. Kung was the master. Although greed was H. H. Kung's specialty, she supported him in his greed so that her children's inheritance would be increased (and, indeed, they ended the war far more than just well off). But in all other matters, Mme. Kung called the tune and her husband danced.

Mme. Kung's strongest links with Mme. Chiang were their common detestation of their brother T. V. Soong and their sister Mme. Sun Yat-sen, although Mme. Kung's children provided links as well, for Mme. Chiang was childless. Among these children, I learned later that the most important was the eldest daughter, Jeannette, whom Mme. Chiang had brought up and regarded as her own daughter. I have no idea what the girl was like or may be like today, but in those days she did not look at all like a girl. When in China, she wore a man's felt hat and a man's long gown; while in the United States, she wore the felt hat and a suit of men's clothes. At the White House, the president kept confusing her with her brothers and calling her "young man." Despite these peculiarities, Mme. Chiang was deeply attached to Jeannette.

All this was important because, as I have already described,

Mme. Chiang effectively controlled the "Palace faction" in the Nationalist government—the generalissimo's Secretariat and others who had such vital functions as securing Chiang Kai-shek's all-important "chop" (or seal) to validate orders. Received wisdom in Chungking political circles held that H. H. Kung was the leader of another faction within the government. This faction was composed of all the most backward-looking elements in the Kuomintang: the horrifying war minister Ho Ying-chin; the rest of the more crooked generals in the Chinese army; and the so-called "C.C. clique," which was civilian and essentially ideological. After my third degree over the Mongolian hot pot, I was convinced that the real leader of this backward-looking—or, if you will, "reactionary"—faction of the Nationalist government was Mme. H. H. Kung, who spoke through her husband because most Chinese of those days would have found it both embarrassing and insulting to receive orders from a woman.

T. V. Soong was hated by his sisters because he gave orders like any Chinese man; but Mme. Sun Yat-sen was hated far more because she had won over Dr. Sun Yat-sen, the great hero of Nationalist China, before either of her sisters was suitably married. Hence, the middle sister lived under house arrest in Chungking in a small villa charmingly fronting on an open sewer. There she held a kind of genteel court, playing host to a steady stream of visitors from every spectrum of the odd Chinese conflict. She was a woman of infinite charm and apparent sweetness, but those who were enchanted by her sweetness did well to remember her cold intelligence.

Like virtually everyone who made the pilgrimage over the little sewer to see her, I liked Mme. Sun enormously. She was very pleasant to me, as she was to General Chennault. However, I learned that summer that she was one of the chief propagandists in Chungking for the Chinese Communists. Yet I must add that almost anyone, not just politically unsuspicious colonels and generals, would have been bemused by her sweet protestations of simplicity, her further protestations that her delicious dinners were "just home food," and the way she talked what seemed like high-minded politics while drawing her little black sweater ever tighter over her shoulders in a pretty gesture.

By the time of her death in May 1981, Mme. Sun had had much experience in house arrest, for she was plainly confined to her house in Peking when I went there in 1972 in the false belief that Mao Tse-tung's terror had come to an end. During that last visit, I tried to send her flowers through an intermediary, although they must have been quite tawdry in the end, for the Foreign Office charged me only $4 for them. As a counterpresent, accompanied by a sweet noncommittal note, Mme. Sun sent me little animals, to be used as children's toys, that she had apparently made herself out of common pipe cleaners. It was then that I concluded that there was more than met the eye in China's political situation; and, in truth, the Cultural Revolution had only been briefly suspended in 1972.

I have now drawn a crude political map of the China I knew in 1943. This sketch leaves out many features such as the very real power wielded by the two or three warlords who still survived and the sheer communications difficulties Chiang Kai-shek faced in commanding and disciplining the governors and army commanders in remote provinces. Warlordism, albeit a periodic phenomenon in China's history, is always only a temporary substitute for other, more stable arrangements. The only significant men deserving the title of warlord when I was in China were General Stilwell's particular hero, General Pai Ch'ung-hsi, who controlled Kwangsi Chuang in the southeast, and General Lung Yun in Yunnan, who had even more local power than Pai Ch'ung-hsi.

The political fate of Free China, however, was to be played out in Chungking. It was there, against this background of factionalism and intrigue, that the conflict between General Stilwell and the generalissimo came to a head in the fall of 1943. It should be pointed out again that within the grand drama of the Second World War, the CBI theater was a tiny show. What was, by the standards of the other theaters of war, a relatively meager allocation of resources and supply was routinely and ferociously fought over by two—and sometimes three—different command headquarters. As I have said, the generalissimo favored General Chennault's plans for an air war in part because they were far more cost-effective than the arming and training of his divisions that Stilwell demanded. General Stilwell's plans also meant a considerable overhaul of the Chinese military system, something Chiang was loath to do since the old practice of tribute and favor among his regional generals helped keep the precarious balance of his own government intact.

By the summer of 1943, Stilwell and Chiang had thoroughly soured on one another. Progress on the Ledo Road, which was being built east from the Indian border through brutal jungle terrain, remained sluggish. Supplies were still being flown in over the Hump, although at a slow pace. That July, the generalissimo finally agreed in principle to back Stilwell's move into Burma, a plan that would receive its final go-ahead at the Allied summit meeting in Cairo that November. In practice, however, Chiang continued to rebel at the idea of using his own military resources (albeit, to a great extent provided by the United States) for an offensive outside of

China. As a result, the troops and supply Chiang had promised Stilwell for his "Y force"—30 Chinese divisions to be trained in Yunnan and used as the second prong of the attack on Burma (the "X force" in Ramgarh was the first)—were slow to gather.

The American general was, by now, in a nearly continuous state of high temper. He habitually referred to Chungking as "the manure pile." In a letter written to Mrs. Stilwell shortly after the Trident Conference, he described the generalissimo as "a grasping, bigoted, ungrateful little rattlesnake." Surely, the generalissimo was beginning to sense that having to rely for his American support on a theater commander who regarded him as a despot and a fool was a positive danger.

General Stilwell's behavior in Washington during the Trident Conference, rightly or wrongly provoked the generalissimo to order T. V. Soong to the White House to recall the American theater commander; this apparently had been Soong's central goal in Washington during the whole of that summer. The result was the first Stilwell crisis of October 1943. This, in turn, would alter the whole pattern of Nationalist China and its factions and political groupings, and, by doing so, come within an ace of causing China to be defeated by the Japanese before the war ended.

T. V. Soong's efforts to remove Stilwell came to a climax in mid-October on the eve of yet another inter-Allied meeting, this time in Chungking to mark Lord Louis Mountbatten's induction as supreme Allied commander for Southeast Asia. The day before the conference was to begin, Soong arrived with Harry Hopkins's promise that a request for General Stilwell's recall would be approved by the president if such a request were made. Soong was elated by his success in securing this promise, but, as Stilwell's own diary reveals, he had been halfway forestalled by his sisters. Beginning in late September, Stilwell's papers show Mme. Chiang and Mme. Kung, about both of whom General Stilwell had previously been decidedly contemptuous, making all sorts of efforts to flatter the American commander into a kind of alliance.

The Soong sisters succeeded, for before very long, the crusty American general took to calling them "Ella" and "May." Jolly tea parties were held at which Mme. Chiang hinted how difficult a husband the generalissimo was; other of General Stilwell's prejudices were also catered to. Sensing that he was in trouble, the general wrote hopefully: "Both [Ella] and May went to bat for me." It is clear from his papers that General Stilwell had not even a vague suspicion of the real motives for these cozy moments with Ella and May: these ruthlessly self-centered women were determined to block their brother T. V. Soong. If Soong could manage to get rid of General Stilwell, his standing with the generalissimo and the standing of his modern-minded allies throughout the Chinese government would increase automatically; proportionately, the Mme. Kung/Mme. Chiang influence would decrease. These being the facts, T. V. Soong's arrival in Chungking with Harry Hopkins's promise to relieve the American commander set off a most extraordinary family fight that went on for a couple of days in the generalissimo's large Chungking villa.

T.V. used to tell me briefly of what was passing when he came home for lunch or over a drink before bedtime. I saw him often because the China Defense Supplies office, where I worked, was in effect an annex of the Foreign Ministry, which was in turn attached to the foreign minister's official house, where T. V. Soong still lived at the time. He always told me he wanted my judgment; and, to some extent, I suppose he did. But I am sure that I would not have been his confidant except for our close quarters and the fact he thought me to be trustworthy—if only because I was unable to betray him to any of his Chinese enemies. If T.V.'s reports of what was happening are to be trusted, the fight at the generalissimo's house occasionally reached extraordinary pitches of emotion and near-violence.

The line taken by Mme. Chiang and Mme. Kung was that General Stilwell must be retained, for if his recall were requested, an enraged General Marshall would then cut off all aid to China. In this, the two sisters were supported by General Ho Ying-chin, the grossly corrupt army chief of staff whom General Stilwell usually denounced in unqualified terms whenever he had occasion to mention him. At first, the generalissimo stood firm, as can be deduced from the fact that he informed an American officer out from Washington, Lieutenant General Brehon Somervell, that he wished to ask for General Stilwell's recall. At one point, he also asked Lord Louis Mountbatten's opinion about the problem. Mountbatten, who would later urgently recommend General Stilwell's replacement, told the generalissimo on this occasion that he thought he and Stilwell could get along, although later, when he had gotten to know his opposite number better, he always considered Stilwell an ingrate because he believed he had saved Stilwell singlehandedly.

The general's real saviors, however, were "Ella" and "May." One cannot quite understand why General Stilwell was so much surprised by the generalissimo's wish for his recall, but it is clear from what happened and from what he wrote himself that he was both surprised and very much shaken after General Somervell had told him what was afoot. In these circumstances, Mme. Chiang and Mme. Kung found it easy to persuade General Stilwell to make what one supposes was a fairly lame apology to the generalissimo, after which Chiang Kai-shek, according to *The Stilwell Papers*, lectured General Stilwell for some time on the relationship between a commander in chief and his chief of staff. Obedience seems to have been prominently mentioned among the chief of staff's duties.

There can be little doubt that the matter of obedience lay behind the extraordinary experience of General Chennault during that Allied meeting in Chungking. The general, who had been summoned for an audience with the generalissimo, was waiting in an anteroom when Mme. Chiang burst out of the generalissimo's office in a state of high excitement. She kept assuring Chennault that General Stilwell had now agreed to "obey" the generalissimo, and in the end she and Mme. Kung made some sort of effort to patch up a friendship between Chennault and Stilwell. I have never understood exactly how this was done or who was present. Poor General Chennault, who was half in love with Mme. Chiang and had no political instincts whatever, was completely bewildered by his entire visit to the generalissimo's house in Chungking.

T. V. Soong, meanwhile, had no idea that his sisters were moving against him. Indeed, he only learned of Chiang's reversal when the visiting grandees took their leave of the generalissimo (the previous evening, in fact) and the generalissimo then informed Soong that he had decided to retain General Stilwell after all. Soong foresaw the consequences both for China and for himself. He felt, too, that he had been sent on a fool's errand when the generalissimo instructed him to seek the president's consent to Stilwell's recall. A very serious personal row resulted, in the course of which the generalissimo shattered a teacup on the floor and more than hinted that he might have his brother-in-law shot. In the end, T. V. Soong returned to the foreign minister's dreary residence in a state of serious emotional collapse, and I found myself called on to try to console him, although I did not in the beginning know what had gone wrong.

This was the first time that I learned that even the most highly placed Chinese were capable of bursting into tears at moments overcharged with serious emotion. Nor can I blame Soong for giving way to his emotions, when I look back on the consequences of this first Stilwell crisis. Stilwell had been saved from recall—and had agreed to be saved from recall—by the forces in China that he and the rest of the Americans so heartily despised.

The immediate consequence of the Stilwell crisis was the triumph of the reactionary group in the Kuomintang. General Ch'en Ch'eng, who had been appointed commander of the "Yoke force" (the Chinese divisions assembled to serve in Burma), was relieved of command. Pei Tsu-yi was driven from the Bank of China; and H. H. Kung, grossly incompetent and dishonest, was given Pei's place—which meant that the last brake on inflation was removed while Kung and his cronies pocketed much of the substantial American loan made to stabilize China's hopelessly weak currency.

The effects of the first Stilwell crisis were not limited to the changes in office and their immediate consequences. The reactionary General Ho Ying-chin had a long-standing feud with General Hsueh Yueh, the commander of a key corps area above Kueilin in southeast China. Ho Ying-chin, now riding very high, left Hsueh Yueh without any supply for a good many months. The Chinese government and armed forces thus sank even deeper into the wartime swamp. By the time all the chits were tallied, the result of saving General Stilwell in October 1943 was the darkest and most demoralizing period the country had seen since the Chinese government had moved to Chungking years before.

This bleak time had its comic-opera side. T. V. Soong remained foreign minister, although he was under virtual house arrest. He could go nowhere without a large detachment of armed goons assigned by Chiang Kai-shek to watch him. The American community in China, beginning with General Stilwell and our ambassador, Clarence Gauss, had not an inkling of the restrictions on Soong. Nor did anyone realize that a crisis had occurred at the upper levels of the Chungking government—a crisis that had changed the entire political environment. T.V. was simply described as having lost influence. General Stilwell, so far as one can make out from his papers, very soon forgot the whole business.

I felt sympathy for T.V. Whenever I had the chance during the ensuing winter months, I would ask him to come out for a walk. Our excursions were a comic business—or so they seemed to me. The official foreign minister of China and I would set off in his official car, followed by another car filled with the goons, armed to the teeth and brandishing enormous weapons. When we got out into the countryside, usually somewhere on the road that ran along the ridge above the Chialing River, we would deploy in the icy rice paddies that covered the whole landscape. During those late months of 1943, this part of China already was in the iron grip of a hard winter.

T.V. was no great walker, for, like the eldest sons of most rich Chinese families of the old days, he had been carried by his amah from place to place until he was at least three years old. All the same, he and I would set off across the rice paddies ridged by the late plowing, and fifty yards behind us, looking very put-upon, would come the troop of goons, who did not like walking for exercise any better than T. V. Soong did. I remember the scene particularly well because on one of these occasions I asked T.V. the question: "If elder sister [meaning Mme. Kung] had been a man, what might have happened?" Soong took this question with the utmost seriousness and crossed another entire rice paddy before turning to answer me.

"If elder sister had been a man," T.V. said, "the generalissimo would have been dead, and she would have been ruling China fifteen years ago."

12

Stilwell's Recall

(December 1943–October 1944)

With T. V. Soong under loose house arrest and his China Defense Supplies operation effectively out of action, nothing was left for me to do in China unless I could get back into uniform. With the new supplies issued after Trident, the Fourteenth Air Force had stepped up the pace of operations considerably during the latter half of 1943. Flying out from three new forward bases in the southeast as well as Kunming, Chennault's pilots managed to establish air superiority over much of China. Aircraft from the Fourteenth also began to do extensive damage to Japanese shipping in the South China sea, while striking military targets as far away as the island of Taiwan. These developments were cause for some celebration in Kunming, although I was still living at the old Jardine, Matheson company house, Kuo Fu Lu, at the time and was party to none of it.

In truth, by the end of 1943, I had grown tired of my attenuated role in the China drama and was beginning to view my life in Chungking as something of a penance. Since my return to China, I had busied myself primarily as an adviser to T. V. Soong. With T.V. now out of the picture, my staff position with China Defense Supplies was all but meaningless. I still held no army rank, and although General Chennault gladly took me in whenever I came to Kunming, I had no official military duties to speak of. A presidential commission was the last avenue of recourse, if I were ever to get officially into the war. And so I waited with more than a little apprehension as General Chennault, who since the Trident meeting was occasionally writing personal letters to the president, as Roosevelt had requested, argued my cause. At times, I am afraid I let my frustration show, for the staff at China Defense Supplies, after an interminable literary conference, had given me the wildly inappropriate Chinese name of "An Szu-po." The literal translation of this was "Uncle Benign Tranquility." They assured me it was both elegant and lucky, and I regret that it did not stick.

The weather that December in muddy Chungking did not help my gloomy mood. It was miserably dank and often bitter cold. Most evenings, I was home with the rest of the Kuo Fu Lu household for the BBC evening news at 6:00. After dinner, usually at the unreasonably late hour of 8:30, there were drinks accompanied more often than not by gossip. I remember the drink best—small glasses of the local vodka with bitters and water. Whiskey was unavailable except for exorbitant sums of money, and the local wine and liquor all tasted as though brewed in chicken dung. Chungking vodka was a weak drink, colorless, almost entirely tasteless, and barely intoxicating even when taken in large quantities. We enjoyed the alcohol's faint effect, nevertheless, and so passed our evenings playing bridge for very low stakes and chatting late into the night.

It was a fretful time for me. Outside of my housemates at Kuo Fu Lu and the few of my Chinese friends who were either in disgrace or deep political disfavor, I cared for only a handful of people left in the capital. To make matters drearier, this number had dwindled steadily. The foreign and press communities began separating into opposing camps as the Stilwell/Chiang relationship continued to fester. General Chennault's relationship with his commander had deteriorated further, especially in the wake of President Roosevelt's concessions at Trident. He—and by inference I, too—had been grouped among the numerous villains in Chiang's camp.

The most vociferous pro-Stilwell claque was based at the foreign-press hostel, where it would soon become fashionable to "tell" on China. The Nationalist government would be made to look worse than ever, often by General Stilwell himself, who was not above going to one or two of the young reporters in Chungking with his frustrations. His particular favorite was Theodore H. White of *Time* magazine, who later edited *The Stilwell Papers*. I always thought of Teddy White, who would gain a considerable reputation as a chronicler of the modern American presidential campaign, as a great reporter, and we were not unfriendly during those long months in Chungking. We came out of our particular wartime experiences with radically different views and prejudices, however. In later years, Teddy and I had to agree not to discuss the China drama for fear one or the other of us would grow apoplectic and seek to do physical harm.

It was the season for villains that winter in Chungking, for it was then that the first bills for the Stilwell crisis of October 1943 came due. They carried heavy interest charges. It already was bad on the economic front. Until then, Pei Tsu-yi at the Bank of China had been doing an extraordinary job keeping inflation in China within reason. The generalissimo, as I have said, had him thrown out because he was a T. V. Soong man and replaced him with H. H. Kung. Kung had obtained the second of two stabilization loans from the United States—a large portion of which he appears to have pocketed for his own use. Meanwhile, he did nothing to prevent the economy from deteriorating with frightening speed as the country's chronic inflation gained appalling velocity.

Moreover, the crisis had further reduced the generalissimo's power to resist Stilwell's wishes and, more to the point, the wishes of General Stilwell's allies in Washington. The American commander routinely threatened to cut off U.S. lend-lease supplies to all Chinese forces except those he himself was training for the march back into Burma. The tonnage coming in over the Hump, meanwhile, flowed regularly to the Fourteenth Air Force. One can assume General Stilwell felt robbed of his command on the mainland by the generalissimo and also by Chennault, and, therefore, decided to wash his hands of the whole business.

In December of 1943, General Stilwell jubilantly led his "X force" Chinese divisions out of India, down the first link of the Ledo Road, and into Burma. To be fair, the Chinese troops fought as they never had before in that war. However, the expedition came up short almost immediately against the veteran Japanese Eighteenth Division, which was dug in along rough terrain around the Hukawng Valley. The British, with whom Stilwell also had difficult relations, refused to go along with the plan, and Chiang withheld the bulk of the fifteen-division "Y force" in Yunnan from the action. Nevertheless, Stilwell stubbornly persisted in seeing the plan through, and for months remained bogged down in bitter fighting. Indeed, the fighting in Burma would last well into the summer after the Japanese counterattacked the British forces along the Burma-India border.

Soon, general theater supplies were being diverted from the Hump to supply both Stilwell's troops and the British in Burma by airdrop. Meanwhile, in February 1944, intelligence reports received in Kunming led General Chennault to conclude the Japanese were at last planning a major counteroffensive in China. The area of the Japanese offensive would ultimately include two-fifths of Chiang Kai-shek's remaining territory, an area that contained three-fifths of his forces. Chennault guessed—correctly, as it turned out—that a main objective of the drive would be the same Fourteenth Air Force forward bases that had inflicted so much damage on the Japanese routes of supply. There were five of these airfields, stretching south of the Yangtze in a long arc between the towns of Hengyang, Kuei-lin and Nanning. To prepare for the expected attack, General Chennault made repeated calls for additional reinforcement and equipment for the Chinese forces stationed in the vicinity beginning just south of the Yangtze in Hunan. This supply had been promised by General Stilwell but effectively vetoed by the War Department in Washington.

In the midst of these grim developments, I finally got word that my presidential commission as an officer in the Fourteenth Air Force had come through. The news came to me under pleasant circumstances. I had traveled down to Yunnan, in the southwestern part of the country, where a group of young officers who were friends of mine had been assigned on detached service. The valley where we stayed could not have been more than twenty-five miles long and ten miles wide. Its floor was as flat as a board and covered with a carpet of little villages, each of which boasted its own small temple surrounded by a tall stand of trees. Temple groves survived because, through the generations, the Chinese, while burning acre upon acre of shrubbery for charcoal, had always spared the trees around temples. Most remarkable, however, were the colors of the land, for each tiny village lay among fields of brilliant yellowish-green rape and blue-purplish beans, all in early flower. Adding to the pleasure of this view were our accommodations, which were set on the soft sloping wall of the valley and were near enough to an old hot spring so that my friends and I could bathe every day in the soothing, highly sulfurous water.

When news of my commission arrived, I immediately set off by Jeep for Kunming to rejoin the general. I was not very pleased when he assigned me a room in his house and told me my job was to be his aide, but I soon found that this was the most useful thing I could do for the time being. Sitting in Chennault's outer office, I functioned as his adviser on matters that fell in his blind spots, particularly political and logistical matters. Every so often, as one of the few who were not afraid of him, I would be called on to put before the general an issue that he did not wish to hear about. It was not the kind of work I should have chosen, but, as I look back, it was probably as useful as any work I was equipped to do in wartime.

I set about busying myself with a variety of office and logistical chores, none of which are worth describing. The worst moment I can recall was caused by General Chennault's belief that his aircraft were rapidly destroying the entire Japanese stock of locomotives in China. A fighter attack on a locomotive produces the most beautiful pictures of pluming steam when the 50-caliber machine-gun bullets go through the boiler. Unfortunately, locomotive boilers are easy to repair, and someone on the planning staff estimated that we had to have destroyed the same locomotives at least two-and-half times over to have met the figures about which the general openly boasted. This would not be welcomed knowledge to the general, who took to sucking his teeth in the angry, idiosyncratic manner he always did when he was mightily bothered. I was drafted to present him with the news, which I did—haltingly. The general sucked his teeth for a record period, then accepted the reality confronting him, and promptly applied for a number of fighter bombers armed with cannon capable of completely destroying a locomotive boiler.

The great drama of those first months back in Kunming was the eastern offensive that General Chennault had feared for so long, which got under way on the seventh of May. The Japanese Eleventh Army attacked south, from the Yangtze toward the city of Changsha, while a smaller force simultaneously moved west from Canton. Of the battles that had begun north of the Yangtze weeks earlier I know little, save that General Stilwell's intelligence staff—we used to receive copies of the intelligence report in Kunming—persisted for some time in describing them as rice raids. Where the Japanese offensive began to matter, however, was south of the Yangtze, beginning with the fall of Changsha in June. The immediate objectives in this region were, indeed, General Chennault's forward bases; but unless the Japanese commanders were mad, their larger object in this offensive, the cost of which increased as it went southward, was to administer a severe shock to the whole Western alliance by knocking China out of the war. More practically, the Japanese also wished to open the first dependable secured lines of communication from Manchuria, down through east China, to their vital holdings in Southeast Asia.

I now know that General Stilwell claimed toward the beginning of this crisis that Chennault had been guilty of insubordination in stating his needs so plainly to the generalissimo. Furthermore, according to General Stilwell, Chennault had stated that Chinese ground troops alone could protect his air bases, with the help of the Fourteenth Air Force. In fact, Stilwell had long argued that Chennault's plans for an air war would come to nothing unless a ground force were properly maintained to protect the bases of the Fourteenth Air Force. Stilwell predicted that once Chennault's planes began to do serious damage, the Japanese would strike at them directly. Indeed, the disagreement between the two commanders over Stilwell's Burma strategy had long since evolved into a running feud over whether offensive air power could have a dramatic effect in the CBI theater. Stilwell no doubt saw the Japanese offensive as redemption for his views. In fact, Chennault had said that Chinese troops, properly supplied, were sufficient protection for his bases, and the narrative of the fight south of the Yangtze makes it apparent that Chennault was telling the truth. What Stilwell omitted was the simple fact that the Chinese ground forces were running out of ammunition and that Chennault was almost daily dispatching telegrams written by me to Chungking pointing out the need to do something about the severe supply shortage that was crippling the defensive effort in southeast China.

The key battle in the Japanese advance, as far as the loss of all of General Chennault's forward bases was concerned, was a remarkably prolonged fight for the small walled city of Hengyang. Located between Changsha to the north and the larger town of Kueilin, Hengyang was within the corps area of the well-respected General Hsueh Yueh. His troops were well trained, courageous, and entirely loyal to the Nationalist government. Unfortunately, Hsueh Yueh was also particularly detested by the corrupt chief of staff Ho Ying-chin, who, no doubt, regarded him as a rival and passed on these suspicions to the generalissimo. According to our intelligence, a month or so before the Japanese offensive actually commenced, General Ho Ying-chin, who did not have quite the power to dismiss General Hsueh Yueh because the latter had strong provincial support, attempted to prepare for Hsueh Yueh's dismissal by cutting off all his money and supplies.

In consequence, the defense of Hengyang was in danger of collapse not more than five weeks after the Japanese offensive had begun. It is impossible, after all, to maintain the defense of even a walled city without ammunition. Considerably before this critical moment, I had begun, as I have said, to compose for General Chennault a series of anguished telegrams to General Stilwell, begging him to pay attention to the situation in east China and to release supplies to the beleaguered Chinese troops there. At this juncture,

General Stilwell's command, inherently distrustful of the central government in Chungking, had not released a single round of American ammunition to any Chinese soldier in China, except for those in the "X" and "Y forces" assigned to help Stilwell in Burma. The Nationalist army, meanwhile, suffered considerably from the bungling and corruption of the leadership in Chungking. Much of the U.S. aid money earmarked for military use had been either embezzled or misspent, while certain capable commanders in the field, especially in the southeast, were wrongly suspected of treason and, therefore, being purposely starved of supply.

Moreover, as pressure on the Nationalist forces increased, Stilwell remained deep in Burma. Attempting to communicate with him was like trying to convey important news by voice power alone across the whole width of the Great Dismal Swamp. Only when the fall of Changsha was imminent did messages from the generalissimo in Chungking induce Stilwell to emerge from Burma. In Chungking, he conferred with Chiang indecisively. He gave Chennault a short half hour in Kunming. Stilwell said no additional forces in the theater would be mobilized to meet the Japanese threat. He did offer Chennault another of the false gold bricks so common in those years in China—1,500 tons of supplies originally allocated to the B-29 project, which was then in its final stages in central Szechwan. The B-29 airfields, which were to be used as bases for the bombing of Japan, were controlled by the very highest level in the War Department and had a priority much greater than either General Stilwell or General Chennault. Chennault made the mistake of not pointing out this fact to Stilwell. I believe he decided to avoid an instant and public row with his commanding officer. As could have been predicted from the beginning, the recommended reallocation of the B-29 tonnage to Chennault's forces was torpedoed the instant it reached the War Department.

Hengyang fell on August 8. The Fourteenth Air Force airfield had been evacuated and demolished the month before by one of General Chennault's own commanders. General Hsueh Yueh promptly began to prepare a counterattack to retake the city on the assumption that he would be provided with the ammunition to do so. In this, however, he would be disappointed.

General Chennault was sufficiently disturbed by now to offer to give General Stilwell a thousand tons of his own Hump tonnage—I thought he should have done so earlier—to replenish Hsueh Yueh's ammunition supplies. The response to this offer came from General Hearn, Stilwell's chief of staff in Chungking. In a telegram to Kunming, Hearn explained that General Stilwell intended to administer to the Chinese government a very serious "face losing," which made it a poor idea to help General Hsueh Yueh in the east. By some very peculiar magic, the phrase "face losing" has been replaced in the official military history of the CBI theater by Charles Romanus and Riley Sunderland with the phrase "face lifting." But this prettification does not alter the real thrust of the telegram, which was that the more the Chinese suffered in east China, the more leverage General Stilwell would have over Chiang Kai-shek in Chungking, particularly in pleading his case to Washington.

Remarkably, General Hsueh Yueh nearly did halt the Japanese drive, and I think he would surely have done so if the telegrams I drafted to send General Stilwell in Burma had received a different reception. In a postwar interrogation, the Japanese general who was in command of the siege of the Hengyang praised the defense of the city as a heroic episode and told his interrogators that he was about to withdraw from Hengyang, leaving it in Chinese hands, when the Chinese finally gave out. Hengyang, in turn, was the key to all the other positions farther south, and their fate was sealed when Hengyang fell. General Stilwell later made an empty gesture by going to Kueilin when nothing could have saved the place except the kind of weapons and aircraft that we did not have in China.

As the situation in China worsened on the ground, General Stilwell's staff drew up their first theaterwide plan for the evacuation of Chungking—a plan so complete that it included the assignment to each colonel of a specific staff car in which to flee. In Washington, the defeats in China led Roosevelt finally to agree to the kind of great experiment that Stilwell's partisans at the War Department had been urging for a long time. It was their view—and the view of General Marshall, too, for he staunchly defended his old friend Stilwell to the very end—that if the battle for China and, by extension, Burma was to be fought with any success on the ground (the Hengyang debacle, they believed, had shown the vulnerability of Chennault's emphasis on air power), Chiang Kai-shek must be persuaded to cede complete control of his troops to an Allied commander. At Kunming, neither General Chennault nor I had any inkling of what was being contemplated. The Chinese, however, had received the first grim telegram from Washington in early July.

The telegram all but asked the generalissimo to make General Stilwell dictator of China—with command of the Chinese armies, including the right to promote and demote, hire and fire, plus total control of the American lend-lease supplies, which in turn would, in all likelihood, have meant providing at least a portion of lend-lease for the Chinese Communists. The extent to which General Stilwell wished the Chinese Communists involved in his fight against the Japanese is a matter of some debate even today. During the summer of 1943, following talks with one of the Nationalist generals, Stilwell submitted plans for a joint Kuomintang-Communist attack in the north. His stated military intent was to divert the Japanese command from driving into east China. As Stilwell's frustrations with the Nationalist army grew, he clearly came to view the Communists as a more motivated, effective fighting force than the troops with which he had to deal. John Davies had suggested that a military observer's mission travel to the Communist headquarters in Yenan in 1943, and there had been talk of trying to broker some form of political coalition between the two warring groups. Even the president was persuaded to apply pressure for negotiations between Chungking and Yenan, and had instructed his vice-president Henry A. Wallace to tell Chiang as much during a visit to China in June 1944.

However, the generalissimo steadfastly refused to join or in any way aid his old enemies. Naturally enough, he feared that any form of compromise would jeopardize his own political position after the war ended. But his position following the Japanese offensive was weak. The group surrounding him in Chungking, who had to consider what to do about Washington's message in July, was dramatically changed from the one that had argued over the Stilwell crisis in October 1943. Mme. Chiang had fled to the United States because she feared the anger of the generalissimo, who made it clear that he felt that none of the current troubles would have come upon him if he had handled the Stilwell crisis of 1943 differently. In addition, Mme. H. H. Kung, her husband the finance minister, and all her children apprehensively swarmed aboard the same plane that was provided for Mme. Chiang, and thus both "Ella" and "May" were removed from the argument in the summer of 1944. T. V. Soong, meanwhile, had been released from house arrest, and the goons had gone home; he had again become the generalissimo's chief civilian adviser, with the effective title of foreign minister.

Faced with the Washington telegram requesting supreme power for Stilwell, the generalissimo and Soong adopted the immemorial Chinese expedient of playing for time. The disastrous results of the Japanese offensive were presented by the War Department as an indictment of Chiang, who, in Stilwell's eyes, resisted attempts to make over his own army while relying too heavily on General Chennault's airmen. Given the severity of the crisis, the generalissimo could not argue, although he undoubtedly noted the telegram's arrogant tone. Oily messages were sent to President Roosevelt explaining that, in principle, this new program for China had a great deal to be said for it but, in practice, the new plans would raise a great number of exceedingly delicate points that needed to be negotiated face to face.

At the end of July, when the Chinese reply reached Washington, General Marshall was on a trip overseas. Thus, the president's first response was, simply, to inform the generalissimo that the negotiators would, indeed, be forthcoming and that he was glad the generalissimo had requested talks. General Marshall returned early in August and, for want of a better candidate, proposed Major General Patrick J. Hurley, who had been appointed the president's personal representative in China. Hurley was a curious figure with a splendid white mustache, an upright carriage, and something of the appearance of a nineteenth-century riverboat gambler. He had made his own fortune in Oklahoma; he had served as secretary of war in the Hoover administration; and he had carried out a series of difficult bipartisan war jobs for Roosevelt, which had won him the confidence of the War Department as well as the White House.

Both the Chinese and General Stilwell had liked Hurley when Hurley first arrived in Chungking in November 1943 with orders to help facilitate relations between the generalissimo and the other Allied heads of state. Both sides trusted Hurley, too, which suggests the old diplomat's most curious trait. Pat Hurley had great confidence in his own abilities to charm and to persuade, even though the kind of colorful frontier language he often used was lost on the Chinese. At times, this confidence got the better of the Oklahoman, with the result that he talked to each particular audience in a way that gave each what it wanted to hear. All the same, he had a large measure of the common sense that, I feel, had been denied General Stilwell; and, at the outset, he took to his new task, sincerely convinced that in Chungking he would win the public praise he had always sought for himself by getting Stilwell all that Roosevelt and Marshall had asked for.

In the early days of Hurley's mission as the president's peacemaker, Stilwell and his friends found nothing to criticize in his negotiations with the Chinese. Hurley quickly perceived that putting General Stilwell and the generalissimo at the same negotiating table would be asking for trouble. Consequently, when the Chinese had conceded "in principle" all the authority requested for Stilwell, Hurley asked the American general to stay behind in Chungking while he and Chiang Kai-shek and their American and Chinese entourages went up to the generalissimo's villa at Huang Shan to work out the actual wordage of a written commission outlining the powers of command.

Before they all moved up to Huang Shan in September, I had

been asked to come to Chungking by T. V. Soong. I was hesitant to do so at first since I was now in uniform. But, in the end, curiosity overcame propriety. Horror replaced curiosity when T.V. explained to me what was to be negotiated at the generalissimo's villa. I said, quite forthrightly and, I think, accurately—General Stilwell agreed—that the grant of authority contemplated for General Stilwell would destroy the generalissimo by the war's end. Soong replied that China's position had been so weakened by the losses in the east and, above all, by continued deterioration of the country's economy that the generalissimo had no choice but to give in.

I then said that I saw no point in remaining in Chungking. But Soong, who had an odd way of regarding me as a sort of talisman, begged me to remain until everything was finally settled on a "just in case" basis. He offered me a bed at the comfortable new house he had built for himself out of town, overlooking the Chialing River. Anxious to see the outcome of the negotiations, which would surely affect General Chennault, I accepted T.V.'s offer. The effect a Stilwell victory would have had on my chief can be guessed by reading an entry in *The Stilwell Papers* written when Stilwell thought he was going to be made quasi dictator of China. He listed the various problems he wished to tackle in the order of their importance, and high on the list, quite conspicuously, appears "the 14th Air Force." From this, one may be quite sure that the Fourteenth Air Force, Chennault, and even I (who was no favorite of either the theater commander or his allies in Washington) would have suffered promptly.

Meanwhile, however, a most mysterious development, still incompletely explained, had taken place in the United States. From the villa at Huang Shan, Hurley was reporting daily to Roosevelt that he was making good progress in reaching some form of agreement; and, indeed, he was, considering the enormous demands that he had to put forward. Chiang, however, continued to balk at the suggestion he send more troops into Burma, a stance that did not satisfy someone of great importance in the negotiations. I still suspect that this someone was General Stilwell and that he back-channeled to General Marshall's staff a suggestion for applying additional pressure on the generalissimo. In any case, in mid-September, a new message from the president, then meeting with Churchill in Quebec, was dispatched to Chiang Kai-shek in Chungking. It still seems to me this was one of the more mysterious and nearly lunatic messages ever used for a high wartime purpose. It did not ask for powers for Stilwell beyond the enormous ones Hurley was already asking for. It did not, indeed, ask for anything except for Chiang

Kai-shek to hurry up and grant Stilwell the powers already requested. However, in the most offensive tone, it put the blame for all China's misfortunes squarely on Chiang. Indeed, this was the reason given for accelerating the process of turning over all military authority to Stilwell.

It was a message such as Roosevelt in health and vigor would never have sent to an Allied chief of state. According to one report, his approval of it was secured at the end of the Allied leaders' conference then under way at Quebec; if so, this approval was secured when he was already desperately tired. On the original that was submitted to Roosevelt by General Marshall, it is easy to distinguish what was added by Roosevelt on the last page: half a paragraph of politeness preceding the president's signature. It seems intended to dilute the effect of what had gone before.

To make matters worse, this entirely superfluous, deeply insulting message was sent not to Hurley, the president's personal representative, but to General Stilwell with the request that he present it to Chiang Kai-shek. Stilwell greeted the message with delight. In his *Papers,* in the entry for September 19, he says, "Mark this day in red on the calendar of life. At last, at very long last, FDR has finally spoken plain words and plenty of them with a firecracker in every sentence. 'Get busy or else.' A hot firecracker. I handed this bundle of paprika to the Peanut and then sank back with a sigh. The harpoon hit the little bugger right in the solar plexus, and went through him. It was a clean hit, but beyond turning green and losing the power of speech he did not bat an eye. He just said to me, 'I understand' and sat in silence jiggling one foot."

Behind this singular entry in General Stilwell's diary, there was a vast drama. First of all, the American commander had taken the trouble to have the Roosevelt telegram translated into Chinese, and, if what T. V. Soong later told me was correct, the Chinese version of the telegram was even more insulting than the English. Second of all, once the translation was ready, Stilwell had gone up to Huang Shan on his own, contrary to his promise to General Hurley not to join in the negotiations there. He halted on the villa veranda and sent into the meeting, which included many high-level Chinese, to ask General Hurley to come out and talk to him. Hurley came out, cast his eyes over the new telegram, and begged Stilwell not to present it to the generalissimo under any circumstances. According to what Hurley later told me, he also warned Stilwell that he would wash his hands of him if he, Stilwell, presented the telegram. "You have already won the ball game" is what Hurley told me he said. God alone knows what the reality was because, according to others who have reported the same events, Hurley told them something quite different.

There is only one reason I am inclined to regard the account of what happened at Huang Shan in *The Stilwell Papers* as distinctly understated. It does not account for the swiftness and violence of the generalissimo's response to the president's message. For if the generalissimo alone saw the text of the message, his face was not blackened before the other Chinese who were present, as Stilwell himself, in another context, insisted. Shortly after the episode, both T. V. Soong and General Hurley gave me the same account—that General Stilwell had started to read aloud his Chinese translation of the president's message and had only stopped when the generalissimo indicated the meeting was over and stuck out his hand to be given the papers as they were.

As for Stilwell's deliberate malice, directed specifically against the generalissimo, it will be found in the most singular poem General Stilwell sent his wife after the event. It is worth quoting in full:

> *I've waited long for vengeance—*
> *At last I've had my chance.*
> *I've looked the Peanut in the eye*
> *And kicked him in the pants.*
>
> *The old harpoon is ready*
> *With aim and timing true,*
> *I sank it to the handle,*
> *And stung him through and through*
>
> *The little bastard shivered,*
> *And lost his power of speech.*
> *His face turned green and quivered,*
> *As he struggled not to screech.*
>
> *For all my weary battles,*
> *For all my hours of woe,*
> *At last I've had my innings*
> *And laid the Peanut low.*
>
> *I know I've still to suffer,*
> *And run a weary race,*
> *But oh the blessed pleasure!*
> *I've wrecked the Peanut's face.*

T. V. Soong, who was the only Chinese the generalissimo asked to stay behind when he broke up the meeting, was my source for what happened next. With everyone gone, the generalissimo burst into convulsive and stormy sobbing. When I heard this from Soong, I remembered him sobbing the same way in October, so I was not perhaps quite as surprised as most people would be by such reports concerning the "impassive" Chinese.

At any rate, when the sobbing subsided, the generalissimo told Soong that after the insult he had just suffered from General Stilwell—he was sure, rightly or wrongly, that the telegram was entirely General Stilwell's doing—he had to reverse his field completely and permanently. He had to ask for General Stilwell's recall. T.V. told Chiang that this was a matter of such importance that he could not venture to draft the generalissimo's message to President Roosevelt and asked Chiang to do so in his own hand.

This was a tall order, for the generalissimo did not use his own hand any more than he had to since his calligraphy was notoriously less than elegant. During the generalissimo's work on the message, T.V. called me, most likely directly from Chiang's Huang Shan villa, where he was staying for the duration of the conference. He asked me to go as soon as possible to the home of Pei Tsu-yi, which was also at Huang Shan.

The result of this call by Soong, plus the orders he had given to his subordinates, was both quasi-magical and downright comic. Arrangements had evidently already been made for my transportation out of the city by Soong's staff. In virtually no time, a government car arrived to bear me in grandeur to the banks of the Yangtze River. A private sampan was waiting there to carry me across the Yangtze. On the other side, another car was waiting to carry me up into the Western Hills. Pei Tsu-yi's villa was charmingly situated about a mile from any road in the midst of rice paddies and a bamboo grove. A carrying chair waited nearby the road to hurry me along the narrow and perilous path through the rice paddies. At the end of this ludicrous journey, I found T.V. on the little porch that ran along one side of Pei Tsu-yi's small house. The foreign minister was positively fizzing with impatience and, with only the most rudimentary greeting, shoved into my hand two documents. One of these was the generalissimo's personal draft of his message to President Roosevelt. The other, which was attached to the generalissimo's calligraphy with a rather rusty pin, was a quick translation of the generalissimo's Chinese words intended for Roosevelt.

The generalissimo lacked any knowledge or real understanding of the Western world. In addition, he had never written his own communications with Western leaders, which was one of the reasons why, in dealing with his Western allies directly, he had always had difficulties. Furthermore, the generalissimo felt an astonishing personal admiration—even reverence—for Franklin Roosevelt. The message that he brushed for the president in Washington resembled a farmer's son's notion of a memorial to the Chinese imperial throne before the revolution of 1911. The opening, which will give the reader an idea of the rest, was "Oh hope of the world! Oh light of the West!"

I looked at the translation and immediately told T.V. that the beginning would probably delight President Roosevelt, who would certainly not take it amiss to be described as "the hope of the world" and "the light of the West"; but it would just as certainly convince Harry Hopkins, General Marshall, and other key figures that the generalissimo was stark, staring, raving mad. Soong allowed that "some changes" might be necessary in the wording of the communication and added that this was why he had called me in to help him. I thought about T.V.'s request for a while and decided it was a case of in for a penny, in for a pound. I further decided that if the Chinese hoped to get anywhere in the climate that then apparently existed in Washington, they would have to take the offensive instead of bowing meekly before every suggestion. Therefore, with full conviction, I suggested they declare General Stilwell persona non grata and blame him, in large measure, for China's fearful situation.

For many years, I believed that the Chinese had sent forward, without revision, padding, or other changes, my draft of the answer to the president's alleged wire to Chiang Kai-shek. I have now been informed, I think correctly, that Hurley felt my draft (which, of course, he did not know was mine) was too severe and too outspoken. My memory is not vivid, but I have a dim recollection of working out with T. V. Soong a tactical approach that I rather admire now. I have read the relevant telegram, which, for a long time I had forgotten and which was partly my own. Using an approach not easy for Washington to get around or under, the telegram began by accepting every demand for an American commander that the president and the War Department had made on behalf of Stilwell. It was extremely precise about the unnamed commander's power to hire and fire and so on. There was no hint of coming trouble until the generalissimo continued by asking straightforwardly for Stilwell's recall and requested his replacement by another American commander in whom he, Chiang, could place his confidence. This was sent forward by General Hurley, sandwiched between a few meaningless words of introduction and Hur-

The family in Avon on the weekend in 1941 before I left for the war. *Back row left to right:* John, Corinney, Stew, myself.

As an officer in the Fourteenth Air Force.

Left: FDR's principal wartime adviser Harry Hopkins. (National Archives)

Opposite right: Chungking under Japanese bombing attack. (National Archives)

Opposite below, rear row, far right: With other newspapermen on the *Gripsholm* en route home from Hong Kong and Japanese internment.

Robert A. Lovett, one of the "Wise Men."

P-40 fighters lined up at the Fourteenth Air Force base at Hengyang, July 1942. (Smithsonian Institution)

The Third Squadron of the AVG at Kunming. (Smithsonian Institution)

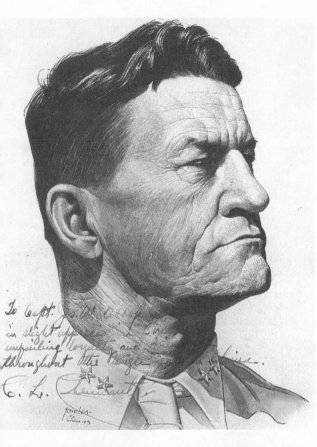

A signed portrait of
General Chennault from
a drawing for *Life*
magazine.

Colonel Chennault
(*second from right,
kneeling*) reviewing air-
defense positions with
some of the pilots.
(Courtesy Charles R.
Bond, Jr., Major
General USAF, Rtd)

General Stilwell sharing
a light moment with
Mme. Chiang and the
generalissimo, April 1942.
(National Archives)

Mme. Chiang strikes a
contemplative pose during
her visit to Washington in
1943. (National Archives)

T. V. Soong.
(National Archives)

Chiang Kai-shek with
Mme. Kung. (National
Archives)

A C-46 transport plane flying over the Hump. (National Archives)

Construction on Stilwell's Ledo Road through northern Burma, 1943. (National Archives)

Stilwell and Chennault during one of their infrequent meetings. (National Archives)

Henry Wallace with Mme. and Chiang Kai-shek on Wallace's visit to Chungking in June 1944. (UPI/Bettmann Newsphotos)

Left: In Kunming with one of my Chinese godchildren, the daughter of General Chennault's chauffeur. *Above:* In Chungking with a member of my four-man chair crew.

My brother Stewart with his bride Tish on their wedding day in June 1944.

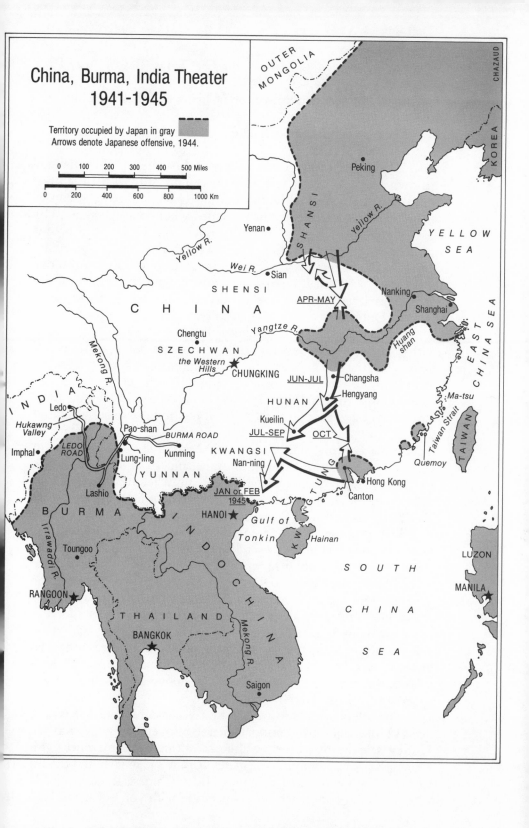

China, Burma, India Theater 1941-1945

Territory occupied by Japan in gray
Arrows denote Japanese offensive, 1944.

0   100   200   300   400   500 Miles

0   200   400   600   800   1000 Km

OUTER MONGOLIA

CHAZAUD

KOREA

Peking

SHANSI

Yellow R.

YELLOW SEA

Yenan

Yellow R.

Wei R.

Sian

SHENSI

Nanking

APR-MAY

Shanghai

C H I N A

Chengtu

Yangtze R.

Huang shan

SZECHWAN

the Western Hills

CHUNGKING

Changsha

EAST CHINA SEA

JUN-JUL

Hengyang

HUNAN

INDIA

Ledo

Hukawng Valley

Pao-shan

BURMA ROAD

Kueilin

JUL-SEP

OCT

Ma-tsu

Imphal

LEDO ROAD

Lung-ling

Kunming

KWANGSI

Nan-ning

Taiwan Strait

TAIWAN

Quemoy

Lashio

YUNNAN

JAN or FEB 1945

Hong Kong

Mekong R.

BURMA

INDOCHINA

HANOI

Gulf of Tonkin

Canton

KWANGTUNG

Hainan

LUZON

Irrawaddi R.

Toungoo

MANILA

RANGOON

THAILAND

SOUTH

BANGKOK

Mekong R.

CHINA

Saigon

SEA

ley's final judgment that Stilwell and Chiang Kai-shek were "incompatible."

The twenty-fifth of September, when the request for recall was sent out, was also the day Hurley went to General Stilwell with what is described in *The Stilwell Papers* as "bad news." The news of his own recall seems, at first, to have caught Stilwell between the wind and the water. Although he must have realized the consequences of his own rash act, he remained wholly unrepentant. "His face is gone over the president's message and he is afraid of my influence in the army," Stilwell wrote in his diary of the generalissimo. On the twenty-sixth of September, the American commander sent General Marshall a wire, no doubt hoping for help from the War Department. On the twenty-seventh, the entry in his *Papers* is simply "Dubbed all day. Hot. Played records."

I had been the opposite of busy all this time, occupying myself with what reading I could find at T. V. Soong's house, and was still there when the first answer from Washington came through. Roosevelt's reply to the generalissimo's request was a very strange wire embodying a kind of "Judgment of Solomon" on the Chinese theater. It suggested that General Stilwell continue to occupy himself solely with the war in Burma while the Chinese provide troops for the Burma fighting. The Fourteenth Air Force was to remain in China, the Hump airlift was to continue, and, to sum up, a situation was to be created that could easily blow up whenever General Stilwell, on the other side of the Hump, chose to order the first inevitable diversions to Burma from the Hump airlift.

The proposal for a Solomonic division of responsibilities reached China on October 6, and after considering it, the generalissimo sent an extremely firm reply on the ninth of October, Chinese time. This message rejected the proposed solution and reasserted the generalissimo's lack of confidence in General Stilwell as well as his obligation to refuse to allow Chinese troops to fight under a foreign officer in whom he had no confidence. There was an additional aide-mémoire essentially repeating the points in my first-draft telegram. In fact, I am inclined to believe that the aide-mémoire, which is long, was the original draft that T. V. Soong approved and Hurley refused initially to transmit.

The telegram went through Hurley, and he ended it with a decisive message abandoning General Stilwell for good and all. Hurley said he had been in almost continuous conference with Chiang Kai-shek, studying the generalissimo's character and the situation. "I am convinced that there is no Chinese leader available who offers as good a basis for cooperation with you as Chiang Kai-shek," wrote Hurley. "There is no other Chinese known to me who possesses as many of the elements of leadership as Chiang Kai-shek. Chiang Kai-shek and Stilwell are fundamentally incompatible. Today you are confronted by a choice between Chiang Kai-shek and Stilwell. There is no other issue between you and Chiang Kai-shek."

President Roosevelt then asked the generalissimo to name the American generals he would prefer to have instead of Stilwell. The result was a fairly laughable exchange between myself and the foreign minister—and, through T.V., even between myself and the generalissimo. Being Chinese—which means that they regarded their country as the eternal center of the entire world—the generalissimo's first impulse, heartily supported by his foreign minister, was to name General Eisenhower alone as Stilwell's desired replacement. I pointed out to them that, at the time, General Eisenhower had other things of great importance that he was undoubtedly locked into doing. I begged them to forget about Eisenhower and to choose someone more likely to be appointed—or at least to add other names to Eisenhower's so that they would not appear foolish in the eyes of Washington.

Stilwell's diary records that the Chinese had asked that he be replaced by "Eisenhower, Handy or Patch." (Eisenhower, of course, was Allied commander in Europe; Major General Thomas T. Handy was a key member of Marshall's staff in Washington; and Lieutenant General Alexander M. Patch was commander of the Seventh Army in France.) The list I was shown a day after my argument with T.V. was much longer and looked as though it had been made up by putting down the names of most of the generals in the European war who had been lucky enough to grace the cover of *Time* magazine. I ventured to suggest one amendment—and this certainly went forward, although it is not mentioned in *The Stilwell Papers.* I said that General Albert C. Wedemeyer, who then served as General Mountbatten's American chief of staff in Delhi, was known to be close to Generals Marshall and MacArthur, and that he admired the generalissimo and, furthermore, detested the Communists. As another point in his favor, I said that it was obvious General Marshall would like to give General Wedemeyer a significant job but had only been able to find him a high place on General Mountbatten's staff.

The president's telegram of October 18 implies that the generals finally requested were Patch, Wedemeyer, and Walter Krueger, who was commander of the Sixth Army in the Pacific. This communication rather testily pointed out that Generals Patch and Krueger were both very busy fighting elsewhere and announced the appointment of General Wedemeyer and the recall of General Stilwell. It also made known the separation of Stilwell's own command into a China theater under General Wedemeyer and into an India-Burma theater under Stilwell's former deputy General Daniel Sultan. The communication was signed by the president and ended with the words "I think all the above is the best solution . . . let me hear from you as soon as possible." Thus, after an extraordinary delay, the second Stilwell crisis was resolved by the general's recall.

I am almost ashamed to confess that before returning to Kunming to explain the month's events to my chief, I could not resist a visit to Stilwell's headquarters to see how they were taking the news. The path from my own quarters to the CBI headquarters passed over a hill. The route ran along a narrow farm path, and the ditch that ran alongside the path was no more and no less than an open sewer. On this perilous walk, I encountered a very hefty and very leftist lady member of the press hostel, a Stilwell supporter, and cheerily asked her what the news might be. The woman did not tell me outright but made her feelings plain by giving me a rather hard push toward the sewer. I managed to avoid falling down into the muck and so continued along the path. I found General Stilwell's headquarters in righteous uproar, rather like an anthill that had been kicked in by an elephant. I stayed there only long enough to ask innocently what the matter was. I received a withering glance or two in return and quickly retreated, first to my own quarters and then back to Kunming as soon as I could pack my belongings and find transport.

13

"Matter of Fact"

(1945–1946)

My years in China, which really began in Burma, were the only ones of my professional life in which I ceased to be a commentator from the sidelines and became a minor actor in the historical process itself. These were certainly the most interesting years of my life, although they were far from being the most agreeable. With the end of General Stilwell's story, my inside view of the intrigues in Chungking ceased. The War Department considered General Chennault partially responsible for General Stilwell's recall and, in time, exacted its revenge on my old chief. General Henry Arnold, who commanded the air corps, ordered a reorganization of the Fourteenth and Tenth Air Forces under a single command in China. Under this plan, which was bitterly opposed by General Chennault, the Fourteenth would be reconstituted as a long-range bomber group and moved to Chengtu, in central China. General Arnold anticipated Chennault's objections and overrode them, with the result that Chennault finally resigned his commission in August 1945, just days before the Japanese surrender.

In the interim between Stilwell's fall and my own chief's resignation, I settled back into the role of air force captain (I never rose above that rank) and served out the remainder of the war performing routine staff work in relative tranquility.

The most cheerful of all my memories of that last good year in China concerns the arrival of my brother John, who came to Kunming to see duty as a combat commando. As I have said, Johnny started in the war as a military policeman, much against his will, and in some devious way or other he eventually managed to find his way into Bill Donovan's Office of Strategic Services (OSS). In July 1944, he made a parachute jump behind the lines in France, an adventure he survived with some comic distinction. Johnny then moved on, via Delhi, to Kunming, where Bill Donovan's men arranged a second excursion, this time into the hills of Japanese-occupied Kwangtung, the southernmost province in China. John was to join a guerrilla group there and help facilitate their activities by providing steadfast leadership and large amounts of capital. To insure the allegiance of his group and to finance their adventures, the OSS had provided John with a huge suitcase filled with Chinese currency. Johnny showed me the suitcase when he arrived in Kunming and remarked innocently that this should last him until kingdom come. I assured my brother that, given the prevailing rate of inflation in Nationalist China, no amount of paper money was safe.

I promptly led Johnny down to the best money changer in Kunming—a little old man with dirty teeth who kept a tiny but very lucrative shop in a side alley of the city. The money changer regarded John's suitcase with vague distaste, opened it, and counted the contents carefully. After he had finished this task, he gave Johnny a smallish bar of gold weighing no more than 7 ounces, sourly commenting that the suitcase would not have been worth nearly so much had we waited until the next morning. I, meanwhile, made careful logistical arrangements to send John and his commandos two bottles of whiskey every week. Two was the essential number because I knew quite well that the Nationalist general south of Kunming, through whom the whiskey would have to be delivered, would take one of the bottles, and Johnny would have no chance of getting his own bottle unless there were two. As for the gold, Johnny told me after the war that it was a magical salvation. Every other week or so, he and one or two members of his guerrilla band would visit the village money changers in the bare and terribly poor hill country where he fought. Invariably, the old man or woman would bring out a scale set with a razor and, with the razor's edge, shave off barely enough gold to weigh. Johnny would then go away to his guerrilla group with yet another suitcase of currency to sustain them for a while.

During that last year, I also managed a glorious vacation to the ancient city of Sian, far to the north of Kunming in Shensi province. Sian is located in the Wei river valley along one of the central trade routes of old China, and over the centuries the valley has, on different sites, been home to five different dynastic capitals. Today, the Shensi city is most well known as the place where Shih Huang Ti, the first Chinese emperor, built his vast tomb with a huge underground army made from terracotta and metal to stand guard—all of which has been discovered only in the last two decades. Even during the war, however, Sian was a dramatic, cultured place and a welcomed change of scene from the mud of Chungking and the rustic military world I was used to as an officer in the Fourteenth Air Force.

I managed to find quarters with Vaughn Meisling, a friend from the Hong Kong internment camp, a journalist, as I recall, and a Dutchman, although when I caught up to Vaughn in Sian he was operating, I believe, in some semisecret intelligence capacity out of a large compound abandoned a short while earlier by American missionaries. Clearly, the missionaries in question—I never did find out what their sect was, although judging by the books on the shelves it must have been some form of fundamentalism—had observed one firm rule during their tour: nothing in the house or garden was to reek of local flavor. Although the garden was ravishing, the plants were all those from China that had become common worldwide, such as wisteria. As for the interior of the house, the furniture was 1920 vintage Sears Roebuck, and the reading texts that I could find were all staunchly Protestant and very menacing, indeed. Entering the rather stiff confines of this compound, then, was like taking a trip in a time machine to an era of my own country that I remembered very well but an era long gone and many millions of miles from China.

Another curious feature of this luxurious missionary establishment was that the only converts the missionaries ever seemed to have made were their servants. When the missionaries fled under the first threat of Japanese attack, their servants stayed on and, to their credit, loyally attended church every morning without their missionaries to prompt them. In the campaign to exclude the merest whiff of China from their doors, the missionaries had also trained their cook in what I would call American church-supper cooking. On each day of my visit, Vaughn and I were given a ritual lunch or dinner containing seven sweets and seven sours—that is, seven different kinds of sweet preserves and seven different kinds of sour pickles—to be eaten with such dishes as mashed potatoes, southern fried chicken and cream gravy, thick country cheese, and apple pie. I never really much liked church cooking at home in my youth, but what a joy it was, after more than a year of wartime rations in China, to sit down in a room full of consciously American things to a supper of richly prepared, home-style American food. Indeed, I was so pleased with the arrangement that I persuaded Vaughn to offer up a regular prayer of grace for the benefit of the devout servants.

The other pleasures of that trip were also material, for Sian was the center of antiquities in China. With the help of a guide provided by the Bank of China, I went from antique shop to antique shop, knowing very vaguely what I wanted and with many a bargain confronting me. In those days, the Sian area was like a huge field that yielded up a rich crop of antiquities every time the farmers tilled their fields. The dealers in Sian were accustomed to sending their rich harvest to Peking for sale to Tokyo, from where the goods would be dispersed to Paris and New York. With each stop on its route to market, an antiquity's price would increase by half. The war, however, had disrupted this lucrative routine, and when I arrived in the city the local dealers had been sadly cut off from Peking for seven years. As a result, their shops were bulging with all manner of beautiful objects, valuable as well as ancient, many of which dated back to the Ch'in dynasty in 200 B.C. Needless to say, the prices were also exceptionally low, which always makes shopping more enjoyable. In this way—alternately browsing among the ruins of China's grand past and resting in the familiar and comforting confines provided by the absent missionaries—I spent a jolly fortnight and returned to my wartime duties immeasurably refreshed.

Among my more somber memories from that last year in China is the staff meeting held by General Wedemeyer in Kunming upon his return from a trip to Washington early in 1945. The meeting took place in the small Fourteenth Air Force auditorium normally used for briefing squadrons on their missions of the day. After the general had run through the routine agenda, he paused as though in doubt about whether to continue and then did so with quiet solemnity. He told us that while he was in Washington, he had had "the honor to see our president," as he phrased it, and he believed he was the last official visitor before the president went for a rest at Warm Springs. Here the general paused again but went on, "I think I should tell you confidentially, our president is now so unwell that I fear he may be lost to us soon." Most at the meeting could not believe Wedemeyer, although I heard one or two who thought him likely to be right draw in their breath sharply. And so we filed out.

In April, news of the president's death at Warm Springs arrived in Kunming. For one long day, I saw a sight I have seen only twice in my life—when President Roosevelt died and when President Kennedy was assassinated: the extraordinary sight of public tears—unexplained, yet totally uncontrolled—coursing down faces both young and old, both American and Chinese. Later, I wrote Mrs. Roosevelt a heartbroken letter of condolence. Her reply, which came almost at once, was one of the most beautiful and dignified letters I can remember, and not the smallest part of its beauty was its generosity about President Truman. I ventured to have it copied and circulated to the staff. At that time, I could not see how a seemingly ineffectual and largely unknown politician from Missouri could measure up to a leader such as Franklin Roosevelt.

I finally departed China with General Chennault on August 1, 1945. The general by then was very near stone deaf and pushing sixty. However, he still refused to give up flying his own plane and so insisted on guiding his staff over the Himalaya Mountains in a C-47 transport that the air-service command had long ago ruled unusable. To please their chief, the air-service command had glued this dreadful vehicle together to the best of their ability, although they could not prevent the wings from flapping a bit—or so it seemed to me. When it came time to depart, we were visibly overloaded by General Chennault's loot, my loot from Sian, and everybody else's loot, along with a fair number of the general's closest junior staff members. I don't think I have ever been so really alarmed as I was when we flew over the Hump in that dreadful plane, although our much later arrival at New Delhi was a close competitor, since the general, who flew this ramshackle C-47 as though it were a 1920s fighter plane, insisted on diving down to inspect every significant building in the city, including the viceroy's house and the other grand old palaces of the Anglo-Indian bureaucracy.

Upon arriving home in Harry Truman's America, I promptly resigned my officer's commission and, after a brief visit to Avon, went straight to the *Herald Tribune,* where they asked me to resume my newspaper column. I had given little thought until then to the course my professional life might take after the war. However, when it came time to choose between journalism or some other, more somber, pursuit, I quickly chose my old trade. Indeed, my experiences in China had reinforced the conviction that a newspaperman was what I was most fitted to be. Although I had done my best during the war to be a team player, it was clear to me that I worked most effectively alone. Just as clearly, however, I relished being involved in large events. Furthermore, when I left the newspaper business to go to war, I was rather callow. By now, I had learned more about how official policy was conceived and implemented; and while this knowledge did not lead me to take a brighter view of human nature or the characters and motives of the great, it would, I reasoned, make me a better judge of the political process itself and the workings of government.

I wanted, also, to continue the column with a partner, as I had done before the war. I planned, to an even greater extent than before, to build my franchise on reporting and reasoned that two pairs of legs would do better in this regard than one. Since Bob Kintner had chosen to become a magnate in the broadcasting business after the war, I suggested to the *Tribune* that they take on my brother Stewart. Although Stew was apprehensive about his lack of experience, he needed a job, and I was confident that he would have great success in journalism.

In time, indeed, my instinct was proved right. My brother wrote beautifully, and although his style was very different from mine and he was not as given as I to dealing with portentous subjects, our outlook and work habits were a good match. Moreover, when Stew finally found his feet in Washington, he was also an incomparable reporter, for he had that rare knack essential to first-rate reporters of seeing that if fact A is related to fact B in such an such a manner, it implies that somewhere or other fact C and fact D must be lurking in a comparable or logically connected relationship. Sometimes, to be sure, we fought like the devil—usually I was in the wrong, now that I look back—but we never ceased to enjoy one another's company, which is the key to any productive relationship.

Stew's life story strikes me as a very strange one. Growing up on the farm in Avon, he had been desperately ill as a little boy—first with eczema and then with asthma. For a year or so as a baby, he never appeared in public without being swaddled like a mummy in yards and yards of bandage, although these only partially smothered the stink of the enormous quantity of cocoa butter—then thought to be good for eczema—with which he was slathered. After infancy, Stew's allergies were so innumerable that the first grand allergy doctor the family consulted in New York suggested to my mother that she had no alternative but to move with her young son to Tucson, Arizona. In answer, my mother pointed out that Stew had a sister and two brothers and she had a husband who was engaged in farming in Connecticut, so Tucson, Arizona, was not exactly an alternative.

Luckily, as children we all had a friend, protector, guide, and counselor in the person of Agnes Guthrie, our Scottish nurse, whom my mother had hired straight off the boat when I was six months old and Aggie, as we all called her, was just eighteen. Anything but a finished English nanny, Aggie was an enormously wise and warmhearted woman who adopted us as her own until we were grown up and then chose our house in Avon as her empire until she died from melanoma when she was in her fifties. Stew, the sick little boy, required more attention, and was Aggie's clear favorite. She watched over him like a mother hawk—not in a spoiling way, but in order to do everything possible to minimize the fiendish asthmatic attacks that sometimes literally caused Stew to turn a strange shade of blue.

I can still hear Aggie, when we would set off to play on the farm in the morning, calling out the window to me her last ringing instructions: "Now, Joe, don't make Stew laugh; don't make Stew run too hard; don't take Stew near the manure pile." These hazards were all known triggers of Stew's asthma attacks, and by constant watchfulness Aggie managed to minimize the attacks so that Stew reached adolescence with his health miraculously intact and without the scarred lungs so common during that time among asthmatic children.

Where Stew acquired his peculiar temperament I shall never know. My brother could be very odd—at least if one thinks it odd to spend an entire year in a New York apartment with an unused motorcycle as the only form of living-room furniture. Stew saved money in curious ways, always wearing secondhand clothes if he could manage to get them yet always managing to look negligently elegant in a way I could never emulate. This natural elegance was enhanced by a genuine, all-encompassing charm, the two main ingredients of which were a quick, forgiving wit and an enormous capacity for gaiety. Stew's gaiety, laced as it always was with an intelligent humor, gave itself to good companionship, gallantry, and a genuine wisdom of heart. Indeed, all his life, Stew was a man who, sometimes in spite of himself, inspired universal affection and, in many people, more than that.

In general, his view of clothing, furniture, and almost all other normal outward ornaments of life were like those of the Boston lady who remarked scornfully, "You don't buy hats! You have them!" At the same time, he could also be extremely peculiar about what was mine and thine in the sense that he always thought that what was his was or would somehow be snaked away from him. Here I am not by any means talking about money, but about the innumerable, often enviable, objects that my family used to possess. Among this vast jumble of odds and ends, Stew had a peculiar fondness for Aubusson rugs and for aged portraits of obscure members from the family's past, both of which I have always done my best to give away but which Stew somehow always suspected me of coveting.

About traveling, too, Stewart was the exact opposite of me. I could not bear taking a working trip with someone else along because this invariably meant arranging two schedules instead of one. Stew, on the other hand, felt greatly depressed and lonely unless he traveled in the company of at least one other person and preferably with an entire troop of admirers. Nor did it matter to Stew who among his innumerable friends and acquaintances composed this troop. On one fairly surrealistic occasion, he proceeded up the Italian peninsula with Randolph Churchill, who was a friend of his, and the old American left-wing populist Governor Culbert Olson of California. The party had managed to have a very jolly time until they got to Florence, where Stew and Randolph decided that Governor Olson's company (the former governor had what Stew in his own memoirs called a "flat hyena laugh") had worn a bit thin. They, therefore, arranged a meeting between the aged politician and the scandalous Mrs. Violet Trefusis, who was the daughter of King Edward VII's mistress, Mrs. Keppel, and the former lover of, among others, the writer Vita Sackville-West. Mrs. Trefusis's enthusiasms had long since inspired the rhyme "Mrs. Trefusis never refuses." Governor Olson, as it turned out, was not refused, and the improbable couple subsequently stayed together for a brief time at Mrs. Trefusis's villa outside Florence, where, by all accounts, they were much cheered up by one another.

At any rate, Stew and I were close friends and had, I think, complementary talents, as brothers often do. The *Herald Tribune* was enthusiastic about our partnership, and so shortly after Christmas of that last war year, Stew and I went to Washington to begin work. On December 31, 1945, we published the first of our thrice-weekly columns—our first offering was a nondescript and embarrassingly dismissive assessment of Harry Truman—under the broad title "Matter of Fact." It was hard for Stew at first to learn the trick of writing a column, which is rather like a debased version of the trick of writing sonnets. Remembering my own strained beginnings, I advised him to write as plainly as possible, using an absolute minimum of adjectives, ornaments, and images, until he felt fully at home in the medium. The best columns, after all, are straight news stories of a rather specialized character, which require extra polish and particularly careful organization but which, nonetheless, follow the normal rules that govern all news stories. Along these lines, I wrote up a brief list of dos and don'ts, which, in very little time, Stew was following better than I:

- Do have a point to make that will increase the information and improve the understanding of the average reader who follows national affairs.

- Do use as much personal, human, and anecdotal material as you can collect to buttress your point.
- Do organize your column with great care, following the rule that the lead must make the point you want to make, the central section must prove the point. The last paragraph or two can then present any conclusion you wish to draw or any comment you wish to make.
- Don't be stylistically fancy.
- Don't make extreme assertions on your own authority.
- And, finally, don't try to imitate me; be yourself.

We chose the name "Matter of Fact" for two reasons. First, Stew and I were starting a fresh venture together and wanted to emphasize this new beginning. Second, we wanted to stress, a bit pompously perhaps, that we would be dealing with facts in the column and not with theory. I wanted to pursue the same line Bob Kintner and I had done—working the town for reportorial stories instead of conjuring analysis from the issues of the day. Although conclusions are the prerogative of any political columnist, I have always thought it ridiculous to draw conclusions, no matter how right-minded or profound, without first providing the facts on which those conclusions are based. After we settled into our working routine, Stew and I would refer euphemistically to the "straw"—i.e., the news that we gathered in order to build the bricks that comprised the body of our columns. This philosophy entailed a great deal of hard work, especially during the early days when Stew was learning the trade and I was trying to rebuild what small journalistic reputation Bob Kintner and I had managed to win before the war.

Before long, however, our partnership had attained very real success, both in Washington and around the country, where we had to make our living by offering the Herald Tribune Syndicate columns good enough to be sold to a substantial number of papers. After Stew found his feet, he never ceased to grow as a newspaperman and came to enjoy the role as much as I did. Indeed, I relished that postwar time perhaps more than any other in my professional life. Washington—still manageably small then—was made all the more manageable by the fact that my chief friends in public life had been made in the Senate before the war and were now highly placed or were to be found high up in the government bureaucracy among the group later called the "Wise Men."

From the Senate, Jimmy Byrnes from South Carolina was secretary of state and Arthur Vandenberg from Michigan was the pillar—indeed, virtually the inventor—of the great American postwar bipartisan foreign policy. Among those who helped conceive this policy, Chip Bohlen had been Franklin Roosevelt's Russian-language interpreter at the wartime conferences in Teheran, Yalta, and Potsdam and was now in very high standing back at the State Department. Dean Acheson, after a brief interval practicing law, would soon become Byrnes's under secretary of state, and like Bohlen and his wife Avis, Dean and Alice Acheson lived two blocks from my house in Georgetown. Although Bob Lovett and Jack McCloy both resigned from the War Department following the war, Jim Forrestal, who was perhaps my closest friend among the group, was then secretary of the navy and in time would become the country's first secretary of defense.

These were civil servants of a type that is no longer found—at least in the Washington that I know today. To a man, they possessed close to a grand passion for public service, which they conveyed both in their work and in the conduct of their daily lives. Although schooled in the great law offices and banking houses of Manhattan and more often than not Republican by inclination, these men tended to be both nonpartisan and, it sometimes seemed to me, almost excessively nonideological. Entering government from a sense of duty, they stayed on for a variety of reasons: for patriotism, for power, but mostly because, in the very long run, they could find no parallel outlet for their considerable talents in the private world.

I remember one visit I made, shortly after the war, to Bob Lovett at his offices at the New York investment firm of Brown Brothers Harriman. Bob had only recently resigned his position at the War Department. He was a brilliant, wise, and intelligent man, and if I had to choose, I would pick him among all those I have mentioned as the single one of the old "Dr. Win the War" group whom I admired most. We had just completed a jolly lunch and were back at the small, surprisingly poky offices of the bank, when Bob rose to say his farewells. "Sorry, Joe," he told me in the softest, most mockingly sardonic tones. "I must get back to my great task for this month: we are underwriting a million-dollar bond issue for a conglomerate in the West." There was no touch of malice in Bob's voice, only a wry trace of regret. During the course of an hour as assistant secretary of war for air, he routinely dispensed of sums ten times as large, with consequences far more important. Clearly, Bob missed his work in Washington, and it was not long before he returned to the capital as under secretary of state to General Marshall.

Stew and I were about as well connected with the government as any newspapermen then working in Washington. Being an insider in a world capital, even a very minor and unofficial insider, was for me a new and remarkably enjoyable experience. Insiders in that Washington of long ago could not help noting that under President Truman it was a strangely organized city. I am still inclined to think that Harry Truman is an overrated president, although he had more guts, more sheer, naked guts, than any leader the United States has had during this century, barring, perhaps, Theodore Roosevelt. However, Truman often was a dreadful picker of people; and when he was liberated from the ghosts of the past by being reelected in 1948, he became a dreadful picker of policies, as he showed during the first part of his second administration.

During his first years in office, however, the president's choices were more than sound. As his main political adviser and strategist, Truman chose a suave young Missouri lawyer named Clark Clifford, whom he found in a rather lowly job in the naval aide's office in the White House. Clifford, who since leaving the Truman administration in 1949 has been a Washington lawyer-lobbyist hardly different from all the rest except that his bills are very much larger, was undoubtedly a most useful adviser to his first chief, and it was not long before all Washington knew it.

This meant, of course, that in the new social alignments after the war, Clifford quickly became one of the most conspicuous and sought-after men in the city. One of his greatest supporters was Mrs. Dwight Davis, the most admired hostess of that period. Indeed, Clifford was so often at Mrs. Davis's dinners that Alice Longworth, who for one reason or another heartily disliked the newcomer from Missouri, took to calling him "Pauline Davis's counter jumper" possibly because of Clark's very engaging good looks. "Counter jumper" was the label applied to department-store clerks during the nineteenth century; these men were usually chosen for their appearance and assigned to woo the clientele, most of whom were women.

Clifford's skills and talents far transcended the mere social, of course, for he was a shrewd judge of political character and a very deft inside operator. Clifford would play a large role in orchestrating the White House response to George Kennan's famous "Long Telegram" and would also be one of the key strategists during Truman's 1948 reelection campaign. In my view, his most important contribution during those first years of Harry Truman's presidency was to stress the theme of continuity. His plea to Truman was to retain all the men like Dean Acheson and Robert Lovett who had been in place and in high office under Roosevelt. And, indeed, Clark had a considerable job to do in persuading the president to keep these men on.

Very few of the holdovers from wartime had the kind of attitude toward Harry Truman that one would normally expect from the subordinates of a president. At parties around Washington where some members of the higher levels of the Truman administration were present, it was not uncommon to hear patronizing remarks of the same indirect but rather snobbish kind Stew and I had made in our first column. Very early on, Stew and I complained in print about how the White House had become "the home of an average man in a neat gray suit, who answers questions briskly and is chiefly marked off from his fellows by such habits as folding his handkerchief into four perfectly symmetrical points." I remember comments by, for instance, Bob Lovett's wife Adele about the odd cut of the president's Hawaiian shirts. This more or less captures the attitude. It was a silly remark, but, like the others made in private, one that surely got back to the president and just as surely infuriated him.

Truman compounded this problem by promoting Jimmy Byrnes, whom he had revered in the Senate, to the highest post in the State Department. As nearly as I can capture it, Byrnes's attitude was like that of the head boy in a school who found himself, by a bizarre chapter of accidents, under the leadership of the man who had been the smallest and least-regarded boy in his class. Byrnes had been a senator from South Carolina long before Truman had entered politics on a national level. Appointed to the Supreme Court by President Roosevelt in 1941, he abruptly resigned his place on the bench for an office in the White House, where, as director of the Office of Economic Stabilization, he spared Roosevelt much of the enormous burden of managing the economic problems of wartime.

During the war years and before, Franklin Roosevelt and Harry Hopkins had been content to run the foreign policy of the United States entirely on their own. I used to think that Roosevelt and Hopkins purposely looked for an ornamental man to serve as secretary of state, one who would do nothing more important than change the colors of the telephones at the old War, State, and Navy Building on Pennsylvania Avenue. Their wartime choice, Edward Stettinius, a handsome, essentially empty man, notable for his extremely fine, thick head of silver hair, fitted these cosmetic requirements to a T.

Byrnes, however, was a character of much greater mettle than Stettinius. Roosevelt had tried to recruit the South Carolinian as a running mate for the 1944 election, a move eventually foiled by the leaders of organized labor. I suspect that Byrnes, because of his long, distinguished record of public service, felt bitter at having missed the chance at the vice-presidency to which he felt entitled. Indeed, he must have been quietly shocked when, after President Roosevelt's death, this plum chance for national leadership fell on the junior senator from Missouri, Harry Truman. For whatever reason, Byrnes, during his two years as Truman's secretary of state, most improperly sought to run American foreign policy on his own, with a minimum of reference to the president and a minimum transfer of information, too. This is always wrong for many reasons, the first being that it flies in the face of the Constitution. Dean Acheson, who was then serving as under secretary of state, was trained to revere the Constitution and was I think secretly shocked by his superior's attitude toward the White House. Indeed, Acheson's long and especially warm relationship with President Truman was built, in part, on the fact that Acheson consistently imparted to the president the sort of information Secretary Byrnes withheld, a practice that got so bad that Byrnes even withheld information from Acheson for fear that Dean would inform Truman. This compounded the strained relationship between the State Department and the White House.

During Truman's first year in office, moreover, consensus among policy men and politicians in Washington over how to confront the erratic and aggressive behavior of Joseph Stalin was almost wholly unformed. Although Stew and I were fringe figures as far as the policies of the day were concerned, we shared the old-fashioned WASP conviction that the balance of power is the mainspring of history and that if war itself was never desirable, then military security certainly was the best way of preventing it. Like most Americans emerging from the war, we also took it for granted that America should—and could—do great deeds in the world. By the spring of 1946, although the Soviets were still taking every advantage of their status as a victorious ally, Stew and I thought we were detecting the first signs that Stalin would attempt to upset the balance of power. One could later argue, as Stew and I often did, that the way the United States let its guard down after the war—first, by the disorderly scramble to demobilize and, finally, by the disarmament program pushed through by Harry Truman's second secretary of defense Louis Johnson and approved by President Truman just before the Korean War—was a key to Stalin's deciding on aggressive postwar initiatives, from the Berlin blockade and the first incursions into Iran and Turkey in 1946 up to the Korean War.

The fact is, however, that when Stew and I started work in the winter of 1946 on what we envisioned as an international column, this country knew little more about the Soviet Union than what it had learned from *New York Times* Moscow correspondent Walter

Duranty. A favorite of the KGB, Duranty had denied the existence of the Ukrainian famine in the early 1930s, when that great reporter, William Stoneman, published the horrifying facts. Stoneman, then in Moscow for the old *Chicago Daily News*, had brilliantly contrived to get to the Ukraine and to send out an accurate account of the horrors of the famine, in which 5 million people were lost. The Soviet authorities thereupon gave Duranty all facilities to go to the Ukraine himself, whence he sent back word that there were no real signs of horror. Duranty would also accept at face value and write about Stalin's wholly faked show trials in a manner that deceived an entire generation of Americans and won him two Pulitzer prizes.

To banish the lingering delusions of the Duranty era, Byrnes authorized his deputy Chip Bohlen to open the eyes of as many Washington newspapermen as could be opened. Very early on in his diplomatic career, Chip had made a calculated decision that so large a national entity as the Soviet Union inevitably would play a major role in foreign affairs. Forgetting about the American posture of his youth—which was essentially one of ostentatious nonrelations with the Soviet Union—he proceeded, entirely on his own, to learn superb Russian and to read Russian history. Chip, whom I had last encountered on my voyage back from the Japanese internment camp, had spent the remainder of his war making a reputation in Washington as the State Department's foremost expert on Soviet affairs. He had served as President Roosevelt's liaison with the State Department and continued in this role under Harry Truman. So situated, he was able to play a major role in our early postwar policy toward the Soviet Union.

Chip was in no sense obsessive or hate-ridden in his judgments of the Soviets and would often say that the USSR was like the act of love: it could never be known or understood by mere verbal description. In those early days in Washington, Chip spent a good deal of time in the company of another man I admired, Isaiah Berlin. Isaiah was in the final months of his assignment to the British embassy in Washington and had just returned, in early 1946, from an extended visit to the Soviet Union. It used to exasperate me beyond measure when the three of us met without others present except Chip's wife Avis, for here were the two men I liked most to listen to, and within ten minutes they could be expected to be talking Russian and to stick to it unless I protested almost tearfully. Isaiah and Chip weren't trying to be rude, of course; they simply shared a delight in the language.

In those days just after the war, during endless talks at the Bohlens' small Dumbarton Avenue house, Isaiah and Chip invented what they called the NCL, the Non-Communist Left. Both men were too knowledgeable and humane to have been deceived by the fashionably approving 1930s views of Stalin's Soviet Union expounded by what Chip always jokingly called the "fellow wanderers." Both men were also too astute and farseeing to believe that the brittle, right-wing, anti-Soviet sentiment that some early Soviet and eastern European émigrés to the West had begun to advocate could have much future. So they invented the notion of a non-Communist left, a view that Stew and I as well as a number of other highly placed newspapermen adhered to instantly.

Nor was Chip Bohlen's active eye-opening limited only to members of the Washington press. While working under Harry Hopkins and Roosevelt, Chip had seen all the State Department cable traffic and had studied it carefully. Wherever Foreign Service officers of promise were being what he considered less than realistic, he took corrective measures, especially if they were men whom he liked and respected. John Paton Davies was one he most liked and respected, and Chip had contrived to send him from Chungking to Moscow in 1945 in order to balance his viewpoint.

In this case, however, the corrective went rather too far. On his return from Moscow, Davies would be assigned to the State Department Planning Staff under George F. Kennan. As I later learned from John, his first act was to write a serious policy paper solemnly advocating preventive war with the Soviet Union at an early date while the United States still enjoyed a nuclear monopoly. "I guess I'd overreacted to Moscow" was how Davies later put it to me. George Kennan, meanwhile, certainly overreacted to John Davies's paper. The horror it inspired in him was such that he insisted not just in collecting all the original copies, but all the carbons on which the copies were made. He even examined with suspicion the platen of the erring typewriter in case the rubber might have retained some dreadful trace of the words recorded on it.

Everything—paper, copies, carbons, though not the platen—were then stuffed into the not-very-flameproof wastebasket in George's office. George himself touched a ritual match to the offending accumulation, marking the fact that it had been assigned to total oblivion. Unfortunately, the resulting conflagration lit the basket itself, and there was some danger, as John later told me, that it would set alight George's entire office. I like to think of the episode nowadays, just as I like to recall the four men I know to have advocated preventive war, simply because they seem such an improbable group. They were, in England, Sir Winston Churchill and Bertrand Russell, who was very vocal about preventive strikes until the

Soviets broke the American monopoly on nuclear weapons; the ferociously tough air force general Curtis LeMay, who did not quite admit it but did nonetheless advocate it; and John Paton Davies, who does admit it, as far as I know, to this day.

It is important to note that Chip's educative program within the government had some serious, broad ramifications. W. Averell Harriman, then ambassador in Moscow, was by no means the hard-nosed, cynical assessor of Soviet objectives and motives that he subsequently liked to think he was. Chip, I think, sensed this in the cable traffic coming back to State from Moscow and so, in the winter of 1946, sent a letter by pouch to his great friend George Kennan, who, before heading the policy planning staff, served in Moscow as the elaborately titled minister-counsellor under Harriman. The letter begged George (for his duties as the embassy's "minister-counsellor" were chiefly administrative) to take the opportunity of Harriman's planned return to Washington for holiday and consultation to write a full, frank, and carefully pondered survey for the American government, in his capacity as charge d' affaires, realistically describing the existing Soviet situation and Stalin's discernible plans for the future.

The result of Chip's prodding was the extraordinary Kennan telegram that so excited then Secretary of the Navy James V. Forrestal that he hand-carried a copy from Bob Lovett to Jack McCloy, from Jack McCloy to Bob Patterson, and so on around the government as it then existed. As is well known, this Kennan telegram and Kennan's subsequent "Mr. X" article for *Foreign Affairs* became the intellectual basis of the containment policy for dealing with Stalin's Soviet Union. I heard about the telegram while Forrestal was circulating it and was provided with a sort of précis before Kennan's article appeared in *Foreign Affairs*.

Averell would later claim that he had come back from Moscow that winter with full knowledge of what George would write. But this, I think, was a calculated tale. Although Averell and I were, intermittently, great friends, he was one of the most self-absorbed and coldly ambitious men I have seen in government. Averell also possessed, to use an ancient phrase of my grandmother's, one of the most remarkable "forgetterys" in Washington. Certainly, he was not at the core of the Truman administration's great postwar foreign-policy decisions. Nor was he consulted by subsequent administrations in the way that the other "Wise Men" were. Averell rarely took a direct stand and was well capable of covering his tracks with a careful reordering or reassessment of the facts when his reputation was threatened. He could be quite brutal about this because, unlike

Lovett, Acheson, and the others, his instincts—and, indeed, his ambitions—were entirely political.

I remember one encounter, indicative of Averell's behavior, that took place at a Washington dinner party attended by a Polish emigré named Teddy Weintal. One of the more heated topics of conversation that evening concerned the efforts of the brave Polish resistance to set up their own exile government in London after Stalin had established the beginnings of a satellite regime in Lublin. In his cables from Moscow, Averell had persuaded the Allies to appease the Soviets on the issue of Polish sovereignty. Weintal, a nice man, peppery and opinionated, was naturally horrified by this official policy and, at this particular dinner, confronted Averell about it. Averell, to the shock of everyone present, responded with an excess of fury. Seizing Weintal, a much smaller man, he shook him up and down by the scruff of the neck and said: "If you wish to destroy me, Teddy, then I'll destroy you!" Weintal, who was a journalist by trade, was not destroyed, nor, of course, was Averell, but the incident was the talk of Washington for more than a day or two.

Many years later, after Chip Bohlen had died, Avis Bohlen told me how the Kennan telegram had been processed through Averell's remarkable forgettery and transformed. In his later life, Chip was very proud about his role in moving Kennan to produce his masterful treatise, and Avis was, too. Both of them knew that Averell had exaggerated his part in the drama, and I think Chip secretly resented it. Yet Avis adored the Harrimans, especially toward the end of her life when she was not always well. They treated her with great kindness, and she usually didn't tolerate criticism of Averell (something not uncommon among the Lovetts, Achesons, and others) in any context. But on this particular day—it was during the 1960s, deep into one of Washington's long, unspeakably sweltering summers—she had been to some sort of social gathering at the Harrimans' swimming pool in Georgetown and returned fuming mad.

I was on hand on one of my weekly visits to keep Avis company after Chip's death, so she told me the story. During the usual idle summer gossip, the subject of the telegram had come up, and Averell had apparently taken considerable credit for it, declaring that he had returned to Washington that February, knowing that the telegram would be written and intending to carry it around the government himself. In fact, Averell had been badly upstaged by George Kennan and was angry about it. In the end, he had made the best of the situation by readily agreeing with everything George had to say and by insuring that Jim Forrestal got an early copy of the cable. Any credit beyond the fact that Averell happened to be ambassador to Moscow at the time was largely coincidental. So this tremendous poolside revision of the past was far from the truth, and Avis knew it.

In the end, however, the credit for the Long Telegram belonged to one man only—George Kennan. I should confess it was not what I then expected from George, for I had met him years earlier, before the war, at a dinner at Chip and Avis's and had come away less than impressed. I remember that there was an extra man at table, so George and I had sat next to one another. I had never heard of George Kennan then and did not know that he was one of the great young experts on the Soviet Union at the State Department; I did not know either that he was one of the sweetest of human beings and, in this respect, at odds with much of Washington society.

I had insufficient experience in those days and still believed in what *Time* magazine called the "striped pants syndrome"—that classic caricature of the cautious, ineffectual, all-too-cerebral diplomat. Moreover, when George Kennan was a young man, he could only be described as pretty in a rather off-putting way. In addition, he had a curious, fluting voice. In short, at first meeting, I was not impressed by George's appearance, and I all but turned my back on him when he opened the conversation by remarking that the United States was doomed to destruction because it was no longer run by its "aristocracy" and had ceased to be responsive to "aristocratic" suggestions. This struck me as about as silly a remark as I had heard at any a dinner table. In Avon, we had been brought up to believe that aristocracies, whether real or imagined, had no place in either the political or social system of the United States; by further family training, moreover, I had the ingrained view that Americans who talk about native aristocracy have something very wrong with them.

Later, George Kennan was to become a cherished friend, but I am afraid I still regard him as resembling the priestess on the tripod at the Greek oracle at Delphi who inhaled the sacred smoke and then held forth. For part of the time, the God spoke truth through her mouth; for part of the time, her speech was sheer gabble. The trouble was you never knew which element in what she said came from the God. And, indeed, the truth is, that in the fifty years I have known George Kennan, he has been more wrong than anyone else and more right than anyone else—and no one, including myself, has ever reliably deduced which was which at the moment of its expression.

My connections with men like George and Chip were made all the more enjoyable because I not only admired them greatly and largely agreed with their views, but genuinely enjoyed their company. Many of these men in government and their wives had known one another before coming to Washington; they all kept similar houses, and they all, in their old-fashioned way, liked to have chums in for dinner. Socially, these first postwar years were a jolly time for me. There has always been a strong touch of the zoo in Washington social life; everyone in Washington likes to see the lions, who also like to be seen, and this rule held true just as much after the war as before it. But the curious old style of Dining-Out Washington that I have described had slipped almost entirely from view during the war years to be replaced by a social routine that was less decorous, less subdued, and, in its own way, just as amusing.

This new social order was less preoccupied with the old snobberies of class and heritage than with one's level of accomplishment or, more specifically, one's proximity to power. Washington after the war was a growing place, more invigorating than the small southern town of old and more involved with the outside world. The old idiosyncratic tales of patronage and pork had given way to a dialogue more global and more self-important. As the United States slowly took up the burdens and distractions of a world power, so, too, did its capital city.

I remember many entertaining stories from those immediate postwar times—several of them relating to dinners I gave—and, with apologies to the reader, I shall indulge myself with them for a little. One of my English friends—I have forgotten precisely who but fear it may have been Sir Isaiah Berlin—asked me to have the Donald Macleans to dinner. At the time, it should be explained, American foreign policy was at its first, great postwar turning point. The Soviets had occupied the northern Iranian province of Azerbaijan during the war and, by the winter of 1946, were showing every intention of staying there. To the vast surprise of the English left, which included Maclean, Jimmy Byrnes had taken an exceedingly firm stand, side by side with the British foreign minister Ernest Bevin against the Soviets in Azerbaijan. Maclean, who was to go over the hill to Moscow two years later, was at this time still a shining member of the British embassy staff in Washington with a reputation for quick thinking and a sharp tongue. He was known as well for a certain left-leaning keenness, although this was no more or less than was then fashionable among certain intellectual circles in Britain.

On the appointed evening, the British diplomat and his small, wan-looking wife Melinda, who, if I am not mistaken, was an American Quaker, arrived late for dinner. The English diplomat's handsome face was already a little flushed with drink, and his anti-Americanism, of which I had been previously warned, was already a bit out of hand. We managed to get through dinner without any breach of the peace, but after dinner, when he had had a stiff glass of brandy, Maclean lost control of himself. His tirade took the form of a vicious denunciation of the United States and all things American, with special emphasis on Secretary of State Byrnes, who was described in a loud voice in terms that are still not printable in any family newspaper. I tried to be polite for about thirty seconds, whereupon I pointed out to Mr. Maclean that he was speaking about a friend of mine and should perhaps choose another subject. This only caused Maclean to redouble his denunciations of Byrnes, whereupon I am afraid I lost my temper altogether and asked him and his horror-stricken wife to leave my house at once. Maclean did so with Mrs. Maclean in tow. This was the last I saw of either of them.

This episode, however, is only half the basis of my claim, which I believe to be unique, that I am the only man who ever threw both Maclean and his co-conspirator in espionage, Guy Burgess, out of his house the first time each crossed the threshold. Burgess would appear in Washington in 1950, a year or so before he and Maclean both fled to Moscow for good. One could see immediately that Burgess was more comfortable with ill-mannered behavior than his partner, for he asked himself to dinner, saying that Lady Pamela Berry and her husband (Michael Berry, later Lord Hartwell was publisher of London's *Daily Telegraph*), for whom I was giving a dinner, had asked that he be invited. I told Mr. Burgess that, alas, I had a full table but would be delighted if he would come in for coffee. Burgess arrived very late for coffee, filthy-dirty in appearance and filthy-talking, too. Drink firmly in hand, he then began the same routine as his colleague Maclean, starting with the denunciation of U.S. policy and ending with the denunciation of the secretary of state, who was, by that time, General Marshall. The end was the same, too, and Burgess left my house on Dumbarton Avenue just as Maclean had before him.

14

A New Europe

(1946–1948)

I look back on Harry Truman's White House years with the greatest nostalgia and delight. Gratitude is not normally a commodity in international politics, but in those days the achievements of our country were so towering, so sound, and so obviously disinterested that they could not be ignored by sane persons in England and Europe. These same sane persons, many of them very highly placed, were always glad to see Americans and eager to show their appreciation for what America had done. In those few years after the war, I went to more places, had more good times, and made more highly placed friends than I could possibly have managed during a normal era. For Stew and his wife Tish, it was the same.

By 1947, Jimmy Byrnes was aware, probably before the president was, that something like the Marshall Plan was desperately needed to stabilize Europe, where U.S. interests were most deeply engaged. Byrnes, however, would have nothing to do with a project like the Marshall Plan because he regarded any such proposal as a political impossibility, sure to be defeated in Congress and unlikely to call forth enough national support to overcome congressional opposition.

However, when General Marshall replaced Byrnes in the winter of 1947, he persuaded the president that the Marshall Plan was essential to prevent the collapse of Western Europe under the combined pressures of economic need and Communist intrigue. Truman revered Marshall and responded to him much as a brave junior officer might in battle. This almost boyish reverence for the general was something we all shared. Indeed, of the great men to serve this country during the second war, George C. Marshall was the figure I admired most. A Virginian in the most proper and gentlemanly sense, he was already in his mid-sixties by the time he became secretary of state. It has occurred to me that Marshall was a man no sculptor could have portrayed properly except in granite because his judgment and his standards had the integrity of a block of granite. I never met him during the war, and if I had, the general, in all likelihood, would have fixed me with a grim and icy look, for he regarded my back-channel maneuvering on behalf of General Chennault in China as most improper—which, of course, from a strictly military standpoint, it had been. We did, however, meet several times during the Truman years, usually at one or another of the three or four very grand, very old-fashioned houses around Washington where he and his wife used to dine.

The hostesses—most often Mrs. William C. Eustis or Mrs. Robert Bliss—had an idea that General and Mrs. Marshall enjoyed the company of young people, and so, given the wisps of significance that still clung to WASPs in those days, I would be asked along, very often with Chip and Avis Bohlen in tow. One lunch in particular stands out in my memory. This was at Oatlands, the large, beautiful country home of Mrs. Eustis, set in the rolling hunt country of Virginia, not far outside Washington. If it was possible, Chip admired the old general even more than the rest of us, tending, I sometimes thought, to regard him as the next thing to God. So he was somewhat put out when, upon our arrival at Oatlands, Marshall moved from his place by the fire to seek me out for conversation.

Marshall may have been curious to inspect this monster about whom he'd heard so much ill from Stilwell and others. He had also, by that time, concluded his nearly hopeless mission to China in the winter of 1946 to try to bring Chiang Kai-shek and the Communists together in some way. I think this firsthand view of China had given him a new respect for the grim diplomatic complexities of wartime Chungking.

In moral and physical style, in pure personal presence, General Marshall surpassed any man I have known. He had a gentlemanly bearing, very calm, very direct, and quite subdued. But even in casual conversation, he conveyed an uncanny mix of intensity and integrity. I am not easily cowed, even by grand figures, but had the general chosen that first moment of our meeting to disapprove of me or in some way to reprimand me, I would have bowed down on the spot in abject and dutiful shame.

As it was, General Marshall wished to talk about basic things, none of which were particularly inspiring or memorable. I did ask him, though, to describe his working relationship during wartime with FDR, which I knew to be different from those of the other military commanders. Marshall replied that while he had admired the president greatly as a man, he made it a special point always to treat Roosevelt with the profound respect due his office. Sometimes this respect came close to the point of aloofness, so much so that Harry Hopkins once asked him why, after years of working together, Marshall still insisted on calling his commander "Mr. President." The reason, the general told me, was as simple as it was shrewd: "I feared that if I let the president call me 'George,' he would soon be asking to appoint my theater and corps commanders, just as he had been doing for years with the navy's admirals."

To return to the Marshall Plan, however, during that spring of 1947, Stew and I had gotten wind of a series of muted but somewhat frantic discussions going on at the State Department over the need to put some sort of practical plan of action behind the "Truman Doctrine," a policy of economic and military assistance first extended in March of that year to counter Communist gains in Greece and Turkey. Dean Acheson, who had agreed to stay on as under secretary of state for several months until General Marshall had settled into his job, was the chief voice in support of some kind of concerted financial-aid program for Western Europe and the defeated countries alike, along with another friend of Stew's and mine, Paul Nitze, who would soon replace George Kennan as head of the Policy Planning Staff.

Stew and I had already made several extended reporting trips to Europe, and neither of us needed any convincing that the situation there was desperate. Very early on in our partnership, we developed a reputation for mild public pessimism, a reputation that would flower in the turbulent years leading up to the war in Korea. Looking back over our dispatches of that period from Paris, London, Athens, and Berlin, our worry seems well founded, for they accurately conveyed the curious mixture of wariness and verve with which Europeans confronted their uncertain future.

At that point, Soviet armies still occupied much of eastern Europe, and although promises of withdrawal had been made, Stalin's troops showed little inclination for leaving. The crisis in Azerbaijan had been forestalled by the withdrawal of Soviet forces—albeit grudgingly—in April of 1946. The diplomatic climate in Europe remained far from cordial, however. In February 1947, just months after my own trip to Europe, Stew brought back the first public, and hence widely circulated, report from Athens of the British decision—relayed by Prime Minister Clement Attlee to President Truman—to lay down the economic burden Britain had been carrying in Greece and Turkey, where the local governments were engaged in pitched battles with the Communists. The consequences of this decision had been obvious at the time. "The United States," as Stew rather bluntly put it, "has got to fish or cut bait, not only in Greece but throughout the whole area."

The grave tone of that time, and the nub of Stew's and my reaction to it, was neatly summed up by Eugene Meyer, the very shrewd publisher of the *Washington Post*. My Washington friends Philip and Kay Graham, took me up for a day's visit to the Meyers' enormous summer house, a very grand establishment in the town of Mt. Kisco in Westchester County, an hour or so from New York City. It was a warm spring day, warm enough, as I remember, to swim, and the Meyers had arranged a large Sunday lunch to which a number of important people had been invited, including the grand and certainly self-important Mr. Bernard Baruch, who, at that time, had ceased advising his old ally Jimmy Byrnes on matters of foreign policy and was our representative to the United Nations Atomic Energy Commission. Of course, Baruch had made his real reputation in the financial world, where he was a millionaire many times over, although he still liked to think of himself as the aged and indispensable adviser to U.S. presidents.

Eugene Meyer was a short, tough-looking man, very funny and very able. He was a wonderful bridge player, and although I never played with him, Alice Longworth did and reported that the stakes were frighteningly high. Outwardly, at least, Bernie Baruch was the opposite of Meyer. He was languid, very tall, vain, and shrewd. Meyer had started as a great Wall Street ally of Bernie Baruch's but came, during the First World War, to think of him as slightly phony. I always thought Baruch a fraud except when he was making money. But in those days, the old magnate's proclamations, although not digested with quite the same eagerness as during the Roosevelt era, still commanded polite attention.

The occasion was not overly formal, and a delicious lunch was accompanied by a good deal of keen and happy conversation. Afterward, the gentlemen separated from the ladies and gathered on the porch of the great house, where both Meyer and Baruch lit enormous cigars. After a perfunctory puff or two, Baruch launched into an admirable description of the situation that lay at the root of the Greek-Turkish aid bill already passed by Congress earlier in the year and that would soon give rise to the Marshall Plan itself—namely, the complete economic and political dilapidation of the whole of Western Europe caused by the war. Baruch said, quite rightly, that start-up money was what was really needed and ended his long disquisition by declaring that he would make a careful study of the whole problem before going to Washington and reporting to the president on "what we can afford to do."

Mr. Meyer was a hell of a magnate himself and, in my opinion, was equipped with more guts, a better national head, and only slightly less ego than Baruch. As I have said, for a long while he had been generally irritated with his old ally. He now grew visibly more impatient as this speech progressed. And when Baruch had finally finished his disquisition, Mr. Meyer waved his enormous cigar at his guest and snapped in a tough, puncturing tone, "I'll tell you what you'd better do, Bernie. You'd better make a study of the problem and tell the president what we can't afford *not* to do." Meyer clearly thought a comprehensive aid program for Europe was crucial, and his is the best one-line justification of expensive steps in national policy that I know of. I doubt whether Mr. Baruch ever ventured to offer his advice in Washington, but if he did, it is to President Truman's lasting credit that he refused to take it.

In early June 1947, I was appointed a marshal at the Harvard commencement and, therefore, was present for General Marshall's famous speech outlining the beginnings of a massive program of financial aid to revive Europe. (Acheson had also spoken publicly on the issue a month earlier in Mississippi.) In line with my duties, I wore the commencement dress that the future Speaker of the House, Nicholas Longworth, then chief undergraduate marshal, had instituted in 1891, when Harvard first abandoned the old commencement dress of white tie and tails. Longworth had objected to this old costume on the ground that he did not wish to look like "a French waiter at breakfast" and had designed a new costume that was worn through the 1970s.

So on that marvelous early summer afternoon, I was present in good order wearing my Longworth-decreed white four-in-hand tie, my Longworth white-linen waistcoat, and my Longworth cutaway coat and striped trousers, carrying a suitable top hat and my white and gold marshal's baton. There had been a jolly and somewhat raucous lunch at the Porcellian Club beforehand, but I had drunk less than the usual amount precisely because I knew General Marshall was going to speak. Had I known that Chip Bohlen had written the first draft of the general's speech, I might have been even more abstemious, for Chip, for all his personal style, had a notorious tin ear and, as a rule, wrote very badly. I listened to General Marshall carefully, within easy hearing distance, and I confess that the wording of the speech was so vague and its delivery so lacking in vigor that I had not the dimmest notion of what the secretary of state was saying, let alone that he was making a proposal that would change the world. Nor, to my knowledge, did anyone else present that afternoon in the Harvard Yard make very much of Marshall's talk—at least so I deduced at the time from the polite, perfunctory smattering of applause.

Since the strict rules governing Harvard commencements had forbidden advance briefings, the few newspaper correspondents who covered the speech had no more idea of the significance of what Marshall had said than I did. Fortunately, the rules had been broken in Washington by the State Department, and the meaning of General Marshall's speech had been relayed to the British embassy, which then had passed word to London, where Foreign Minister Ernest Bevin's response had been worked out in advance. It was only when Bevin's statement was published the next day that everyone realized Marshall had offered something very important.

Up to 1948, when President Truman's European Recovery Program was finally implemented, Stew and I, like many Americans of our generation, still hoped that the country's national life would again resume the old easy, inward-looking course that everyone who was of age when the war began regarded as normal and proper. But by the end of Truman's first administration, it had become apparent that nothing would ever be the same again. This passage of a great, unseen divide affected every aspect of the American political process, and, naturally, as reporters, we were affected, too. But nowhere was the change greater than in the newest branch of our trade as columnists: foreign reporting.

When I reflect on the constant traveling abroad that I did when I was a fairly young man with a column on my hands, I find myself unavoidably remembering what I think was Sophie Tucker's most famous vaudeville line: "Turn on the lights! Turn on the lights! I'm up to my ass in pygmies!" Immediately after the war, the Western nations for some reason had leaders who seem to me now twice the size of their immediate modern successors. It is startling, for example, just to consider Western Europe. And, with the reader's indulgence, I will do so, for nowadays, in my advanced old age, more

than the events, it is the people from that era and their odd characteristics that stick in the mind.

For all his innate modesty and reluctance to speak, Clement
Attlee, who served as Britain's prime minister from 1945 to 1951,
was a courageous and big man, although he did not look big in
person. Ernest Bevin, as foreign minister, was an undeniably big
man, heroic in physical proportion and heroic in character. Sir Stafford Cripps, who was the chancellor of the exchequer, may have
been a misguided doctrinaire, but he was certainly one of the most
courageous and powerful intelligences I have ever encountered.

In Germany, Konrad Adenauer's shrewdness and longevity in
rule prompted Stew to transpose Lord Acton's famous phrase from
"Power corrupts" to "Power preserves, absolute power preserves
absolutely." One could not help but admire Adenauer, partly for his
adroitness as a political leader but overall for his stoutness and
strength of political leadership. Here, too, one must add his considerable and sometimes arrogant wit. I remember waiting in the anteroom of the Chancellery in Bonn, while the former mayor of Co-
logne harangued his cabinet like so many bumbling aldermen. In
these circumstances, he almost always excused himself for being late
with the same turn: "You must not blame me, Mr. Alsop. You must
blame the Lord God Almighty, for he made men with limited intelligence and unlimited stupidity."

Among the grand figures of postwar Europe, however, none
was grander than Sir Winston Churchill, and it is a pleasure for me
to describe my only personal glimpse of the great British leader and
to steal my brother Stewart's Churchill story for good measure. My
encounter with the great man took place in London during the
spring of 1946. I was staying at the Ritz, where my friend Ronald
Tree had gotten me a room overlooking Green Park. Ronnie's son,
Michael, asked me to luncheon with his mother, Mrs. Nancy Lancaster, who had a large flat near Berkeley Square. I am willing to
swear on Bibles to this day that Michael said one-fifteen. At any rate,
at one-fifteen on a beautiful, sunny day, I dutifully arrived at the flat
to find myself in very bad odor indeed because I was fifteen minutes
late. Sir Winston was in a darkened side room with two or three
ladies. The rest of the large luncheon party was huddled in the
drawing room clumped in restive groups and already obviously
severely prejudiced against any latecomer.

After hasty introductions, we went downstairs to the dining
room, where I found myself sitting next to Lady Churchill. Mr.
Churchill was at the far end of the table, looking silent and grumpy,
not unlike, I thought, a great old owl who had been dragged, much

against his will, out into the bright sunlight. He was seated between Mrs. Lancaster, who was a good-looking and witty woman, and the very pleasant, statuesque Mrs. Oswald Birley, wife of one of Britain's more prominent contemporary painters. This was almost immediately after the end of the war, so all the relief organizations were still in being, and Lady Churchill, quite naturally, was enmeshed in several of them. I was barely seated and still gazing about when she chose Russian relief as her topic and started to discuss it at great length and from every angle.

Meanwhile, out of the corner of one eye, I was watching the extraordinary proceedings at the other end of the table, where Mrs. Lancaster and the painter's wife, Mrs. Birley, alternately filled Mr. Churchill's glass in an attempt, I concluded, to induce artificial respiration with champagne. The old man remained hunched over and hardly said a word, although a plump pink hand would reach out for the glass at fairly regular intervals and bring it to his lips to be drained.

By my calculation the great man must have had near to a bottle of champagne before luncheon was over, whereupon he began to utter for the first time. Unfortunately for me, Lady Churchill had not gotten to the end of Russian relief, and so I was in the exasperating situation of listening out of one ear to the man I would rather have heard more than anyone on earth, and out of the other ear to a detailed discussion of a subject that did not interest me in the least. I hope I remained polite until Lady Churchill, at long last, got up to go, saying she had many things to do that afternoon. No one else was in the same plight, apparently, so brandy succeeded brandy, and then champagne came back again as the afternoon lengthened and Mr. Churchill talked on.

I cannot possibly call to mind the innumerable subjects he touched upon during this curious verbal display. I can only say that it was like a marvelous, never-boring, always-fresh-and-funny personal charade. The old man evidently enjoyed talking; and when he had nothing very serious he wanted to talk about, he chose to perform a kind of vaudeville turn. I have retained only a single fragment of his long and amusing routine, and this concerned the weather in general and Britain's lack of sunshine in specific. "Above all," declared Churchill, "I believe these islands would be vastly improved by a five and twenty percent increase in their annual allowance in sunshine." When the party at last broke up late that afternoon, I went away reflecting that it was the first time I had ever heard the weather discussed with such wit, albeit decidedly ignorantly—for a yearly increase of five and twenty percent in sunshine would have been enough to turn a sizable portion of British crops a light golden brown.

My brother Stewart's experience with the great man followed by many months and was infinitely more significant although much more problematic. Randolph Churchill ran into Stew in London and asked if Stew would like to come down to lunch with his father at Chartwell. It was not an invitation that Stew was likely to refuse, although I am sure there were moments after he and Randolph got to Chartwell when he wished he had. To begin with, they both found themselves strikingly unwelcome, for Randolph had had some sort of row with his father that had not been patched up, and this being so, it was a great added offense on Randolph's part to have brought an unexplained stray American home to dine.

Nonetheless, the small party sat uneasily down to lunch. Once again, champagne was served, and this time Mr. Churchill, who looked, according to Stew's report, like an ancient angry baby, was pouring the drinks. He gave none to Randolph, who was on the wagon, he gave the bottom of a single glass to Stew, and he reserved the rest to quench his own thirst. Through the three or four courses of lunch, Mr. Churchill refilled his champagne glass regularly and ate his food, but he made no effort to converse with his guests. Stew, like myself, was fatally imbued with the old-fashioned New York brand of politeness that thought it the worst kind of bad manners to allow a dead silence to occur; and since Randolph did not seem to care and ate his lunch in silence like his father, Stew simply babbled through the three or four courses, touching on topics, I fear, far more desperate and ineffectual than Russian relief.

When lunch was mercifully over, the bottle of champagne had been consumed, and coffee and brandy were on the table, Mr. Churchill at last showed signs of being about to talk. By then, Stew, who was so desperately nervous that he could not stop talking, said to Mr. Churchill that he had come to England to report on the political situation and would like Churchill's opinion on who among the younger Tories were worth seeing. The old man glowered at him. "Younger Tories?" he said. "Younger Tories? Hmmm. Well there's Hogg [Quintin Hogg, later Lord Hailsham and chancellor of the British courts]—he's an ass. Younger Tories? I don't know any of their names." Whereupon the old leader returned to his glass of brandy and once more silence fell upon the table.

This time, however, the silence did not last, for Mr. Churchill somehow or other hoisted aboard the fact that Stew was an American, and an American, moreover, who had strongly supported both Roosevelt and Truman. I cannot reproduce the discussion, but I can at least offer the climax, which was quite splendid enough. "The United States," said the old man, "reminds me of a great and noble horse dragging the cart of civilization up the hill against heaviest odds and amidst the direst circumstances. Often I ask myself—I ask you [he glared at Stew] whether the horse can stay the course?" Stew answered that he thought so. And that was the end of that, although once he got started, Mr. Churchill talked almost without pause—never falling into the trap of repetition, never for an instant being boring, never for an instant being trivial either—for about two hours.

The great political figure in France then, out of power but still as much of a national presence as Churchill in Britain, was Charles de Gaulle. De Gaulle had resigned his provisional presidency in January 1946 and would not return to government until his people called upon him to do so during the Algerian crisis, a full twelve years later. His office, in those days, was in the same building as one of the city's great old restaurants, a warren of little private rooms where the food was frightfully good, very unpretentious, but also very expensive. I presented myself for an audience at the proper time and was led by a Gaullist gent to a stuffy little anteroom, where I cooled my heels for nearly an hour. At last, the Gaullist motioned me to enter, which I dutifully did.

General de Gaulle's office was not as tiny as the anteroom had been, but his enormous physical size made it seem even smaller. He loomed up over his desk, looking quite glum, and waved me to a low-slung chair near the window. As with General MacArthur, this arrangement insured that I spent my entire time peering up at de Gaulle from knee level. His rhetorical style was similar to MacArthur's, too, for he did not so much discuss events as expound on them. And so, for nearly an hour and a half I sat with my nose in the air, looking upward, as the general paced to and fro about his tiny office. His subject, of course, was France, for no man was less a citizen of the world and more a citizen of his own country than Charles de Gaulle.

Most Americans do not understand the French because the French are, by our standards, so improbable. French logic—Frenchmen always talk about "la logique française"—has two basic propositions. The first is that if events do not proceed exactly the way the French want them to, then there is bound somewhere to be a plot. The second proposition is that the leaders of the plot, when it is uncovered, are bound to be their dearest friends and warmest supporters. There were tinges of this kind of thinking in de Gaulle's analysis, which forecast, among other things, the creation of an Allied security pact much like NATO and predicted France's unwillingness to join. His tone, I remember, was very funny and quite sardonic, and his delivery was highly personalized and eccentric in the way Churchill's had been. I would encounter de Gaulle much later on in my travels, during the crisis in Algeria, and come to have great respect for him. But sitting in my low little chair in that dim little office, listening to his booming prognostications, I must confess I thought that the great man was near to being half crazy.

France, of course, had not paid Britain's enormous wartime price for victory over Hitler, and Americans, for a brief time, stood just as high in Paris as they did across the Channel. After the Marshall Plan, for instance, my old friend David Bruce enjoyed a privilege that I never imagined could be accorded to an American ambassador. French governments came and went with deceptive and dizzying rapidity. Each time a new government was being formed, an emissary would be sent along to the American embassy to ask David Bruce whether the replacement government would be acceptable in Washington. David used to have one of his staff with him on these occasions so that he would have a witness in case he were misrepresented, for he recognized the extreme delicacy of his situation.

I would have liked nothing so much as to be under the desk to hear David's customary reply, as he recounted it, to the officials who brought the government list, always delivered in his very richest and most Virginia-country-gentleman tones: "Gentleman, ahm deeply honahed that you've come to consult me, but ahh must point out to you at once that the United States does not considah that it has any role whatevah in the internal politics of the great French people. These decisions are yours to decide, it is not mine to criticize or have second thoughts." The French would then do a little French turn of protestation and politeness, and David's frankness would be broken down a bit.

"Well, gentleman, since yah asked what would make the Washington govehnment confident of these great French people's future, ahh will answer you in all frankness. In all frankness, any French govehnment that has Robert Schuman at the Quai D'Orsay, Maurice Petsche at the Finance, and Jean Monnet at the Plan will command the fullest confidence of my govehnment at home." And, indeed, that trio remained at their posts, producing what was in fact a stable French government, while the ridiculous political revolving-door act went on month after month after month.

I would encounter this ever-changing group of bureaucrats and politicians at the home of the finance minister, Maurice Petsche,

who, during my first postwar visit to France, took the fairly flatter-
ing step of holding a luncheon party in my honor. The guests at the
Petsches' lavish apartment included the entire French cabinet, except the other permanent members, Robert Schuman and Jean
Monnet, who rarely had time for lengthy midday meals. The table
was headed by the president of France's provisional government
Georges Bidault. Maurice Petsche was a short, brilliantly intelligent,
odd-looking little man, full of dynamic bounce and fun. He had a
high sense of mischief and a low sense of pomp and self-importance.
I don't know why, but he had taken a liking to me, as had his rather
rich, ample, and effusive wife Suzanne, who was fond mostly of
talking about food.

Our party met in the garden court of the Petsche apartment,
where great quantities of iced vodka, caviar, and buttered toast were
consumed. We then moved to the dining room and went on with
the most delicious meal that I can recall for something on the order
of an hour and three-quarters in addition to the vodka time. I remember only two things about the occasion, and I think it creditable
that I remember so much. None of the ladies was present except
Suzanne Petsche, and she set the ball rolling by asking what on earth
she was going to tell her chef to feed poor Sir Stafford Cripps. Sir
Stafford, at that time, was suffering terribly from the cancer that
eventually killed him. Petsche, who had a great liking for the old
Labour statesman, had loaned him his château outside of Paris for a
period of rest and recuperation, and he had sent a chef and sous-chef
there to cope with the appalling, nearly insoluble problems of feeding a vegetarian.

Mrs. Petsche pointed out that Cripps was a rigorous vegetarian
and said she did not know how on earth she was to strengthen him
by feeding him up, so to say, while he was staying in the country.
The French cabinet addressed this vital problem with extreme solemnity for near a course and a half. I cannot remember what other
solutions were offered, but I do recall that the Gordian knot was
finally cut by Petsche himself. The finance minister had been on a
diet and was eating an enormous steamed truffle, black as tar, large
as an asparagus, and absolutely delicious. Looking up from his plate,
he cried with happy intuition, "Mais Suzanne, il y a toujours les
truffes!" whereupon the cabinet burst into rounds of applause, and it
was agreed that a major truffle dish would be included in all of Sir
Stafford's menus except breakfast.

Suzanne departed lunch with the coffee, whereupon every single French minister dozed off except for Maurice Petsche. I was also
conscious and still sitting upright, and felt as though I were one of

the two last survivors on a stricken field. Lunch adjourned only after Bidault, then president of the Republic, woke up and prodded the rest of his slumbering cabinet into action.

I do not want to make it sound as though the time just after the war was a continuous misplaced version of the duchess of Richmond's ball. However, there is one last episode among the wonderful times I had in those happy days that I cannot resist describing. It was during this time that I became close friends with Duff Cooper and his wife Diana, whom I had last, of course, seen aboard their old little imperial train in Burma. Duff, who was then Britain's ambassador to Paris, was a most remarkable man in his own right, but having known Diana well makes me feel more and more as though I had known Helen of Troy, although Helen must have been a singularly heartless woman, whereas Diana was profoundly learned in her odd way and had a heart as big as the world.

She also had a knack of giving her guests a marvelous time. After our encounter in Burma, we met again through my old friend Bill Patten, with whom I had shared rooms in New York, and his enchanting wife, who would later become my wife, Susan Mary Jay. The occasion was a luncheon at the British embassy in Paris to which I and the Pattens went. This huge greathouse on the rue du Faubourg-St.-Honoré had been either built or redecorated by Maria-Paulette Borghese, Napoléon's sister, who was a luxury-loving woman. When the Duke of Wellington purchased the house shortly after Waterloo, he received all the Borghese furniture, with the result that the modern embassy looked like an early Napoleonic Paris hotel, ravishingly preserved in amber.

It was summer, and the small luncheon party dined near an open window in a bright, breezy room off the main dining hall. President Roosevelt's former adviser Ben Cohen was there, a little out of place but enjoying himself greatly along with Averell Harriman and one or two others. All in all, it was an unmanageable mixture, but Diana managed it perfectly, getting everyone stirred up in a happy manner and enjoying being stirred, too. The grand climax came at the end of lunch, when Duff, who was involved in lengthy and futile negotiations with V. M. Molotov and others, asked the embassy butler to bring another bottle of champagne.

Diana, rather horrified, said, "But darling Duffy, if you have any more champagne you will go straight to sleep the minute you get to the meeting."

To which Duff Cooper replied, "Diana, darling, that is my purpose."

Indeed, I later found out that among the newspapermen covering the ghastly Anglo-Soviet and Franco-American meetings during the summer of 1946, there used to be a pool on the number of minutes and seconds it would take Duff to go to sleep after the meeting began. He always wore enormously high, extremely supportive starched collars so that his head did not loll, and he later boasted to me that he got more useful rest and avoided more boredom through these working siestas than in any way he could remember.

For a reporter, however, no European city during that immediate postwar period offered as much political drama or as much odd otherworldly allure as did Berlin. The city in many ways was a crucible for the great themes of that time, for nowhere on the Continent did the stark outlines of Europe's past and the startling dangers of its immediate future come into sharper focus. Beginning in the summer of 1946, I visited the city for four consecutive years to watch as the infinitely dangerous game of cat and mouse unfolded between the Soviets and the occupying Western powers. By the spring of 1948, it was easy enough to see that something like the Berlin blockade would come about. Stew predicted as much in a column written early that June. And, indeed, within weeks the blockade did come down to be followed shortly by the great Berlin airlift, which I covered in the fall of that year. (The lift would be orchestrated by the same air-force planners who had planned the supply flights over the Hump in China.)

The most memorable visit I paid to postwar Berlin, and the one that had the most profound consequences as it applied to my journalistic life, occurred during my first postwar trip to Europe in August 1946. I had been to Berlin a year earlier on my way back from China with General Chennault. The city, as Chennault and I found it, had been in ruins, full of gutted buildings, piles of blasted rubble, and battalions of inebriated Soviet troops. Strolling down the Kurfürstendamm, marveling not a little at the devastation of Hitler's empire, I had come upon a most bewildering scene. Three Soviet soldiers, obviously very drunk, had commandeered a rattletrap old carriage, probably from the carriage house of some old East Prussian grandee. To this contraption the three men had harnessed a horse and a camel in tandem. The soldiers sat atop the carriage, alternately hooting at and cajoling their ungamely team. In the back of the carriage, piled high in prominent display, were their unlikely spoils: a large load of top-quality German toilet seats.

The scenes I found when I returned to Berlin as a journalist in August 1946, were just as incongruous and only slightly less bizarre. After a day's tour of the city, I filed the following description for publication in a column that appeared on August 26, 1946: "Berlin is a harsh summary of the state of Germany one year later—and a grim lesson in the meaning of defeat in World War II. In outward appearance, as some one has said, it is a city of the moon. The rubble has been neatly stacked. A year's rains have washed off the stains of battle. The endless streets of ruins, which once composed the bustling center of one of the richest cities in the world, now have a sort of cold, impersonal lifelessness which is beyond description. Yet behind this dead facade a kind of life goes on. The people of the city shelter themselves wherever they can find four walls and a roof in patched-up holes and cellars. They have their rations provided by the military governments. They can live and even work. They work for the allies, or in the few industries which have been reestablished, or in the little, miserably furnished shops, squalid nachtlokalen (night clubs) and poverty stricken restaurants in which a kind of parody of the normal metropolitan pattern has been obstinately recreated. The black market men and those who have attached themselves to the Allies have scrambled up above the uniform low level. But for the rest, Berlin is now a large, well managed soup-kitchen."

In contrast, the Americans in Berlin could buy anything that was purchasable with a carton of Camel cigarettes from the PX, although there was very little worth buying in the ruined city. Against this backdrop of general devastation, the life of the American community in the undamaged suburbs, complete with hot dogs, country clubs, Coca-Cola, and Saturday-night hops, seemed unreal. The grand foreign ghetto was called Dahlem. There, it was not easy to find a single major or captain who would not have benefited from a severe diet, just as in the city of Berlin itself it was not easy to find a man or woman who showed no trace of undernourishment.

I spent as much time as I could during that visit at the home of one of the political officers on the occupation staff, a White Russian named Nicolas Nabokov, whom I had met through Chip Bohlen. A musician by trade, Nicolas was a wonderfully eccentric man, very funny, very intelligent, and very noble-minded. We shared a fondness for parties and entertaining, and he gave me a standing invitation to come to his house in one of the grander military sections of the ghetto. Nicolas did this in part because the powerful army females in charge of housing were convinced that he had no right to so large a house, and he believed that as a well-known newspaperman I could help smooth his way with the U.S. military—which, indeed, I managed to do.

Almost daily, a lady in military boots would crump down the path through the front garden in an audibly disciplinary way, and I would be summoned to tell her that Nicolas was, like myself, a personal friend of the deputy chief of the U.S. military command in Berlin, Lucius Clay. In measured and confident tones, I would assure her that if she questioned the general's staff she would find that Mr. Nabokov's duties warranted his present quarters. Meanwhile, whoever was left among those writers, artists, and bohemians of the city who could speak a little English would be gathered upstairs in quiet celebration. I do not remember any of their names except that a young philosopher named Wolfgang Harich, was a regular there, usually in the company of his beautiful Japanese mistress. For some reason—I think to annoy the mistress—Harich had dyed his hair the color of a brass bedstead. Wolfgang was very vocal, very pessimistic, and on the verge of throwing in his lot with the East Germans. Later he did so and was promptly rewarded by being clapped in jail.

The general riot that prevailed at Nicolas's had a serious undertone, however. This was provided mainly by Nicolas himself, who was convinced that the occupation staff in Berlin was riddled with Communists. He kept begging me to raise the subject with General Clay as soon as I was received by him. Our postwar occupation governments were run and managed according to "directives"— policy guidelines—drawn up in advance in Washington. In large measure, too, the occupation staffs, especially in the more civilian-oriented sections, were largely manned by graduates of schools set up during the latter part of the war to train personnel for the tasks of military occupation. For Germany, one of the early guidelines was the "pastoralization" policy, which Secretary of the Treasury Henry Morgenthau, Jr. had persuaded President Roosevelt, then already cruelly overtired, to propose at the Quebec conference. This called, in effect, for the all but complete reduction of populous, industrialized West Germany to the status of a preindustrial agricultural region.

The "pastoralization" decision was shamefully vindictive and foolish, although the emotions that led to the decision were (and are) easily understandable. Naturally, the Soviets sought to dramatize it locally, in occupied Germany, as an example of what the citizens might have in for them under Western rule. It would not have mattered so much, however, if the military government school for Germany, set up in Camp Ritchie, Maryland, had not been deeply penetrated by members of the U.S. Communist party. In Berlin, this, in turn, produced a considerable percentage of "goat pasture" fanatics—American Communists sent from Camp Ritchie to take up positions on the occupation staff. According to Nicolas, this group had used its leverage to influence the appointment of the boards of trustees that then ran German newspapers following their "de-Nazification." Thus, the three great newspapers in the American zone, the *Frankfurter Rundschau,* the *Stuttgarter Zeitung,* and the *Rheinische Zeitung,* were heavily influenced by and in some cases effectively under the control of German Communists. The line these papers took was so extreme, furthermore, that the American newspapermen in Berlin habitually referred to the *Frankfurter Rundschau* as the "Frankfurter Pravda." Nicolas's point was that if General Clay did not move soon to correct these conditions, there would be a public row at home in the United States.

I was shocked by what Nicolas told me, and, as he had urged me to do, I took it up with General Clay as soon as I met with him. A West Point man from Georgia, Lucius Clay was a highly competent and accomplished soldier who a had reputation—unearned, I felt—for arrogance. (Whatever arrogance Clay could muster would come in handy two years later, when he helped to orchestrate the U.S. response to Stalin's blockade of Berlin.) I had letters to the general from Jack McCloy, so we talked with one another almost as friends from the first moment we met. But when I raised the matter of the Communists on the occupation staff and the German Communist control of the press, General Clay said, "I know, Joe. I am told you are a friend of Nicolas Nabokov's, and no doubt you got this from him. I am moving to correct the situation as fast as I can, but I have to go carefully because I have to take into consideration what *PM* will say."

PM was a decidedly left-wing afternoon New York tabloid founded by Marshall Field. To anyone coming straight from the United States like myself, the general's worry about what *PM* might say was inexplicable. The publication had never gained a particle of influence nationwide and had a minuscule circulation even in New York. The general's concern for *PM* was more understandable in Berlin, however, for *PM* was the only American newspaper that reached the city in time to be read with morning coffee by the officers and officials on the occupation staff. There were other U.S. papers available in the quarter, to be sure, but *PM* had a respected place among them, and this was far more than the publication deserved.

General Clay did finally muster the nerve to challenge *PM* and to clear the Communists from his staff. It was an incident and, indeed, a news story of little note. At the time, I wrote a column about the German newspapers. I also wrote a column about a man named Russell Nixon, a deputy in the labor section of Clay's occupation staff who had happily betrayed two German Socialists to members of the German Communist party. The German Socialist parties were, at that point, under considerable pressure to join forces with the Communists, and some went more willingly into this alliance than others. These men had gone to Nixon to express their fears in confidence, thinking that, as an American, he could be trusted. Nixon listened to their tale with apparent concern, showed them the door with repeated assurances of his support, and, as soon as they had gone, handed their names over to the Communists, thereby insuring that the two men knuckled under.

The Nixon incident is as tawdry an act as I can remember in over four decades of reporting. But the general Communist infiltration of the occupation staff would not matter a damn if not for one curious point. The responsibility for these appointments lay, at bottom, with Franklin Roosevelt. But the first occupation commander—indeed, the man who, officially, had allowed these people to handle de-Nazification in such a way that the German Communists gained temporary but rather absolute control of the press and radio in the American zone—was Lucius Clay's predecessor General Dwight D. Eisenhower. I had not yet heard of the young Wisconsin politician Joseph McCarthy. Nor could I imagine a time in Washington when all public servants, up to and including the president of the United States, might be held accountable for even the most obscure oversights in their professional past. So I did not register the import of Eisenhower's small role in this drama until years later, by which time, as I will show in a later chapter, Joe McCarthy had registered it, too.

15

Truman's Washington

(1948–1950)

Had Stew thought to ask him directly, I have no doubt Winston Churchill would have credited President Truman with "staying the course" during his first years in office. However, by the time the presidential campaigns had gotten under way in the early summer of 1948, Harry Truman was being given no credit at all by the American press—including, I regret to say, Stew and myself—or by the American public for the enormous achievements of his first administration. Most of the praise had gone to the great officials of the past like Marshall, Dean Acheson, and Secretary of State Jimmy Byrnes, who stayed on in government after President Roosevelt's death. Indeed, Truman's destined opponent, Governor Thomas E. Dewey of New York, so firmly believed in Truman's foreign and defense policies that he sent a private offer to Jim Forrestal to continue at the head of the newly created Defense Department, should the governor be elected president.

While his low public standing could not have pleased the president, it positively shocked his compatriots in the Democratic party. Indeed, the Democrats were so sure they would be beaten in 1948 that Franklin Delano Roosevelt, Jr., Arthur Schlesinger, Jr., and several other leading intellectual liberals took the fairly bizarre step of getting up a "draft Eisenhower" movement. The Democrats' distress was matched only by the unparalleled smugness of their opponents. At the Republican convention, held in Philadelphia in June, the GOP put on an unusually confident display of cool, mechanical, big-money politics. Dewey and his slender, precise chief of staff Herbert Brownell managed, with a minimum of ruckus, to coopt the right-wing traditionalists of the party, led by Senator Robert Taft of Ohio. Earl Warren, the progressive governor of California and future Supreme Court justice, was named as the vice-presidential candidate, further depriving the Democrats of any chance to exploit isolationist, conservative candidates like Taft or House Speaker Joseph W. Martin, Jr. As for Dewey himself, his record as chief prosecutor for New York County and as governor of the state was impeccable—indeed almost too clean. Coming out of that convention, he and Warren were considered a glittering, nearly unbeatable pair by all of the fashionable Washington prognosticators, including Stew and myself.

Meanwhile the Democrats seemed to be paying far too much attention to the notices their opponents were getting. Perhaps as a result, their own 1948 convention, which was also held in Philadelphia, in July, was one of the outwardly saddest and generally most dank political gatherings I have watched. Precisely because it was so lacking in good humor and good spirits, however, the Philadelphia convention lent itself to memorable pictures, many of them somber and eccentric. The most somber of all of these—and, indeed, the most indicative—took place toward the end of the session, when President Truman was waiting to make his acceptance speech. There had been some delay; the speech was delivered, finally, early in the morning, when most of the nation was fast asleep. Before he took the platform, Stew and I spotted the president. He was wearing a pressed white linen suit and waiting, completely alone, on the freight loading platform at the rear of the convention hall. Truman appeared to be as jaunty as ever, but at long intervals he took a pull on a half bottle of liquid that was in his pocket. The president, I learned later, had a stomach ailment that night, and, in all likelyhood, this was some form of medicine. Stew and I noted the picture but, of course, did not report it. Seeing the president of the United States reduced to such a lonely plight was deeply depressing.

Only days before, Justice William O. Douglas had, in a humiliatingly public way, refused the president's offer to join him on the Democratic ticket. Indeed, the general unenthusiasm for the incumbent had been such that, at one point, a good many of the leaders in his own party had advised Truman not to accept the nomination for fear he might be heckled off the platform. Truman had replied by saying that he was not a quitter, just as he had answered the other leading Democrats months before when they warned him not to run. The speech, when at last he delivered it, was a strangely uplifting affair. For the president finally abandoned the rather stilted, elevated tone that he seemed to have thought suitable to his office and began to rail at his opponents in that high, barking voice of his. Stew and I reported the next day that Truman had begun to campaign "as a county Sheriff in the Ozarks might campaign." This was a good thing, too, although none of us realized it at the time. Harry Truman had finally become himself that night, and this change would have far-reaching consequences—consequences that would become clear only four months later, on the day of the general election.

The principal news to come from that convention, besides Truman's defiant new "Give-'em-hell" style—a style embodied in his decision, taken under Clark Clifford's counsel, to call the hostile "Do nothing" Republican Congress back to Washington for a special legislative session—was the defection of the party's old conservative southern wing. Already, the Left had been battered by the formation of the Progressive party under Roosevelt's vice-president and Truman's former secretary of commerce Henry Wallace. The fashionable wisdom at the time held that with the southern wing of the Democratic party also divided, Truman had no chance. In fact, in the end the southern split achieved exactly the opposite for Truman.

Wallace had declared his presidential ambitions well before the Democratic convention. But in the months leading up to the meeting in Philadelphia, Truman's men had battled fiercely with the southern conservatives in the party, who opposed the inclusion of a civil-rights plank in the party platform. It became an open split at the convention, when a good portion of the Alabama delegation and all of Mississippi's walked out of the convention hall to found the Dixiecrats, who ran the durable Governor Strom Thurmond of South Carolina that year.

The challenge from Henry Wallace was, in its way, just as serious as the one posed by Strom Thurmond and the Dixiecrats. The Democratic party that Truman had inherited from Roosevelt contained a fairly large doctrinaire left wing, including a substantial number of Communist party members and fellow travelers. The tough anti-Soviet foreign policy of Truman and Jimmy Byrnes naturally horrified these people, a horror that had grown from the first hardening over the Soviet invasion of Azerbaijan in the winter of 1946.

Some members of the dissaffected Democratic Left turned to poor Henry Wallace for help. I had known Wallace in China, when, as FDR's vice-president, he had been sent out to Chungking and Kunming to inspect the Stilwell-Chiang tangle. In China, as far as I could tell, Wallace had spent a good deal of his time trying to persuade the Chinese to invest in American tractors, for he was an Iowa man and primarily an agricultural expert. On matters of general political substance, he was less than deft. Indeed, the more I saw of Henry Wallace, both during his famous mission to China and afterward, the more I came to believe that he was a man whose judgment could never be trusted when he strayed more than six feet from a manure pile.

By assiduous flattery, the radical American Left had persuaded Wallace to become the Truman administration's leading pro-Soviet figure. In that capacity, the former vice-president made speeches bitterly and openly criticizing U.S. initiatives abroad. In September 1946, Wallace took a draft of the last and worst of these speeches to the White House and effectively cleared it with Truman—which shows that Truman hoped to go into the 1948 election with the party's left wing still behind him. When delivered by Wallace at Madison Square Garden in New York, however, the speech provoked Secretary Byrnes to confront Truman with a naked ultimatum. It was simple: if the president did not show Wallace the door, Truman would lose his secretary of state and Byrnes would explain his reasons for leaving publicly to the press and suggest that Truman was giving way to the extreme Left.

I do not suppose President Truman enjoyed being confronted with such an ultimatum (people rarely enjoy ultimatums). Nevertheless, he acted with dispatch and quickly showed Wallace the door, probably because he thought this the least bad alternative. It turned out to be the cruelest blow Truman could possibly strike at Dewey, who had counted on being able to talk at length during his campaign about the infestation of the Democratic camp with members of the extreme Left. With Wallace gone and even setting up his silly third party, Dewey had nothing to talk about (for he believed, by and large, in the government's initiatives overseas) except the beauties of motherhood and the horrors of the man-eating shark.

Truman, meanwhile, managed to seize the center, which has always been the key to American politics, and, having seized the center, he stood upon it and crowed. The Republicans that year gave the voter no real reason to support them save for Dewey's glittering exterior and what they claimed was Truman's incompetence. In the final analysis, for all of Dewey's polish, he was not the sort of political leader to arouse personal fervor or affection among his followers. He was against sin and for virtue, against waste and for economy, against hunger and for plenty, and so on ad infinitum. But on any major problem of special policy, to forecast Dewey's solution was to wander through the realms of misty speculation.

Sad to remember although Stew and I reported all this, it in no way changed our conviction that President Truman had no chance of victory. In advance, the election of 1948 was judged to be the dullest in modern memory. Those of us whose business it was to speculate on such things were so dead sure of the outcome that, by mid-October, we had stopped paying attention. Indeed, by that time, Stew and I were regularly referring to the Republican candidate as "President Dewey" in our columns. For our readers on the day of the election, we solemnly predicted a Republican victory and fretted about how the country might survive the final weeks of Harry Truman's presidency.

My brother and I took little comfort in not being the only journalists that day to pre-elect Tom Dewey president. After the magnitude of Truman's victory had become clear, we made a joke of our mistake in the next day's column, hoping that a bungle of such proportions would be remembered in a good-natured way. This happily contrite column (in it we discussed the pleasures of eating crow) had its desired effect, although we learned two things from our mistake: never predict an election without a prearranged escape route; and never pay attention to the received wisdom of the day, for it is almost always wrong. Thankfully, our franchise as columnists did not suffer from the disaster. Within weeks, I was off to Berlin to report on the progress of the airlift there, leaving Stew to shore up the column's good name in Washington.

To his credit, President Truman did little gloating over his surprise victory. But I suspect that, with the exception of General Marshall and Dean Acheson, he could not wait to get rid of the Roosevelt leftovers from his first term, now that he had been elected in his own right. James Forrestal, of course, also stayed on; he had been named the country's first secretary of defense when the various departments of war were unified under that broad rubric early in 1948. But the president never fully trusted Jim, and when Forrestal was dismissed in the first months of the new administration, the choice of the former West Virginia lawyer and American Legion chief Louis Johnson as his successor exposed Truman as a relatively weak judge of character when left to himself.

Jim Forrestal once called himself "a victim of the Washington scene," and I suppose he was, for Jim was a man of zealous and, in the end, desperate dedication. To understand what finally broke Forrestal and drove him to his tragic suicide in May 1949, one must go back to 1948, his first full year as head of the new "national military establishment." When it was first created, the office of secretary of defense was a much less powerful post than it is today. Although effectively under one roof, the various branches of the military still coveted, and in many ways flaunted, their independence. Under the letter of the National Security Act, the army, navy, and air force were permitted to contrive their own budgets, which they did in an open and unrestrained spirit of competition. Officially, these demands were submitted to the secretary as recommendations. The services were under no obligation to trim or prune the budgets to a realistic level.

One cannot understand the fiscal mentality of the old military unless one realizes that, for over a century, the U.S. armed services had a pattern of growth not unlike that of a desert plant. Time and again during peacetime, American armed forces died down to a withered nub, like a desert plant in the dry season. Then, when a new national danger arrived, like rain to the desert, there arose a new and extraordinarily lush growth in armaments. During the course of this blossoming, the military, like the plant, rapidly scattered seed. With luck, some of this seed took root and survived the next dry season, to flower when the rains came again. This curious pattern of regeneration would end with the Korean War, when it became obvious that U.S. military preparedness was of constant and global concern. But in the interim after the second war, this odd pattern remained ingrained in the American military mind.

In spring 1948, the budgets Forrestal received from the three services totaled $28 billion, still a vast sum by the standards of those days. Jim was well aware that he would have no chance of getting these numbers past the White House (Truman had set a $15-billion ceiling for spending on defense), let alone through Congress. Just as surely, he was convinced that the threat posed by the Soviets (the Czechoslovakian leader Jan Masaryk had fallen to his death under wholly suspicious circumstances in March of that year during Stalin's effective takeover of the country) demanded a higher degree of military readiness than was being acknowledged. The Joint Chiefs of Staff—a group who, in my opinion, cannot be matched for arrogance when the wind is blowing their way or for a quality of abject ass kissing when it is not—refused to moderate their demands. Looking to the White House for guidance, Forrestal requested a clear blueprint for the country's security needs. President Truman refused this request, telling Jim to get on with his business.

I will never forget that summer of 1948, for I greatly admired Jim and often would meet him for dinner after his long hours of work at the extravagant new Pentagon headquarters building in Virginia. We had been introduced first through mutual family connections in Middletown, but I got to know him and his wife Josephine just before the war, when Jim went to work for Colonel Frank Knox at the Navy Department. I gathered that Jim and his wife's private life together was not a happy one, for he had his darkly intense side, while she drank a good deal and could be very cutting. But in public, they made a lively, kinetic couple, and we saw a good deal of one another in those early days, when the members of the "Win the War" group were first beginning to raise their voices around Washington. Intellectually, Forrestal was the equal of any in that group. He had the courage, certainly, of a Dean Acheson, yet could be as subtle and sardonic as Bob Lovett. I would learn, too, that he was as moody in his way as George Kennan, although in a far more active and obviously destructive manner.

In those days, the old service budgets were enormously detailed and badly organized. Forrestal had to pore over the lists line by line, taking into account everything from outlays for old soldiers' homes to the cost of the latest generation of high-performance air-force bomber. He did this while carrying on the other duties of the secretary of defense, which meant that a normal working day lasted nearly eighteen hours. Between fits of feverish work, he would occasionally find time to meet me for a late supper. One could see that Jim was desperately tired. I have always believed that this prolonged period of intense overwork and its sequel pushed him over the edge. For in the end, President Truman turned the budget down, and months later, in March 1949, he personally dismissed Jim in a brusque, almost cruel manner.

Forrestal's replacement was Louis Johnson, a man who was as self-serving and unscrupulous as his predecessor had been dedicated. I remembered Johnson as a large, bluff, falsely genial man who had worked under Harry Woodring at the old War Department before serving as chief of the American Legion. Johnson had come to Truman's aid as treasurer for the 1948 campaign after a series of others had turned the position down. This act, combined with the fact that he raised large sums for the campaign in a short period of time, quite naturally earned him the president's gratitude. Johnson was, however, a practiced liar, without a scruple I was able to discover. He intended to use his office as secretary of defense to lay the groundwork for a bid for the presidency itself and the return of the country to what President Harding had called "normalcy," symbolized by enormous cuts in military manpower and investments to their ridiculous prewar levels.

Unlike Jim Forrestal, who was desperately wary of the Soviet threat, Johnson was only too willing to accede to President Truman's general wishes for a large cut in defense. Johnson's call, essentially, was for a balanced defense budget. Indeed, it is easy to forget, since Louis Johnson was luridly close to being a truly evil man, that the Johnson program was also the Truman defense program. Dean Acheson, when he became secretary of state in January 1949, was plainly aware that defense investments were to be cut to the bone, but he was still able in those early days to pin his faith on the American "nuclear monopoly," which was recognized as both real and enormously significant. It was further believed, at the very highest levels, that our monopoly would be long-enduring because the Soviets were little more than ignorant muzhiks, unlikely to achieve as complex an engineering-industrial feat as building a nuclear weapon.

My own views had long been fixed through lengthy social debates with George Kennan, Chip Bohlen, and others. These talks could become quite animated, and often I would follow them the next morning with a letter, occasionally apologetic in tone, reiterating my stand of the evening before. To me, it seemed logical that the Soviets, who believed that a remorseless historical process was doing their expansionist work for them, were not planning an outright attack. On the other hand, I could not help but feel that if a day came when the Kremlin felt it had a wide superiority in military strength, Stalin, based on his recent behavior, would be unable to resist giving the historical process a good, sharp nudge—that, in short, the Kremlin would be tempted to undertake the kind of international bullying that ultimately could only be resisted by force.

Imagine our horror, then—and it was a horror shared by all of official Washington—when news of the first Soviet nuclear test was announced in September 1949. When I recently reread the columns we wrote on the news of the Soviet bomb test, I found the tone too shrill. The announcement of the test had filled both Stew and me with a sense of doom that only deepened during that winter and spring of 1950. In February, we began criticizing the secretary of defense and his policies. Our stance culminated in a series of columns published under the headline "Mr. Johnson's Untruths," the word "untruths" having been decorously substituted for the word "Lies" at the urging of the *New York Herald Tribune*'s lawyers.

Using the detailed, unspeakably boring line budgets submitted by the Pentagon to Congress, we reported Johnson's heavy cutbacks in air-force wings, navy sea-and-air units, and marine divisions. What we reported put the lie to his repeated claim that he was "cutting defense fat without cutting muscle." Johnson, who at the beginning of his tenure as secretary of defense had offered us use of a direct line to his Pentagon office, reacted to our attacks by spreading a story that Stew and I had turned against him because we were not allowed the same confidential access given to us by James Forrestal, adding further that the source of our information was none other than his formidable enemy Dean Acheson. This was an absurd claim. In fact, Dean and I were not then on speaking terms.

I had known Dean Acheson from Middletown—where his father presided, rather conspicuously, as bishop of Connecticut—and later, before the war, when he first made a name in Washington as an anti-Roosevelt lawyer with a handsome wife. Dean had been made to go to Groton School because my father and uncles had gone there, a fact I do not think he held against me, although he was never happy at school. I have always thought that, secretly, Dean would have liked to be one of those old-fashioned dashing, imitation-British fellows so prevalent during his time at Groton. Initially, however, he lacked the money to support such habits. Thankfully for us all, he chose the public life, where he retained some aggressively Anglophile traits, including, to my dismay, very strong imitation-English views about secrecy.

Dean had a largely imaginary, idealized picture of expert Foreign Office officials placidly treading their way through the intricacies of British diplomacy behind the tough screen of Britain's official secrets act. As secretary of state, he held firm to this principle of "no newsies" and made it clear that Stew and I were to shrink into the social and professional woodwork until his public life had ended. Having seen a great deal of Dean and Alice prior to his ascendancy, I thought his attitude arrogant and a little insulting, and by the time the columns on Johnson appeared, Dean and I were no longer speaking.

The facts that so bothered Louis Johnson came not from Acheson, but from the comptroller of the Pentagon, a very pleasant man named William McNeil, whom I used to visit regularly with questions on various components of the published budget and their effect, in practical terms, on army training time, equipment for specific divisions, and so on. Johnson also suspected his own subordinate, Secretary of the Air Force Stuart Symington, of traitorous tendencies with regard to the press and once righteously ambushed my brother Stewart when he was on a rare visit to Symington's Pentagon office.

According to Stew, Johnson closed Symington's corridor office door behind him and loomed up like the Commandant in *Don Giovanni*. Johnson, who was a large and physically intimidating man, said nothing and began slowly to nod his huge bald head up and down with a virtuously accusatory air. The unhappy silence was at last broken when Symington attempted an introduction, at which point Johnson, pronouncing the hated name loud and clear, cried, "I know Mr. Alsop!" A second accusatory silence followed before, at long last, the secretary of defense turned slowly on his heel and left the room.

Like many in the government, Johnson had a remarkably simplistic view of what is now referred to as a "leak" by reporters and officials alike. In high-level reporting, it is almost always wrong to talk about "leaks" unless the leaker in question is being blackmailed by the reporter, something I suspect has happened more than once during my working lifetime. The best way for a sensible reporter to secure new and important information is to know his topic as well as it can be known without his having read classified papers. The way, then, to attain what everyone calls "a leak" is to pick up two in one place, to see the ghost of another two in another place, and then to recognize, "By God, two and two equal four." In order to do this, however, one must be able to recognize two as well as to surmise that lurking beneath mounds of paper and doubletalk there may, indeed, be such a thing as four. Invariably, a so-called "leak" is more a corroboration than a statement of fact, and, as such, it involves very little magic and a good deal of hard work.

It was said, after the outbreak of the Korean War had exposed the secretary of defense's policies for what they were, that the Alsops "got Louis Johnson." This was nonsense. The facts got Louis Johnson; we aired them publicly, painting him in harsh colors as the great disarmer, so that when events caught up with the real dangers inherent in his defense program, as they would that summer when fighting broke out in Korea, he could not survive. Our sole boast is that we persisted in publishing these facts because we thought they were important, although readers and editors were bored by our persistence and the column's circulation dragged badly.

We got little encouragement from official Washington. But we learned enough to know that the administration was being torn to bits by a fearful subterranean struggle between Johnson and Dean Acheson over defense appropriations. The two men nearly came to blows during a now-infamous briefing at the State Department over a document authorized by Dean advocating increased military spending and known obliquely as NSC-68. Until this time, Dean had gone along with Johnson's disarmament plan, but the news that the Soviets had the bomb had changed his views.

In the early months of 1950, Dean ordered Paul Nitze and his colleagues on the State Department's Policy Planning Staff to write NSC-68 in order to sway high government policy (much in the manner of Kennan's Long Telegram) toward a vastly greater outlay in defense spending. The paper advocated spending between $40 billion and $50 billion to counter the Soviet threat, which was described as not just local—meaning Europe—but global in nature. To diffuse potential trouble with Johnson, whom Acheson and Nitze knew would be violently opposed to the proposal, a briefing for the secretary was held in late March. According to legend, Johnson, who had brought the Joint Chiefs of Staff with him to the meeting, sat stonily listening to Nitze's presentation for a minute or two. Suddenly, he burst up from his chair and began berating both men for attempting to circumvent administration policy. His fury grew so intense that he finally stalked from the room, the Joint Chiefs numbly in tow, as Nitze and Acheson looked on in shocked amazement.

One can imagine that Dean's Anglo sensibilities were deeply disturbed by Johnson's attack, and, indeed, he later let it be known that he thought Johnson mad. But at the time, the incident had highly disturbing implications concerning the direction and fate of President Truman's national defense policy.

I can still remember talking one evening to Paul Nitze shortly after I learned about the existence of NSC-68. Aware that the tough principles outlined in the paper had been passed on to President Truman, I said to Paul, "Well, now at least the decision has been made to try and get on a sensible footing, and the outlook is a little better."

To this Paul replied, "The outlook is not any better, Joe. If anything it's worse." In those days, there was no use fussing with Paul Nitze for details. So one stored up what he said and looked elsewhere for explanation, and even then Paul was very gnomic—it was easy to misinterpret what he said.

Nitze's general gloom and apprehension was surprisingly confirmed that spring by the new British prime minister Clement Attlee, whose Labour party had succeeded in ousting Churchill's government in 1945. When interviewing men of Attlee's stature and responsibilities, I made it a rule—provided they deigned to see me at all—of boiling down, to the best of my ability, everything I wanted to know to three questions.

The British prime minister had received me twice before in the long cabinet room at 10 Downing Street, and each visit had followed the same curious pattern. Seated in the prime minister's chair under the imposing portrait of Sir Robert Walpole, Lord Attlee would greet me with elaborate politeness and then lean back as though to indicate he was ready for questions, all the while smoking his pipe so fiercely that loud, gurgling noises were emitted from time to time. The first question would be asked, the pipe would be removed from the clenched jaws just long enough to permit the word "Quite" to pass the prime minister's lips before the jaws clenched shut again and the gurgling continued through the next, more-nervously-stated question. This process generally left the conversation rather flat and not much further forward. And after the prescribed number of polite mumblings, I would say, "Prime Minister, I think I have asked you the questions I wanted to get answers to. I have to thank you for giving me this time," and we would mutter our good-byes.

On that spring morning, not long before the attack in Korea, the same dialogue was repeated three times over. But the fourth time, being preoccupied with the issue, I used the phrase "Western defense" in a question, and the result was like bursting the bung out of a barrel. Out flew the pipe for good and all, and the prime minister launched into an eloquent, closely informed discussion of Western defense and its weaknesses, the risks the latter created, the remedies that should be applied, and the need for America "to give a lead" because Britain, with her strained finances, could not give "the lead I'd like to give." Before very long, the young men who generally order the public lives of high officials began hovering about the door of the cabinet room, hoping to move Mr. Attlee on to his next appointment, only to be waved away by a prime minister too absorbed in his subject to worry about his next meeting.

From my own perspective, the drama leading to Korea came to a head at my house (I had moved, following the war, into a large, fairly eccentric house that I had, with infinite trouble, designed myself; it was on the same 2700 block of Dumbarton Avenue) on a beautiful early summer evening in June 1950, shortly after I had returned from Europe. Several days before, I had spent two hours in my Dumbarton office with George Kennan. George wanted to explain to me his reasons for leaving the State Department, a decision that he had made some time earlier but that was to become effective that month. I knew then, in very crude terms, that Kennan, in his capacity as head of the Policy Planning Staff at State, had sent out a circular memo, a kind of questionnaire, to U.S. troop commanders overseas asking, very roughly, where a Soviet attack might occur should Stalin try to push forward a satellite army. The answers had come back saying an attack might occur just about anywhere, the most likely spot being Yugoslavia and the least likely, thanks to General MacArthur's lordly intelligence services, Korea.

George was an emotional man and not above self-pity. Often, his moods were linked to his status at the department, real or imagined, or to the seriousness or lack thereof with which he felt his views were being received. On this particular afternoon, his pity took the form of a long, gloomy monologue on the perishable nature of democracy and the hopelessness of coherent policy making in the face of the country's confused and conflicting political demands. George was, in those days, an unashamed elitist who thought the proper course for national action was best charted by a select and knowledgeable group—preferably including himself—free from the noisy deliberations of the masses.

Although I was naturally expected to affirm George's view, I instead asked him and his wife Annelise to a dinner I was giving that Saturday evening for Mike Handler of the *New York Times,* an invitation that was declined but that effectively blunted further disquisitions on "terrible rancid democracy."

Among the other guests that evening were Justice Frankfurter; my old adversary from China, John Davies; Dean Rusk, then assistant secretary of state for Far Eastern affairs; John McCone, under secretary of the air force; and Frank Pace, officially secretary of the army but that night in effect the acting secretary of defense since Louis Johnson, like Dean Acheson, was out of Washington for the weekend. Altogether, there were about twenty of us—a large party for me—and I remember we had finished a very jolly dinner and were engaged in lively discussion out on the garden terrace, when my Filipino butler Jose announced a telephone call for "Mr. Rush."

(I had hired Jose from a Washington taxicab in 1946, and he and his wife Maria would stay with me until Jose's death shortly after President Kennedy's inauguration. In time, they became well-known figures in my little Washington world. Jose, in particular, gained a reputation for such kindness and competence that several of my regular guests, including Jackie Kennedy, sometimes seemed more preoccupied with his welfare over the course of a dinner than that of my other guests. Although he took pride in his abstemious ways, Jose's singular failing, aside from a very light head, was the habit of drinking the heeltaps left in the wineglasses after dinner. He had indulged this habit to excess on the evening of Mike Handler's party, when, bowlegged with drink, he came tottering out of the dining room with news of this curious call.)

Being identified as the probable callee, Dean Rusk went indoors to the telephone, which, in the garden room of my old house, was visible from the terrace. As Dean listened to the call, I saw his face turn the color of an old-fashioned white bed sheet. Frank Pace and John McCone were summoned to the phone in a rather stricken manner, where they, too, promptly turned ashen-faced. Speaking for the three, Dean Rusk asked me to make their apologies to the ladies. There had been a rather serious, as he put it, "border incident" in Korea, and he and Pace would have to go down to the State Department to see what was what. McCone ran off to the Pentagon, likely to call some sort of an alert, and we stragglers gathered at the end of the garden to speculate over what the news might be.

I never thought it the journalist's prerogative to gloat over gloomy predictions come true. God knows I have been wrong enough times during thirty-seven years of reporting to avoid the habit. I suppose, too, that if a columnist keens long and loudly enough, bad news will be bound to come his way. Certainly, on that evening, I never imagined that war had broken out on the Korean peninsula. When the news did come, Stew and I felt vindicated on a basic level, for we had hammered so long at the evils of Louis Johnson, the need for a strong defense and the danger of a war coming from this state of military disarray, that our professional reputations had begun to be impugned. When the North Korean attack confirmed our worst worries, we were only glad in the knowledge, as Dean Acheson was and Jim Forrestal surely would have been had he lived, that Harry Truman, so challenged, would fight back with every available ounce of firepower at his disposal.

Several days later, many of the same people who had been at my house on the evening of the Korean attack were gathered to celebrate the twenty-fifth wedding anniversary of Dolly and Bob Hooker, a diplomatic couple with many friends in Washington. In the interim, U.S. naval and air forces sent to the peninsula had quickly lost ground to the North Korean onslaught. Given the severity of the situation, most of us felt that President Truman's decision to commit General MacArthur's occupation forces from Japan was imminent. I happened to arrive outside the Hookers' the same moment as George and Annelise Kennan did. Although he regards himself as a total contemplative, I have always observed that George makes his best sense as a man of action, when there is a good, loud cable machine at his elbow clacking out horrible problems all over the world. When George broods, he becomes a little silly.

On this day, the cable machine had been clacking madly, and George was dancing on air because MacArthur's men were being mobilized for combat under the auspices of the United Nations. He was carrying his balalaika, a Russian instrument he used to play with some skill at social gatherings, and with a great, vigorous swing, he clapped me on the back with it, nearly striking me to the sidewalk.

"Well, Joe," he cried, "what do you think of the democracies now?"

No matter how well intended, it is never pleasant being knocked about, and I replied quite crossly, "I think about democracy exactly what I always have, but not what you thought when you came to see me."

With that, we all three proceeded into the Hookers' party, which was a wonderful success. Three days later, on Friday, June 30, 1950, President Truman instructed MacArthur to begin an attack on the North Korean forces, by then well south of Seoul. Two weeks later, I was crossing the Pacific for what would be my first taste of a real shooting war.

16

In Korea

(July–October 1950)

"A good war" is not a phrase that carries much currency today, and I am alone and, I suppose, somewhat guilty in feeling nostalgic about a time when it did. My father and, indeed, both my brothers held to the notion that when their country was at war, gentlemen tried their best to go out and shoot at the enemy, a process that generally entailed some risk. Johnny, Stew, and I had all enlisted well before Pearl Harbor. Like myself, brother John suffered from some form of high blood pressure and had to appeal his draft classification thirteen times just to make it into the military police. After a short time with the MPs, as I have said, he joined the OSS and parachuted behind enemy lines to join the French Resistance. Stew made one jump—alone, as it turned out—into occupied France, and Johnny traveled on to a disputed part of China's Kwangtung province, where his small guerrilla group had to fight both the Japanese and the Communists.

I never boasted about my war, and the truth is I envied Stew and Johnny their fighting experience, no matter how disagreeable it may have been. I had joined Colonel Chennault because staff work with the Flying Tigers was nearer to being in combat than dining out in Bombay. Other than my ludicrous introduction to firearms in Manila, the only time I came near real military trouble in the second war was when the Japanese sent a night-equipped single plane to strafe our landing strip in Kunming. Alerted by his air warning system, General Chennault, as was his nature, drove out to the airfield in an open Jeep and rode up and down the runway, peering into the black sky for a look at this new enemy weapon. As we were making our curious tour, two large bangs sounded off to our side, sole evidence, as it turned out, of the Japanese attack and my sole experience, until Korea, of enemy fire.

When the fighting broke out in Korea, I felt very strongly that this infantry war should be covered in our column. However, Stew had had his share of combat and was now responsible for a beautiful wife and the beginning of a family of six children. So I decided to go myself and, in a queer way, looked forward to doing so. The necessary preparations were made: transport was arranged; khakis and notepads were packed along with reading matter suitable in length and theme for the hours of travel as well as the hours of nervous waiting, which I knew, from secondhand, were so much a part of war.

I flew out in late July 1950, only weeks after the first North Korean attack. With all the busyness of preparation done and out of my mind, the full weight of my predicament—the fact that I was going to Korea, with no experience and no training, for a shooting infantry war—finally hit me and came close to reducing me to a quaking wreck. Fortunately, on my plane going to the peninsula via Tokyo was the great *Life* magazine combat photographer Carl Mydans. I was gloomy about the battle's outcome and, on a far more basic level, desperately preoccupied with the dual terror of doing my job in erratic and unfamiliar circumstances while facing gunfire and, quite possibly, death.

I have never known a case of real physical cowardice that did not show through to the naked eye, and I fear I was no exception. Sensing my apprehension, Carl listened patiently to my nervous chatter, and when we landed within the Pusan Perimeter, the very small territory the U.S. and South Korean troops then held, he kindly let me attach myself to him like a limpet.

Carl held my hand with great kindness until we reached Taegu, the grey little town, fifty-six miles inland from Pusan, which served as provisional capital of South Korea and headquarters for the American field commander, Lieutenant General Walton H. Walker. The world press was also congregated there in a small makeshift hostel. From my days on the *Tribune,* I already knew two of the luminaries there. Marguerite Higgins I had last seen in Berlin, where, at age twenty-six, she had taken over the paper's local bureau. Among journalists in the occupied quarter, Marguerite had a reputation as a ferociously combative and competitive reporter with a special social fondness for highly placed generals. She was a pretty woman in a popular sort of way but scruffy around the edges. Her fingernails were always dirty, and she suffered from a chronic eye condition that gave her eyelids a pinkish, irritated look. But she had always been kind to me, and despite the hostile reports I had heard from her male competitors, I was glad to see her in Taegu.

Marguerite was by then in a celebrated and bitter competition with her colleague on the *Tribune*, Homer Bigart. Homer was widely known then—and, indeed, now—as the best combat reporter of his day. He had been a copyboy at the paper when I arrived in 1932, but we had only known one another from a distance. Because he had a stutter, Homer was able to cultivate a self-effacing manner, although at heart he was a Vermonter with the tough, hard-bitten core of a far-northern Yankee and no doubt thought of me as a cosseted child of privilege—which, of course, I was. For my part, I had always admired Homer Bigart's work enormously, while thinking him a curious but brilliantly competent man.

As the *Tribune*'s bureau chief in Tokyo when the Korean War broke out, Marguerite covered a good deal of the early fighting on her own. But Homer had won his title as the *Tribune*'s reigning combat correspondent in repeated action in the Pacific during World War II, and he was naturally protective of it. When U.S. troops went into the thick of the fighting in Korea, Homer was sent out by the *Tribune*'s editors ostensibly to replace Higgins. But Marguerite knew the value of the story and refused to be budged. So this very odd pair spent a measure of the war chasing up and down the front, each taking the most hair-raising risks in an attempt to undo or unseat the other. The end result would be some startlingly good reporting, especially from Homer.

Later on, when I became as acclimated to war as one could, I would fly out to U.S. Army headquarters in Tokyo to file my columns. I remember one trip in particular, right before the Inchon landing in early September. There was heavy fighting around the defensive perimeter of the U.S. and ROK (Republic of Korea) forces. As the action developed, I was startled to see MacArthur's staff officers running into the press room and ripping the takes of Homer's file from the telex as they came clattering in over the wire. Homer, it turned out, was their quickest and most reliable source of information as to what was happening along the front. I never told him about it, and I doubt that he would have been flattered, but to this day I have never seen a greater testament to any reporter's skill in the field.

I never hoped to match Homer Bigart. Indeed, his presence at Taegu exaggerated my growing fear that I would be unable to cover the war properly. Nor was I greatly comforted when the only close friend I found in Taegu, Ian Morrison, correspondent for the London *Times* and an acquaintance from my travels in Europe, was killed on a trip to the front not long after our Taegu reunion. Unknown to me then, Ian was carrying on a torrid affiar with the now-mercifully-forgotten Eurasian writer Han Suyin, who was in Hong Kong and already becoming a worshipful Maoist. In her book *Love Is a Many Splendored Thing*, she chose to publish Ian's last letter to her. In it, I appear, not so inaccurately, as a harried member of the combat press corps, clutching the Oxford pocket edition of Thucydides I had chosen for Korea reading, clearly despondent about the future.

The news was exceedingly gloomy during those first days of the Korean War. The initial American military problem was, of course, to keep from getting pushed into the sea by the North Korean invaders. The early fighting consisted mainly of desperate, improvised defensive actions by exhausted and overdriven American and South Korean troops. In early July, the Twenty-fourth Infantry Division of General Walker's Eighth Army attempted to engage the North Koreans along the line. This turned out to be a great mistake. In his usual grand manner, MacArthur had vastly underrated the invaders' tenacity and firepower. Our ill-equipped, ill-trained troops were no match for the latest Soviet T-34 tanks. In two weeks of bitter and confused fighting, Walker's men, along with what remained of the South Korean forces, were pushed pell-mell back toward the southeastern corner of the country. By July 23, roughly half of the 16,000 U.S. troops put into combat were either dead, wounded, or in enemy hands. Six days later, Walker himself issued a widely publicized statement, commanding the Eighth Army to retreat no farther, and his soldiers held.

By the time Mydans and I landed in Taegu, Walker's "stand or die" line stretched some 150 miles in an elongated L—from the southernmost coast of the Korean peninsula to the east coast. The front itself started 25 miles due west of the port city Pusan and ran north up the Naktong River for 100 miles before bending east through the mountains toward a town called Yongdok, not far from the Sea of Japan. Early in August, with U.S. reinforcements still trickling in from Japan and Hawaii, the North Koreans sought to blast their way through the Pusan Perimeter in a series of savage armored attacks. All of these were beaten back, although some of the battles along the Naktong River had come perilously close to going the other way.

Morale among Walker's men was not high. In spite of their brave stand, they were a defeated, downcast group, ill trained and ill prepared for combat. Tales of their running in the face of the enemy, called "bugout fever," did little to dispel my fears, and so I had not gone out to the front on the day Ian died or on the day after that. On August 1, however, word came to the press that Walker was moving one of his divisions, the Twenty-fifth, down to the southwest corner of the perimeter.

Later, I would learn that our military intelligence service had already broken the North Korean codes. Walker knew that the invaders had split their main attacking force in half. Aware that Taegu was now no longer vulnerable to direct attack, he decided to deploy the Twenty-fifth. Its objective: to open some breathing space in the far southwestern part of the perimeter, then the most vulnerable of our defensive flanks. The front there was only a little more than 20 miles from the port of Pusan itself, which was of vital importance as the entry point for all American military supplies. I decided to go along.

Military historians would later hail Walker's maneuver as one of the most inspired of that early stage of war. But to my inexperienced eye, the trek seemed muddled and interminable. We moved out from Taegu by convoy late on the night of August 1—line after line of transports, tanks, and mobile guns, all crawling in pitch darkness over narrow mountain roads, past deep precipices. In the jolting trucks, the mood seemed at once tense and exhausted, for almost all the men were too young to have experienced combat and—such was the haste of preparation—very few had had much sleep in the last few days.

By dawn, we had reached our objective at the southern front. I still retain a vivid picture of the battlefield along the southwest Korean coast. It looked curiously like a mixture of the coast of Maine and a Chinese romantic landscape. There were precipitous, pine-clad mountain slopes, luminous blue bays among green cliffs, and narrow, terraced valleys, where thatched mud villages seemed to grow from the brilliant-green rice paddies. In all, it seemed to me that the irregular topography of rocks and crags made this land far better country to look at than to fight over. But I said little and milled about on my own with the rest of the force, trying to get my bearings as the morning heat set in.

Somehow I became entangled with the Fifth Regimental Combat Team (an RCT was a self-contained force of three infantry battalions with its own tanks and artillery). This green and uncertainly led outfit had been given the mean task of occupying the crest of a sugarloaf-shaped mountain that commanded the route of advance along the two roads that traversed the coast toward a village called Chinju. The Fifth RCT was to spearhead this push and had not gone far toward its objective before our offensive posture became decidedly defensive. We were pinned under a furious North Korean counterattack and so spent the day in the rear shelter of our stony, sugarloafed hill, whose crest we had so nobly set out to occupy.

For me, it was not an encouraging introduction to combat. We were led into battle by an empty-headed, formerly handsome man who, at some point or other during his military career, had been given the rank of colonel. His orders were vague and his command of the men haphazard, although at that point in my own military career I had no way of knowing this. Our little group milled about in a dispirited way for much of the morning until we were at last brought under fire. At this point, the colonel and his aide, both of whom seemed to possess the only shovels in the outfit, marked off for themselves the only soft ground in the immediate neighborhood of our rocky cover and began to dig like moles. As the shells fell about us, they continued to dig until their foxholes were big enough to make them all but invisible.

So abandoned, the rest of us huddled fitfully on our exposed rock, listening for incoming mortar shells and doing our best to watch as the fight for the hill unfolded. Communications broke down repeatedly, but at intervals the telephone brought news of one company cut off, another halted, another threatened by infiltration on its flank. To the inexperienced observer, the battle seemed wholly composed of isolated scenes and incidents: an infantry company clambering up a naked mountainside, while smoke from our shell fire plumed upward from the enemy lodgment on the crest; a huge tank turning slightly aside to let pass a medic's Jeep-load of wounded; a worried knot of truck drivers consulting while sniper fire snicked the bushes by the roadside.

The battle lasted on into the night. I was exhausted but slept very little. For what seemed hours, I lay in the dark, waiting for some sign to move on or out, praying for the banging to stop and for the shells to fall somewhere far away.

The truth is, I had never been so frightened before in that sort of way. I had been a fat child, both physically incompetent and timid. Physical timidity is much more important in the makeup of character than people suppose, for cowardice spoils most other human attributes in the same way courage adds to them. I have always observed that courage in and of itself is not a particularly attractive personal quality, but that its absence, like the absence of salt in cookery, can be devastating in its total effect. Every major gain in my life, from adolescence on, has involved the conquering of some childish fear—whether of horses or people or unruly explosions—and in each case, the remedy has been direct experience.

It may have been peculiar to the times in which I grew up or to the profession I chose, but the older I become and the more I see of the new world in which we live, the more I cherish my memories of being unceremoniously packed off to Groton, of being hurled into jobs without preparation, of going off to war and being, in stages, imprisoned and then released to return to China. The truth is, the members of my generation enjoyed a range of experience altogether remarkable by the standards of today. The Korean War would be the final episode in a long series that convinced me that true value in life comes from facing head on whatever experience one's life brings along. For me, these were liberating episodes in the sense that I found out about myself and, with each new discovery, could cross off the list one more damn thing it was foolish to be afraid of.

My fear that night was a sheer and unadulterated physical terror. It was a residue of my awkward youth—a terror not of death, but of pain and unpleasant bruises, not unlike (ludicrous as it may seem) the fear of getting on an unruly horse. Nor did the terror end after the shelling had stopped and the heights above Chinju been taken. The next morning, a ranking officer appeared and broke our unhappy colonel on the spot for failing to answer repeated calls to his command position. We later learned that the man had been broken once before under similar circumstances during the second war. Those early crimes had been forgotten, and, apparently, he was a very agreeable officer who knew how to suck up to command, for, in a supreme example of peacetime decay in the armed forces, he had been made colonel again. For some unimaginable reason, he had also been given command of a combat team, which, to my mind, seemed both an incompetent and wicked thing to do.

That first taste of fire shook me a great deal. When I got back to Taegu, I was still shaken. So, in line with my motto of experience conquers all, I decided on a radical treatment. Like a child plunging into a swimming pond without proper instruction, I asked permission to travel up to the northernmost tip of the perimeter, where the Twenty-seventh Regiment, commanded by a brilliant young colonel named John Michaelis, was covering the main corridor of attack to Taegu.

Colonel Michaelis's regiment was known as the "Wolfhounds." In those early days of combat, there was very little to cheer about, and so the few spots of bright, successful fighting received a great deal of attention from the press. Thanks in no small order to the efforts of Marguerite Higgins, Michaelis and his men had won a substantial reputation for hardiness and bravery during their capture and defense of a crucial point far up in the northwestern tip of the UN line. Here, the Naktong River, the natural barrier for much of the western front, fell away into rough mountain terrain, which the North Koreans constantly probed for routes of attack. It became clear, early on, that only a few of the mountain passes were wide and flat enough for tanks to run through. Michaelis and his men straddled the biggest of these, a place called Chanp'yongdong valley. Here, they were under constant pressure from enemy armored assaults, which, since our forces maintained absolute air supremacy, usually came late at night.

This much I knew as my Jeep moved north, up twisting dirt roads toward the makeshift regimental headquarters. When I arrived, one company was lined up for supper, and the smell of good food hung in the clear, bright air. Farther on, beyond a solitary scar of charred, still-smoking thatched huts, the Chanp'yongdong valley opened funnelwise upon a glowing prospect of distant hills and sky.

Here, I encountered Michaelis, a tall, impressive, blue-eyed Californian who, at age thirty-seven, was the youngest regimental commander in the U.S. force. He had won distinction early in his career as a member of General Maxwell Taylor's 101 Airborne force, which helped spearhead the Normandy invasion. Later, he parachuted into Arnhem, and by war's end he had been wounded twice. Michaelis was given command of the Wolfhounds after the previous officer was abruptly removed. Already Michaelis's outstanding performance had earned him one battlefield promotion—to full colonel—and within six months of our meeting he would be promoted once again in the field, this time to brigadier general.

Entering the peaceful valley, it was hard to believe that no-man's-land began just down the road or that the occasional snicking sound above the chow line was really a rather inefficient sniper to whom nobody paid much attention. The local battalion commander was Lieutenant Colonel G. J. Check, a short, wiry, businesslike man with a wry, unpretentious manner. Check, too, had distinguished himself early on in the fighting and had already been put up for a Distinguished Service Cross by his commander, Michaelis. But there was in Check no swagger of the hero; indeed, the lieutenant colonel welcomed me to his forward position much in the manner of a suburban householder. He said that he had once worked for the

Agriculture Department and "just stuck" in the army after the war. We dined on passable food, and then, as dusk fell, I was given a tour of the battalion's troop and tank dispositions covering both the valley approach and the flanking mountains.

Check's command post, called the Persimmon Grove, was set in a narrow, rocky draw above the valley floor. A South Korean company defended the mountain crest far above, while, in nearby foxholes, Check's men nursed 3.5 bazookas. Tanks squatted heavily by the roadside and the streambed, menacing the far valley door with their guns, as the positions of the battalion's three rifle companies—Able, Baker, and Charlie—bristled along the valley's fringing hills. Indeed, the entire narrow valley, called "the bowling alley" by the troops, had been efficiently transformed into a grim trap for the enemy armor and infantry hoping to gain the main road south to Taegu.

Just as we were returning to the battalion command post, the North Koreans announced their intention to test this trap. There was a loud whistling sound and a tremendous crash on the flank above us. With a happy grunt, Colonel Check began barking into a tangle of field telephones that looked like something one might have encountered in the bowels of the Ritz Hotel around 1911. I had been assigned an unpleasant foxhole that felt like a half-filled bathtub with rocks at the bottom, and it was a relief to leave these sodden quarters no matter what banging was going on. So I spent the first hours of the attack sitting on a rock, desperately smoking cigarettes, trying to master my nerves and track the flow of battle as best I could.

With infinite incident and endless uncertainty, the fighting continued all through the night. At one point, the South Koreans on the mountain crest called for support, and our big mortars spoke. At another, the forward observers reported a tentative enemy advance. Colonel Check ordered flares, and, as our firing testified, the attackers hastily retreated, peevishly blasting away with their flat trajectory guns. Linemen went out to repair broken communications among the dark precipices; runners came and went; the noise of fighting rose and fell. Not even the wisest observer could be sure of what was happening—whether the artillery really had knocked out its target; whether the enemy really had turned back or was creeping across the rice paddies; whether the South Koreans still held the mountain crest on our exposed flank.

The attack peaked at 3:30 A.M. with the full North Korean advance. Enemy mortar rounds exploded around the Persimmon Grove. There followed a curious coughing crash from all our mortars, all our tanks; then, after a few minutes, an explosion like a giant firecracker blowing off; and after that, for half an hour, the wild rattle of machine-gun and rifle fire.

A major enemy attack, of course, is not conducive to general calm, but gradually my apprehension gave way to a robust fatalism. The soldiers, although frantically busy, did not seem overly worried, so neither, I concluded, should I be. As the night wore on, I discovered the truth of Winston Churchill's immortal observation about combat—that being shot at was rather enjoyable, provided one did not get hit. I discovered, too, that being hit was moderately unusual—if you happened to be dug in behind a strongly fortified defensive position and merely a bystander, as I was. Then, near to 5:00 A.M., the firing subsided. As the pale dawn was just beginning to spread in the sky, the North Koreans withdrew. The battle was over, and in the command post men lay down to doze on the hard rocks.

Because it was exhilarating to do your job when you doubted you could do it and because nothing, on balance, is nicer than winning, I count the three days I spent in the Chanp'yongdong valley among my most memorable as a newspaperman. The columns were well received back home—A. J. Liebling in the *New Yorker* likened me to "a rich man's Ernie Pyle"—and my standing rose (albeit only momentarily) among my colleagues in the field. In the following weeks, I would spend time with several outfits along the perimeter. After each experience at the front, I would then fly back to Tokyo to file two or three columns before heading out again. This routine continued through the first week of September, when I was advised by General MacArthur's people to stay in Tokyo along with the rest of the press and hold myself in readiness for "the big show," which, it was hinted, would be coming soon.

Within days, I found myself aboard some form of navy warship bound under night sail for an unspecified and darkly secret landing on the peninsula. We were headed, of course, for the port city of Inchon.

The press was given the specifics of the landing in a briefing on the eve of the attack. After the briefing, I sat up half the night with Keyes Beech of the *Chicago Daily News,* sharing a bottle of whiskey we had managed to smuggle on board. Keyes and I argued over two grave subjects: which of the landing waves we should go in on (the dangerous first ones or the "official" initial assault that followed); and whether Keyes should marry my old *Herald Tribune* colleague Marguerite Higgins, with whom he had been carrying on a furious affair. If I recall correctly, I argued in favor of the latter proposal (they never did marry) and for the first wave both on the grounds that this would be the distinguished thing to do.

Inchon city lay on the lower end of a long, bow-shaped harbor. The port itself was protected by a peninsula, flanked by the island of Wolmi. This island, which had been heavily fortified by the North Koreans, was the first key to MacArthur's plan of attack. And it was toward this target that the initial waves of the assault were directed. (The "first wave" manufactured for press purposes would come much later.) Indeed, we were not scheduled to go off until well past three o'clock in the afternoon. By this time, Wolmi had been taken, the preliminary, mechanized waves were already ashore, and the air above Inchon was alight with flame and smoke from a steady air-force bombing.

That morning, the narrow, island-studded harbor was all grey under a mauve-grey sky. The troop transports with marines pouring down their sides into their Higgins boats huddled at the head of the channel. Cruisers and destroyers lay farther offshore, filling the air with the roaring crash of naval gunfire. Flights of aircraft, black against the overcast, marked the presence of the distant aircraft carriers. And on either side of our control vessel, where the first waves of amphibious tanks and tractors were taking off like orderly squadrons of water beetles, two rocket-carrying cruisers were sending an endless, terrifying rain of fire inshore.

We spent much of that day peering ashore in an attempt to divine what was happening. As the day lengthened, however, a thick fog moved in and hung on the water, obscuring our view of the battle. My wave was to take a long stretch of sandy beach south of Inchon. The beach was wide and passable but buttressed at the city end by a heavily fortified seawall. Neither the beach nor the wall was visible as I clambered down the great rope netting into the landing craft full of marines from the First and Second Platoons of Baker Company and steered off into the fog. Sadly, our steersman, who was leading the other boats in, made some type of navigational error, and within minutes of leaving the main ship we found ourselves separated from the rest of the wave and completely alone. Enveloped in thick fog, we groped bravely toward a battle we could barely hear, much less see.

After several tense minutes, the enormous seawall, not the beach, loomed up at us out of the fog. The wall was a great, battered structure, nearly twelve feet high at that moment of tide. Luckily, it was made from large granite boulders that permitted hand- and foot-holds, and so allowed our startled troop to scamper up. We clambered hastily up along the wall and discovered that we seemed to have established our own beachhead.

Murderous defense works, trenches, machine-gun posts, and bunkers covered a long sandbar emplacement separated by a lagoon from the mainland. A photographer from the Hearst papers immortalized our little group's arrival at the top. The city of Inchon, still in flames, stood to the rear of the abandoned enemy trenches. I remember perfectly well turning to one of our bewildered assault leaders and saying: "Surely, Lieutenant, they put us on the wrong beach." The Hearst man snapped a picture of this earnest conference. The resulting shot of my enormous nose silhouetted against the city in flames was flashed back to the waiting American public.

The reality was less dramatic, for there was no shooting at all, and we wandered lonely as clouds back and forth among the abandoned fortifications, sheepishly wondering where our enemy had gone. Slowly, we crawled into the occasionally flame-shot darkness, across a breakwater that connected our sandbar with Inchon and where a sniper was interested in any visible silhouette. We waited a long time in the dew-damp vegetation while a machine gun somewhere rattled and the platoon ahead engaged a party of the enemy established in a small stone building. We had the gathering sense that our landing-craft wave leader had, indeed, taken us to the wrong beach. At one point, I went back to our original landing point with a young runner from First Platoon to find "where the hell the other marines is at." We failed to find other marines, and after the whispered consultation of the platoon leaders peering at too small maps under a poncho and the return trudge along the sandbar, our leader, Sergeant Herbert Brink, offered a judicious summing-up: "Well," he said, "no son of a bitch can say he hit this damn beach before we did."

At length, the captain of our group raised the command center and was told that he had, indeed, lost his way and that the assault beach was too far to sprint to. For the time being, there was nothing to do but settle down for the night, which was pretty near hell in itself. The weather had turned bitterly cold, and I had with me for the landing the same tropical kit that had been suitable for the deep August heat in the first weeks after my arrival. The men huddled together in heaps for warmth in the drizzle and tried to sleep in the enemy's rock-filled trenches. At the first dawn, the First and Second Platoons cleaned their weapons and reconnoitered, poking long sticks into previously invisible bunkers and flushing out ten hidden, starving North Koreans. No one grumbled over the botched attack the night before. In fact, the marines seemed fresher and more enthusiastic than ever as they prepared to join the big attack inland.

Only after our successful reconnoiter and after we had settled into some semblance of routine onshore did the stunning success of

MacArthur's Inchon landing become clear. I would later learn that the Joint Chiefs of Staff had behaved in their usual stricken manner by putting every conceivable block in the path of the plan before the president gave his final approval. In fact, all of the much-discussed drawbacks of the proposed landing, including the possibility that our invasion fleet might be stranded by Inchon Harbor's fickle tides, were overcome, thanks to the precision of MacArthur's planning, to the skill of the invasion force, and, as is often the case in the world of war, a good degree of luck. In the end, the American landing forces had achieved a nearly complete surprise. Not long thereafter, they succeeded in splitting the invading North Korean forces in half, cutting off those in the south from their routes of supply and sending the bulk of the dispirited troops who had occupied Seoul reeling back toward the border.

Indeed, when I managed to reach Seoul several days later, the brutal battle for that city had practically ended. The initial marine assault had been followed by three days of close-quarter, house-to-house fighting. Set high in the surrounding hills, heavy U.S. artillery poured sheets of fire into the city. Thousands of civilians died in the brutal crossfire, and when it was over much of the city lay in smoldering ruins. So our conquering force received a perfunctory welcome. The people of Seoul displayed no overwhelming emotion that I can remember, no great dramatic scenes of ecstatic cheering and brightly tossed bouquets. For our troops, the capital was an objective, attacked and taken, and the question for most of them now was where to go next.

I myself resolved to fly back to Tokyo. The fiercest fighting under way now was back at the Pusan Perimeter, where the Eighth Army was in the process of breaking through to meet up with the marines from Inchon. The South Korean government was officially reestablished in Seoul on September 29, but weeks before the Joint Chiefs had authorized MacArthur to send his troops across the 38th parallel and into the north. As it turned out, two South Korean divisions already had moved into the north and had encountered little or no resistance. In either case, it was obvious to me that the next great questions of the war would involve issues of strategy and that these would be played out at command headquarters.

After I arrived in Tokyo, I sought and obtained an interview with General MacArthur at his Dai Ichi headquarters. I wanted to decide what my next step would be and thought it best to get a reading from "on high" (and when one spoke of General MacArthur in Tokyo in those days, "on high" was a phrase one had to use) as to whether the recapture of Seoul meant—as, indeed, everyone on the peninsula was saying—that the war was for all intents over.

I had sampled the atmosphere of MacArthur's headquarters in Tokyo sufficiently to realize that the daily air that he breathed was laden with enough incense to make even Louis XIV retch. Indeed, Dai Ichi was proof of a basic rule for armies at war: the farther one gets from the front, the more laggards, toadies, and fools one encounters. The great general had chosen his subordinates in the main from the "Bataan gang" of his Philippine days. For the most part, they were insipid men, arrogant with the press, wary of each other, and generally incompetent. Their tone toward MacArthur was almost wholly simpering and reverential, and I have always held the view that this sycophancy was what tripped him up so badly in the end. The general had shown enormous guts when he landed his forces at Inchon in defiance of the Joint Chiefs' nervous warnings. All his calculations after the fighting began had been justified by the outcome, and he did not deserve to end his military career with so gigantic a mistake as his misreading of Chinese intentions. But anyone who encourages those around him to tell him over and over again that he can walk on water and has this judgment reinforced by a major success will have a tendency to believe that, indeed, he can walk on water—a monopoly the Lord has not shared with humans.

MacArthur's personal setup in Tokyo was an odd reverse of the one I had seen in Manila just before Pearl Harbor. Although the Dai Ichi complex was vast, the general's own office looked like a cell compared to his usual grandiose standard. Nor did he have a dais to sit on, as he had when he received me in Manila. Instead, the contents of the modestly sized room were carefully arranged so that he sat between his guests and the only openly lit window. Squinting into the glare, the general's guests could thus contemplate his noble profile without observing, generally, that the outrages of time had been perpetrated on him, as on everyone else.

We know now that MacArthur was being warned from various quarters not to go too far up the Korean peninsula because of the danger of Chinese intervention. After a brief spate of flag-waving, George Kennan had gone back into a characteristically gloomy pose and was one of those (rightly, too, as it would turn out) who counseled caution. But in the afterglow of the Inchon landing and with the capture of P'yongyang imminent, General MacArthur was in no mood to listen. When we met, he welcomed me into my low chair and proceeded to give me a thumbnail analysis of the situation, not failing to point out that his landing at Inchon had changed everything or to hint that the plan might have been blocked by the Joint Chiefs if he had not taken a strong stand. He talked of the possible

Chinese reaction, making very little of it, as he would to President Truman and others after he saw me, and he wound up our interview with a delicate flattery: "As a matter of fact, Alsop," he said, quoting the title of our column, "if you stay on here, you will just be wasting your valuable time."

MacArthur was deadly wrong, of course—and so, for that matter, was I. At the time, it seemed to me foolish for the Chinese to intervene at that late stage of the war, when they had already had the chance to do so—and with much more decisive effect—early on, before the United States had committed ground forces. Even if they did come, as they were threatening, as far north as the Yalu River, I reasoned that the untested Chinese forces could not get very far against the battle-tough UN troops. So I nodded vigorously as MacArthur gave me his views, just as I had done years before in Manila on the eve of the Japanese attack on Pearl Harbor.

I confess there was another reason for my acceptance of MacArthur's advice. I longed to get home. Shortly after my audience at Dai Ichi, I managed to hook a ride with a retinue of high-ranking air-force officers from the Pentagon who had come out to see what their people were up to in Korea. I thus reached Washington in great comfort and very short order.

I never saw Douglas MacArthur again, but I am inclined to think that President Truman was dead right to recall him when he did. The famous meeting with Truman on Wake Island, in which the president of the United States was all but summoned to a theater of war by one of his own generals, only increased MacArthur's sense of invulnerability as well as his contempt for his political superiors. In early November 1950, after the first probing attacks south of the Yalu by Chinese troops, the Joint Chiefs offered a timid protest over MacArthur's move north of the 38th parallel. As he had done at Inchon, the great general arrogantly dismissed them.

In all fairness to MacArthur, however, when I returned to Washington in mid-October, I found little evidence of worry over the ability of our forces to complete their invasion of North Korea. Indeed, nearly all of official Washington had joined in applauding President Truman's decision (in reality, the decision was MacArthur's more than Truman's) to order the troops north. Only George Kennan, who was experiencing one of his fits of prophecy, protested that the military invasion was both hasty and dangerous since the Chinese would be unlikely to tolerate American power so close to their northern borders. It had always been the official intention, at the United Nations, to reunify the Korean peninsula. Overtly, at least, the American government was much more cautious; there was considerable confusion and disagreement over whether to cross the 38th parallel and, if so, to what end. Dean Acheson, I later learned, was advocating, with General Marshall, a fairly cautious move north in order, in the words of the Joint Chiefs, to insure "the destruction of the North Korean Armed Forces." Of course, MacArthur had grander plans and never allowed the Joint Chiefs, Dean, or, for that matter, President Truman to get a word in edgewise until after the Chinese launched their fatal attack.

Dean's attitude toward the matter, however, was indicative of the casual arrogance that we all shared after General MacArthur's first stunning victory in the weeks leading up to China's decisive attack in late October. The Chinese, at that point, were using the Indian ambassador to Peking, K. M. Panikkar, to relay their public threats of action to the UN command. Panikkar was not highly regarded or trusted in Washington. I can still remember Dean Acheson at a dinner he was hosting then, in his most archly aristocratic form referring dismissively to the Indian diplomat as "Panicker."

It is no surprise, then, that when the disastrous Chinese attack did come, everyone, including Stew and myself, was caught flat-footed. Exposed, outnumbered, and outflanked, Walker's Eighth Army was sent bowling back down toward the south. Far up on the peninsula's northeastern coast, the marines of X Corps began their famous, bitterly cold retreat from the Chosin reservoir. An atmosphere of grave crisis came over Washington thanks, in no small part, to General MacArthur's own public, nearly hysterical misgivings. Stew and I were no less party to these than others, but in our column of December 4, 1950, we placed the blame for the defeat squarely on the old general, while noting that "this may displease those who like to believe he has attained some sort of divine attention."

I must confess that MacArthur's demand for reinforcements with an eye to attacking China did not seem as wrongheaded to Stew and me at the time as it would later on. But we in no way supported his subsequent attempts to undermine the authority of President Truman and were glad, on April 11, when the old soldier was at long last sent home to his clamorous and altogether undignified welcome. I never went back to the front in Korea and am a little sorry now that I did not. The truth is that I was happy to have led the kind of life I did as an overaged combat correspondent but gladder still to be done with it all.

17

McCarthy's Washington

(1950–1952)

Coming back from Korea on the comfortable air-force plane, I thought repeatedly how nice it would be to take it easy for a while in Washington: to tend my garden, to make my social rounds, to watch events unfold as I imagined a political columnist should—with a leisurely concern and a minimum of personal worry. I was dreaming, of course. The next months—and, indeed, the next four years—would be among the busiest of my professional life. As I look back, I wonder at the reserves of energy I must have needed to pursue all the different strands of action that I did during that time. Some of these strands were professional, others highly political. But to the extent they wove together or joined in a coherent pattern, they did so in response to the grim assaults being waged on the government by Senator Joe McCarthy.

In all, the McCarthy period lasted from February 1950, when the junior senator from Wisconsin made his first celebrated accusations in Wheeling, West Virginia, until the late months of 1954, when his colleagues voted at long last to censure him. At times during the intervening years, it seemed to me the sewers of our public life had burst and the accumulated filth was flowing in the streets. For McCarthy and the men who operated as his allies and henchmen, such as Senators Pat McCarran of Nevada and William Jenner from Indiana, succeeded in bringing down on Washington attitudes of cowardice and recrimination that I had never before seen or even dimly imagined. In the end, their willful paranoia spread to the very highest levels of government, threatening, as my brother and I saw it, to engulf even the president of the United States.

In the end, we felt obliged to go further than journalists generally do. We took on a real role in opposing the McCarthy witchhunt. The decision to do so was mainly mine because among those accused of betrayal by McCarthy were John Paton Davies, Jack Service, and John Carter Vincent, three of the young Foreign Service officers who helped make our wartime policy in China. I knew that these men, like Stilwell himself, had become disgusted with the generalissimo's regime. I knew, also, that at one time or another in their capacity as political advisers to the American commander, Davies and, in particular, Vincent considered the Communists a more palatable and, indeed, a more viable alternative for U.S. military aid than Chiang. I disputed their judgment privately at the time. I disputed it publicly after the war in my own lengthy account of the Stilwell-Chiang schism published in the *Saturday Evening Post* in January 1950.

I am not sure now that I was right to do so. Davies and his colleagues held the view that the generalissimo's government was already past saving. If this were the case, the question became not how to prevent a Communist Chinese victory, but how to come to terms with it. Davies also knew one thing I did not: Mao and his Communists had developed their party and their policy in isolation from—and sometimes in defiance of—the Kremlin. In short, Davies saw that Titoism was possible before Marshal Tito ever came to power. In theory, American aid could then be used not just for battles against the Japanese, but to wean Mao even further away from Moscow. History has shown this to be a moot point. Peking and Moscow never managed to stay allies for long. In the hands of General Stilwell, moreover, military aid to the Communists would undoubtedly have caused real havoc in Free China as it was constituted during the war.

The fact remains that Davies's recommendations contained a good deal more foresight than I had realized during our policy debates in Chungking. No man "lost China," including Joseph Stilwell, whose personal hatred of the generalissimo irrevocably tangled an already desperate situation. Moreover, for the American representatives in Chungking, wartime guidance from Washington was so limited and vague that we were all operating in a policy vacuum. We improvised as we went along, and I improvised more than most. As a junior officer under General Stilwell's command, my own actions during the war in service of Colonel Chennault had been grossly insubordinate by any basic military standard. In short, I was conscious that if these men had been guilty of impropriety in China, then, surely, I was, too.

As time went on, almost all the occupants of the opposition "backroom" in China came under attack by the McCarthyites. The careers of Davies, Service, and Vincent were ruined, a fact that made me lividly angry. I testified for every one of the men I had known in the China years, helped to get lawyers for as many as I could, and in general enjoyed the chance to be combative. It is proof of the nastiness of that period that I was repeatedly asked why on earth I testified for Jack Service and John Davies when I had disagreed so flatly with them. The obvious answer, which people in the McCarthy camp found difficult to understand, was that even though I did not always share their opinions, they were friends of mine, and I had never had the faintest doubt about their loyalty to their country.

Loyalty was not something Joe McCarthy cared a great deal about. Stew and I had known the senator first as the big, raw-boned pride and joy of the real-estate lobby, which is where he found his friends when he first came to Washington. Quite obviously, McCarthy adored attention and as a politician had tried to get it several different ways before finding his voice that famous February evening in front of the Ohio County Women's Republican Club in Wheeling. I was on a reporting trip in Europe when the senator's first confused accusations surfaced concerning 205 (the number was later amended to 57, although the actual count fluctuated, depending on the senator's mood) Communist agents who lurked in the Foreign Service.

My brother recognized this kind of headline hunting for what it was and responded with outrage. Indeed, from then until I returned from Korea months later, Stew bore the brunt of the McCarthy story, and did so with great guts and character. His first column on the subject, published less than a month after the Wheeling speech, would set the tone. After conferring with officials at the State Department, Stew predicted: "McCarthy will get his head so thoroughly washed that neither he nor any of his like-minded colleagues will soon again use this particular vote-catching technique."

McCarthy did get his head thoroughly washed that very spring when the Senate convened a special subcommittee to investigate his claims (it was chaired by Senator Millard E. Tydings of Maryland) and found no factual evidence whatsoever of Communist infiltration within the State Department. However, McCarthy managed to regain his political footing by three cleverly combined methods. First, he was grossly, quite shockingly, rude to any one who questioned his behavior on the Senate floor, like the venerable and far-from-tough Herbert H. Lehman of New York. Second, he did everything possible, by every method possible, to bring home to his fellow senators the admiration he was earning (from misguided and ill-informed fellow citizens) all across the country. Third, and most important by far, he cold-bloodedly undertook to frighten his fellow senators out of their wits by showing that he could single-handedly defeat one of their number at the polls. The Louisiana Kingfish, Huey Long, one of the cleverest American politicians of the twentieth century, had intimidated the Senate in this manner in 1932, when he had successfully backed the simpering Mrs. Hattie Caraway, the widow of Thaddeus Caraway of Arkansas, against the chosen candidate of the local state politicians. Based on what I saw of McCarthy in action, I would bet any amount of money that he had never even heard of Senator Hattie Caraway. Nevertheless, McCarthy went into Maryland that year and campaigned hard for John Marshall Butler, the Republican opponent of the arrogant Millard Tydings, just as he had promised. And just as McCarthy had promised, Tydings lost his election by a tidy margin of 40,000 votes, an outcome that caused the rest of the Senate to take note and tremble.

I did not discover for myself the vile flavor of McCarthyized Washington until October of the next year, 1951. For much of the time since the Tydings episode, I had been on reporting trips abroad—first as I have said, at the front in Korea and then in Europe and Iran. Not long after my return from London in the late summer of 1951, I was bewildered to read on the front page of the *New York Times* that a certain Louis Budenz a former member of the Communist party and, at that time, an assistant professor of economics at Fordham University, had charged former Vice-President Henry A. Wallace with being under "Communist guidance" during Wallace's celebrated "mission" to China in the summer of 1944. The "guidance" was allegedly supplied by a Foreign Service officer I had known in the China days, John Carter Vincent, who was accused by Budenz as having contacts with the Communist party.

The venue of this attack was a meeting of the internal security subcommittee of the Senate Judiciary Committee, presided over by McCarthy's ally, the aged and bitterly prejudiced Senator Pat

McCarran of Nevada. It was odd, of course, that Budenz had shirked a whole series of other opportunities to denounce Vincent. After leaving the party in 1945, he had worked closely with the FBI, helping agents to discover or confirm the activities of such key Soviet agents as J. Peters and Gerhart Eisler. By his own estimation, Budenz had spent some 3,000 hours on these cases, serving as expert witness a number of times in regular court proceedings before ascending to more rarified duties on Capitol Hill, where his accusations could carry great political weight without suffering the nuisance of strong, legal cross-examination.

Budenz was first summoned to the Hill to testify before the Tydings committee through Alfred Kohlberg, the wealthy silk merchant who was resident China specialist among the feverish coterie surrounding McCarthy. It was through Kohlberg, no doubt, that Budenz targeted first Owen Lattimore, also in China during the war and later an academic at Johns Hopkins, and then Vincent. Budenz, of course, had ample opportunity during his long hours with the FBI to search every nook and cranny of his memory for the names of these lurking traitors, and it seemed odd to me that they came up only in the wake of McCarthy's ranting accusations. Further, Budenz, in his accusations, never offered specific proof, saying only that he knew "from official reports" that both Vincent and Lattimore were Communist party members.

Budenz plainly did not know that he was going dangerously far with a lie when he attacked Vincent. He evidently was entirely ignorant of what had happened in Kunming, when Vice-President Henry Wallace came to visit General Chennault with John Vincent as his embassy chaperon. I knew this quite simply because I was there. I also wrote Wallace's final report on China for him from General Chennault's headquarters in Kunming. So if the vice-president was guided in any way while in China, I was the man most responsible.

Henry Wallace's mission to China in June 1944 had been a perfectly ridiculous episode. The vice-president, as I have already noted, was an agronomist at heart. His work on hybrid corn had made him a great fortune, and he was an excellent secretary of agriculture. As the record shows, however, he was without any real diplomatic skill and almost entirely devoid of political judgment. Wallace was sent to China by President Roosevelt with instructions to promote goodwill between Chiang Kai-shek and the Communists in Yenan. From the first, however, the vice-president seemed more preoccupied with a scheme for solving China's food problems by importing to the mainland large numbers of American tractors.

While in Chungking, he had journeyed out of the city to view the great irrigation project on the Chengtu plain, a magnificently engineered network of sluices and dams inaugurated in the third century B.C. When I visited the plain, the damming was still done as it had been centuries before, with huge woven bamboo baskets filled with rocks, pulled into place by armies of 10,000 men apiece, dragging them forward on bamboo ropes to hold back the headwaters of the Yangtze until the season of need. An American tractor would have found little room to maneuver among this careful management of the water flow, a fact Wallace surely realized.

As it happened, Kunming was Wallace's last stop in China. The vice-president had already spent several days in Chungking in conversation with the generalissimo. Although Chiang had quickly dismissed any notion of compromise with Mao's forces in Yenan, Wallace, when I encountered him, had not yet formed the overall opinion about the political crisis in Free China that his position required him to express.

Since I had known Wallace before the war and Vincent through my visits to Chungking, General Chennault asked me to act as subhost during their visit to our headquarters. Lattimore, a man of great learning but slightly befuddled politics, was along on the trip as a representative of the Office of War Information and served, in effect, as Wallace's public-relations officer. Upon the arrival of the American party, Lattimore promptly went off to stay with Chinese professor friends in Kunming City, while the vice-president and Vincent settled down in two rooms in the general's little guesthouse among the rice paddies outside Kunming.

During the standard, ghastly VIP tour—which Vice-President Wallace managed to vary by dragooning reluctant sergeants into volleyball games—we fell into discussions of the Chinese situation. Never one to shrink from such an opportunity, I offered my view on the Allied war effort in China. I recounted the decline of the Stilwell-Chiang Kai-shek relationship and pointed out the problems, as I saw them, with the offensive in Burma. As I was both near at hand and the only American in the country he had really known before, Wallace listened to me.

It will be remembered that by the summer of 1944, the allied effort in China was precarious. The Japanese offensive was in full swing, and Roosevelt was perpetually concerned that Chiang might decide to drop out of the war altogether, thereby freeing Japan's China forces for use elsewhere in the Pacific theater. General Stilwell's efforts in Burma had yielded little in the way of solid military gains, and Chennault's operations were being devastated by the new round of Japanese attacks. The generalissimo had long ago made plain his wish to see Stilwell recalled by the U.S. command. Of course, Chennault and I agreed with this view, and I took the opportunity to reiterate our position to Vice-President Wallace. My answers seemed both to startle and impress him, and he promptly called both Vincent and me to an informal conference at General Chennault's house. There I pressed the vice-president to send a cable back to President Roosevelt outlining his new position, and he, somewhat to my surprise, consented. I brought my typewriter into General Chennault's living room and made my draft for Wallace on the basis of my "guidance," passing the pages to Wallace, who then passed them to Vincent.

I knew Vincent only slightly as a diplomatic bureaucrat who showed the marks of many fairly easygoing years as a China specialist in the Foreign Service. Until the possibility of a cable was mentioned, he had attended the proceedings with an air of being amused that Wallace should presume to form any judgment whatever on China's complex problems. As the cable was composed that recommended, in the boldest terms, that General Stilwell be removed from his post, Vincent made no objection except to giggle from time to time, which did not surprise me because I had always thought him a very amiable but basically frivolous man.

When my work was completed, I had an embarrassing moment because Wallace wished to recommend replacing Stilwell with General Chennault. I felt that this would have been a great mistake. Chennault was quite unprepared by previous training for the vast responsibilities that had been entrusted to the even more unprepared Stilwell. Furthermore, it was obvious that proposing my chief as Stilwell's replacement would cause a maximum row at the Pentagon, with General Marshall digging in his heels in a way that would have alarmed President Roosevelt and Harry Hopkins. With great embarrassment, therefore, I had to persuade Wallace to forget my chief and propose General Albert Wedemeyer as the new commander in China. Henry Wallace made no argument and signed the cable as I had drafted it, whereupon Vincent took the message to the American consulate in Kunming and filed it as a personal communication from Wallace to President Roosevelt.

Such were the facts of Henry Wallace's famous mission to China as I knew them. I would have charged Budenz publicly with perjury if the *Tribune*'s lawyers had permitted me to. Instead, I contented myself with an open letter to Senator McCarran's committee and demanded in print the opportunity to testify. In October of 1951, I was finally called to do so, and during an entire day of testimony I answered the charges against Henry Wallace as best I could. I outlined the political and military situation in wartime China as I knew it and pointed out to McCarran and his cronies that replacing the anti-Chiang General Stilwell with the anti-Communist Wedemeyer was about the most unwelcomed step the president could have taken from the Communist viewpoint. I made it rather plain, also, that my own influence on Wallace had been a great deal more direct than Vincent's alleged Communist guidance.

To my enormous surprise, Senator McCarthy, who had been present for most of the morning's proceedings, followed me into the elevator after my testimony and, smiling his black-jowled smile, offered to shake my hand. I ignored the proffered hand and did my best to give an imitation of Old Stone Face. I have never seen anyone more surprised than McCarthy was by this kind of rejection. I was also greatly surprised myself to see that the newspapermen who were going down to lunch in the same elevator also were shocked.

I was not so innocent as to imagine that Senator McCarran would abandon Budenz in the face of my testimony. I did think that the national press—in particular the *New York Times*, which had given enormous play to Budenz's charges against Vincent and Wallace—would at least declare that these charges had now been challenged and, on base, disproved. The morning after my testimony, I found nothing on the front page of the *New York Times* and discovered that the whole subject of my testimony had been covered in a four-paragraph notice under a small-sized head on one of the inside pages.

It was my introduction to the weakness of the press in the face of McCarthyism. I do not deny that the charges made by McCarthy with such total irresponsibility were news and that printing them was part of the job of the newspaper business. But with very little hard work, it was entirely possible to prove that the man was a practiced and habitual liar. Although he told so many lies and varied the tune so much from lie to lie that it was difficult to pin down and counter his claims, the job could have been done. There were those, like my colleague Drew Pearson, who devoted a good deal of energy and reputation to attacks on McCarthy. But Drew, who, of course, came to blows with the senator at the old Selgrave Club in Washington, was the exception and not the rule. If the newspaper business had had the guts to follow back over the trail of McCarthy's rise and to show him up as a liar over and over again, I doubt very much whether he would have inspired such terror.

Prior to the McCarran hearings, I wrote Henry Luce, publisher of *Time,* urging him to devote his magazine's considerable resources to exposing McCarthy and his cronies. (It is a general rule among publishers that they believe what their own publications tell them, and since their publications more often than not tell them what they want to hear, they often begin to live in an unreal world. Although this rule may have applied less to Henry Luce than to some others, he was certainly a man with peculiarities, and these would surface from time to time in his magazine. As it turned out, *Time* would become critical of McCarthyism, although I found their early editorial treatment of the senator sadly tepid and noncommittal. The magazine would whip up a good deal of public sentiment against Alger Hiss and his supposed protector Dean Acheson. Although Luce knew McCarthy to be a demagogue and a fraud, he did not begin selective criticism of the senator until late in 1951, a full year and a half after the speech in Wheeling. General attacks did not begin in *Time* and *Life* magazines until much later, when Luce's real hero, President Eisenhower, was beginning to be threatened by McCarthy.) Mr. Luce's early reply to my letter was, I think, indicative of a prevailing attitude among journalists. "I agree with all you say against 'McCarthyism,' " Mr. Luce wrote to me in September 1951, when the controversy was still brewing, "but, if I may say so, you don't deal with all the facts: you do not, for example, deal with the fact that millions of your reasonably decent fellow citizens condone or approve of most, if not all, of Joe's doings."

Senator McCarthy went so far as to charge that Stew and I were, in fact, Communists. We would read these allegations with shocked amusement, for Stew and I had never been accused of such a thing before. In fact, as the senator well knew, it was our implacable anti-Communist credentials that allowed us to open our prolonged attacks upon McCarthy. These personal skirmishes did not matter in the long run, however. What concerned me most of all—and Stew agreed—was the increasing seriousness and tolerance with which the views of the senator and his political supporters were being treated.

Late 1951 saw the spectacle of Senator Robert A. Taft marching forward to the Republican nomination, flanked by the *Chicago Tribune* publisher Colonel Robert McCormick and Senator McCarthy, preceded by William Randolph Hearst's favored columnist Westbrook Pegler and radio commentator Fulton Lewis, Jr., beating their peculiar, anti-Communist drums. At no time was there any public suggestion that Senator Taft was keeping just as dubious company as President Roosevelt had when he failed to repudiate Communist party support during his presidential campaigns; on the contrary, if a politician chose to wrap himself in the cloak of anticommunism, he seemed to rise above the standard rules of civilized conduct, becoming a sort of chartered libertine, freed from all normal restraints of justice, fairness, decency, and truth.

For these reasons, I was strongly against Robert Taft in his drive for the presidency, although I always admired the senator as a man. Indeed, Robert Taft was one of the most curious and truly American political phenomena I can recall in my more than forty years of reporting. Taft's physical appearance was astonishing. He was a large man who appeared to be badly fitted together, and one had to conclude from his wardrobe that he went to a tailor who sought to emphasize his peculiar construction. He was also bald, or nearly so, and for some reason he grew three or four hairs on top of his head very long. Whether or not the aim was to persuade people he was not bald I never figured out, but this floating lock and the bald head that supported it made a very odd effect. The nearest one can come to a description of Senator Taft's voice on the stump was an angry quacking; and if the senator was asked to suffer fools gladly, the quacking could grow very loud, indeed, and take on a strong overtone of outrage.

Outwardly, Bob Taft was not the kind of politician that the modern image makers regard as easy to handle. Although quick-tempered, he was a man of native charm—far more so than General Eisenhower. Frightfully down-to-earth in both character and professional outlook, he was doggedly true to his own narrow set of beliefs in a way I have not seen since in politics. Even the Second World War had not shaken his belief that the United States would be best served by minding its own business and no one else's. A critic of the formation of NATO and of the Korean War, Taft seemed to take positive delight in opposing Dean Acheson at almost every turn. In matters of domestic policy, Robert Taft was, of course, a champion of labor and a strict party man; indeed, his furious political allegiance earned him the title "Mr. Republican." He always played election politics rough because that was the way it had been played when he was young. Taft's failing was his willingness to tolerate people like Joe McCarthy. He knew they were morally repugnant but thought their existence a part of practical politics and so made the best use of them he could.

Taft's essence was neatly described by a rather willowy BBC reporter whom Stew, never able to be alone on the road, had taken along with him when he went to Ohio to cover the race that sent Taft back to the Senate in 1950—a victory that automatically made the old campaigner a contender for the presidential election. Stew and his BBC friend arrived home from Ohio toward the end of a dinner party given by Alice Longworth. Everyone wanted to hear what they had to say, and Stew made an untypically conventional report. But the BBC man gave a surprisingly memorable summation. Choosing Mrs. Longworth, a strong Taft supporter, for his audience, he said in a fluting voice, "I really can't understand, Mrs. Longworth, the way people talk about Senator Taft. Everybody says he's a man of sterling honesty and no charm whatever. I must confess that I thought he was distinctly dishonest but ravishingly charming."

For a time it appeared that Taft would get the Republican nomination by acclamation if General Eisenhower could not be induced to run. Hence, tremendous pressure was put on the general by Republicans who could not stomach Taft's aggressive isolationism. This second draft-Eisenhower movement began with greater promise and a more willing draftee. General Eisenhower's new-found enthusiasm for politics amused me because by then I had had a glimpse of the conflicts between the old soldier's ego, the values he had learned from his patron General Marshall, and the effects of his sudden, nearly intoxicating elevation to supreme Allied commander in Europe on the eve of the great war.

Eisenhower's ambivalence about the game of politics was best suggested by an incident that he described to me himself during the early Truman years, shortly before he laid down his immediate postwar task as chief of staff of the U.S. Army in February 1948 to become president of Columbia University. Dwight Eisenhower was a hero to me in those days, as to everyone else, and as a columnist I had done my best to make him a friend—a task at which I think I succeeded briefly. He thought well of our column in those days, and, if I recall correctly, I was invited to pay him a farewell call at his office in the Pentagon before his retreat to the Columbia campus in New York City.

The general greeted me amiably, and we had a long, pleasant exchange ("Good-bye, good-bye, so sad to see you go"—that kind of talk). Finally, when my audience was up, I said, "General, if you have got the time, there is one question of a business nature I would like to ask you." He told me to fire away, and so I asked him for his views on the rumors then circulating in Republican and, oddly enough, liberal Democratic circles that he might be drafted for a run at the presidency in 1948.

Then, as later, the general's face resembled a deep pink rubber mask. He had a way of twisting his features into different expressions that always astonished me, and at the mention of politics and the presidency this mask turned the brilliant red that, I think, anger always brought. General Eisenhower then told me a story that I have never forgotten, partly because it was so instructive and partly because I thought it was so amusing.

The general's story to me mainly concerned his visit to Tokyo, one of his stops on an extended procession through the Far East in the spring of 1946. There, General MacArthur, as viceroy of the East, gave his old staff officer what must have surely been one of the more macabre dinner parties in the history of Western entertainment. The party was held in the beautiful American embassy in Tokyo, which, when it still stood, was one of the little-known triumphs of Art Deco architecture. Over thirty people attended, all Americans or from various Allied units, with no Japanese present. No drink was served, and the food, as someone who was there has told me, was just what you'd expect from a good army mess sergeant. After the dinner, as General Eisenhower told me, the two viceroys simply forsook their guests—over thirty people, mind you, with not a drop to drink and nothing to do but stare at one another. With elaborate ceremony, MacArthur led his guest into a small side room.

Before the war, Eisenhower had served as MacArthur's aide in the Philippines, and the two men were, in many ways, complete opposites. Eisenhower, of course, was understated in manner and temperament with none of the shiny, boot-cavalry panache that General MacArthur went in for. However, the supreme Allied commander had a considerable ego of his own, while MacArthur, God knows, had an ego bigger than all outdoors. The success of his old subordinate must have caused the Pacific commander silent fits of envy. Then, from his days in Manila, Eisenhower undoubtedly knew of MacArthur's penchant for self-promotion long before most and no doubt disapproved of it. The two must have clashed somewhere earlier because the tension was palpable in their Tokyo meeting.

As General Eisenhower recalled the experience to me, General MacArthur's first topic in the side room was a rumor that a certain number of five-star admirals had succeeded in getting military honors that were not accorded to five-star generals. Eisenhower, who was genuinely not interested in that sort of thing got rid of the issue by saying that, in his view, all distinctions and honors ought to be abolished, that he did not care about them and thought that everyone should get the same salutes, the same ruffles and drum beats, from brigadier general on up. To which General MacArthur replied, "That's all right, Ike. Just so long as those navy sons of bitches don't get ahead of us, I don't care."

General MacArthur's next subject was rather more interesting. If Eisenhower quoted him correctly, he said that either he or Eisenhower unquestionably would be president of the United States before very long. He added, very shrewdly, that he, MacArthur, was debarred. The reasons for this were twofold: although he was a Republican by birth, the Republican party of those days was an oligarchy and MacArthur believed in strong, personal leadership, not oligarchy. To this, he added that he was still very busy as viceroy of Japan. It was a very big job that he wished to finish, and his duties were still such that he could not possibly tear himself free by election time in 1948.

The old general then pressed Eisenhower, saying that since he himself was out of the running, Eisenhower was a sure thing for the presidency, should he choose to run. Perhaps because MacArthur sensed that this line of questioning irritated his guest, he kept up the pressure until Eisenhower was angry enough to counter with a lecture to MacArthur. He reminded his host of the desirability of total divorce of the military from politics, a standard principle of General Marshall, a name perhaps chosen to irritate MacArthur. Eisenhower continued with a lengthy and, one cannot help but imagine, self-righteous statement to the effect that not only did the military have no business in politics, but also he, Eisenhower, felt that at this point in his life and career, the United States had given him everything he could possibly hope for or deserve. Therefore, he announced, he had no intention whatever of running for the presidency.

At this point, to my amazement, General Eisenhower broke off his recital to me, turned the color of a boiled beet from sheer remembered rage, and said: "Joe, do you know what that man said to me then?"

"No, General," I said.

"He leaned over, he patted me on the knee, and he had the nerve to say, 'That's all right, Ike. You go on like that and you'll get it sure.' "

I replied, "I can hardly believe it, General. I wish you all good luck." And with that, our conversation ended. It is still one of the funniest political episodes I have heard. I had it from Eisenhower's own lips, and I have not exaggerated. MacArthur, of course, was dead right. Although he may have been egging his old adversary on, he no doubt spotted General Eisenhower's self-deprecating brand of vanity long before any of his fellow Republicans chose to exploit it. Often, as that 1952 campaign unfolded, I imagined the old soldier sitting in fitful and bitter retirement. As Eisenhower moved ever closer to his party's nomination and then the White House, MacArthur might have smiled to himself in rueful remembrance of their Tokyo meeting. I know I did.

As it turned out, I would contribute in a very minor way to Eisenhower's successful bid to beat out Taft for the 1952 Republican presidential nomination. The tactical turning point of the party battle occurred in Texas. The Taft organization, alarmed by the strength of the grass-roots movement for Eisenhower in a state they had counted on, decided to nail down the Texas delegation without further delay. The place appointed for the nailing was an ancient and dusty resort in the Texas hill country called Mineral Wells. Henry Cabot Lodge, who was to be Eisenhower's floor manager at the convention that July in Chicago, asked me to go to Mineral Wells. He argued that certain bad dealings expected from the Taft people would make a good story for a syndicated columnist and also might present an opportunity to exercise considerable capacity for public outrage, something that other reporters would not be able to bring out so clearly under the rules governing political reporting in those days.

As the Eisenhower campaign gained momentum through that spring of 1952, Texas produced an outpouring of support for the general on the Republican side, and the question was, of course, whether this support was to be reflected in the delegation that the state sent to the Republican convention. The Taft forces, led by the state's chief Republican National committeeman, a tough old bird from Fort Worth named Henry Zweifel, had decided that this upstart movement would not be reflected, not even by a compromise delegation. Thus, a drama of old-fashioned American political bullying was enacted against the ideal backdrop of the Mineral Wells Hotel with its gimcrack 1880s charm, by now going rapidly to seed.

On the day of the voting, a number of burly deputy sheriffs guarded the hallway doors, blocking entrance to anyone not conspicuously displaying a Taft button. As Zweifel pushed his troops on to outrage after outrage, I wrote what was happening for all it was worth—and it was worth a lot. Without departing from the facts, I reported that the selection of the Republican delegation at Mineral Wells was a ruthless vote steal on a huge scale. At the convention that July in Chicago, the Eisenhower strategists made the vote on whether or not to seat the Taft delegation from Texas a prime issue. The Taft people failed to attain a majority against what Eisenhower's lieutenants called the "Fair Play Amendment"; and, with that, their chances of winning the nomination were gone.

When the vote was in, Cabot and I had a jubilant drink together, and Cabot flatteringly told me, "You made the Texas vote-steal issue, and now we're going to win on it." I should add that making the issue was easy enough to accomplish. The Eisenhower people in Texas had expressed polite outrage at their treatment, some of which had been blandly reflected in the national press, although at nowhere near the indignant level I had managed to attain. The national news magazines, in turn, had been waiting in the wings to pick up and echo my material, and they also were for Ike. I still ask myself whether this kind of political intervention was appropriate for a reporter like myself. I find myself answering, "I don't care," although during those Eisenhower years that followed I sometimes wondered whether it might not have been better to leave the events at Mineral Wells in the dark.

What followed was a bitterly disappointing general election. In one of my own letters to Isaiah Berlin from that period, I compared following the 1952 campaign to a "trip through the Paris sewers." In the back of my mind, however, was the long shadow of Joe McCarthy. Many of us believed in those days that only the Republicans had the power to directly confront the senator. As I wrote Isaiah, "I find myself constantly blackmailed by the virtual certainty that we shall have a first class fascist party in the United States if the Republicans don't win. The real need for a change in this country arises, not from the decay of the Democrats, but from the need to give the Republicans the sobering experience of responsibility."

Nevertheless, with Taft out of the way, Stew and I briefly entertained high hopes for Adlai Stevenson, then governor of Illinois, during the period when President Truman was seeking to recruit him as the Democratic candidate. We even went to Springfield to see him before the Democratic convention but were alarmed by his tendency to bring Abraham Lincoln into the conversation, for we had a steadfast rule that when American politicians began bracketing themselves with Abraham Lincoln it was always well to send for a psychiatrist. Our alarm was not erased at the 1952 Democratic convention in Chicago. In fact, it was strengthened by Stevenson's famous acceptance speech in which he compared his agony in reaching his decision to run for the presidency with no less than Christ's agony in the garden following the Last Supper.

Indeed, when he used Christ's anguished plea to our Lord "Let this cup pass from me!" as a highlight in his speech, I am afraid I was driven, quite literally, to drink. This convention was only the second to be played out on television, a development that proved startling both to the participants and to long-time hangers-on like Stew and myself. If truth be known, I was briefly caught on television in an unbecoming posture, for my beloved sister-in-law Patricia used to insure Stew's and my occasional refreshment on the convention floor by going to her gallery seat with my grandfather's large silver flask. There she would attach a stout string to the container (already filled with an alcoholic beverage) and dutifully lower it over the gallery rail on request. I was later told that this highly functional arrangement made an amusing scene on the television news coverage of the convention.

From my own rather insular perspective, the hero of the 1952 election turned out to be my brother John, who that year directed the Eisenhower campaign in Connecticut. It was Johnny who (a bit maliciously, perhaps) gave Stew the immortal quotation "All the eggheads love Stevenson. But how many eggheads do you think there are?" John was also the author of Alsop's law of political oratory: "The important thing is to be able to say 'Most oranges are round' and sound as if you meant it." In the end, Stevenson's inability to fulfill Alsop's law was his real political weakness. The governor was always remembering—he was even hinting to his audience—that no orange is absolutely round, that oranges only seem round, that they have pores on their surface, and so on and on. The overall effect was beautiful to hear but lacked impact. The "message" of Stevenson's campaign was, in the end, dull and indistinct, something today's highly paid political "spin doctors" could have doubtless remedied for a sizable cash fee.

As the campaign progressed, I found myself thinking less and less of Adlai Stevenson, so much so that when the time to choose came that November I decided not to cast a ballot. The more I saw of Stevenson, the more I thought of the world he came from: the cultivated, old-fashioned, only-WASP-family-in-town world where cast-iron deer adorned every front lawn and ladies in white lace dresses and lingerie hats took tea and finger sandwiches under the elms. American upper-class genteel was the note, and I had long ago concluded that one could not be a serious politician and be genteel.

I suppose I would classify myself as a lifelong Democrat although I have never voted in a partisan way. Indeed, it seems to me that if neither of the great political parties of the United States cares to offer a candidate able to send one to the ballot box with any real enthusiasm, nonvoting is a sensible response. Perhaps, too, my judgment had been corrupted by early experience. When election time rolled around in the old days, Mother would write letters to both Stew and me, pointing out that in this softer time the citizen's task had been eased by the provision for absentee ballots, which she enclosed and urged us to fill out. We always filled them out and returned them to Mother, whereupon she would remove her maternal cap and put on her party cap as the Republican town chairman of Avon, Connecticut, a post to which she had been elected on the day women got the vote. Without further ado, she would then put Stew's and my filled-out ballots in the fire, for we rarely then, as later, followed the family Republican line.

Mother was forced to confess her crime when Stew tested her by voting for the Socialist candidate Norman Thomas. He then waited eagerly to see whether a Socialist vote was registered in Avon. When no Socialist vote was recorded, Stew charged Mother with political skullduggery, and she calmly replied that she had a very poor opinion of anyone who went into politics without being professional about it.

In further self-defense, I must add that my nonegghead failure to see the charms of Adlai Stevenson was nothing compared to my outrage when candidate Eisenhower gave a warm greeting, with no hint of rebuke, to Senator Joe McCarthy. That infamous meeting took place in October 1952, according to prearranged plan, in Milwaukee. The year before, Senator McCarthy had escalated the level of his sordid rhetoric by attacking Marshall on the floor of the Senate. This meandering, wholly scurrilous speech later appeared in printed form, under the title *America's Retreat from Victory: The Story of George Catlett Marshall.* Although the great general was never directly accused of treason, it was suggested that Marshall and the Communists were in tacit alliance, a charge so absurd that all but two senators present for McCarthy's original diatribe on the subject had fled the chamber by the time he had finished. As for candidate Eisenhower, one would have thought this attack against his old mentor Marshall was enough to earn McCarthy a stiff rebuke.

However, not once during the entire campaign did Eisenhower speak out. Indeed, during the candidate's final whistle-stop tour through Wisconsin, Senator McCarthy found his way to Eisenhower's side. As members of the general's staff told me later, they thought Eisenhower could not avoid appearing with McCarthy on the platform at the big party gathering in Milwaukee. But they planned not to invite McCarthy to travel through Wisconsin on Eisenhower's train. In order to emphasize the general's stand, Eisenhower and his staff had included high praise of General Marshall in their first draft of the general's Milwaukee speech. However, at the pleading of Wisconsin governor Walter Kohler, Jr., a moderate Republican who feared McCarthy's power in his own state, these passages were deleted. Instead, Eisenhower gave vent to his own views on the great Communist menace, words that he no doubt believed but that also gave new legitimacy to the hometown senator who stood grinning at his side.

That infamous meeting in Milwaukee was bad business, and, like many around the country, Stew and I were incensed when we got news of it. For no other reason than base political cowardice, the candidate chose to give a warm greeting to the man who had just imputed near treason to General Marshall—not only the greatest and most honorable American of our time, but also the virtual creator of Eisenhower. When he was pressed about it, Eisenhower blamed Kohler as well as his own staff for forcing him to make the fateful changes in his speech. However, President Truman saw the incident for what it was and quickly denounced Eisenhower as a coward. This was no less than the truth, and for a time even Eisenhower's men referred to their candidate's appearance in Milwaukee as "that terrible day." In some ways, however, the candidate's action presaged even worse, for the cowardice shown by Eisenhower during the election was of little importance compared to the cowardice he showed once he was in the White House. By the time the old general took office that January 1953, it was difficult to find a corner of government in the city of Washington free of intimidation from Joe McCarthy and his vile crowd.

18

Ike's
Washington

At the deepest level, McCarthy's success was made possible by America's recoil from the discovery that the world was a very dangerous place, even for those favorites of fortune—Americans. We had never had to consider an external military threat; we had never been without vast continental spaces waiting to be developed and exploited; we had, in fact, as Bismarck said, been taken care of by God Almighty. The Korean War, with its losses and frustrations, brought home the disagreeable fact that this country was no longer being taken care of by the Almighty and, therefore, had to face all the unpleasant necessities of taking care of itself in a larger, much less hospitable postwar world.

But that does not alter the fact that prominent, respected American politicians could not resist the temptation presented to them by Joseph McCarthy. As I have already said, few men in politics have been more decent or more honorable, in my judgment, than Senator Robert A. Taft. But the way Taft responded to McCarthy reminded me of the behavior of the kind of drunk who cannot resist "just one more for the road." Taft was not alone in his weakness. But among those politicians who contributed to the double-talk and appeasement that predominated at the highest levels during McCarthy's bull's rush to prominence, none was more feeble in his response or less defensible in his actions than President Eisenhower.

I will not bore the reader with a rehash of well-known history. Suffice it to say, the opening months of the Eisenhower presidency were among the most peculiar the American government has ever passed through. The new president's rule for dealing with Congress was "I speak my piece, and then it's up to them." His "piece" was, to some extent, influenced by the isolationist views of Senator Taft; for until his illness struck him down, Taft, in effect, exercised a power of veto on all the administration's actions. This situation did not make Eisenhower happy. Indeed, he gradually became so disgusted with his own party that he began to talk in private of the need for a new party, vaguely formed of men of good will. But the president's unhappiness was not remedied in the usual way—by a firm assertion of the great powers of the presidency.

As a consequence, McCarthy continued to run roughshod over the new government. Going back over those days, both in the many books that have subsequently been published and in my memory, mulling over the events and trying to find coherent patterns in them, I think it can be argued that the reason Dwight D. Eisenhower dealt with McCarthy and his crew with feebleness for so long and agonizing a period was not because he was confident that McCarthy would destroy himself if given enough rope, but simply because McCarthy, his allies, and their methods frightened Eisenhower deeply. And, I have slowly come to believe, the truth is that President Eisenhower had good reason to be wary, given the lunatic atmosphere of that time.

When Eisenhower took office in January 1953, no one in Washington was quite prepared for the way the city would change. Eisenhower's Washington closely resembled a company town with the president as the chairman of the board, a rather remote and frequently absent figure. The domestic side of the company was entirely under the control of Secretary of the Treasury George M. Humphrey, and the foreign side was in the hands of Secretary of State John Foster Dulles. In this company town, a clear line was drawn between those who served the company and those who did not. The people in the company, including the wives, were an organized hierarchy. For example, Pam Humphrey, George Humphrey's wife, who would have been an exceedingly agreeable woman in any other setting, was a kind of despot with whom no one dared to argue except Janet Dulles, whose husband, after all, had his own company pasture where she, too, reigned supreme.

I will admit in all honesty that I and, to a lesser extent, Stew viewed the arrival of this new administration with real apprehension. All our working lives we had been thoroughly familiar with the officials of each administration. The Truman administration, so far as its high officials were concerned, had been a continuation of the Roosevelt years. Stew and I had had our quarrels with government officials; we had criticized and had been criticized. However, with the exception of Dean Acheson, we had never been denied access to the top echelons of government. But, as all working newspapermen know, there comes a time when the old wires that one has strung are cut. This was our first total unplugging, however, so we—I should say I, for Stew, to his credit, took a more placid and measured view of his work—spent the first Eisenhower months in something of a lather.

Once acclimated, I did not like what I saw. Possibly from spite, possibly from a nostalgia for my Truman friends, I privately described Eisenhower's cabinet as being composed of eight millionaires and a plumber. The secretary of labor, Martin Durkin, was the plumber, a man who received the bulk of his political training as head of the plumber's union in Chicago. Without exception, the other members of the cabinet were millionaires, all of them drawn from the upper reaches of the business world. An extreme self-righteousness prevailed among many of these newcomers. They behaved as though they were somehow sanctified because they had sacrificed their often large business jobs to serve and live in Washington. The Roosevelt holdovers in the Truman administration had, after all, also sacrificed potentially enormous incomes to work for the government for many years and did not go around patting themselves on the back with a sacerdotal air because they had done so.

At a dinner party early on in the Eisenhower administration, a famous encounter took place between Phil Graham of the *Washington Post* and Treasury Secretary George Humphrey's wife Pam. The two had been seated next to one another at table and, by all accounts, were having a very civil discussion until Mrs. Humphrey brought up the subject of her husband's decision to give up his duties as head of a large corporation in Cleveland and come to Washington as a member of Eisenhower's government. The choice, it seemed, had been an agonizing one and was still viewed by the Humphreys—in any number of ways, including financial—as being a great sacrifice. Phil Graham, who regarded government service as the highest point of honor and who, like myself, had been great friends with a number of high-ranking officials in the Truman administration, listened at length to this disquisition until, evidently, he had had enough. "Mrs. Humphrey," he said in a firm tone, "making that kind of remark down here in Washington is like belching in Shaker Heights. We think of serving the United States of America as a privilege, not a sacrifice." Mrs. Humphrey, who had apparently never thought of her husband's new duties in this way, turned all the colors of a dying dolphin with Phil's remark and, as those who were present told me, seemed to gasp for air during the rest of dinner.

John Foster Dulles was perhaps the most curious man on the Eisenhower team. The president had wanted to appoint Jack McCloy as his secretary of state. He ended up choosing Dulles on the advice of his old friend Lucius Clay, who thought the rather severe Republican lawyer would be a more palatable choice to Senator Taft, who, after all had been no friend to McCloy's old ally Dean Acheson. In character, Foster Dulles was a very unchanging man. He could be amiable and unpretentious in private, although one had the constant feeling that he was never entirely at ease with his surroundings. Indeed, Dulles's key trait was a kind of angular, self-righteous charmlessness. In appearance, he was "a solemn looking man," as Stew described him, "with a long, early American face, a penchant for green tinted suits and a habit, when deep in thought, of making small clicking noises with his tongue." He must have had a very hard time of it as a young man, for his younger brother Allen had enormous personal charm and was likely everybody's favorite when the two boys were growing up. Foster, although he clearly had considerable talents, acted like a man who had been neglected or disparaged in some subtle way and who, because of this treatment, had resolved to rely on no one but himself. I never thought Foster was a very trusting man, although as one watched him in action, it became clear he had great ability. At the end of his life, when he was dying of cancer, Foster also showed that he was a man of great physical courage, for he went on working in agonizing pain without the faintest flinch.

A noted New York lawyer, Dulles had served as a delegate to the initial United Nations meeting and had also spent a brief time in the U.S. Senate, where he completed New York Senator Robert Wagner's unexpired term before losing in the 1950 election. Dulles was brought into the State Department as ambassador-at-large by Dean Acheson and President Truman, who wanted to add a bipartisan guarantee to their policies. Despite negotiating the peace treaty with Japan in 1951, he had not won many friends at State, and in time the inner group of Foreign Service officers who tended to dominate the higher, career positions took a hearty dislike to him. In fact, Chip and Avis Bohlen once repeated to me a little song that was sung quietly when Dulles was in Paris on some duty or other and behaving particularly deviously, "Doooles, Doooles, you take us for fooles," went the ditty. No doubt Dulles heard these lines intoned by the young diplomats further down the gilded corridor, and it cannot have increased his attachment to the Bohlens.

As this song implies, Foster Dulles was capable, despite his almost clerical façade (he had at one point presided over the Council of Churches), of being entirely unscrupulous. One of his first acts as secretary of state was to allow into the department an overtly McCarthyite goon, Scott McLeod, who proceeded to institute lavish security proceedings in an effort to make McCarthy's insistence that the Foreign Service was full of Communist spies and sympathizers appear to be true. These so-called "loyalty boards" soon became the bane of the department. In time, as I have said, many of my old adversaries from China, like Jack Service, would be hauled before them. Following the course I had chosen with Budenz, I assisted these men in finding legal help and, as I have said, testified on their behalf.

In particular, I testified several times over the next two years on behalf of John Paton Davies, whose career, by then, was well on its way to being ruined. During one of the dreary waits in dingy State Department loyalty-board rooms for still more dingy interrogators, John told me one of the oddest stories I can remember. On the eve of Theodore White's publication of *The Stilwell Papers* in 1948, which are in fact extracts of Joseph W. Stilwell's private diaries and letters during his China period, John, as he told me, became seriously concerned about the possible contents of the book. In consequence, at his own expense (which was heavy for a young officer in the State Department), he flew out to Los Angeles to see Mrs. Stilwell at her house on the West Coast.

John made his pitch that harm might be done by publishing General Stilwell's private papers since the general, as I have documented, was a choleric man and passages in his diary no doubt contained facts and expressions that he would not have wanted to make public without more mature reflection. Since General Stilwell was then dead at least two years, John was a little astonished to be told by Mrs. Stilwell that "the General has always had a high opinion of you, John." Still using the present tense, she added that General Stilwell would doubtless appreciate John's decision to come all the way to the West Coast to offer his advice and then concluded, "But the final decision must rest with him."

Thereupon, as John told me, Mrs. Stilwell retired to the rear of the house and either meditated upon the problem or consulted some form of psychic medium. Meanwhile, John sat uncomfortably in the living room, wondering what his host could possibly be up to. When Mrs. Stilwell at last returned, she informed John that although the general well understood John's worries, he nevertheless wished to go ahead with the publication of his memoirs. John Davies grinned when he told me this and said, "What could I do. You can't argue with a ghost." Indeed, he could do nothing, and after a polite interval, he begged Mrs. Stilwell good-bye and returned to Washington—again at his own expense.

I did my best for John and for the other Foreign Service officers I had known in China who were now coming under attack during that grim time. Stew and I both wrote a number of bitter columns on the subject of the State Department purges. Well before the Davies case, however, it was obvious that Dulles was determined to have no trouble with Senator McCarthy, even if it cost him the respect of his peers. From the upper levels on down, many in Eisenhower's new government followed suit, albeit to varying degrees. It was not long before this mixture of offhanded appeasement, along with the attempt to claim some sort of acquired sanctity, inspired a good many rebellions among the more permanent members of the Washington community.

The most forceful outburst I ever witnessed against one of the new Eisenhower recruits came from Chip Bohlen. This occurred during what we came to call the "tea-table episode." The tea table in question was Chip Bohlen's, and the venue was the little house he and Avis shared down the street from me on Dumbarton Avenue. Robert Cutler, whom Chip and I had both known in the Porcellian Club at Harvard, had been asked to tea by Avis and Chip, and I was included as a fourth guest for makeweight. Bobby Cutler, it should be understood, was a self-important Bostonian who had come to Washington to be secretary of President Eisenhower's National Security Council. The office was newly formed in those days and without an established portfolio. Lacking defined duties, Cutler found solace in the imagined rituals of his office. Before long, he had transformed the National Security Council into a virtual nest of Byzantine ceremony, with a sacred agenda and other trappings that would have suited the Foreign Secretariat of a Byzantine emperor.

On a personal level, Bobby Cutler was a nice enough man, but he brought with him from Boston a well-established reputation for having what the eminent English historian Edward Gibbon called "incorrect tastes in love." (There may have been something to this, for when he died Bobby left a large part of his fortune to his ever-loyal personal masseur.) At the time of our little tea party, Chip had already been appointed ambassador to the Soviet Union by the president. The appointment had yet to be confirmed in the Senate, however, thanks largely to an inspired innuendo attack by McCarthy, who was suggesting to anyone who would listen that Chip, too, of all people, had incorrect tastes in love. It was a charge incredible to anyone who knew him. Chip was a married man, closer to his wife than almost any man I knew, with a well-deserved reputation, before he met Avis in Moscow, as one of the most successful ladies' men in Europe.

Later on, Bob Cutler would help to call off the McCarthyites, but at the time of the tea-table episode he was highly sensitive to the prevailing political winds and still fearful. So as tea was being poured for our little party at the Bohlens', Bobby, to my amazement, ventured to discuss the subject of the attack on Chip. More incredibly, Cutler took the line that Secretary Dulles and the president—who had known Chip well from their time together in Paris, as golfing partners—were showing nobility by staying steadfast behind Chip's nomination for the Moscow embassy in the face of these grave charges.

While it was true President Eisenhower had offered Chip continued public support, Dulles had, in fact, done the exact opposite. Chip was enraged by this exhibition of self-righteousness, as I could tell from the muscle in his cheek, which used to announce his anger by bouncing detectably. As his face hardened, I held by breath, for I could see that Chip was about to remind Bobby of his own incorrect tastes and that, in the upshot, unforgivable things were likely to be said. Fortunately, Avis saw the same signs and took the rather drastic measure of a sudden movement that knocked the tea tray off its precarious perch on the coffee table. Amid the broken tea cups and general need for tidying up, the conversation mercifully changed and the meeting ended amicably enough. Chip, after some drama, ended up getting the Moscow embassy and performed there with great distinction. Recently, I reminded Avis's daughter, another Avis, of this story, and she replied, "Now I know why we don't have any teacups that match."

During that first Eisenhower year our major preoccupation as newspapermen continued to be the outright attacks being waged by Joe McCarthy and his cronies on all levels of national government. We were most concerned with the continuous appeasement of Senator McCarthy in the face of the clearest evidence that McCarthy was the enemy of Eisenhower and everything he stood for. Fear, political or otherwise, could not be the president's sole motivation, for Eisenhower was a soldier after all and had never been a cowardly man as far as we could tell. Being a far more devious man than Stew, I began to question the president's motives and, in time, I came to believe the old general had more to hide from Senator McCarthy than was generally known at the time. The story of this tentative discovery was for me the major drama of the entire Eisenhower presidency.

It began in a roundabout manner in the spring of 1953, when I traveled downtown from my office in Georgetown to meet with Admiral Lewis L. Strauss. The occasion of the interview was the admiral's imminent appointment by President Eisenhower as chairman of the Atomic Energy Commission. For his own peculiar reasons, Lewis Strauss pronounced his name as though it described the bedding usually provided for horses. An investment banker before obtaining a civilian-in-wartime commission as admiral under President Roosevelt, he was short, natty and energetic in appearance and a very able and frighteningly ambitious man.

Stew and I had written a great deal about the Atomic Energy Commission before the admiral's nomination as its head. During the late Truman time, we had dragged into the open the controversy within the administration about whether the hydrogen bomb should be built. In 1952, we had also broken the news of the devastating effects of the first H-bomb on the Pacific island of Eniwetok. Strauss had evidently decided that I was a dangerous character and had better be pacified in advance. So he had asked me to come to see him in the temporary office he occupied in the old Executive Office Building before his appointment as AEC chairman had been confirmed by the Senate. I accepted his invitation because I had never known him well, even though he had been a friend of Jim Forrestal, who had made him an admiral, and had served in the AEC under President Truman as a member of the commission.

For half an hour, while he told me at great length about my virtues and the fine work Stew and I had done, I wondered why Admiral Strauss had invited me to meet with him. Finally, unlikely as this may seem, I grew tired of being flattered and ventured upon serious questions of policy having to do with the AEC. I forget what my opening question was, but I well remember the admiral rearing back in his chair and, with an air of putting me in my proper place, saying that I was attempting to talk about "substance" and adding, "Surely, Mr. Alsop, you can't expect me to talk about that sort of thing now, especially as you're a member of the press."

Since Admiral Strauss had asked to see me and the interview was entirely his own doing, I was more than a little angry and broke in to say, "In that case, Admiral, you have asked me to see you in order to waste half an hour of my time." So unburdened, I rose from my chair and left the office.

Strauss made this something of a dinner story in Washington, increasing my own already impressive reputation for arrogance. This reputation I have never coveted although, admittedly, at times it has been deserved. I still believe my treatment of Admiral Strauss was warranted, however, since he was the initiator of the interview and had taken me for a damn fool by his obvious assumption that I could be taken into camp by the application of a little grease. I wondered at the time—and I still wonder now—whether Admiral Strauss's reason for this application of grease was his knowledge that Senator McCarthy and his crew already had confronted him with the option of jettisoning the brilliant physicist J. Robert Oppenheimer or becoming a McCarthy target himself.

I should have realized that there might be an Oppenheimer connection when Admiral Strauss extended his invitation. I had become a fairly close friend of Robert Oppenheimer when we served together as members of Harvard University's board of overseers. When he was in Washington during the early days of the AEC I made it my business to see him often. I had an interest in both the man and his subject, for he was, after all, the father of the atom bomb. By November 1953, however, the FBI was known to be gathering information on Oppy largely because of a letter sent to them by a former member of the staff of the Joint Committee on Atomic Energy, William L. Borden. In this document, which I saw much later, Borden cited a mishmash of stale facts and unsupported conclusions before asserting that "more probably than not J. Robert Oppenheimer is an agent of the Soviet Union."

Strauss may have gotten wind of this investigation long before Borden's letter was ever sent. At any rate, whatever the exact timing may have been, it was natural for Strauss to respond with some desperation to this news—news, no doubt, already known to McCarthy—for Strauss himself had approved Robert Oppenheimer's security clearance several years earlier while serving as one of President Truman's atomic energy commissioners. His choice, therefore, was either to stand up for his past judgment and for Oppenheimer or to offer Oppy, bound on the altar, as a sacrifice to appease McCarthy's wrath.

Attacking Oppenheimer instead of standing up to McCarthy was made yet more tempting to Chairman Strauss by another set of facts that now seems to me almost lunatic. In brief, Oppenheimer, during his early days on the Atomic Energy Commission, had become deeply interested in the problems of the air defense of the

United States. These problems were being tackled in those days by a government-funded scientific enterprise known as Project Lincoln. Dr. Jerome Weisner of the Massachusetts Institute of Technology (he later would become president of that institution) had given me enough of an idea of how much Project Lincoln had accomplished to produce a series of news stories that Stew and I wrote for the *New York Herald Tribune*. And these, in turn, brought down upon me—I can think of no better expression—one of the strangest experiences I have ever had.

This began with a summons to the office of an old friend, Tom Finletter, who was secretary of the air force until Eisenhower went to the White House. Tom warned me, ominously but somewhat mysteriously, about having a care to avoid evil associates; and he then passed me on to the chief of air force staff of those days, General Hoyt S. Vandenberg, who was also a dinner-party friend of mine. Vandenberg forthrightly charged that Stew's and my Project Lincoln stories were Communist-inspired.

Vandenberg's accusation made me hot enough under the collar to say I must ask for an immediate explanation in full or would be forced to leave the room forthwith. Vandenberg then said that Robert Oppenheimer was an associate of Dr. Weisner in sponsoring Project Lincoln and that Oppenheimer, in the past, had been a Communist. I replied rather rudely that this charge did not seem in line with Oppenheimer's effort to insure the air defense of the United States. Vandenberg answered that the real purpose of air-defense advocates was to take funds away from the air force's coveted long-range bomber programs and, hence, their nuclear capability. I am afraid that I answered the general rather shortly and left without delay. But at least the episode revealed why Strauss—a staunch big-bomber, big-bomb advocate—would single Oppenheimer out for attack and could count on the alliance and support of the air force in doing so.

It was Strauss who went to the president without consulting his colleagues and came back that December with the dramatically phrased order putting a "blank wall" between Oppenheimer and all classified data. It was Strauss who called the still-unsuspecting Oppenheimer to Washington to notify him that his AEC clearance was suspended. It was Strauss who accelerated the secret trial of the case months later in the spring of 1954. And it was Strauss who manipulated the proceedings in such a way that the AEC counsel during the Oppenheimer hearings would be a lawyer named Roger Robb, best known as counsel to Joe McCarthy's chief journalistic incense swinger, Fulton Lewis, Jr.

Oppy told me almost as soon as he had been warned by the AEC that he was to be proceeded against as a security risk. But he told me in confidence, and so the story was broken by James Reston of the *New York Times*, who, I believe, had also been told it in confidence. I all but threw up my hands a little later when Oppy proudly announced that his lawyer was going to be Lloyd Garrison, an impeccably virtuous man but exactly the sort any sensible man would not hire to contend with Lewis Strauss represented by Roger Robb, a fiercely effective lawyer who would stop at nothing to win. An eminently well-groomed New Yorker, Garrison was the epitome of high-mindedness, and it is always a mistake to pay for high-mindedness when you are hiring a lawyer. In the end, Garrison allowed himself to be so hustled by Robb's well-practiced nastiness that he failed even to get it squarely on the record that Strauss had studied all the evidence at length only a year or two before and had seen fit to approve Oppenheimer's security clearance only a little before the case was brought on.

When the case became public knowledge in April 1954, Stew and I would write a great many indignant columns about it, and in the end we accumulated enough data to produce a book—which we called *We Accuse!* in a ridiculous imitation of Emile Zola's "J'accuse." Long before this, however, we had begun to discern a deliberate pattern in Joe McCarthy's actions. This pattern—it can only be called high-level intimidation—had first become noticeable with McCarthy's shocking attack on General Marshall, which General Eisenhower, under pressure from conservative Republicans, failed to refute during his 1952 campaign.

Stew and I thought that it was not entirely a coincidence that McCarthy's activities had increased dramatically following the presidential election. He and his cronies had undertaken a series of frontal attacks on the new Eisenhower administration. What we observed and reported was a planned attempt to cut the new president down to size to make it possible for McCarthy to go after President Eisenhower himself. As I would later write in a private letter to Foster Dulles concerning the Davies case: "I am certain you and the President will be the next victims if the administration continues to build up McCarthy by surrenders and seeming surrenders to him. . . . It does not matter what you say or do; if Davies is now dropped from the Department, you and the administration will be universally regarded as bowing down to Moloch's temple in the most public and decisive manner."

I do not think so shrewd and farsighted a strategy was likely to have been worked out by Senator McCarthy himself, who was basi-

cally what my father used to call a "chancer," incapable of any kind
of long-range plan. Following the election, however, McCarthy had
at his elbow a New York lawyer named Roy Cohn, who was then a
very young man, all too eager to use his position with McCarthy to
build a sleazy yet highly profitable career. Cohn was brilliantly intelligent and one of the truly evil men I have ever watched in action in
American public life. Hence, I suspect that the long-term strategy
was Cohn's.

Whether Cohn or McCarthy knew of them at the time (and my
guess is that they did), Oppenheimer's troubles were bound to create a dilemma for the far-from-courageous new chairman of the
AEC. At bottom, however, the real dilemma lay with President
Eisenhower himself. When he learned of the accusations against
Oppenheimer in December 1953, he acted with uncharacteristic de-
cisiveness: he issued the orders blocking Oppenheimer's access to all
classified material and also ordered the FBI to begin its own secret
investigation into the matter, which he no doubt hoped would pre-
empt any attempts by McCarthy and his men to dig up the same
material and make it public.

By that time, Dwight Eisenhower was the only man with
enough power to stand up to McCarthy. Eisenhower's motives and
actions, as such, were one of the keys to the senator's political success. It was a puzzle to me, as it was to others, why the president so
consistently and resolutely failed to stand up to McCarthy in public.
Historians have since traced Eisenhower's hesitancy to a number of
factors: a desire, during the general election, to keep the Republican
party together; a fear, during the Oppenheimer affair, that some of
the "evidence" marshaled by Strauss—specifically, that Oppenheimer, labeled a "red," had deliberately slowed the development of
the H-bomb (which, of course, he had done, although from personal
conviction, not under orders from the Kremlin)—would be taken
public by McCarthy; and a belief that any presidential response to
McCarthy's methods would drag the office down to the senator's
debased level.

All these elements of the McCarthy problem must have played
in the president's mind through that early winter of 1954, leading up
to the decisive Army-McCarthy hearings in late April. Another vital
thread in this ugly pattern was the situation I had seen in Berlin in
1946. Eisenhower then was coming under rising criticism for having allowed Soviet troops to take over Czechoslovakia, preventing
an Allied march on Berlin, and in other ways setting the pattern for
postwar eastern Europe. One may be sure that Eisenhower was very
sensitive about this, for the subject is covered at great length in his

grandson's biography of him, which I take to mean that in the circle around the general there was a good deal of defensiveness on the subject.

But in looking back over the president's career—and, indeed, over mine—Stew and I found another and, I think, more basic key to President Eisenhower's behavior. For argument's sake, let me backtrack to the period of my visit to postwar Germany in the late summer of 1946, the same year of my first visits to London and Paris. Allied occupation headquarters in Berlin was, as I have already said, home to a number of American Communists. It will also be recalled that some of these men and women were appointed to their posts during General Eisenhower's brief tenure as commander of the U.S. occupation forces in Germany. What would have happened, I asked myself, if Dwight Eisenhower had stood up to McCarthy when Eisenhower had first had the chance—when the senator attacked General Marshall, the great man who had plucked Eisenhower from obscurity in the army and made a great career for him? How would it have been if McCarthy had then challenged the candidate himself? Indeed, how would it have been if McCarthy had said in response to the candidate's attack, "No wonder Eisenhower stands up for the fellow-traveling General Marshall when we have to ask whether he isn't a fellow traveler himself"?

This was a ludicrous charge on its face but an undeniably potent one, given the fetid political climate of that time. By the early winter of 1954, McCarthy and his men had chosen the U.S. Army as a general target. Their point of attack was an obscure army dentist by the name of Captain Irving Peress. Peress had evidently been a Communist, for he took the Fifth Amendment on the subject. It did not seem to occur to anyone that the politics of a man who had been filling the neglected teeth of GIs really mattered very little. McCarthy made a great stink about the fact that this Fifth Amendment dentist had been promoted to major when he left the army, and I still remember the eight-column front-page headline that McCarthy's stink produced in the New York Times: "Who Promoted Dr. Peress?"

The nation, it seemed to me, had simply taken leave of all sense of proportion. It was a climate in which the facts about Germany could have been desperately damaging to President Eisenhower. What Stew and I began to discern that winter, in fact, was a progression in McCarthy's strategy. It began with the attack on General Marshall that forced Eisenhower to knuckle under, going on to the open intimidation of Foster Dulles and the State Department combined with deliberately veiled threats to take on the AEC, and ending with the attack on the very institution closest to Eisenhower—the U.S. Army.

McCarthy's attacks on the army began to escalate through the early months of 1954. As the pitch of debate rose, there began to be a palpable feeling in the town—entirely justified, as I thought then and think still—that great issues were at stake. The man most directly involved in the drama was Secretary of the Army Robert Stevens, a textile manufacturer far from notable for either intelligence or guts. He had no political experience and not a trace of political guile. If the attack on the army was to be successfully parried, it was clear that the White House would have to intervene. From Cabot Lodge, who was then U.S. representative to the United Nations, Stew and I learned that the White House was dangerously divided. Vice-President Nixon, who knew his own star might rise and fall with McCarthy's, was for giving way to the senator, as was the Eisenhower staff member in charge of congressional liaison, General Jerry Persons, a sly, morally sinuous man with deceptively agreeable manners.

The whole matter came to a head when McCarthy, largely at Nixon's behest, agreed to meet the unfortunate Stevens for a peacemaking lunch at Senator Everett Dirksen's office on Capitol Hill. The issue discussed over the lunch (fried chicken was served) was McCarthy's brutal bullying of the army officers he called to the stand, most notably General Zwicker, a decorated combat veteran who had had the bad fortune of being Irving Peress's commanding officer at the time of the dentist's automatic promotion. Stevens had ordered Zwicker not to testify further, whereupon McCarthy threatened in private to go after the Secretary himself. Wishing to head off such a confrontation, Nixon tried to guide the two parties toward some form of compromise. In the end, however, Stevens caved in completely and agreed that McCarthy could continue questioning whomever he wished so long as he promised to be polite. The uproar resulting from this ludicrous agreement was so bad that Stew and I, who had obtained a step-by-step account of the meeting from Stevens's legal counsel John Adams, compared the event in our column the next day to the Reichstag fire. We cast the silly Stevens in the role of the Dutchman Marinun van der Lubbe, whom Hitler's people had used to set fire to the Reichstag.

Admittedly, the comparison reflected our flair for the calamitous, but I had chosen it because it conveyed the real and desperate gloom that Stew and I were feeling that winter. Up to that point, our repeated public attacks on McCarthyism had come to little. Ever since the election, the column had been losing subscribers by the month, and because we habitually split costs with the *Tribune*, we were beginning to feel the effects. But none of this seemed to matter after General Stevens's public display of appeasement. It is hard to believe now that the American press and public were capable of such excesses of folly, but they were. With each new frenzied headline, one had the grim sense that the government was sinking further and further into crisis. This gloomy view was reinforced—and, indeed, embodied—by the president's resolute and continued failure to confront Joe McCarthy.

By now, because we suspected that there was more to all of this than met the eye, Stew and I had been going down the old trails to check the appointments on Eisenhower's German occupation staff and to get the names of the newspapers and the names of the de-Nazified governing boards that had created the grim situation in postwar Berlin. Cabot, with whom we were then in constant touch, grew frighteningly gloomy after the Stevens-McCarthy lunch. I knew from him how deeply divided the White House was at that point. Both Cabot and I believed very strongly that if Eisenhower chose to stand up and fight, McCarthy could be stopped. I also believed, as I wrote Foster Dulles, that if the president continued to sit on his hands, McCarthy, having beaten down the institution closest to Eisenhower, would have the courage and momentum necessary to go after the president himself. So, with Stew's approval I decided to take action on my own.

I got hold of the only member of the Eisenhower staff whom I knew well, a young man named Charles Willis, and asked him to arrange a meeting with Eisenhower's chief of staff, the former governor of New Hampshire Sherman Adams. I told Willis that I wished to see the governor as a matter of personal privilege and for reasons having nothing to do with my being a columnist. The appointment came through rapidly for 10:00 A.M., as I recall, on the nineteenth of February.

It was a cold, grey morning when I found myself marching into the governor's White House office. Adams was a little man with a face that looked frost-bitten and manners that everyone would have called downright bad if they had not assumed them to be natural in rock-bound northern New England. I greeted the governor, made an apology for asking for his time, and accepted an invitation to sit down. On a foolscap pad, I had made my notes of the names and offices of the Communists who had been important under Eisenhower's German command. I now withdrew the list and placed it on my knee. I explained to the governor that I was not after information, but rather possessed information that I thought he badly needed and might be without. Adams showed no great emotion at my pronouncement. After a brief silence, he nodded as though to signal me to go ahead, and I started reading from my pad.

I droned on undiscouraged for fifteen minutes. I explained the situation, as Nicolas Nabokov had laid it out for me years before, at Camp Ritchie, Maryland, listed each of the suspect newspapers, and ran through all the names of the Communist party members on the various governing boards and military staffs which ran occupied Germany. When I reached the end of my notes, I handed them all over to Governor Adams. Adams, more frosty than ever, accepted the notes.

After a brief silence, he inquired, "Why do you think I need to know this, Mr. Alsop?"

I replied that with the army now under attack, my brother and I were convinced that McCarthy was planning to make the president his next victim and we had reason to believe that the president might be able to use the material I had just read.

I added that I had only one question. My brother and I, I said, were sure that all this material would be spread upon the record by McCarthy unless the White House stood up and fought for the U.S. Army. We were equally sure, I said, that if the White House stood and fought, McCarthy would be beaten and sink back into insignificance. We had considered, therefore, publishing the material in our column because if it were to appear so publicly and in such a straightforward way, it would not cause the kind of sensation that McCarthy was reaching for. We might still publish it, but before we did so we thought it best to seek some kind of signal from the White House as to whether the president was, indeed, going to fight.

Whereupon Governor Adams, looking still like a frost-bitten quince, said, "Alsop, we'll fight."

I replied, "Well, that was all I came to find out, Governor. Leaving my notes with you, I have forgotten the conversation already."

I got up to go and was halfway across the room when Adams stopped me with a question that surprised me more than almost anything I can think of in my whole working life. "Wait a minute, Alsop," he said. "Do you believe in God?"

For some reason I thought this question was exceedingly impertinent and not a little odd, and I heard myself replying, "Governor Adams, I believe in this country, and that is all I need to say to you. Good morning."

I have never known—and do not know to this day—whether this modest intervention on my part made the difference of a feather in the balance of the decision, but two weeks following my appointment with Adams, President Eisenhower asked his attorney general Herbert Brownell to begin laying the legal groundwork for the issuance of an executive order that would cut McCarthy off from members of the executive branch and all documents pertaining to the executive branch. When it was finally issued three months later, this order turned out to be among the most extreme invocations of executive privilege in the nation's history. Given the closeness of the argument in the White House, which Nixon and Persons had always won before, I like to think that Stew's and my venture did have at least some influence on this outcome.

From the day of Eisenhower's executive order on May 17, 1954, the road was downward for the ugliest prejudice peddler the United States has known in my time. The story ended, of course, with the Senate's censure of McCarthy in December, after which the senator's claws were drawn and he consoled himself with drink so lavishly that he died in obscurity in less than two years. It may be that Stew and I were a bit presumptuous to think that our ten-cents worth helped precipitate McCarthy's decline. Nevertheless, my brother died proud of his part in this little drama, and I am proud of it to this day.

I do not for a moment claim that my visit to Governor Adams was decisive. It can be said, of course, that it was the sort of intervention that reporters have no business making, but it was always our view that reporters were citizens of the United States like everyone else and had the duties of citizenship like everyone else. When I came away from Adams's office, I felt I had done my duty. And so did Stew when I recounted to him with some glee what had passed between the governor and myself.

Being only human, we regretted being closed off from writing the planned series of columns on how the president, by the prevailing standards of the McCarthy years, was just as open to criticism as anyone else in public life. In one column published that winter, we did hint—obliquely—at the Berlin connection. But since both Stew and I liked a fight, the pattern of my curious encounter with Governor Adams mainly gave us a great deal of pleasure. And although we both knew it was wicked to exult in the collapse and death of another man, we could not resist a drink together when, some years later, we got the news of the end of McCarthy.

19

The Weather
in the Streets

As a journalist, I always followed the rule I laid down for myself in China in 1941: to go and see for myself when trouble became serious enough abroad to make the trip worthwhile. I went abroad at least twice a year until I retired after Stew's death from leukemia in 1974. At no time, however, were these travels more hectic or more diverse than during the 1950s. From our early visits to the postcolonial trouble spots like Iran and Indochina to my semipermanent move to Paris after the Suez crisis in 1956, Stew and I were often on the move. We were still young then, still able to survive the rigors of a Malayan jungle patrol, stomach the hottest foods, and drink the strongest liquor. We never tired of going abroad, and, indeed, we relished the opportunity to get away from our stodgy Washington rounds.

For the most part, I went where the news of the day took me and, as columnist, was rarely bound by daily deadlines and was hardly ever refused access to those I wished to see. In preparation for travel, I would pack a huge bag with almost enough clean linen to take me around the world, a portable typewriter with an adequate supply of paper; and a huge book bag with books enough to occupy me in flight and let me read myself to sleep at night for two months. The distances traveled seemed greater then, the going more settled and sedate, the destinations more distinct and exotic. Even the half-improvised transocean planes of the 1940s and 1950s were somehow more comfortable, more pleasant than their quick and cramped successors; and the airports, too, were downright heaven compared to the vastly sanitized, vastly overrun airports of today. Upon arrival, I could linger a little, sample the best a place had to offer, and then move on. As I look back over the old columns, my recorded impressions—often somber, occasionally insightful—are of less interest than the odd sights seen along the way, and it is to these peculiar dramas that I now turn.

Very often a solitary journey will unfold as a story—by turns dull, aggravating, adventurous, or purely comic. So it was when I went abroad; and although my travels contained long stretches of boredom—punctuated by the usual frustrations of missed appointments, disagreeable foods, and late arrivals—I seemed to have a knack for attracting the ridiculous, even during the most difficult and hair-raising circumstances. Often (and this was especially true during the early postwar years), I sought destinations—such as Berlin, Saigon, Teheran, and Athens—that seemed on the verge of some great conflagration. Invariably, the promise of disorder or conflict threw the more mundane adventures of daily life as I found them in these countries into heightened, sometimes absurd, relief.

One such experience took place toward the beginning of Stew's and my career together, when I traveled to Greece in 1947 to witness the progress of the civil war there. Arriving at the front gate of the American embassy in Athens, where I was to stay, I found a thoroughly bewildered American sergeant who seemed to be in command of a large flatbed truck containing a giant mule. The man asked me for the address of the U.S. embassy. I replied that he was standing in front of it and, to the man's obvious relief, proceeded to ring the doorbell. Entering, I gave my bags to the major domo and told him that both man and mule outside seemed also to be looking for the embassy. His face showed a glimmer of awed comprehension, and he promptly disappeared, leaving my bags in the vestibule.

So stranded, I had no real choice but to stay and witness the eruption, from the front hall of the residence, of my hostess for the duration of my stay in Athens, the ambassadress Mrs. Henry F. Grady. Lucretia Grady was an old friend and, I knew from previous experience, a remarkably masterful personality. She paused not at all to greet me, however, and as she flew through the doorway, I saw that she was bearing in her hand a large perfume atomizer. To the extreme alarm of the sergeant and myself, Mrs. Grady briskly climbed into the truckbed with the mule. The arrival of Mrs. Grady did little to improve the mule's mood, for he appeared a sullen animal and showed a strong tendency to begin kicking. Unawed by the great hooves that I feared threatened her, the ambassadress sprayed the mule with the perfume atomizer, crying loudly, "I christen thee Greece!" I thought the sergeant might well faint dead away, and I feared for the mule, too, before Mrs. Grady mercifully finished her odd little ceremony and clambered down from the truck to greet me.

Later, I found that Mrs. Grady had forced the U.S. Army to send its remaining mules to Greece for use in the fearful mountain fighting that was a major feature of the civil war there. In fact, the delivery of the mules to Greece had been perfectly sensible—indeed, inspired, as it turned out—for when the animals did get past Mrs. Grady and her perfume atomizer and into the mountains, they proved very useful in battle. I often remember Mrs. Grady and her mule when the appearance of oddity suggests the absence of common sense; for the truth is, oddity and common sense tend to co-exist in this world far more easily than stupidity and practicality.

Mrs. Grady was again one of the players in a nearly surreal visit to Teheran I made in the spring of 1951, when Reza Shah Pahlavi was in only tenuous control of his country and the old nationalist politician, Premier Mohammed Mossadegh, threatened from his rumpled bed to take charge. In those days, American policy was built on the expectation that Britain would remain this country's great power partner indefinitely. It was quite obvious that this could not happen if Britain lost her control of Middle Eastern oil, which was, indeed, threatened by Mossadegh's new government in Iran. Moreover, by dint of its strategic location next to the Soviet Union, any instability in Iran, whether Soviet-inspired—as had been the case during the Azerbaijan crisis—or not, was viewed, then as now, as being of crucial importance to the Middle East.

I was worried by these developments, possibly to the point of gloom, and in preparation for my journey I had gone in London to see Sir William Fraser, the head of the Anglo-Iranian Oil Company, whose operations Mossadegh threatened to nationalize. It was not a reassuring visit. Sir William was an arrogant and stony man, and he asserted rather haughtily that by the drift of my questions he could see I had a tendency to needless worry. "You'll see, Alsop," he said, "in a little while, probably six months and no more, my Iranians will come to heel like whipped dogs." I was sufficiently upset by this extraordinary remark to dare to point out that his Iranians seemed to be showing a strong tendency toward the opposite. Whereupon, the staff of Anglo-Iranian who were present when Sir William received me all went white with horror because I had come perilously close to arguing with the aged godhead.

Nor, after this unpleasant meeting with Fraser, was I quite prepared for what I found in Iran. Although parts of Teheran were horrible slums, the city as a whole was not densely occupied, nor was the bulk of its inhabitants desperately poor like the people, say, of Calcutta. The streets were relatively clean, and gardens in the more affluent sections showed trees above the high walls to give variety to the generally dusty urban scene. However, the city, as it existed before the unfortunate shah rebuilt it during the 1960s, had one essential and shocking feature. The buildings were clustered on a hillside, and in almost every case the higher block of houses was the richer one. Furthermore, the old water system consisted of large, open channels that coursed along the sides of the streets. From these channels, the residents of each house took whatever water they needed and put back whatever refuse or slops they had to get rid of. What these channels must have been carrying by the time the city tailed off at the bottom of the hill I always shuddered to think but never dared to investigate. However, it seemed to me that this arrangement, in which the poor drank the slops and worse of the rich and the the rich drank the slops and worse of the very rich, did not enhance Iran's chances for long-term social stability.

I arrived in Teheran to find the American embassy staff entirely obsessed with the subject of Mrs. Grady again. This time the animal in question was an elephant. Quite reasonably, but with less practicality than in the case of the mule in Greece, Mrs. Grady had persuaded her friend Pandit Nehru (Henry Grady had also served in India) to present her residence with a large Indian elephant. The elephant, she argued, might offer comfort and diversion to the very poor of Teheran, for she had seen the slums just as I had and knew what brutal conditions existed there. Precisely how the elephant would offer comfort to the poor was a mystery.

When I got to Teheran, the arrival of the elephant was imminent, and the members of the embassy staff found themselves faced with a series of grave logistical problems. Since none of the country's narrow-gauge railroad cars was large enough to carry the animal, alternative transport had to be arranged. The elephant also ate nearly a ton of grass a day, and, as today, there was no grass in Teheran. Nor was it at all clear that the elephant would be accompanied by a mahout—a man trained to keep elephants in order—and the second secretary of the embassy, a timorous man, was obviously terrified that Mrs. Grady would cast him in the dreadful role of elephant trainer. Somehow, the American embassy's preoccupation with an elephant struck me as being just as improbable, on the eve of the takeover of the Anglo-Iranian Oil Company, as Sir William Fraser's wrongheaded political analysis had sounded in London.

As for the political crisis, itself, the British would soon blockade Iran in response to the nationalization of Iranian Oil. This action did not cause the Iranians visibly to "come to heel," as Fraser had predicted, however. Indeed, Mossadegh would remain in or near to the seat of power until 1953, at which point the Eisenhower administration, worried by his close ties with Iran's Communist Tudeh party, would successfully arrange for his overthrow. My cousin Kermit (Kim) Roosevelt would play a leading role in orchestrating this coup, following which the shah was returned to his throne, Iranian oil was happily diverted back to U.S. and British companies, and general peace reigned in the country until the real revolution finally took hold more than two decades later.

My curious adventures in Iran, however, were nothing compared to what I would find when I made my first extended visit to French Indochina two years later. On January 27, 1954, Stew and I published a column entitled "Where Is Dien Bien Phu?" The remote jungle valley, of strategic importance because it commanded the approach from Laos into northwestern Vietnam, had been overrun by French parachute units just two months before. In the firm belief that the Viet Minh would never attack a strongly defended French position, the French high command ordered its new position fortified and reinforced. Theoretically, the position would prevent further incursions into Laos and serve as a launching point for attacks on the main Viet Minh supply roads. Shortly thereafter, Viet Minh forces, under the direction of General Vo Nguyen Giap, performed the remarkably difficult feat of dragging a considerable amount of heavy artillery, including howitzers and 37- and 40-millimeter antiaircraft guns, over the mountains and into position around and above the valley perimeter.

Ours was one of the first detailed accounts of the Dien Bien Phu operation to be printed anywhere, including the French press; and it concluded with the suggestion that the battle that was just starting might well turn out to be "the Yorktown" of Indochina's revolutionary war. When Eisenhower and Foster Dulles managed to get their final settlement in Korea in 1953, the international focus shifted to Vietnam, as I had foreseen it would, and for this reason our column caused a minor stir at the time. What I remember best about that story was not the "discovery" of Dien Bien Phu, however, but my own visit to Vietnam the month before and my adventures there with a company of French Foreign Legionnaires in a small corner of northern Indochina called Phu Nho Quan.

The Saigon of those days was an enchanting place, for, except in the highest quarters, the city as yet had no smell of desperation or impending defeat. Instead, the Flame of the Forest trees, the celebrating troops on furlough, the crowded restaurants, and the omnipresent opium dens gave Saigon the air of a jolly provincial town, not without its dramas. The streets themselves were far from beautiful, for most of the old city was composed of officials' villas in the Louis XIII style, a form of architecture that does not lend itself to stylistic imitation. Even by 1953, the more prudent members of the old colonial French community were already pulling up stakes and going home to France. The newspapers were full of real-estate advertisements, most of them proclaiming the houses for sale as having a "fumerie charmante," which meant a special room where the host and his guest could smoke opium before dinner.

Although one could find a number of decent restaurants in the city, the streets teemed with small, open-air cafés. Not long before my arrival, many of these installed wire-mesh nets drawn down between the tables and the street to prevent grenade attacks by the Viet Minh. The French Deuxième Bureau took care of this danger by, quite literally, selling the city to a local sect of gangsters called the Binh Xuyen, who drove the Communists out with great ease. The nets came down, and the Binh Xuyen had celebrated by building a gigantic gambling palace known as the Arc en Ciel. There these gangsters held court until the new president, Ngo Dinh Diem, drove them out two years later. At any rate, there was little outward sign of trouble in the city's cafés as I found them. So in the evenings I could sit at leisure, enjoying a cold bottle of beer and a bowl of what soon became my favorite Vietnamese dish, Soup Chinoise—a tangy mix of noodles, bits of seafood, ham, and vegetables, all floating in a thick and marvelously spicy chicken broth.

By 1953, the French had been fighting the Viet Minh for nearly seven years and to very little effect. The quite substantial amounts of military aid provided by the United States were obviously grossly inadequate for what had quickly become a large-scale conflict. For example, the French relied heavily on air power to discourage the Viet Minh; yet outside Saigon, in that very wet countryside, they did not maintain a single airfield with a permanent runway surface. The soldiers of the French parachute units and the Foreign Legion, and also the inadequately appreciated Vietnamese soldiers, fought with great courage, but it should have been clear at once that they had an impossible task on their hands.

I got a hint of what was to come when I traveled inland from the northern port city of Haiphong to Hanoi, where the bulk of heavy fighting was then concentrated. Most French military operations took place around and along the Red River delta, which flowed through the northeastern section of the country, past Hanoi, into the Gulf of Tonkin. One month before my arrival in Vietnam, French paratroopers dropped into Dien Bien Phu, to the surprise and delight of General Giap, who promptly ordered a series of masking diversionary attacks as he moved the bulk of his forces in to envelope the valley. I knew nothing of the French operation at the time and so made my way cautiously up to the front, south of Hanoi in the Tonkin delta. I had hoped there to be able to gauge the fighting performance of the French by tagging along on a combat mission and soon found genial guides in members of the Moroccan *tirailleurs,* a battalion in the French Foreign Legion.

On the morning I found them, the Moroccans were part of an operation I would have recognized as being completely ridiculous had I known anything about guerrilla war. After weeks of effort, the French troops had succeeded in poking a very long, thin finger into the enemy-held countryside. They had reached Phu Nho Quan, a small town that was supposed to be the Viet Minh's provincial headquarters. The setting for the operation, in the pearly light of early morning, was an incomparably beautiful valley of flat, green-golden rice paddies enclosed by dark hills. Early that morning, there had been a sharp skirmish at a bridge crossing the Sang Long River. By the time I arrived, the battalion, complete with heavily armored tanks and a Jeep for the commander, had rumbled into position not far from a disorderly thicket of bamboo, palms, papayas, and ragged-leaved banana trees bordered by rice paddies. The thicket, I was informed, was the first of several small villages that comprised the suburbs of Phu Nho Quan.

When the forward elements of our group advanced to within forty yards of the village's lush green fringe, the firing began. The enemy remained perfectly invisible, but the effect of their fire was not. Several of the soldiers creeping through the rice paddies made the sudden convulsive gestures of the wounded. As the intensity of gunfire increased, the battalion commander, a lean, whipcord-tough-looking man named Proudhom, barked a command in Arabic to his troops. As the order—a simple flanking movement—was carried out, the enemy fire died down. Before very long, the whine of rifle fire and low rattle of burp guns ceased altogether as the Viet

Minh troops gave up the village and melted invisibly toward the rear.

Hours later, the Moroccans pushed cautiously on to the ruined mud houses and battered brick temples of Phu Nho Quan. Always we moved to the muffled sounds of rifle fire. Never did we catch sight of the Viet Minh. "It's always like that," the major told me later. "The enemy in front, on both sides, and in the rear, too. That's our war here." Later that evening, the battalion effectively gave the town back up to the enemy and returned to the river-crossing scene of their first early-morning firefight. There, the Moroccans were joined by a French parachute regiment that had dropped into the valley earlier that day. Before long, an unimaginably delicious dinner was produced in a shop commandeered to serve as the French officers' mess. We had marvelous fresh bread and, what was more unlikely, delicious fresh butter, excellent veal cutlets with fresh vegetables, and mountains of fruit accompanied by plenty of wine. I knew we were not living off the country, so I asked who the mess officer was, thinking he should be complimented for producing such a feast. This turned out to be the plump and smiling chaplain of the French parachute regiment. I asked him how he managed to provide fresh butter and fresh bread for his customers in such rough surroundings, and the plump, smiling little man thrust his small finger toward the sky and answered, "Ça tombe du ciel, mon fils. Ça tombe du ciel."

Of course, as the chaplain spoke, General Giap's artillery was being wheeled into position in the hills around Dien Bien Phu, and in no time the sky itself would fall in on the French effort in Indochina. It was already evident to me, however, that French power in Vietnam was at more than full stretch. Back in Saigon, I asked to be briefed by a member of General Henri-Eugène Navarre's intelligence staff. The intelligence officer whom I saw agreed that French forces were already at the limit of their capabilities. He then remarked rather casually that besides the Viet Minh troops already inside Vietnam, it was necessary to consider three full divisions of Viet Minh that had been operating in a fairly menacing manner just above the (Laotian) Chinese border. It was evident to me that if these additional divisions were thrown full into the fight, the French effort soon would reach the breaking point.

I then went to see General Navarre himself. Although he had been in his post only seven months, the French commander had gained a modest public reputation for optimism and perseverance. In person, however, the general made no such impression, for he was a sad, grey man with pallid features and a languid, almost ef-

Jimmy Byrnes during his tenure
as secretary of state.

George Kennan at the State
Department. (National Archives)

John Paton Davies in 1952.
(UPI/Bettmann Newsphotos)

Dean Acheson. (Warder
Collection)

Above: General Marshall at Harvard on the day of his famous speech in June 1947. (Warder Collection)

Left: Myself, under the wing of an aircraft, waiting for transport during the Korean War in 1950.

Opposite top: Chip Bohlen *(right)* with President Eisenhower and John Foster Dulles following Chip's appointment as ambassador to Moscow. (National Archives)

Opposite bottom: General MacArthur *(right)* and George Marshall leaving MacArthur's headquarters in Tokyo, 1950. (UPI/Bettmann Newsphotos)

"McCarthyism,"
a cartoon by
Ed Holland published
in the *Washington
Times Herald.*

A drawing of me by
Ed Holland (1951).

Posing with Stew outside the State Department during the 1950s.

Our reputation for public gloom was well established by the time this cartoon appeared in *The New Yorker* (1959).

Kick Kennedy with her husband Lord Hartington at the time of their marriage, May 1944. (UPI/Bettmann Newsphotos)

Jackie and John Kennedy on the night of the president's inauguration, January 20, 1961. (UPI/Bettmann Newsphotos)

President Kennedy and *Washington Post* publisher Philip Graham. They were my closest younger friends.

South Vietnamese president Ngo Dinh Diem. (UPI/Bettmann Newsphotos)

Secretary of Defense Robert McNamara. (National Archives)

En route to Paris with Susan Mary in 1961.

The garden room at 2720 Dumbarton
Avenue. The cage that housed my
belligerent toucan is on the left.

The three Alsop brothers with Tish and John's wife Gussie *(back to camera)* shortly before Stew's leukemia killed him (1974).

In the study of my last home in Georgetown, 2806 N Street.

feminate, manner. I asked him straight off about the strategic import
of the Viet Minh divisions in Laos. In reply, the general got out a
map of the north and put his finger on a straight, little valley near the
border, marked by a village called Dien Bien Phu. He explained that
he was going to assemble a sizable force there, fairly near the border,
and would stop the Viet Minh with ease. I asked what would happen
if the invading divisions possessed modern artillery, something the
French troops had not yet encountered in enemy hands. General
Navarre brushed the question aside.

In Paris at Christmastime, I rounded out my reporting on the
Dien Bien Phu story and, in late January, filed the column from
Washington. Within three or four weeks General Navarre's little
valley had become temporarily famous. As the record now shows,
Giap's Viet Minh divisions had, indeed, occupied the hills surrounding Dien Bien Phu. There, they had begun pounding the French
units below with artillery for which the French were unprepared
and to which they had no answer.

A momentary crisis occurred in Washington when, just before
Giap's final attack in early March, the chairman of the Joint Chiefs
of Staff, Admiral Arthur Radford, suggested the use of nuclear
weapons to get rid of the offending Communist divisions. Eisenhower vetoed this recommendation, and with this, the French attempt to maintain the status quo in Indochina came to an end.

I would witness a drama of a more local kind during my second
visit to Saigon in December 1954, just about one year after the
French had first overrun Dien Bien Phu and had taken Phu Nho
Quan. The Geneva Accords, which officially partitioned Vietnam
into two countries, North and South, were not yet five months old
at the time, and remnants of the French colonial contingent—in
particular, the French intelligence service—still retained political
influence in the South. Not all were in favor of Ngo Dinh Diem, the
brave nationalist chosen to serve as prime minister of South Vietnam.

Diem's chief American adviser was Colonel Edward Lansdale,
who two years before in the Philippines had all but invented a president, Ramón Magsaysay, to counter and crush the Communist-con-
trolled insurgency of the Hukbalahaps. I had been involved with
this story, too. Frank Wisner, a great Washington friend of mine
who then was in charge of operations for the Central Intelligence
Agency, asked me to stop at Manila on the way to the Far East.
Frank wanted me to write a column or two about the international
disapproval that would be felt if the old political bosses in Manila
insisted on crooking the election, as had been their habit in the past.

This was not a job I minded doing for the simple reason that I agreed with Frank about the situation there. As far as I remember, my columns from Manila, although of doubtful influence on the election outcome, were true to the facts.

Lansdale was in Vietnam to do the same kind of job he had done in the Philippines. However, the facts in Saigon, to the extent I was able to piece them together, were a good deal more complicated. At Lansdale's urging, Premier Diem would soon begin his large-scale military campaign to ruin the Binh Xuyen gangsters in Saigon as well as two quasi-religious sects in the deep south, the Hoa Hao and the Cao Dai. The Binh Xuyen maintained some 5,000 men under arms and also controlled the police. The Cao Dai and Hoa Hao each boasted armies of 20,000 men or so and exercised feudal power in several of the country's provinces. Despite their obvious idiosyncracies, these groups had been effective in fighting the Viet Minh during the French occupation. Therefore, when Diem took after them, remnants of the French intelligence still in Saigon took after Diem and his American mentor Lansdale in a subversive, although ultimately ineffective, way.

Going to Lansdale's dreary little compound on a Saigon side street always amused me. Lansdale himself was a well-mannered, laconic-seeming man whose casual appearance masked both a real intelligence and a keen instinct for decisive action. At that time in Saigon, he was an air-force colonel on loan to the CIA. As a member of Bill Donovan's OSS during the war, he had seen a good deal of behind-the-scenes combat and, therefore, was more than comfortable in the chaotic and menacing atmosphere of postcolonial Saigon. Lansdale's main house was a low-lying, rundown structure, the interior of which was very unkempt and disorderly. The same Filipino lady was always present, advertised as Lansdale's cook but who did more, I think, than mere cooking. A score or so of beardless young Americans, most of whom either had worked with Lansdale in the Philippines or were on loan from our forces in Korea, streamed in and out of the house or simply lounged cheerfully in the various rooms and discussed the events of the day.

When I visited them later, in April 1955, during the height of the Binh Xuyen fighting, the group was in high good humor and reported to me that several nights before, representatives of the French intelligence—possibly the Binh Xuyen themselves—had thrown a grenade into the Lansdale compound as a warning not to interfere. The colonel and his young men had searched out and found a number of hideouts of the old French intelligence network in Saigon. With this information in hand, they had gotten rather tipsy with drink and at three o'clock in the morning had loaded a Jeep with hand grenades of their own and proceeded to careen around the city, grenading as many of the major intelligence installations as they could find. After this, there were no further hostilities between the two groups, and the Binh Xuyen in time were wiped clean from the map.

Well before then, however, it was clear that the real battle for Indochina did not center in Saigon, which was, at root, a Chinese city with a thin veneer of Franco-Vietnamese local color. The real center was in the countryside, where, thanks to the Viet Minh, the vast, obscure, somewhat formless processes of historical change were already well under way. At the time of my second visit to Vietnam, in December 1954, the geographical "regrouping" agreed to at Geneva was not yet complete. The French army still held the North Vietnamese seaport of Haiphong, and the Viet Minh retained their own enclaves in the lower Mekong Delta at the extreme southern tip of the country. The largest of these, on the Camau (now Quan Long) peninsula, was not purely military in nature, but social and political as well, with a loyal population of nearly 2 million, a powerful regular army, a complete civil administration, and all the other normal apparatus of established governmental authority.

Max Clos, the gifted West German correspondent whose work out of Indochina appeared for many years in *Le Monde,* was one of the few Westerners to have visited Camau. After some days frantically chasing political stories in Saigon, I sought Max out and asked him about the likelihood of arranging a similar excursion for myself. So began a series of meetings with one of Max's Viet Minh contacts, a plump, pompous Saigon dentist who had only recently jumped aboard the Communist bandwagon to save his skin and fortune. This man, who had developed strong conspiratorial tastes during his brief time with the Communists, was a great imitator of French ways and a fine illustration of the rule that when Asians imitate Westerners they generally choose the worst models. After days of intrigue, this man arranged for my journey south and provided as my guide a thin, courteous man named Hinh.

At length, Hinh and I arranged to set off at dawn the next day in a hired car for the ten-hour drive south. Our destination was a place called Phung Hiep, a delta town on the bank of a muddy canal where French authority ended and, on the other side of an officially demilitarized zone, Viet Minh authority began. After an interminable, winding passage to the perimeter, we boarded a *chaloupe*—a big wooden canal boat with an alarmingly asthmatic motor. Such barges provided the main means of public transport within the Viet Minh zone. Besides pigs, chickens, ducks, and several tons of inanimate cargo, our *chaloupe* carried about fifty passengers, jammed together in overpowering intimacy. Hinh, being a kind and agreeable man, suggested I store my bedroll as we passed through the Communist customs office some twenty minutes outside of Phung Hiep. There, I picked up a second official companion—a youthful, smooth-faced cadre called Nha. Managing to look almost dandified in his billowing guerrilla uniform of black pajamas and solar topee, Nha explained that he had been sent to escort an important unnamed visitor to Vinh Binh, a main Viet Minh administrative center seventy-five kilometers away. Hinh welcomed his comrade with vigor, explained I was surely that visitor, and promised me that together he and Nha would see us safely through all the subsequent Viet Minh control points on the way down to Vinh Binh.

In the golden afternoon sun, we set out down the canal through a strange but lovely countryside. An enormous swamp until the French drained it in the 1870s, the lower Mekong Delta was—and undoubtedly still is—an immense, perfectly flat checkerboard of emerald rice fields, neatly squared off by drainage canals. The canal's narrow levees are the only really dry land. Hence, the little delta hamlets are almost continuously strung out along the canal banks in thick groves of palm and bamboo. As we moved slowly south, the whole life of the region spread out before my eyes. We floated through a Catholic village, where the inhabitants were preparing to celebrate a Feast of the Virgin with a superb array of decorated boats. Next were endless views of sweeping rice paddies dotted with an occasional water buffalo and, closer to the river, peasant families taking their afternoon meal together in the front yard of their palm hut.

The *chaloupe* chugged into Vinh Binh well before dawn, and I slept briefly in one of the canal-side hostels before Hinh escorted me to an isolated palm hut on the far side of the bank. I noticed that the hut was guarded, but Hinh explained the guards as "the usual protection from French agents provocateurs given to distinguished visitors." I was allowed to take a bath in canal water. I was given a fine breakfast of noodles with chicken and hot peppers, and strong, sweet French coffee.

The world was just beginning to look wonderfully good through the smoke of the first postcoffee cigarette when a small, elderly, exquisitely courteous Viet Minh official appeared at my door. Hinh introduced the man as Dr. Pham Thieu and then promptly receded into the background, which did not alarm me since Thieu, whose arms looked like pipestems in his flapping black pajama sleeves, had a worn, humorous, intelligent face. Until break-fast was finished, Pham Thieu played host in the most graceful man-ner. Then, still without putting off his host's role and as though sadly embarrassed by his deficient hospitality, he announced that the arrangements advertised by my Saigon go-between had been pure fabrication. My friend, Hinh, had had no authority to pass me up the canal to Vinh Binh. The Viet Minh, in fact, had never guaranteed safe conduct of any kind. With profuse apologies perceptibly tinged with mockery, Pham Thieu added that perhaps I had better not leave the palm hut until the Viet Minh Civil Affairs Bureau decided what to do with me.

From that moment on, I was, quite plainly, under a gentle form of house arrest. But since Pham Thieu chose not to be coarsely frank about my status, I rather desperately played the part of the unlucky guest who accidentally inconveniences his host. I insisted that the man to blame was Max Clos's Saigon contact—as, indeed, I still think he was. Hinh, who mildly remarked that I was in "a rather ambiguous situation," bravely backed me up; and with his help, I convinced Pham Thieu that I had come in honest belief that my visit was properly authorized and not as a spy or in defiance of the Viet Minh.

That same evening, after a day of nothing to do except read, sunbathe, and wonder whether I would be hustled off to one of the grim local "reeducation" camps, the chief of the Civil Affairs Bureau came across the canal to hear my case. Dr. Vinh, as he was intro-duced to me, was an emaciated man with a sharp face and ears like batwings. With him was my old friend Nha and a second "assist-ant"—a youthful Viet Minh cadre of almost feminine good looks who carefully seated himself with his profile outlined against the guttering lamp. In the suddenly solemn atmosphere, Pham Thieu joined the others at the table, and court was convened. In as pleasant and as unconcerned a manner as possible, I apologized for my intru-sion among the Viet Minh and asked for authority to stay, if that could be officially granted. I said that if it could not be granted, I wanted to return to Saigon immediately—which was an extreme understatement. The court quickly divided into two camps. Nha and the other young assistant were plainly hostile. Pham Thieu and Hinh, just as plainly, did their level best for me. Dr. Vinh said nothing during the proceedings and continued to say nothing for some time after the others had fallen silent. Clearly, the old man was very much of two minds about letting me depart, and I could hear my heart pounding when he at length gave his judgment: "It is very irregular—but you may go."

Nor was this the end of the story. The next day, in the brilliance of the early tropical morning, Hinh and I boarded the *chaloupe* that was to take us back up the canal to French territory. The boat was packed with the usual assortment of farmers and their livestock, merchants and their wares. I had chosen that morning to wear shorts, which, in themselves, were no oddity. But to the smooth-skinned Vietnamese, who, during the whole course of their nine-year war, had seen no Westerners, the appearance of my naked, hairy knees on the canal boat produced about the effect you would expect if a friendly chimpanzee suddenly appeared aboard the *Twentieth Century Limited.* A wizened grandmother was the first to stroke my knees experimentally. The whole boat joined her in her incredulous laughter, and before long about half of the passengers had climbed over their neighbors to imitate the old lady's experiment. Since there did not seem to be anything else to do, I touched their smooth arms as they came up for inspection and laughed right back at them. The silly, simple, shared joke produced an immediate cozy intimacy. Hinh described to all and sundry my misguided visit to the Viet Minh. The passengers, in turn, told me, through Hinh, all about their small affairs, and so we proceeded up the canal in great delight with one another.

This camaraderie and good cheer would prove useful. Toward noon we reached a fairly big market town, the site of a large police post. Almost at once, a squint-eyed security policeman with a glittering mouthful of gold teeth came forward and asked for my papers. When Hinh produced my exit permit, a regular canal-side soviet of policemen, black-uniformed and forbidding, gathered on the pier to examine it from every angle. At length, looking really distressed, Hinh informed me that I was about to be arrested. Apparently, one of Dr. Vinh's assistants had left the official seal off my exit permit, rendering it worthless. I took the papers from Hinh and saw they were not only unsealed, but were made out in the name of a certain "M. Muller, journaliste progressive français." I shuddered to think what might happen if this hard-core cadre were to choose to search my bedding and find, by my passport, that I was not an entirely imaginary French fellow traveler, but an American.

To my intense relief, however, my new friends on the canal boat spoke up. They said, in effect, that anyone who was so amiable about being a monster was really most unlikely to be a spy. They protested that high Viet Minh officials had been seen happily waving good-bye to me when I left Vinh Binh. This prompted more questions directed at Hinh, who, brave and loyal as before, energetically swore that the omission of the seal on my exit permit was a mere accident. There followed the most edgy hour I can remember. First, the canal-side soviet said I could go. Then they declared I must be arrested. After each new decision, they argued loudly with one another. When, after a time, a third permission to depart was granted, the captain of the canal boat, strong in the knowledge that he had public opinion behind him, abruptly pushed off, leaving my squint-eyed, gold-toothed would-be captor black with anger.

So I was saved, quite literally, by the hair on my knees, and my adventure with the Viet Minh ended. The other passengers were much relieved to be under way and happily congratulated me. Hinh gave a broad grin of relief and delight. And so, in time, we made our way up the canal toward French territory without incident. I never saw Hinh again after we arrived back in Saigon. Nor did I manage to catch up to Max Clos's turncoat dentist, for after filing several columns on my adventure, I made my way out of the country.

That year, 1954, was the beginning of the great "Asia crisis," embodied in the conflict between Communist China and the Nationalists on Taiwan over the disputed offshore islands of Ma-tsu and Quemoy. In September 1954, after a series of threats and counterthreats, the Communists opened fire on the Taiwanese-held island of Quemoy. Although this initial barrage soon died away, the dispute, which caused Eisenhower to send much of the U.S. Pacific fleet into the area, would drag on for several months. Congress passed the Formosa Resolution in late January 1955, which permitted the president to maintain a general military defense of the offshore islands, provided the Communist attack was aimed at Taiwan itself.

I visited the islands, which, to my great surprise, were never attacked, and, judging from my old columns, managed nevertheless to register a high level of alarm. I also traveled to other points in Asia, including Thailand, Singapore, and, for the first time since the war, Rangoon, which still retained some of the old, oddly clean, stuffy prettiness of the British time. It amused me, on that particular trip, to count up the characteristics by which one could identify the departed colonialists. Dutch officialdom had left in Indonesia the unique feature of forms having to be filled out in septuplicate—generally in tiny little airport buildings resembling the steam rooms of Turkish baths with riots taking place within the walls. In the ex-French possessions of Indochina, the bread, butter, and mayonnaise were always superb. In ex-British possessions, one's shoes were shined impeccably, one's clothes were beautifully pressed, but the food was unspeakable. Proper postcolonial meals, particularly in Burma, tended to begin with the most disgusting of all British culinary inventions—Brown Oxford Soup, a concoction resembling nothing so much as dark-brown mucilage.

That particular excursion through Asia took in all some six months and was indicative of the kind of leeway Stew and I enjoyed as reporting partners. One of us could mind the news in Washington, leaving the other free to report on so-called "trouble spots" around the world. Since Stew had a devoted wife and all of six children by this time, I always volunteered to go overseas, although until the Eisenhower time, we ended up splitting the duty in a more or less even way. The overseas routine reminded me of what the Red Queen sternly said in *Through the Looking-Glass:* "It takes all the running you can do, to keep in the same place. If you want to get somewhere else, you must run at least twice as fast as that." In 1957, not long after the Suez crisis, I went abroad for an entire year in the spirit of the resolution I made in Chungking so many years before. Some of the events of that journey will be told in the next chapter.

Politics aside, however, there are pictures from that time that break my heart as I look back and compare them with what I know of the world today. I have seen Bangkok, once one of the world's most enchanting cities, idling along its canals under the Flame of the Forest trees, transformed into an open sewer with the canals filled in for highways and the flame trees all but decimated by pollution. I saw Saigon go bad in a more drastic way, for it was, as I have said, a small and exquisite place when I first traveled there in the late French time. So many of the larger cities in Asia—and in Europe and the Middle East, for that matter—have followed Hong Kong, which in the past decade or two has turned from a half-Victorian and altogether agreeable anomaly, which I knew so well from having been interned there, to a jumble of automobile traffic and competing skyscrapers.

But there is no use lamenting the past once one has taken plain note of the ugly changes that have occurred almost everywhere. Nor do I mean to sound like an apologist for colonial times. The world I was born into was, quite simply, a beautiful place. The world I shall leave before long is downright ugly, except in patches protected by their remoteness. But this is an all-too-fashionable complaint, and, after all I have experienced in a life of travel, there is no use wailing.

20

Suez
and Beyond

Few things irritate me more than the failure of memoir writers to describe how they lived day to day. So I will turn briefly to my private life on Georgetown's Dumbarton Avenue, where I had been based in one house or another since 1937. The first house I owned, which I purchased before the war, was very agreeable but had proved too poky and inconvenient to suit my purposes. That house had a pretty garden; and although the rooms were very narrow, I had taken great care by using rather small, low furniture to create a false feeling of space. With the help of one of Washington's more voracious lady real-estate sharks, I sold it for the asking price to a comfortably rich couple who liked the garden but did not notice that the house's interior would make their very large, solid furniture look as if they had turned a herd of elephants loose in the rooms.

In 1949, I bought, at the modest price of $17,000, a large parcel of land across the street from my first house. I decided that I myself would design the house that would occupy this land, which measured sixty feet by one hundred; it was to be built in a style that I would eventually christen "Garage Palladian." In working up the blueprints, I focused all my attention, as I believed all architects must, on the proportions of the living space and on how the light fell into each room. As for the actual construction, I soon found that the best building materials available were nearly all prohibitively expensive. As a result, the materials I eventually used were very much like those that might be needed for the construction of a sturdy commercial garage. My new home, when at last complete, made a fearful stir among the self-appointed guardians of architectural taste in Georgetown. They considered a cinder-block house—which did look fairly awful until the planned planting had softened its outlines—to be an outrage among the neighborhood's Victorian and Federal façades. Indeed, the Georgetown Citizens Association got a law passed against me—the so-called "Georgetown law"—which, for a long time, prevented anyone from building in the area except in a "pseudo-Georgian" style.

All the same, it was a nice house, and I was happy in it. The rooms were far from poky, and the garden, about which I took great care, was particularly pleasing and productive. Although life in Washington under Eisenhower was not as jolly, in a social way, as it had been under Roosevelt or Truman, the house and garden gave me a very pleasant life. Jose and Maria thought nothing of producing very good dinners for anywhere up to twenty people, and I had plenty of outlets for my tribe's passion for rather indiscriminate hospitality. Indeed, it was during that time that I devised "the bore factor," the only contribution I can claim to the rules of entertaining in Washington.

The bore factor is important in Washington because most dinner guests there wish to see men in high office, and men in high office have a tendency to retain the wives, often very boring, whom they married when they had no office at all. It is a simple rule of thumb that with eight people at table you cannot have so much as one bore; with ten you can have half a bore; with twelve a whole bore; with fourteen a bore and a half; and so on. Half a bore may seem an odd concept, but the world being what it is, plenty of them exist. I count as half a bore a very dull but powerful man or a very stupid but pretty woman. The mindless rich, if very rich, also count as half bores.

I usually arranged these gatherings for my own pleasure and not, as has been imagined, for the sole purpose of furthering my own effectiveness as a newspaperman. It is a myth that many government secrets are leaked at Washington dinner parties. Having people in power at your table is important and useful for two basic reasons. In the first place, one might get a line on the character of a person in power by seeing him or her informally at the dinner table. Second, especially if he or she sees you at your own dinner table, the official may get a line on what kind of a person you may be and can decide, on the basis of this, whether you are trustworthy. This, in turn, lays a foundation for the right business relationship between the reporter and the man in power. However, this business relationship is to be conducted strictly in daytime business surroundings, which, since Washington is a very uncivilized city, include luncheons.

With the help of Jose's excellent cooking and by dint of the strictest observance of my own reportorial rules—which were never to put on the record what had been said off the record and never to ask business questions unless the person to whom I was talking clearly understood that they *were* business questions—I managed to build up a considerable list of officials well worth talking to about the politics of government, even in Eisenhower's Washington. Thus, all through the Eisenhower years, I was able to follow my reportorial rule each working day, which was to see and talk with at least four people in or close to public life or the government.

My daily routine was simple. I breakfasted every morning in the garden room, where I drank an enormous cup of strong black coffee and glanced through the morning's newspapers. I then made the short commute to my office in the back of the house and took to the telephone to fill in any gaps in that day's schedule of appointments, based on the morning's news or, if I had a full day ahead of me, to make appointments for the next day or two. It was a taxing routine, one that Stew also followed. But at least it meant that we seldom found ourselves without "straw to make our bricks," as we called the situation that arose when we lacked the solid material from which to build a column and had to do a story that we dragged out of the blue, which is always the hardest kind of story to do and the least worth doing.

In the years following McCarthy, straw for our columns was plentiful because of the various crises, real or imagined, with which Stew and I occupied ourselves. Chief among our concerns was the gradual and alarming discovery that Eisenhower, who had campaigned on an anti-isolationist platform, proved to be a rather tepid advocate of a strong defense and an aggressive foreign policy once he ascended to the White House. From the first, Treasury Secretary George Humphrey and Eisenhower pressed their decidedly stupid friend, Secretary of Defense "Engine" Charlie Wilson, to reduce defense spending. Indeed, they became dissatisfied with him because he did not do so fast enough. Nonetheless, great reductions in the country's defense outlays were made during the era of Eisenhower's "New Look." In taking a more cautious approach to military commitment and expenditure, the president, it is fair to say, viewed the effect of high budget deficits on the economy—and their potential, as he put it, to "destroy what we are attempting to defend"—to be of more importance than any immediate military threat posed to the United States and her allies by the Soviet Union.

Stew and I both believed Eisenhower was overly prudent in this matter and said so countless times in the column. Indeed, at times, it seemed to us (debatably, as it turned out) that President Eisenhower's so-called "New Look" at American defense policy was really a decision to have almost no defense at all except the nuclear deterrent, and then to neglect the nuclear deterrent so badly that the American lead in that most vital area risked being lost altogether. In fact, the U.S. Army in 1955 stood at 1 million, roughly one-third below the 1953 figure, and the Soviets were close to completing their own hydrogen bomb. The military planners in Moscow, aside from rapidly expanding their current atomic stockpile, had also begun to put great emphasis on air power—in particular the development of a long-range tactical bomber force.

For these reasons, Stew and I focused a good deal of our energies during the Eisenhower time on defense reporting. It was a branch of our trade that the average American editor—let alone the average American reader—did not at the time regard essential. In those days—and, I believe, still—a good defense reporter required the reconstructive imagination of a paleontologist. Besides requisite doses of knowledge and experience, one had to be able to take a rear molar and a bit of fossilized femur and some other scraps, and combine them to make a reasonably accurate picture of the whole animal. In 1954, for instance, certain indications in the Soviet press led us to make an intensive study of the available data on the Soviet rocket program. We were aware that the Soviets had begun an all-out missile development effort in 1946, and we also knew that by 1954 the United States had only begun to make an effort. According to Eisenhower administration estimates, the Soviets would be ready with some form of their own intercontinental ballistic missile (ICBM) by 1959 at the earliest. We printed our own conclusion that the Soviets would reach their goal as early as 1957, which proved, with the launch of their sputnik that year, to be at least partially correct.

During this period, Stew and I wrote other such stories on military subjects, some more prescient than others. But what I remember best about our early work in the defense field were the indignant cries of "leak" that invariably went up after a particularly notable find. In each case, the discovery in question had proceeded from a more or less well-defined clue. Just getting the clue took a lot of hard work. Scores of interviews were needed to produce a single clue of any interest; spotting the clue for what it was took a lot more hard work; and following up the clue took still more. A belief in leaks, therefore, implied a disbelief in a reporters' energy, intelligence, and power to acquire knowledge on his or her own. Yet this belief was an article of faith, particularly among President Eisenhower's men. And in time, Stew and I learned to swallow the implied insult and even to be amused by it.

On at least two occasions, the Eisenhower administration followed its accusations with full-blown security investigations. We had already been inspected by members of the FBI during the Truman administration and so were not alarmed. One of these incidents, which took place in the spring of 1955 upon my return from Asia, is worth recalling here, if only because it was so amusing. On the week of my scheduled arrival, my closest friends Frank and Polly Wisner had gotten together a weekend party at their farm in Galena, Maryland, to welcome me back to Washington. Stew and Tish were to be there, and so were the Dick Bissells, for Dick was an old friend from Avon and Groton, and was in the CIA with Frank Wisner. Dick Bissell had charge of the CIA's aerial surveillance of the Soviet Union and was at the time busy shepherding the first long-range U-2 reconnaissance flights into action. Later, he would brilliantly manage our spy-satellite program.

During this time, all official Washington was secretly debating the question of whether or not we ought to have a major satellite program to match the Soviet's decision to do so, about which news had finally reached the West. The issue was not so much the satellite itself, but the missile driving it, for this meant the Soviets would possess a ballistic capability and could conceivably launch any menacing form of warhead they pleased. Stew, who had first helped break the story, invented a series of alarmist headlines of the sort he felt might be published if the Soviets put up a satellite before the United States did. He was taken with these bogus headlines and with the predicament they described; and when Stew, who disliked waste, had a good turn of phrase, he liked telling it more than once. He must have imparted his headlines to eight or ten dinner tables in the period immediately before my return. Evidently, one of these dinners was attended by a member of the National Security Council staff, and, as a result, the worst happened.

In his own wonderful book of memoirs published not long before his death, Stew compared the process of writing a political column to climbing a ladder that has no end and on which one can never see more than one rung or two ahead: "When nothing very much is going on, writing a political column can be agonizing—you reach up for the next rung and there isn't any. During the two Eisenhower administrations, there were many long placid stretches when hardly anything at all was going on. There was hardly anything to write about, and thus no rungs on the ladder to grasp." This description contains a good deal of truth, and since I was the one in our partnership who assumed the bulk of the traveling during the Eisenhower period, Stew, as a rule, endured the agonies of the ladder more often than I did.

On this occasion, having no fresh rungs in sight, Stew published a column including two of these imaginary headlines. "The most cogent pro-satellite argument can best be understood in terms of a couple of headlines," he wrote innocently enough: "SOVIETS CLAIM SUCCESSFUL LAUNCHING OF EARTH SATELLITE," and "U.S. RADAR CONFIRMS EXISTENCE OF SOVIET SATELLITE." As journalism, Stew's venture was purely speculative for he used this device to set up a largely theoretical argument. The column might not have been written had I managed to arrive home on time because we agreed that the partner who had been abroad took over and wrote at least a week and a half's worth of columns on his return—and after that particular trip through Asia, I had plenty to write. However, as I recall, I was delayed and landed on a Friday evening, looking forward to my jolly welcome-home weekend. I found Stew's column waiting for me. But what was infinitely worse was that on that same morning President Eisenhower evidently had found on his desk a National Security Council paper discussing the pros and cons of the much-discussed satellite program, including all of Stew's bogus headlines, which the Security Council staffer had evidently remembered from dinner and found intriguing enough to include in his own summation of the issue.

Almost simultaneously, someone put on the president's desk for his attention Stew's columns with the same headlines. The president flew to the conclusion that Stew had been consulting Security Council papers himself, instead of making jokes in the presence of government officials. And what followed was the worst security investigation we ever had. This, in turn, aborted my welcome-home weekend. That same Friday, Allen Dulles, who ran the CIA, summoned Frank Wisner and Dick Bissell to his office and told them that the heat was just too high to allow any such reunion of old friends without causing some kind of explosion. And so Stew, Tish, and I spent a somewhat bewildered and solitary weekend together.

The investigation never unraveled the mystery because, of course, security rules prevented anyone from telling us why on earth we were being investigated or, indeed, even officially admitting to us that an investigation was afoot. We only pieced the story together much later, and then only with the help of the wives of the high officials involved, who could not be kept silent for long—even by Allen Dulles.

By the end of the first Eisenhower term, the so-called "missile gap" was not yet the full-flowered—and, as it turned out, overblown—issue it would become four years later. The voters, in fact, seemed far more concerned with the state of the president's health. Stew and I found it hard to believe in 1956 that President Eisenhower would seek reelection after the severe heart attack he had suffered in Denver the year before. However, the theory among those endlessly prodding and cajoling the old general to run a second time seemed to be that being president during the next four years would not be overly taxing and might even prove to be a sort of health cure for Eisenhower. Certainly, the 1956 election—which was one of the dullest I can remember—did not prove taxing for the president. Richard Nixon, having weathered former Minnesota governor and perennial Republican candidate Harold Stassen's silly attempt to dump him from the ticket, was only too willing to do the bulk of the campaigning.

For their part, the Democrats' second nomination of Adlai Stevenson in Chicago seemed to us, as we wrote at the time, "like a man marrying his mistress, long after the flames of passion have flickered and gone out, because he is used to her and badly needs someone to darn his socks." In sum, Adlai did not come to Chicago looking like the great, high-minded, reform-minded intellectual hope of his earlier campaign. He was now simply another Democratic politician— and a vulnerable one at that since former President Truman had come out in favor of Averell Harriman, who was running for the presidency as a Democrat for the second time. This time around Adlai Stevenson very much wanted to be president of the United States, a fact that some of his closest supporters had doubted four years ago. In Chicago, the candidate, therefore, worked like a nailer to get his nomination approved in a tough, practical way. And when this was done, he inexplicably threw the choice of his running mate open to the convention. The party's choice was Senator Estes Kefauver of Tennessee, although the young Massachusetts senator John Kennedy very nearly took the vote.

The 1956 campaign was the first in which we experimented with a solution, adopted initially by Stewart, to the problem of election coverage. It consisted of imitating and sometimes going along with the professional pollsters. For a time, we became almost obsessively enamored of the process—so much so that Edwin Lahey, an astute journalist of the period, jokingly compared the Alsop brothers' attempts at polling to the story of a rockbound New Yorker who, for personal reasons, must travel to California for the first time. "You ain't gonna believe this," the New Yorker assures his other rockbound New York friends upon returning from the West Coast, "but the whole Goddamn place is full of people."

I would like to think that our labors that summer and fall carried more journalistic weight than Lahey allowed, although, in retrospect, I am not entirely convinced he was wrong. Stew and I spent much of that second Eisenhower campaign tramping separately or together from house to house throughout the cities and suburbs of the midwest and the northern Pacific coast. Early on, we discovered that the chatty, friendly demeanor we had supposed all pollsters must use in their work got us nowhere. So at the suggestion of the great pollster Lou Harris, we adopted the brusque, professional demeanor of a small-town clerk. We even took to dressing as unobtrusively as possible—Stew later compared our costume and manner to that of a senior sewer inspector.

As a general rule, Stew's natural attitude and appearance was always somewhat less startling to outsiders than mine, and so he managed this charade better than I. In the end, also, he got better results. "Oh, I'll go for Ike," one prophetic man told Stew in the suburbs of Chicago. "I know he's been sick, and he goofs off a lot—sometimes seems like he's hardly minding the store. But he's the kind of guy I'd like to invite over for a cookout. Can you imagine inviting that Adlai for a cookout?" So our polling led us to the conclusion that the voters would reelect the president by a "fairly handsome majority," although in the end, Eisenhower's majority was far larger than we supposed it would be.

Any tendency to sit back and analyze the outcome of the 1956 election quickly evaporated when the Suez crisis, which had been brewing all spring, drew to its ugly conclusion. A great deal has been written about the Suez war, and I do not intend to add to it here. As lifelong Anglophiles, neither Stew nor I was prepared either for the destruction of Great Britain as a great power or for the overt way in which the United States participated in its demise. My view was that once the French, British, and Israelis launched their operation to take the canal, simple self-interest forbade recrimination among the Western allies. Of course, even by 1956, this was an old and decidedly unfashionable opinion. It was fueled, in part, by a healthy detestation for the Egyptian leader Gamal Abdel Nasser, whom I had interviewed during an excursion through the Middle East earlier that year. Nasser, of course, was gaining wide attention at the time for his bold appeals to Arab nationalism. His hallmark gesture was to lean forward and knead one's knee in a very disagreeable manner, proclaiming, "My principills are very simpill, Mr. Alsop." When he did that, one knew he was telling the biggest lie ever, and one could lie back with hearty impunity and expect very little news of use to come from the rest of the interview.

John Foster Dulles, of course, had precipitated the crisis by first refusing to sell arms to Nasser and then by withdrawing support for the building of the Aswan Dam just when the Egyptians were getting ready to accept it. Nasser then retaliated by seizing control of the canal, and Israel, in tandem with Britain and France, launched its attack on Egypt. I sympathized with this decision at the time, not the least because I thought Nasser a dangerous man. It appeared then that the Arab world could be hostilely organized if this ferment were not contained. I think, for a time, that Foster Dulles believed this also, although in the outcome, even Nasser learned the general rule that it is impossible to organize Arabs.

The Israeli attack may, with hindsight, be dismissed as reckless, but it is also worth remembering that, with the Americans now seemingly gone from Egypt, the European powers felt they had little choice but to fight for their access to the old waterway. Only when a furious President Eisenhower intervened to stop the conflict (Krushchev had threatened to use missiles to blast the invading troops from the desert) did the full extent of the miscalculation come clear. The culmination of Foster Dulles's dealings with the British is worth reporting, for it illustrates the fundamental altering of perceptions that took place on both sides of the Atlantic after the crisis had ended.

In the wake of Suez, the British ambassador in Washington was replaced. The new man, Sir Harold Caccia, was invited by Secretary Dulles to the State Department for a cooling talk after Caccia was officially installed as ambassador. The talk was not a long one because Caccia, an old-fashioned, passionately patriotic man who was still fairly attached to the notion of empire, was so enraged that he had to leave the room (so he told me) to avoid resorting to physical violence. Dulles, clicking his teeth in the curious way he had, opened the conversation with the ambassador by saying that, of course, for moral reasons he had disapproved of the Suez war, which was aggression pure and simple. But, he added, there was one question he had never been able to answer to his own satisfaction. Caccia inquired what this question was, and Dulles (who had been ill in hospital during the crisis) said that he had never understood why, once the decision had been made to fight for the canal, the British did not go ahead and win. The ambassador turned bright scarlet, and said, "Because you threatened to pull the plug on sterling," as indeed, President Eisenhower had done by refusing British access to desperately needed capital in the International Monetary Fund until all points of the UN cease-fire resolution had been met. As it happened, I saw Harold Caccia almost immediately after this conversation, and he became virtually incoherent as he described it.

I was then preparing to go to Paris to set up a sort of foreign bureau for the Alsop brothers' column. Stew and I were convinced that the Suez war was likely to be the beginning of a long series of crises, and, indeed, Suez had occurred almost simultaneously with the brutally suppressed uprising in Hungary. From a personal standpoint, the decision to part for a year was not difficult for me. I was nearly intoxicated by my role as world-wandering columnist. My brother, for his part, was patently glad to be rid of me.

January 1956 marked our tenth anniversary together as columnists. And although the partnership had proved a rewarding one, it was not without its combative side. As a family, after all, the Alsops (and the Robinsons on my mother's side, too) held very strong views and did not always agree with one another. One could not participate in a conversation around the dining-room table at Henderson unless one was prepared to shout. Then, again, the living room of the old farmhouse in Avon was shaped like an L with an entrance at either end. My father invented the debating tactic, which the rest of us subsequently employed, of exiting an argument in a towering passion through the most remote door, only to come banging back through the nearest to begin the argument anew. This family habit was not absent from Stew's and my professional life. Over the years, we had a number of foot-stomping rows in the two-room study we shared in my Dumbarton Avenue home. After a decade, we had never ceased to work together. But the strains and tensions of the relationship had begun to tell (I think more on Stew than myself), and so he was not at all hesitant when I suggested the move to Paris.

Just two things are worth recording here about my year in Paris. My close friend, Bill Patten, with whom I had shared an apartment long ago in New York, lived in the city then with his beautiful wife Susan Mary and their two children—my godson Bill Jr. and Bill's beautiful but emotional sister Anne. I loved the whole family, but I had a special weakness for Susan Mary, who would become my wife after Bill died in 1960. As for the children, getting to know them in Paris was a tremendous plus because when Susan Mary and I married at the beginning of the Kennedy years, they became my step children and are still like son and daughter to me. Their own children, in turn, call me "Grandfather" because "Step-grandfather" is too much trouble. I call them all my "extra dividends" for they have added enormously to the richness and delight of my fortunate life.

Susan Mary and Bill, in turn, introduced me to their Paris friends, and since I was an extra man and able, within reason, to speak French, I soon enough had a large circle composed of friends of theirs and friends of mine. I can still remember the excitement of the big evenings when Susan Mary and Bill would take me out to parties given by their friends in the reviving city. The overture to such an evening was always the same. Susan Mary, besides being beautiful herself, wears clothes beautifully and takes great care with them, facts that were not lost on Christian Dior, then the widely worshiped inventor of the "new look" in fashion. Dior used to dress Susan Mary to show off his clothes. And so the prelude to these splendid Paris evenings would always be the arrival of an elegant lady bearing what looked like a vast white cardboard coffin containing the dress that M. Dior considered suitable for the evening in question. The coffin would be taken solemnly upstairs and opened, and the dress removed for wearing before being returned the next day.

During that winter of 1957, I made my first visit to the Soviet Union, a journey singly remarkable for the fact that the Soviet authorities allowed it to occur. Despite Suez and the savage events in Hungary, relations between Washington and Moscow had settled that year into something of a holding pattern, perhaps in anticipation of the new "era of peaceful coexistence" promised by Nikita Krushchev. I was not for one moment deluded by this promise. After Suez, it was clear that the world order was almost completely bipolar, with the United States the dominant power in the West and the Soviets maintaining strict control over the East bloc. Western diplomacy, therefore, tended to focus on possible points of crisis in the Middle East and Asia. On the other hand, not much was known about the internal state of the Soviet Empire itself—its economy or its people. Nikita Khrushchev, although seemingly far more pleasant than Joseph Stalin, remained, to Western eyes, a mysterious, unpredictable man.

Naturally, therefore, Stew and I tried to arrange a visit to the Soviet Union, although we never considered ourselves to have much chance of succeeding. Stewart had managed to obtain an entry visa in 1955 but only by taking the unconventional step of putting his request in a personal letter to Khrushchev. However, our anti-Soviet record was well known in the Kremlin. Even after my brother's short visit, we had not been treated kindly by the Soviet state press. Indeed, not long before I arrived in Moscow in January 1957, *Komsomoskaya Pravda*, the newspaper of the Young Communist League, referred to Stew and me as "the robber brothers." "Assassins, robbers, pirates and rapists of all flags and nations," declared *Komsomoskaya Pravda*, "have been put to shame by the Alsops."

My official introduction to the country was far more cordial. My arrival in Moscow coincided with that of China's premier Chou En-lai as well as a number of East German officials on hand for the formal signing of a new Soviet–East German accord. A state banquet was given in their honor at St. George's Hall in the Kremlin Grand Palace, and I managed to secure an invitation. Like many inexperienced travelers of the era, I was surprised to find that the Kremlin looked like a particularly gay decoration by the great artist and set designer Léon Bakst for one of Diaghilev's early ballets. The low, ornately crenellated walls were not iron grey, but a rich, dark strawberry red. The high, decorated guard towers struck me as pure, medieval fantasy. Within the walls, the ancient churches rose to happy riots of colored and gilded domes. The palaces, too, were neither drab nor institutionally dreary; they were a bright butter-yellow picked out with white.

St. George's Hall is one of the biggest rooms in the world, a czarist legacy with tall, gilded doors and white plaster decorations so elaborate one has the feeling of being inside a gigantic wedding cake. Around the walls, long lines of tables offered supper to the 1,500 or more persons present. There were caviar and every sort of cold dish and sweet Russian wine and brandy and vodka and the admirable Russian ice cream and champagne as well. Despite the amplitude of the supper, the immensity of the party, and the grandeur of the hall, the occasion lacked pomp. Indeed, the festivities had the hospitable, curiously cozy feel of a parish hall at Christmas. Partly this was due to the daily children's parties in the Kremlin, for which the fantastic room had been decorated with a splendid fifty-foot Christmas tree and an enormous but very parish-hallish snow scene above the stage at the farther end. But chiefly, this feast produced its curiously cozy effect because the 1,500 tucked in the eatables and drinkables with such visibly cheerful enthusiasm.

Members of the Soviet Presidium and their wives occupied a

sort of semienclosure of their own beneath the snow scene, where they played host as though on stage. The Soviet upper crust—State Premier Nikolai Bulganin along with Khrushchev and the rest of the politburo—consisted of mostly stout, solid people, darkly and respectably clad (Invariably, the very top leaders were short, for Stalin would have no tall men around him.) These short, smiling men ate and drank with zeal all the while working hard to make the party "go." They succeeded without much trouble. A jolly time was being had by all when Premier Bulganin, looking the very image of goateed benevolence, rose for the first toast of the evening. Thereafter, with only occasional pauses, the speaking and toasting continued for almost three hours. The unending oratory, however, prevented no one from chatting and drinking. Even Chou En-lai, after listening to the speakers with formal politeness for more than an hour, broke down to the extent of holding his own private reception for Asian diplomats. At length, the massive golden chandeliers in the hall were darkened. Concealed lights astonishingly transformed the painted snow scene into a red and green and pink and blue and silver aurora borealis. And so, with a round of applause for the aurora and one final toast, the party came to an end.

My Soviet hosts would have been glad for me to continue on indefinitely in this genial way, fighting for smoked salmon at the Kremlin banquet tables. I had asked repeatedly, however, for permission to travel in the country, and at length the Intourist officials in Moscow announced—a bit peevishly perhaps, for I had refused their offer of a standard packaged tour—that I could visit western Siberia. Vast, fertile, and uncommonly frigid, this territory contains some of the world's largest coal and iron-ore deposits as well as a good portion of the country's new industries. I was permitted a three-week tour in the company of a state-supplied interpreter and guide. Precisely because the trip was off the beaten path, however, it had its penalties: there would be no running water nor any modern indoor plumbing from Kuibyshev to Barnaul (a five-day journey), a particular problem since the temperature in mid-January was so cold that everything that could freeze did so instantly.

Following the southern line of the Trans-Siberian Railroad, we passed through Kuibyshev, formerly Samara—where young Lenin hung out his lawyer's shingle—and headed eastward into the virgin lands and beyond. The solemn journalistic results of the trip can be found in my old columns and are not worth repeating here. In the Siberia of those days, it was a curious rule that a man was marked as successful by the simple fact that his clothes fit him. The bitter cold was not a serious hazard, providing one brought along a too conspicuous John Held–era coonskin coat. On the other hand, the hotels were like barracks, and the traveler who felt lost without a bath was due to feel continuously lost. As for nourishment, the standard Siberian menu listed pickled herring, pickled tomato, borscht (which was often delicious), and an undefinable substance known as "cutlette"—a nameless piece of meat, heavily fried in what appeared to be leftover machine oil.

I enjoyed myself immensely and took great delight in the overwhelming Siberian hospitality. I think particularly of one town, where I called on the mayor in the late afternoon just before I was supposed to go to dinner with a young local newspaperman. As I rose to leave for my dinner party, His Honor indicated the next room with an expansive gesture and announced firmly: "First, we must have just one glass of vodka to drink the health of our two countries." In the next room, a table was literally covered from end to end with vodka bottles, glasses, and plates mountainously heaped with zakouskis, a Russian hors d'oeuvre. That evening, the zakouski-eating continued without a moment's pause for three hours. Then, at last, I tottered off to consume a second feast with the newspaperman, which was delicious but, by that point, entirely superfluous.

My Soviet hosts through the course of this journey were generally decent and often impressive human beings. I was allowed to see and talk for hours with almost anyone I liked—industrial managers, bankers, educators, doctors, newspaper editors, and so on. The only two groups under an interdict were military officers and members of the party apparatus. So it is not surprising that the only truly unpleasant encounters I had were with my little, pasty-faced interpreter. He was a nasty, suspicious man who wore five shades of underwear, all visible at his wrist—pale pink, Nile green, baby blue, cream-colored, and grey—all of which were a uniform dirty grey by the time we got back to Moscow. He neither washed himself or his clothes for three weeks. He was also undoubtedly a KGB man and evidently had orders to keep me away from Party committee members.

The behavior of my vile little interpreter reinforced a view that, even then, was a fairly common one regarding the Soviet Union. Throughout my public career—if one can call it that—I have never been under the illusion that the Soviet form of government was anything but inherently aggressive and, for the most part, ferociously repressive. This particular journey did little to change my view, although, as I made my way west, it became clear that the further one strayed from the so-called "party line," the better the chances were for leading a productive, addle-free existence. In general, the laborers I met along the way, the factory technicians, agricultural experts, and lumberjacks were sensible, sound men and women, every bit the equal of their counterparts in the West.

On the other hand, the party *apparatchiki* to my mind appeared patently dull, mean-spirited, and foolish. In general, these characters were kept from my view, although I did manage, in the town of Kustanay, to corner three members of the local Communist Party Committee. I asked Comrade Popov, who was the local first secretary, whether it was not a bit of a gamble to plow up 90 million acres of semiarid steppe, a measure then being instituted with fairly mixed results as part of the virgin-lands program. I ventured to point out that expecting crops to grow over such an enormous area in a region where water was never plentiful may, in the end, prove to be a mistake. Comrade Popov considered my question for a barely a moment before he answered, in effect, that the weather would just have to follow the party line, like everybody else. I thought then, as I do today, that the myopic flavor of these men, their dim arrogance and altogether lunatic outlook, constituted a primary Soviet problem.

Before leaving the Soviet Union, I was summoned to party headquarters in Moscow for an interview with Nikita Khrushchev. The Soviet leader was short, round, and well scrubbed. In attitude, he exuded an almost playful energy. Indeed, with his small, shrewd eyes and his three prominent wens, Khrushchev seemed for all the world like a jovial clown at a party. He greeted me with a natural, jolly enthusiasm and then began, after a polite offer of tea, a very boring and uninformative disquisition on Soviet foreign affairs. After an hour had passed, I got up to go, thinking I had already taken enough of the chairman's time. When I did so, however, Khrushchev looked positively disappointed and said, "But you are leaving too soon, Mr. Alsop."

I replied that I would be delighted to stay but did not wish to waste any more of the party leader's time. His eyes sparkling with pleasure, Khrushchev waved this preposterous notion aside and proceeded, in the most animated terms, to give me the first rundown ever received by a foreigner on his scheme for the radical decentralization of Soviet industry. This scheme would have a good deal to do with the near success of the so-called "antiparty" group in hurling Khrushchev from power in June of that year. The Soviet leader was obviously unconcerned with any opposition his plan might arouse; indeed, he seemed to gloat over the impending discomfort among the Soviet upper crust. "Just think, Mr. Alsop," he told me with great cheerfulness, "these gentlemen are now to be sent out into the provinces to do more productive work."

This Soviet journey was both a highlight of my year overseas as well as a kind of finale. For in September 1957, after several more months of dashing from one overseas crisis to the next with pleasant but all-too-short intervals in Paris, Stew called me with news that I had been half-expecting. The fact was that as partners in a column, dividing the proceeds with no additional source of outside income except magazine writing for the *Saturday Evening Post,* we were ceasing to be able to support ourselves comfortably.

Columnists nowadays can do very well, what with the lecture circuit, a link with television, and the annual paid symposia that some of them organize. Stew and I had made the mistake of avoiding television because the appearances we were offered were never paid for. This, in turn, made us less saleable on the lecture circuit, which Stew worked for a little every year because he had a family to support. By then, also, Stew had his own professional identity to maintain. He was a more relaxed and discursive writer than I, and he chafed far more than I did under the narrow stylistic strictures imposed in writing a column. When the *Saturday Evening Post* offered him a very generous salary for a full-time job, he accepted it. I could not argue against this because the salary was substantially more than he was ever likely to make from the column. Although I very much disliked breaking up the partnership, I bade him Godspeed and prepared, in the spring of 1958, to return to Washington.

It proved to be a good move. Although I had no family to support, I was glad of the larger income that I was now receiving from the column. Stew was an enormous success at the *Saturday Evening Post.* And when the *Post* went the way of all the big-circulation magazines, he managed even better as a columnist for *Newsweek* until the end of his life. At first, I must admit, I was a little fearful of working without a partner, for working alone inevitably makes a columnist's writing plans much more rigid. But I found I could do it well enough to maintain my list of newspapers and to keep the wolf from the door. I tried a semipartnership with Rowland Evans for a while, but it did not fall into a working pattern as Stew's and my partnership had. So Rolly went off on his own to found a highly successful independent column with Robert Novak. Meanwhile, I soldiered on alone.

21

Senator
Kennedy

In recent years, the Eisenhower presidency has come under a good deal of historical scrutiny. In this modern era of aggressive military spending and general fiscal worry, it is fashionable to view Dwight D. Eisenhower as a splendid man, prudent, clever, and generally everything this country wants in a national leader. By my tests for a president, however, he comes out looking a good deal less grand than his newly fashionable advocates might wish. There is little doubt General Eisenhower was a superlative military politician, and that kind of eminence cannot be achieved without intelligence. However, I always doubted whether his grasp of broader issues and policy went beyond a rather narrow range.

Throughout his eight years in office, Eisenhower's "image" (I hate that awful word like poison) was of being a kind of heroic national grandpa, much beloved by all except for a few cynical people like myself. It still appears to me today, however, that Eisenhower's performance in office did not meet any common-sense test for a president. To be sure, he ended the Korean War. But by the time he took office, Chinese losses had been so horrendous that Peking must certainly have been eager to make a settlement, and the lever President Eisenhower employed to get his settlement was a discrete but undoubted (and unprecedented) threat to use nuclear weapons.

As has been said, America's prosperity at home and effectiveness abroad are the real tests of presidents. When Eisenhower was inaugurated, this country was enormously prosperous; and when he went off to his retirement at Gettysburg eight years later, the economy was stable but decidedly sluggish. In 1952, the United States had seldom stood so high overseas; eight years later, planned presidential visits, like the Eisenhower visit to Japan in June of 1960, were being canceled because we stood so low. This humiliating position of the United States abroad would, in my view, be directly reflected in the aggressive Soviet behavior that led, during Kennedy's administration, to the raising of the Berlin Wall and the Cuban missile crisis.

Most Americans, meanwhile, were made to feel that all was well with the world. The situation reminded me of a standard plot in countless bad nineteenth-century European novels. The wicked or negligent steward is called upon to handle the affairs of a great family estate. He fills his own pockets assiduously while urging family members to live on caviar, to swathe the women in sables, to treat diamonds like pebbles, and to acquire expensive mistresses and even more expensive gatehouses. The negligent steward then abruptly dies or disappears from view, and the family finds that the roof atop the palace is in an extreme state of disrepair, no debts have been paid, and the family affairs are generally a frightful mess—which is more or less the situation John F. Kennedy faced when he took office in 1961.

One of the first things I did upon returning home in the late spring of 1958, after Stew went to the *Saturday Evening Post,* was to make a careful review of the potential presidential candidates who might have the heavy task of picking up where General Eisenhower left off. I went through the usual motions of looking for a candidate who seemed to me a reasonable and successful nominee and examined the likely alternatives to the best of my ability.

I did not even consider the Republicans that year, partly because I used to regard myself as a Democrat and partly because it was already obvious that Richard M. Nixon, whom I disliked heartily, would be the GOP nominee. After I was confident I understood the main elements of the political situation, three men among the Democrats remained on my short list. One was Lyndon Johnson, by then Senate majority leader and one of the strangest and ablest men I knew. The other two were Senator Stuart Symington of Missouri and Senator John F. Kennedy of Massachusetts, a dark horse because of his relative inexperience and his Catholic background.

Looking back, I think my first choice would have been Lyndon Johnson, had I not been convinced that he was too southern a political by half to win a national election in the United States of those days. Senator Symington struck me as too shallow to be an acceptable presidential candidate. Indeed, he based his not-very-active candidacy on a precarious calculation—that Kennedy would be barred by his Catholicism, that Johnson would be barred by his southernness, and that he, Symington, could maintain good relations with both men and, in the end, inherit the nomination the other two were actively seeking.

As for Kennedy, I added him to this short list at the suggestion of Stew, who, during the course of his own polling experiments, had discovered that, of all the likely Democratic candidates, Kennedy registered the strongest sentiment when paired opposite Vice-President Nixon. I brought myself fully up to date on the senator's obviously nascent candidacy and took into account the strength Kennedy had shown when he all but won the vice-presidential nomination at the Democratic convention of 1956. Other signs suggested to me that the Catholic vote was one the Democrats had to worry about and could no longer take for granted, for most of the Catholic "ethnics" were becoming increasingly and conspicuously successful within the larger context of American society. Moreover, they were exhibiting an intense, aggressive patriotism and a tendency to drift toward the Republican party. Few had noticed this change, and little had been written about it at the time.

Senator Kennedy's staff, however, was alert to this trend and very ready to interpret it with a bag full of rigorous and largely impenetrable statistics. Kennedy's men reasoned that the Democrats could not hope to regain the White House without this critical bloc of support. Evidence of the Democratic party's new worry had been totted up with an amplitude of facts and figures by Ted Sorensen, then and thereafter Senator Kennedy's principal issues man. Sorensen worked me over with such effect that I invited the senator—as his staff called John Kennedy then—to have a drink with me at Dumbarton Avenue and give me the benefit of his views on this novel interpretation of American practical politics.

I can still remember John Kennedy that evening, looking inordinately young on the sofa in my big living room in Georgetown, talking with great eloquence about how the Democratic party had better change its ways or it would end without a single Catholic vote, either Irish or Italian, Lithuanian or Polish. He seemed very confident of his own future when we said good-bye on the high stoop of my house. I remember that some of my neighbors came to their windows, recognized my guest, and clapped. This made the senator smile with delight, for he liked applause, especially spontaneous applause. I told him that he had convinced me of the seriousness of his candidacy and that I was sure he would be offered the vice-presidential nomination at the next Democratic convention.

The senator started descending the steps at a half run, for he was always rather showily athletic if his back was not hurting him. Near the bottom of the steps, he suddenly stopped and turned back with an enormous grin on his face. "Thank you, Joe," he called back to me. "I enjoyed myself this evening. But you have to remember, I am completely against vice in all forms." That was how I learned that if I were to take Kennedy seriously, I would have to take him seriously as a presidential candidate. After some further thought about the matter, I concluded that he could be highly successful as the Democratic candidate and, with luck, could be elected president.

President Kennedy—I have a horror of the people who always refer to him as "Jack" who would never have dared to call him "Jack" to his face in the White House—was, I suppose, one of my better younger friends in Washington by the time he was inaugurated. By the time he was assassinated, the other younger friend I depended on was Phil Graham, publisher of the *Washington Post,* so soon to extinguish his own brilliance in one of his dreadful depressions. But these are personal matters. Stew would say in later years that I admired John Kennedy "this side of idolatry—and not much this side." I suppose this was true.

I had known the senator and his family for some time before their rise to prominence. At the end of the war, however, I had no relationship with any of the Kennedy clan, nor did I want one. Indeed, what I knew of Joseph Kennedy's last months as American ambassador in London had made my flesh crawl and had led to a mortal quarrel between him, me, and my then-partner Bob Kintner. Ambassador Joe Kennedy's war record has long been public knowledge. He was the opposite of brave during the blitz. When he was not crouching for hours on end in his ambassadorial bomb shelter, he was firing off ultraisolationist telegrams to President Roosevelt. When the president at last recalled him from London, he became an active though secretive isolationist propagandist. Bob Kintner, who had connections in Hollywood, kept hearing that the old man told his Hollywood friends, who were mainly Jewish, that the British were far more anti-Semitic than the Germans—a well-chosen lie not calculated to endear him to anyone who felt strongly about the war, as Bob and I did.

Oddly, both of us had known Joe Kennedy fairly well and admired his work when he served as chairman of the Securities and Exchange Commission. But we did not welcome him home from London, and a final break came soon thereafter when he gave an interview to Louis Lyons of the *Boston Globe*. Evidently thinking that speaking to a newspaper then mainly read by the Boston Irish amounted to a kind of private chat, Kennedy made no attempt to conceal his isolationism or the crass, money-based fears in which it was rooted. Lyons himself, if I remember correctly, called the interview to Bob's attention, and we used it as the basis of a bitterly critical column in which we wrapped up all the information we had gathered on Kennedy's post-London activities.

Demonstrating the way Washington can work, Kennedy then went to Arthur Krock of the *New York Times* to ask him who tipped us off to his interview with Lyons. Arthur unhesitatingly informed him that the guilty man was certainly Justice Frankfurter, whom Arthur vigorously despised. For their part, the Frankfurters, even when dining in the same house as the Krocks, used to refuse to acknowledge the Krocks' existence. This astonishing situation— which would give me malicious amusement whenever it arose, as it did about once a month in those days in Washington—stemmed from a specific incident. Krock, it seems, had gone personally to Hyde Park to beg President Roosevelt not to appoint Frankfurter to the Supreme Court on the grounds that the appointment would promote a backlash of anti-Semitism in the country. The president listened to the argument with apparent imperturbability and then, as soon as Krock had departed, telephoned Cambridge and gave a full description of Krock's attack to Frankfurter, who, naturally enough, never forgot it.

At any rate, from the day Bob and I published the Lyons material in our own column, our relations with the founding Kennedy came to an end. Indeed, I might not have met John Kennedy until he became president had I not encountered and been immensely amused and impressed by his sister Kathleen on my first postwar trip to London. Kick Hartington was one of the most enchanting women I have ever known. She was not beautiful, but she was pretty, witty, and wonderfully gay in the old sense of the word. She made other people enjoy themselves and feel better for having been with her; and for these excellent reasons, she was much loved.

Kick's story in itself is interesting, for her connection to the future president was the strongest among all the Kennedy siblings and had, I think, some bearing on his career. She and the duke of Devonshire's eldest son, the marquis of Hartington, had fallen deeply in love during Joe Kennedy's time as ambassador to the

Court of St. James's. Their courtship had been bitterly opposed by the groom's family, the Cavendishes, one of the viciously anti-Catholic, grand English families in the tradition of the Whigs who had driven James II from his throne and replaced him with William III of Orange. Kennedy Catholicism, on the other hand, belonged to the old, hard-shell style of American Irish-Catholicism. And because there could be no agreement between the two families that the Hartingtons' children would be brought up as Protestants, the love affair came to nothing before the war.

But when Kick returned to London as a wartime Red Cross worker, predictably she and Lord Hartington met again and fell deeply in love a second time. Kick thereupon left the Church to marry, causing a temporary rupture with her own family. Unhappily, this was just before Hartington went off to fight in Europe, where he was killed by sniper fire in France. As his widow, Kick was a considerable personage in postwar London, and it did not take her long to fall in love again. I had met Peter Fitzwilliam, her leading man in this new drama, in Washington with his first wife just before the war. He was as near to being a colorful character out of a good romantic novel as any man I have ever met: astonishingly good-looking, wonderfully easy and jolly, and with that curious aura of glamor sometimes conferred by great possessions long held and a great place in the world long maintained.

It was said of Fitzwilliam's main country house, Wentworth Woodhouse, that one needed half an hour to walk completely around it, for the main façades were each near to a mile long. From the eighteenth century onward, the Fitzwilliams had been one of the tremendously rich and powerful Whig families in England. In this, they resembled the Cavendishes. The trouble was that Fitzwilliam was a married member of the Church of England; in the eyes of the Catholic Church as then constituted, Kick could not marry him. Mrs. Rose Kennedy, who seems to have had the final say about questions of religion within the family, took the position that if Kick married outside the Church a second time, Mrs. Kennedy would never speak to her again and, furthermore, would cut off all relations with any members of the Kennedy family who did not cease relations with Kick.

I learned of Mrs. Kennedy's view of the affair and its possible consequences by wonderful accident on a flight to Europe in the spring of 1948. In the seat next to me was an old lady from Boston who took her lace-up boots off as soon as we were in flight, a step that made the air in the cabin no fresher. Mildly curious, I asked my neighbor about herself. She was going home to Ireland for her vacation, she said (our flight was one of those that stopped first in Shannon) and added, quite gratuitously, that she had never been more glad to get out of the house than she had this time. Naturally, I inquired whose house she was talking about. With an air of surprise, she informed me that she worked as a maid for the Joseph Kennedys.

Without any further prodding, my neighbor then proceeded to paint a macabre picture of the consequences of Kick's romance, of which I had vaguely heard. Apparently, the Church had been mobilized by the threat of the eldest Kennedy daughter again marrying in defiance of clerical rules. "Sometimes," my neighbor said to me, "ye'd be fearful of drawing the curtains in the morning, lest ye'd find a Monsignor behind them." Apparently, too, the mobilization had been successful, for my neighbor, who was agreeably forthcoming after she got going, told me that Mrs. Kennedy had laid down the rule I have already cited: if Kick again married outside the Church, Rose Kennedy would cease to speak to her and, further, would cease to speak to other Kennedys who did not follow her own example.

I had all this is mind when, a day or so later, I read of Kick's death with Fitzwilliam in a small-plane crash. The two had been on their way to the Riviera from Paris for a final meeting with Kick's father in Cannes in which the views of the Kennedy family would be made clear. So, as it turned out, Kick went to the graveyard at the Hartington family home in Derbyshire, Chatsworth, and the rest of the Kennedy family did not have to choose between maintaining relations with their parents and maintaining relations with Kick.

Years later, after President Kennedy had reached the White House, he and I were talking, as we sometimes did, about Kick and her charm. I said—without explaining my source—that I had heard that Kick's intended marriage to Lord Fitzwilliam threatened to cause a permanent split in his family and perhaps only failed to do so because Kick was killed before the split could develop. I asked the president which side he would have been on. He said, "With Kick, of course."

I have no idea whether this choice would have caused the family schism forecast on that flight to Shannon. There was at least a chance, though, that John, who was closest to Kick, would have been implacably isolated by his mother. Had the future president stuck by Kick, moreover, thus parting with his own tribal tradition, I have always wondered whether he would have been removed from the succession that he rather reluctantly inherited when his brother Joseph P. Kennedy, Jr., was killed in the war.

Kick's death and her burial at Chatsworth were still a year in the future, when I met young John Kennedy in Washington in the late spring of 1947. As was expected of him, the young man had entered upon a political career, and in some sense his future was fixed, although there was only a small glimmer in the man then of what would come later. Because we had become friends in London, Kick had asked her sisters to invite me to dinner when she returned to Washington that spring to stay in the small Georgetown house where the sisters lived with their newly elected brother the congressman.

Of course, I accepted this invitation, and it proved to be one of the odd experiences of my life. I arrived at the specific hour—7:30, I think—in my best bib and tucker, and was shown into a living room that appeared to have suffered recently from the ravages of a small, particularly unruly tornado. The room's general dishevelment, the maid explained, was the final consequence of "the young ladies and gentleman" having done a series of competitive exercises on the floor earlier that afternoon. I concluded that exercise made the Kennedys hungry, for aside from scattered pillows and oddly placed chairs, there were also two half-eaten hamburgers on the mantelpiece. I felt I must have mistaken the day of my dinner invitation or possibly have come too early, but the maid assured me that I was on time and expected. So I sat down to wait amid the ruins, and one by one the occupants of the house, each more astonishingly good-looking than the last, strolled into the living room.

In time, the hamburgers were sent away, the cushions plumped, and the exercise competition explained and recounted. Kick was the first to arrive, and she apologized effusively for keeping me waiting. Her sisters followed, and for looks in those days there was very little to choose between Jean, Patricia, and Eunice. The new congressman was the last to come down, obviously just out of a hurried shower and looking exactly what he was: a handsome young man. Young John Kennedy's sisters all quite obviously adored him, and until he had joined us the party did not really begin. It proved to be one of the most agreeable evenings I can remember. Kick was in her best form—her gaiety stimulated an answering liveliness and wit in the future president. The sisters all joined in, and I limped along behind as best I could.

After this, I saw a good deal of the young congressman. Besides being decidedly ornamental, he was obviously extremely intelligent, although I thought him surprisingly unambitious and uninterested in politics. He was plainly not entirely well either. I remember one time, still in the late 1940s, during the early years of our acquaintance, when he turned a strong shade of green; this odd skin color combined with his hair—still decidedly reddish—to make the congressman look rather like a bad portrait by Van Gogh. I could not resist asking him why on earth he was green. He replied in the most stoic tones imaginable that he was believed to have some kind of slow-motion leukemia. The disease, he explained, was a kind of blood cancer for which the doctors kept prescribing chemicals to cure. The latest chemical, he felt, had turned him green. He added in a flat tone, "They tell me the damn disease will get me in the end. But they also tell me I'll last until I'm forty-five, and that's a long way away."

President Kennedy, of course, did not have leukemia. His condition was diagnosed as Addison's disease and ceased to be a worry after 1949, when the drug cortisone was discovered as a cure. But I remember the scene as though it were yesterday. In the same way, I remember his estimate of the time that remained to him, for one could not hear that from so young and so vital a man without it sticking in one's mind like a burr.

What the young politician believed about his own future seems to me significant. It explains the apparent lack of ambition, which, in turn, led to his lack of interest in the political dinners I used to give—dinners that certainly interested most of my Washington friends of those days, many of whom were considerably more importantly placed than Congressman Kennedy. I stopped asking him, in fact, when he complained to me about the dearth of pretty young girls at my table. I explained that it was difficult to combine young girls with the kind of key figures in the Washington political scene whom I normally invited to my house. Although we remained friends, John Kennedy and I stopped being in regular touch with one another until he married Jackie Bouvier in September 1953.

Jack Kennedy, Jackie, and I easily resumed the friendships of the old days when I returned to Washington after Stew went to work for the *Saturday Evening Post* in 1958. Marriage obviously had a calming effect on the senator. His character and temperament were more settled than I had remembered, and his political ambitions were more settled, too. The inward seriousness of the man was apparent now beneath the surface wit and charm. For Kennedy, the work of a congressman had in no sense been an absorbing passion. As a senator, however he was far more engaged, although in point of fact he had no great interest in becoming a senator after the manner of a Lyndon Johnson. To join the true elite of the so-called "Senate Club," he once told me with a wry grin, one must be willing to make deals of which one was ashamed without showing the smallest sign of shame. Even so, by the time we reconnected, Jack Kennedy was very much in the swing of Washington political life and also very much intent—as our conversation that summer evening on my front door step showed—on becoming president of the United States.

By that time, the whole working atmosphere in Washington had been changed radically by the departure of Eisenhower's self-satisfied businessmen to their respective businesses. The appointments of Christian Herter as secretary of state and Tom Gates as secretary of defense made a particular difference to me, for they were old friends whose presence in government changed the Washington ambiance in the sudden way it sometimes does. By the end of the Eisenhower administration—given the fact that Eisenhower was very much isolated in the White House—Washington came to resemble the Truman era, when the great figures now known as the "Wise Men" dominated the Washington scene.

Gates, a far abler man than is remembered, and Herter, a far tougher man than he looked, were both closely akin to Truman officials like Bob Lovett, Jack McCloy, and Dean Acheson in their outlook and style. Stew and Tish were particularly close to the Herters, and this brought me into their circle. The Gateses were friends, too. And so when I came back to Washington from abroad, I soon had the kind of connections in the government that I had so much enjoyed and benefited from in the early days—connections, in some sense, more comforting than practically useful. Although I came by the straw for my columns in the usual way, I was now at least assured a higher and more like-minded audience.

The darkest cloud on the foreign scene was Khrushchev's threatened blockade of Berlin, about which he grew so alarmingly arrogant that Chris Herter and Tom Gates were driven to recommend to the president a quick cure in the form of an increase in American defense appropriations. Then, there was what may be called the political charade, alluded to briefly at the beginning of this chapter, of the last phase of the Eisenhower presidency. The president, although no more active than before in any real sense, had taken to making what can only be called presidential processions abroad—mainly, I think, for political purposes.

At first, President Eisenhower was wildly welcomed in Western Europe as the man who had directed the Normandy landing. The huge pro-Eisenhower sector of the newspaper business then used the presidential tours as proofs of his vast success as "the leader of the free world" (the fashionable phrase of the moment). Indeed, to read *Time* magazine, which was particularly strongly biased toward Eisenhower, was almost like reading the Vatican's official newspaper describing the tours of the pope. I made myself unpopular by pointing out that the presidential tours meant nothing in real terms and suggesting that we were really losing standing abroad behind the façade of the newsreels of the smiling president in an open car receiving the cheers of the English, French, or West Germans.

Alas, this was only too true, for the tour device was used once too often and finally blew up in the faces of its inventors in the White House. The first sign of real trouble appeared when Richard Nixon went to Venezuela in 1958 and had to show very real courage when he was all but mobbed by "rent-a-crowds" massed, in all probability, by the KGB. Then there was the overseas tour, ending in Japan, which the president himself planned for the summer of 1960. He was originally scheduled to visit Moscow, but the trip had been canceled when Khrushchev, at the aborted Paris summit in May 1960, announced that the American president would not be welcomed in the Soviet capital. This summit, which came shortly after the downing of the U-2 reconnaissance flight over Siberia, had lasted barely long enough for Nikita Khrushchev to harangue President Eisenhower and stalk from the room. Perhaps to raise his own spirits, the president had then decided in June to visit the Philippines, Taiwan, and South Korea, with a final stop scheduled for Japan. The Japanese Communists, however, had organized substantial and viciously violent street protests against the signing of the new Japanese-American Security Treaty, a revision of the original defense cooperation pact signed in 1952.

The signals that this was sure to lead to embarrassing, if not seriously dangerous, trouble were so obvious that the Japanese government was driven, in effect, to withdraw its invitation to Eisenhower—indeed, to beg him not to come on the grounds that it could not be responsible for his safety. So the Japanese leg of the trip was canceled, a clear indication, it seemed to me, that the United States, which had stood so high abroad at the end of the Truman administration, had sunk to an alarmingly low level in the rest of the world as the Eisenhower administration drew to its close.

This low assessment of the president's progress was fueled at home by the lengthening controversy over the so-called "missile gap," a battle in which Stew and I played a considerable part. The dispute had begun in earnest in October 1957 with the launching of the Soviet's sputnik. The event caused something like panic in the country, to which the administration responded by widening the scope of the Gaither committee, headed by H. Rowan Gaither, Jr., former president of the Ford Foundation. Members of the committee sought to gauge the prospects for U.S. security "in the broadest possible sense of survival in the atomic age." Their conclusions were bleakly pessimistic. As sober-sighted a man as William Foster, who was Robert Lovett's aide and a member of the committee, remarked to Stew of his long weeks working on the final report: "I felt as though I were spending ten hours a day staring straight into hell."

According to the Gaither report, the Soviets were very near to producing an intercontinental ballistic missile, assuming they had not done so already. If this trend continued, the Soviets would have the capability to launch a crude first strike within two years. In other words, unless the planes of the Strategic Air Command were protected by a permanent airborne alert—a hideously expensive step and technically all but impossible—the Soviets would, in theory, have enough nuclear weaponry to knock out a full three-quarters of our bombers on the ground. The Gaither committee, therefore, recommended a major national effort to build better ICBMs (the American Atlas and Titan were of relatively little value for a variety of reasons) and to undertake a large, expensive program of air-raid and fallout-shelter building. Yearly defense appropriations should be increased by some $10 billion. Total expenditures for the civil-defense program would be about $30 billion over a five-year period.

To anyone educated in the Munich choice between fighting like a cornered rat or submitting to the demands of a stronger competitor, these conclusions were deeply alarming. On the basis of the highly secret U-2 reconnaissance flights, however, President Eisenhower chose not to be alarmed. The U-2 could, in theory, take satisfactory photographs of most of the Soviet Union, provided all surrounding allied bases deployed them. But "most" is the key word here, for the U-2 could not cover the entire Soviet Union. In addition, Eisenhower's reluctance to authorize regular flights reduced the coverage to a low level. The result, as was said at the time, was like extrapolating a picture of the United States from good air photographs of Greenwich, Connecticut.

A great nation that can afford to defend itself and fails to do so is responsible for the consequences. I shall go to my grave convinced that it was deeply wrong of President Eisenhower to sweep the Gaither report under the rug and ignore the real life-or-death issues of that time. Furthermore, the constantly repeated claim that the missile gap did not exist and that, therefore, the issue was a false one is both misleading and partly untrue.

What matters in issues of life or death is what you know with certainty. There was no certainty whatever in the conviction that the missile gap did not exist because of the findings of the U-2.

Certainty came when the first reconnaissance satellite was put into orbit, programmed to look at the gaps of doubt that still covered the map of the Soviet Union. The first launch of this satellite took pace in August 1960, shortly before President Kennedy was elected. Conclusive intelligence did not come until the next winter, at which time I admitted my error in print. The missile gap did not exist. Public humility, after all, was a small price to pay for peace of mind.

Politically, the timing of the discovery that the missile gap was nonexistent is important. President Kennedy would probably not have won the 1960 election without the supposed "missile gap" issue to aid him. Much later, during Kennedy's first year in office, I ventured, while dining one evening at the White House, to ask the president what he would have done had the reconnaissance satellite revealed clear evidence of the missile gap we had both feared. He briefly looked very grim and said, "Sometimes I wonder about that, and when I let myself do so I lose most of my night's sleep."

As it happened, the young candidate and I were not the only ones unnerved by President Eisenhower's seemingly casual attitude toward the missile threat. By 1958, the Soviet arsenal of short-range missiles clearly posed a danger to NATO forces in Europe. Tom Gates and Christian Herter grew increasingly alarmed as Khrushchev's behavior became more and more aggressive. President Eisenhower, however, tended to be curiously touchy about the cuts in the military budget that he had carried out in the years when he had George Humphrey at Treasury and "Engine" Charlie Wilson at Defense.

Although it was not recognized at the time by most people, Dwight Eisenhower was an angrily vain man who held the view that he, having commanded the Allied forces in Europe, knew better than anyone else how to manage the defense of the nation. He was disinclined to listen to any advice on the subject. Nonetheless, by the last year of Eisenhower's presidency, Gates and Herter were sufficiently unsettled to decide that the only remedy they knew of—a substantial increase in the defense budget—must somehow be achieved.

That summer of 1960, before the election that brought John F. Kennedy to the White House, was a critical time. Khrushchev's threat to inaugurate a second Berlin blockade was repeated month after month with increasing violence of language. Both the Republican and Democratic campaigns for the presidency were also in full and voluble swing. Meanwhile, President Eisenhower in effect turned his back on the practical affairs of government by going to Newport to play golf with his friends. Chris Herter asked for an appointment with President Eisenhower at Newport, which was granted grudgingly because the president did not like to have his golf game cut short. As Chris used to tell the story—and I heard him tell it myself nearly a dozen times after he had retired to private life in Washington—President Eisenhower received his secretary of state at the golf course in Newport—on the nineteenth hole, so to speak.

With many a concession to the president's attitude, Herter then began to present his case. He warned that although the U.S. defense program was entirely adequate, if the Soviets thought they were a great deal stronger or more determined that the United States, the odds on a move on the access routes to Berlin were much higher. Consequently—and this was the grand climax—he told the president that he, as secretary of state, and Tom Gates, as secretary of defense, had agreed that prudence required a $4 billion increase in defense appropriations to show the Soviets that they had been fooling themselves about American weakness of will.

President Eisenhower, as Herter later described him, was irritated by this proposal. But, after closely questioning Herter about Gates's views, he said in the end that if it was really true that his secretary of defense and secretary of state were agreed on the necessity of a $4 billion increase, he, as president, felt compelled to agree.

At this point in the story, Eisenhower's press secretary James Hagerty—a man who knew ten times as much about politics and Eisenhower's temperament as Herter—suggested that the decision taken at the Newport Country Club be announced to the press without further delay. To his eternal regret, Herter replied that this was not necessary. In his overgentlemanly way, he said that he would like several days to "staff out" the proposed budgetary increase with Tom Gates so that some idea of the specifics of how the money might be used could be presented when the proposal was made public. The president replied that this would be just fine with him.

From Newport, according to Chris Herter's account of this extraordinary episode, the scene changes to Vice-President Nixon, who was then on his way from Camp David to New York to meet with Nelson Rockefeller, his rival for the Republican presidential nomination. For Nixon, this was a crucial meeting for two reasons. First, he was by then as strongly inclined as most in Washington to believe that the Eisenhower/Humphrey disarmament plan had been proved a serious mistake. More importantly, the Democrats, who were then meeting in Los Angeles, had been saying as much in public, hammering at the Eisenhower administration's lack of initiative in combating the so-called missile gap. Nixon already had his own party's nomination well in hand. He was, however, rightly fearful that Rockefeller, who considered the missile gap a genuine issue as well as a politically potent one, would start an intraparty row over the matter at the soon-to-be-held Republican convention in Chicago.

When he reached New York, Nixon proceeded at once to Rockefeller's large Fifth Avenue apartment. He first offered Rockefeller the second spot on the Republican ticket, which the New Yorker refused, as Nixon knew he would. Then the two men sat down to negotiate the Republican party platform. They talked through the night. Nixon was acutely aware of the fact that he could not go too far in his agreements with Rockefeller for fear of rousing the ire of President Eisenhower. In the end, they jointly approved what came to be known as the "Treaty of Fifth Avenue," in which Rockefeller agreed to retire from the presidential race in return for a series of assurances from the vice-president. Among these was the assertion that "there must be no price ceiling on America's security," a point that carried implied criticism of President Eisenhower's defense policy to date.

What happened next was precipitated by Rockefeller's adroit move in giving the text of his agreement with Nixon to a waiting reporter from the *New York Times*. The specifics of the agreement were there for all to read in the special edition of the morning paper, flown to President Eisenhower at Newport. The president read the article with mounting fury. He swore to all within earshot that after what had happened in New York, his agreement with Herter counted for nothing. Indeed, any government decision now for a substantial outlay for defense would amount to an implied acceptance of the criticisms of Rockefeller and Nixon. Nixon was quickly called and told to repudiate his statement, which he did. And so the proposed increase was scrapped.

At the Republican convention in Chicago, Eisenhower loyalists busily and angrily tried to block any attempt by Nixon and Rockefeller to make their views the views of the Republican party. To avoid losing the remnants of President Eisenhower's support, therefore, Nixon's campaign was forced to fight the Democrats' assertions that the American defense program was inadequate. Very few politicians feel comfortable and can wage a good campaign when they are not convinced of what they are saying. Some are phony enough to put on a show, but it is not common. In the 1960 election, Richard Nixon had a difficult time putting on a show.

I am always curious about the "ifs" of history. I later asked

President Kennedy what would have been the result if the defense outlay agreed to by Eisenhower at Newport had been authorized instead of being derailed by the Nixon-Rockefeller meeting. The young president replied: "If that increase had gone through, we would have another president of the United States. Don't forget, I won by a very narrow margin." I concurred with this assessment. Nor, in the end, was I unhappy with the results of the Nixon-Eisenhower feud, for by the summer of 1960—and, indeed, well before the Republican convention and all that led up to it—I had found a political favorite in John F. Kennedy. While Chris Herter and Tom Gates were working diligently to persuade their president to take the rational course, I, in my own way, was working just as diligently to see my man into the White House.

22

Election
Politics

By the time of John Kennedy's reelection to the Senate in 1958, I had concluded that he was the most likely Democratic nominee for the 1960 election and resolved to help him in any way possible to win the presidency. By the strict laws of journalistic propriety, I suppose this decision was improper. However, it had been my nature, since the first interventionist days of the "Win the War" group in FDR's prewar Washington, to promote actively causes in which I believed. Kennedy's viewpoints on foreign and domestic policy were essentially identical with my own (always an endearing trait in any presidential candidate), and I was convinced that he had a strong chance of winning the general election. So I joined in the long campaign fight and relished doing so, although my duties, for the most part, were limited to that of a mostly ineffectual, advice-giving elder.

My early conviction that Kennedy would win strengthened after further talks with Ted Sorensen and careful study of the Kennedy campaign. The principal tactical duties were divided among Sorensen, the intellectual speech-writing wizard; Larry O'Brien in general charge of the practical political side; and

Kenneth O'Donnell, a very smooth operator who worked as O'Brien's partner. The ambassador, as they all invariably called Joseph P. Kennedy himself, interfered constantly—mainly to try to make his son's candidacy more tolerant of what remained of McCarthyism. For a time, these interferences worried me a good deal. However, I soon came to realize that the ambassador's contributions, except for his many large checks, had no real effect on the basic direction of his son's presidential drive.

During those early months, the consensus among political pundits and hangers-on in Washington held that the nomination of a Catholic was impossible. It was a certainty believed by those who talked only to one another. Kennedy's candidacy was being treated as a trivial phenomenon, hardly worth attention. At about the time I came to the conclusion that the ambassador's influence was not worth bothering about, I also concluded that this conviction among the wiseacres in Washington was a sign of success for John F. Kennedy.

My decision to support Kennedy did not mean that Kennedy's close-knit group received its new recruit with open arms. Even to Ted Sorensen, I think I seemed too worldly, perhaps too pleasure-loving. Until we became friends and began to trust one another, Kenny O'Donnell plainly regarded me as a journalist of dubious WASP origins. Larry O'Brien, who was chief campaign strategist and much broader-minded on some issues than his partner, felt the same way about me at first. The hardest of all of the young Kennedy men to know, however, was the future president's brother Bobby. Although clearly a man of large heart, he was fiercely loyal and protective of his brother's small political circle and naturally suspicious of outsiders. In time, however, we, too, became friends, and before long I was a not-infrequent guest at Hickory Hill, Bobby's rambling family home across the Potomac from Washington in McClean, Virginia. There, I had to keep a sharp watch on my rear to avoid being plunged into the swimming pool or being bitten by Broumis, the large, ferocious Kennedy dog of those days. I loved Hickory Hill probably because I love children, and the numerous tow-headed Kennedy children were all young then and hopelessly endearing.

Before long, I was being treated as an informal member of the Kennedy preconvention team. I suspected then—and I still suspect—that the future president as well as Bobby often asked my advice not because they thought it was worth having, but because John Kennedy particularly had a strong respect for what may be called "WASP Establishment opinion." I think he used me as litmus paper with which to test WASP reaction to his ideas and initiatives. I was a willing sounding board and much enjoyed being a spare part on a team of intelligent, vital, and very likable people all much younger than myself.

The presidential campaign began to move into high gear in the late winter and spring of 1959. By that time, Senator Kennedy's chief opponent among the Democrats was Senator Hubert Humphrey, then, as later, the nicest man in American politics though by no means the toughest or most adroit. Humphrey enjoyed the support of most of the northern liberal Democrats, who reacted to Lyndon Johnson in their usual Pavlovian manner. The exceptions were Arthur Schlesinger, Jr. and John Kenneth Galbraith, both of whom had been persuaded with some difficulty to give their support to Kennedy because the liberal hero, Adlai Stevenson, kept protesting that he wanted no part of another campaign for the presidency.

Stevenson, therefore, was excluded from the Wisconsin primary, the first great test of strength in the 1960 political season. Wisconsin, Minnesota's neighbor state with a similar farm population and similar political tendencies, should have been Hubert Humphrey territory. However, the Kennedy campaign people had been working Wisconsin since the previous year, sparing neither effort nor dollar. When, in April, the senator and Jackie went there to barnstorm, I went, too, because I was nervous about the primary and wanted to see what was happening on the ground.

The prelude to my journey was unforgettable. In Washington, I had made friends with the Minnesota senator Eugene McCarthy and his wife of those days, Abby. They were wonderful company, constantly enlivening, and I, as always, liked having them as guests at Dumbarton Avenue. Thus, I was aware that the senator was anything but enthusiastic about the Kennedy campaign. What stuck in his craw, I think, was that Kennedy was the first Catholic candidate to be taken seriously for the presidency, whereas he, McCarthy, a far more devout Catholic than Kennedy and, thus, a much more suitable representative of the Church if there was to be any Catholic candidate at all, was being snubbed.

As it happened, McCarthy and I were on the same flight to Milwaukee. There was an empty seat next to me, and the senator came back half the length of the plane to join me for, as he put it, "a talk." He sat down and made himself comfortable. Beyond this approximation, his purpose was soon evident. We exchanged empty pleasantries for a brief time. Then the senator proceeded to tell me a series of mildly discreditable stories that he had heard about the Kennedys' personal and political past. Although, I suppose, harmless, these tales were not without venom and reminded me of the stories about my cousin Eleanor that Senator Peter Gerry of Rhode Island used to enjoy peddling with thin bile.

I reminded Senator McCarthy once or twice that he was talking about close friends of mine, and once or twice I said I did not fully believe this story or that. Finally, I lost my temper and became a bit pompous. I pointed out hotly that I did not enjoy hearing what the senator was saying about people whom I admired and, in point of fact, to whom I was very much attached. As might have been expected, this made him as angry as I. He rose without a word, returned to his own seat at the front of the plane, and there got out the very largest missal I have ever seen. It held an astonishing collection of long and elaborately decorated Sacred Heart page markers, one of which, I remember, was a meticulous embroidery of the Veil of Saint Veronica. For the rest of the trip, the senator held the missal very high in front of his face so that all would be sure to notice what he was studying.

When we landed in Milwaukee, senator McCarthy and I had nothing further to say to each other. I could hardly wait, though, to get to the hotel where my candidate and his wife were staying in order to describe to them what seemed to me an odd experience. We shared a bottle of champagne in the hotel suite as I told the story of my comic encounter and described the senator's display of missal and page markers. Neither Kennedy blinked at the one or two really nasty stories that I repeated. Jackie merely giggled, and the future president went no further than a wry grin. Then he got in his tag line.

"Well, Joe," he said, "now I know you haven't spent much time with Irish politicians. My grandfather always used to tell me, 'Watch out for any Irish politician who reads his missal on the trolley car.' " Jackie and I burst into roars of laughter. I still laugh when I remember it. Jackie poured another round of champagne, whereupon we toasted one another and went down to dinner.

After this episode, what I best recall of the Wisconsin primary was the horror of door-to-door polling in the suburbs of Milwaukee in near-zero-degree weather. I went door-to-door with Stew and, because of the weather, had wrapped myself in the fur hat and fur gloves I had acquired for use in Moscow two years before. Stew and I had been admitted together to the house of a large, brisk lady who had simmering on her stove a delicious-smelling dish that plainly included quantities of cabbage and a great many highly spiced sausages. We asked the usual questions about the election, and then I asked if she would mind telling me the nature of her delicious-smelling dish.

I cannot recall the woman's answer except that the dish was a Polish specialty. But she then rounded on me with a question of her own that delighted Stew so much I must have heard the story from him a hundred times. "Mister," she said, "you mind if I ask you why do you speak so broken?" I had never heard quite this description of my own curious New England accent and voice, but it was worth being accused of speaking "broken" because of the enormous pleasure that it gave my brother both then and thereafter. I should add that the lady in question proved an enthusiastic Kennedy supporter.

Kennedy won in Wisconsin, but the smug self-confidence that the win generated in the Kennedy camp was soon to be rudely dissipated. Lou Harris and I went from Milwaukee to Huntington, West Virginia, to test the waters of the Democratic primary there. Our discoveries proved to be a marvelous demonstration of the unreliability of polls taken before the voters are up against serious choices. Lou's polls—he was working then for the Kennedy campaign and was generally thought to be the best in the business—had been showing Kennedy far ahead in West Virginia. The numbers were promising, it turned out, because the senator's and Jackie's images, freshly minted for *Life* magazine, had proved irresistibly attractive to the voters there.

Lou and I soon learned that these prospective voters knew nothing whatever about the man they said they were "for." What finally filtered through from Wisconsin to West Virginia was the unwelcomed news that the young candidate was a Catholic. In that ferociously Protestant state—I saw a time-battered copy of Foxe's *The Book of Martyrs* on the dresser in a miner's house—it had suddenly sunk home to voters that Kennedy was what their forefathers in the old country used to call a "papist."

Altogether, those days in West Virginia with Lou Harris added up to an experience both sad and lurid. The condition of the state and of very large numbers of its people was downright heartbreaking. The little mining valleys, to my surprise, were outwardly pretty. But when you called at the shacks in which the people lived, the effects of grinding poverty and recurrent unemployment were easy to see. They were etched in acid on the faces of the people. Young wives looked pinched and apprehensive, and the flocks of fair-haired children, instead of being jolly and full of life, were too obviously hungry and already disciplined to near-apathy.

In every valley, Lou and I heard the same story from the people we polled. They had thought Kennedy was a "nice guy" but had then found out he was a Catholic; and, of course, they would finish, "We can't vote for him now." The resulting poll conducted by Harris (which was, of course, confidential) stung the Kennedy organization into volcanic response. Anyone could see that an anti-Kennedy vote in West Virginia might persuade leading Democrats all over the country of the truth of the Washington adage that a Catholic could never win the presidency. Kennedy operatives swarmed into the state, many of them, I fear, carrying bags bulging with greenbacks. West Virginia's county system leant itself comfortably to a reasonable degree of political corruption, and on that occasion the county system was worked to a fare-thee-well.

Meanwhile, my columns on what I called "the prejudice issue" had their effect, too. Because it looked as though the Kennedy bandwagon might be forever checked in West Virginia, reporters and television people swarmed into the state in the wake of the Kennedy workers. During those early weeks in April, in every miner's valley earnest young men and women were asking astonished housewives for their thoughts on religious prejudice, and on some days it seemed as though half the pitheads in the state were close to being obstructed by television crews.

All this was cruelly unfair to Hubert Humphrey. There were plenty of signs that he had hoped to take advantage of West Virginia's ingrained religious prejudice in a quiet, seemingly respectable way. But it is not possible to exploit religious prejudice, even gently, in the full glare of television lights and in the midst of squadrons of young reporters brandishing tape recorders. I suppose, too, I ought to have been shocked at my own role in generating the controversy. It was certainly unfair that Humphrey should be so hampered in exploiting his main advantage, whereas Kennedy had no difficulty in exploiting his own main advantage—his father's fortune. But the po-faced standards by which the newspapers and television now measure political behavior have never made a great deal of sense to me. Perhaps because I've come from political families on both sides, I have always accepted practical politics as just that. Nor have I been very much worried about it, for whenever American politics have grown excessively corrupt in my lifetime the corruption has somehow been self-correcting.

In the end, Kennedy won West Virginia, and, as convention time approached, his prospects for winning the nomination grew more promising. I became sure of this later, during that beautiful summer when I went to visit Jackie and the candidate at their house in Georgetown. They were nowhere to be seen when the maid let me into the house. I was left with little Caroline, who undertook to be my hostess. I long ago had taken on the role of universal uncle, and so we had an agreeable chat until the candidate arrived to supply the fixative that has always kept the image of that afternoon in my memory. He and Jackie breezily walked in, handed me a drink, and told me in confidence that Mayor Daley of Chicago had at last made a solid commitment to give his support to Kennedy. This news made it fairly certain that I had been right to bet on John Kennedy to win the Democratic nomination.

I was uncertain about the size of Kennedy's lead until later on that July, when I went to see one of my close political friends, Senator Herman Talmadge of Georgia. It is no longer fashionable to say so—for he tragically mismanaged his life and, in then end, forfeited much of his considerable promise to drink—but Herman Talmadge was the ablest of all the political leaders of the South in his era, with the possible exceptions of Johnson himself and the senior senator from Georgia, Richard Russell. Certainly, Russell was a finer man than Talmadge; but equally certainly, he was a southern senator of the old school and, therefore, more inflexible than Talmadge and in many ways far less practical-minded. In the Lyndon Johnson camp, where I foresaw that Kennedy would meet with his most serious convention opposition, Talmadge was the most astute member of the strategy board guiding the Senate leader's preelection fortunes.

I went to see Senator Talmadge shortly before the campaign drama was transferred to the convention in Los Angeles. My purpose was simple. At no political convention I have attended could a reporter reach any significant leader on the officially listed telephone lines since they were continuously jammed with supplicants of every kind. To cover the story adequately, therefore, newspapermen had to go to the leaders we knew best and beg for the secret numbers reserved for them and their staff members.

But when I went to Talmadge's office on Capitol Hill to ask for his unlisted numbers in Los Angeles, I got a shock. "I ain't going to Los Angeles," Talmadge firmly announced to me in a tone of considerable bitterness.

I protested at once that I could not believe he was going to leave his friend Johnson at so crucial a juncture.

"Well, Joe," he went on, "I ain't going to Los Angeles because I know exactly what's going to happen there."

"Well, what exactly do you mean?" I asked.

"Kennedy's going to be nominated on the first ballot with a thousand votes or maybe a few more. He's going to offer the vice-presidency to Lyndon. Lyndon's going to take it. And I just don't want to be there to see it happen. So I'm going huntin' and fishin' in the Great Dismal Swamp. And if you want to know my opinion during the convention, you'll just have to get a canoe and come find me there."

I could hardly believe my ears, particularly when I heard his prediction that the all-powerful Senate majority leader would be offered—and would accept—the vice-presidency under Kennedy. I protested to Senator Talmadge that this scenario was unthinkable, to which he replied, "Well, Joe, you damn well better begin thinking about it because it's going to happen." That led me to think about it long and hard. Fortunately for me, I had long since adopted a simple rule as a political reporter—namely, to believe those who knew a great deal more than I did even if what they said struck me at first as incredible. So I journeyed out to Los Angeles with the vice-presidency very much on my mind.

It was a wonderfully odd convention. First, Adlai Stevenson, with exceptional fatuousness, plunged into the fray as a last-minute candidate, doing, only when it was a hopeless thing to do, what all his friends had begged him to do for months. Then Johnson, who, of course, was himself a candidate for the Democratic nomination, grew bitter about Kennedy's impending victory, although he did not normally permit himself public bitterness over contests within his own party. Finally, the grapevine told me that the other main Democratic boss of those days, David Lawrence of Pennsylvania, was going to end in Kennedy's corner as Mayor Daley had done earlier. This would give Kennedy the first-ballot majority Herman Talmadge had predicted.

Much has been written about my role at the convention, and so I should like to set down what really happened. Phil Graham, who was the publisher of the *Washington Post*, myself, and Phil's wife Kay had made arrangements with one another to lunch every day at the same table in the dining room of the Beverly Wilshire, the least unpleasant of the convention hotels. To secure a table—and following a lesson I had learned from Alice Longworth many years before—we had paid the head waiter a substantial sum in advance. As I remember, it was an especially substantial sum because the Graham children were with their parents for the convention; the table had to be a large one.

I had concluded that Kennedy would make a bad mistake if he did not offer the second spot on his ticket to Lyndon Johnson. By the longest possible chalk, Johnson was, after Kennedy himself, the biggest figure in the Democratic party. To pass him over would be dangerous for that reason alone but also would imply abandonment of all hope for southern votes in the electoral college. After a little research, I had concluded that substantial numbers of Kennedy's closest advisers were advising him passionately to avoid any sort of offer to Johnson. (Senator Stuart Symington of Missouri was the alternate choice most often mentioned.) So I laid my conclusions before Phil Graham. He agreed with me on every point. I, therefore, suggested that we go to Kennedy's suite at the Biltmore to give the candidate our advice—for what that might be worth.

Phil was at first reluctant to join me because he did not then know Kennedy intimately. But I pointed out to him that as a recognized and time-tested liberal, and as publisher of the *Washington Post,* he was important to Kennedy. So we set off to the Biltmore through the fearful convention-time crowds. With luck, we secured places on an elevator that took us to the floor where the candidate's working office was located. Two Connecticut politicians, John Bailey and Senator Abraham Ribicoff, were already in the reception area, biting their nails as they waited to see the candidate. There was general disorder in the room—by then, full of John Bailey's cigar smoke—and an atmosphere of triumph as young members of the Kennedy camp, flush with the early glow of victory, wandered in and out.

We were passed into the Kennedy suite after I was recognized, and I told the senator's private secretary Evelyn Lincoln, by then a friend of mine, that Phil and I would like a few minutes of the candidate's time. A seedy double bedroom was the waiting room for those about to be admitted to the very small sitting room Kennedy was using as his office. Phil and I sat on one of the beds in this dreary anteroom before being called into the office. I had thought a lot about how the presentation ought to be made and had decided to reserve just two subjects for myself and to leave Phil, a far more eloquent man, to do most of the talking.

In time, the candidate received us in his own disorderly room. He looked fresh and ridiculously young, and did not seem particularly tense or overdriven, despite the hectic events of the day. He had a gift for making one come to the point, which naturally we wanted to do. My first subject was difficult because Kennedy was so vital and so young that a reminder of mortality seemed strikingly out of place. Nonetheless, a reminder was essential because I wanted to bring home to him that in choosing his vice-president he might perhaps be choosing the next president of the United States. I was concerned he might make a too-easy choice that could also turn out to be a bad one.

Symington was the too-easy choice I had in mind. As I have said, "Symington for vice-president" was now the cry from many factions of the Democratic party, chiefly the liberal ones. I am afraid that what I said to the candidate was "You know damn well that Stu Symington is too shallow a puddle for the United States to have to dive into." The comment made him grin, and this left me fairly sure that the people who were touting Symington all over Los Angeles were due for a disappointment. I then went on to say that precisely because we thought as he did—that these were dangerous times— our recommendation for the vice-presidency was Lyndon Johnson. I added that although I would leave the arguments for having Johnson on the ticket to Phil, I had one closing point to make.

I recounted, as briefly as I could, my talk with Herman Talmadge, whose intelligence I knew Kennedy respected. I concluded by begging Kennedy not to make a vice-presidential offer to Johnson unless Kennedy was entirely ready to have it accepted, for it seemed to me—I believe rightly—that making an offer and then lamely withdrawing it would only make matters worse for the difficult campaign that lay ahead. I then turned the floor over to Phil, who made a most eloquent and intelligent presentation of the electoral advantages of a Johnson vice-presidency.

The candidate seemed to absorb Phil's arguments, but I concluded that he had already made up his mind. He was glad to hear our arguments for what he already was proposing to do. I do not believe that the advice Phil Graham and I gave to the future president made any difference except to increase his confidence in a decision already reached.

Our visit to Kennedy had one important consequence, however; Phil was closer to Lyndon Johnson than I was and, since he was not officially a reporter, could easily join the Johnson party at the majority leader's hotel headquarters and serve there as a continuing liaison with Kennedy. The candidate saw the virtue of this idea and at once gave Phil the entire assortment of his super secret telephone numbers. This proved to be desperately important later, when Kennedy's choice of Johnson became known and triggered a series of outbursts of rage within the liberal Democratic camp—first and foremost from Robert Kennedy, who claimed that he had given a commitment against Johnson to organized labor. (I believe that John Kennedy had been less than forthright with his brother; very likely, he did not want an exhausting fraternal argument during an already stressful time.)

At any rate, Robert Kennedy was allowed to go to Johnson headquarters and beg Johnson to withdraw from the vice-presidential contest. This seeming reversal of the offer that had already been made added dangerously to the turmoil in Johnson's private headquarters. According to Phil's eyewitness accounts, it was close to a madhouse. Fortunately, however, Phil was there when Bobby met with Johnson and wounded the latter's touchy feelings. So Phil used the secret numbers to ask Bobby's older brother whether John

Kennedy had meant or did not mean the original offer he had made to Johnson. Kennedy asked to talk to Johnson, who came on the line. Kennedy assured him that there had been some misunderstanding, that his offer had been a genuine one, and in his masterly manner he smoothed Johnson's feathers.

So the Democrats came out of Los Angeles with the Kennedy-Johnson ticket I had argued for. For that very reason, I suspect, the candidate invited me to come to Hyannis Port where he and Jackie were planning a short spell of rest and recuperation before beginning the general campaign. To Kennedy's evident annoyance, I refused the invitation. Other newspapermen, I reasoned, would certainly find out I had been staying with the Kennedys after the convention and would be made more than a little angry by the special treatment and extra advantages offered to one of their number. Kennedy apparently understood because he told me that he would arrange for me to stay with his sister, Eunice Shriver. I agreed.

What I remember of the experience, however, is no more than a mildly funny story at my own expense. At my first breakfast at the Shrivers', my companions at table were assorted Kennedy and Shriver children, all of whom were very young, angelic-appearing, and good-mannered. I was enchanted by all of them, and they felt my liking and promptly returned it, as children do. Altogether, we had a most agreeable breakfast until the plain speaking at the close. As the children were leaving, young Robert Shriver turned to me in the manner of a spokesman for the group and pronounced his verdict on the meeting. "Well, good-bye, Mr. Alsop," he said. "We like you very much, but why do you have so little hair?" I could think of no adequate answer except that I was beginning to be an old man. I felt a bit diminished.

Those two days at Hyannis Port were exhilarating partly because everyone there suffered from overconfidence. On the one hand, Kennedy disliked and always tended to underrate Richard Nixon, as I did, too. On the other hand—and, I think, more importantly, although I cannot prove it—I believe that the polls consistently gave Kennedy an exaggerated lead simply because so much had already been made of anti-Catholic prejudice. Persons polled were reluctant to admit the prejudice they felt. Prejudice apart, they preferred Kennedy over Nixon—but only prejudice apart. As it was, the anti-Catholic problem surfaced openly only in Texas, where Kennedy went in person to address the issue and made a wonderful impression.

Thus, the only moment in the course of the general election when I lost confidence was on the occasion of the first televised election debate in Chicago. I was in the audience that evening and did not see the television transmission. As has often been stressed since by political analysts, Nixon seemed to do very well to those of us who watched him in person or listened to the debate on the radio. It was Nixon's appearance, evidently, that cost him so heavily. I was used to Nixon's appearance and did not make allowances for its effect.

I might have lost a good deal of my overoptimism, nonetheless, had I not called Alice Longworth at about 3:30 that morning. I wanted to know her opinion because I considered then, as I still consider, that the three best political handicappers of their era were the three first cousins Alice Longworth, Eleanor Roosevelt, and my mother (who never failed to call the vote of her home state, Connecticut, within a margin of error of 2,500 votes). Alice Longworth did much of her handicapping as a television watcher. I knew she had been watching the debate and had time to make conclusions about it because she habitually stayed awake until 5:00 or 6:00 A.M., generally reading philosophy if there was no television worth watching. I got a happy shock when she came on the line. She had recognized my voice from the first "Hello," and her opening remark was decisive.

"Well, Joe, your man's in, my man's finished [she had admired Nixon since his days as a congressman]. I don't see why they bother to go on with the election. Dick has finished himself off." As it turned out, this was very much the majority view. Indeed, after the debate, numerous Republican leaders immediately bombarded the vice-president with dire warnings that he had "looked awful" and had "sounded like Tom Dewey." In point of fact, the real Nixon was vastly more interesting, impressive, and formidable than his popular image. As a man and politician, Nixon was intelligent, not platitudinous; withdrawn, not folksy; ambitious, not humble. This kind of complexity proved too powerful a package for televised politics, even in its nascent form, and the candidate suffered accordingly.

At any rate, because of this judgment of Mrs. Longworth's and because the strength of the Kennedy camp was persistently overrated by many charmed members of the media, including myself, I was overconfident right down to Election Eve. Phil and Kay Graham and I convened at Phil's office to hear the early returns as they arrived. Presently, however, we returned to the more comfortable surroundings of Dumbarton Avenue, where it was agreed that Kay would be allowed to leave when she had had enough, but that Phil and I would stay until we knew the outcome, however long that took. Unless I am mistaken, we somehow procured a television set (I still prefer the written word and have never owned a television set), and we settled in for a very long and very drunken evening.

Phil Graham was a man in whose company it was impossible to be bored. He possessed a brilliant and extraordinary mind as well as an exceptional ebullience. There was an infectious quality to his enthusiasm; and when he became animated he tended to carry everyone else in the room along with him—like surfing, perhaps, or what I imagined skiing would be like if one was good at it. So even as the early returns, beginning with Connecticut, showed Kennedy the winner and caused the networks to predict more of the same, we had a lively time shouting about the United States and the state of the world.

We had a private celebration when Kennedy carried Texas, for we felt that this was our doing—at least, up to a point—and, indeed, no one argues nowadays that Kennedy could have won without Johnson to help him with the big Texas vote. In the early hours of the morning, the returns began to go sour, and it was still uncomfortably neck and neck until near 9:00 A.M., when Phil at last went home to Kay. I had one more scotch and soda to keep me going until the outcome was finally decided. When Michigan gave Kennedy a bare majority, thus insuring him of the presidency, I went wearily off to bed.

For me, the immediate aftermath of the election was almost as exciting as the election itself. The president-elect was strongly inclined from the first to refuse Adlai Stevenson's request to be the new secretary of state. Many within the new government regarded Stevenson's appointment as automatic, a view, it turned out, that was shared by Stevenson himself. He was openly discontented when asked to become ambassador to the United Nations.

With Stevenson out as secretary of state, those who were already forming a kind of Stevenson wing within the Kennedy government were pushing for Senator J. William Fulbright of Arkansas. When Kennedy asked me whether he had any obligation to give Fulbright the State Department, I replied that I did not know. I did say, however, that for all his laudable qualities, Senator Fulbright was also a very vain man and that vanity was the first step toward disloyalty, especially by the strict standards of Jack Kennedy's politics. Of course, this was exactly what Kennedy had wanted me to say, for I am sure he had the same view of Fulbright as I did. A little later on, it would become apparent that Kennedy wished, like Franklin Roosevelt before him, to keep the focus of the country's foreign policy well within the walls of the White House. So the job of secretary of state went finally to Dean Rusk, a competent man who lacked the stature and public confidence of Fulbright and was, therefore, easier to control.

Then there was the matter of who was to be secretary of the treasury. Kennedy, who wished to make one bipartisan appointment, wanted to offer the post to New York banker Douglas Dillon, a Republican who had served as under secretary of state in the Eisenhower administration. The Stevensonites, already disappointed by their candidate's fate, were dead set against Dillon and had offered as an alternative Senator Albert Gore of Tennessee. Kennedy's main concern (because this had been the chief point of attack of those opposed to a Dillon appointment) was that Dillon would prove to be disloyal. He mentioned the Gore candidacy to me. I answered that in considering the senator, he would do well to remember a little song that used to be sung at my club at Harvard when anyone at a club dinner began to indulge in drunken oratory: "It's a terrible death to be talked to death, it's a terrible death to die; It's a terrible death to be talked to death, it's a terrible death to die."

Senator Gore, I concluded, combined fashionable shallowness and extreme loquacity to an improbable degree. As for Dillon's loyalty, I said that he might be a Republican, but would prove far more dependably loyal than Al Gore and others like him. This evidently made up Kennedy's mind, for he asked me to get Phil Graham to get in touch with Dillon immediately and tell him of the offer. The Dillons were giving a huge dinner that evening. Most of the guests were arch-Republican, and it did not seem desirable for Phil to erupt into the middle of such a conclave. So the arrangement was that the window to the left of the Dillon's front door would be left open for Phil to enter by, and Douglas Dillon would meet him alone at a given hour during the early course of the dinner. The window in question admitted Phil to the large downstairs bathroom-cloakroom of the Dillon house, and it was there that Dillon, with obvious delight, received the president's offer.

For the rest, since I did not want to seem to interfere except when requested to do so, my only contributions to the future Kennedy administration were Averell Harriman and George Kennan. For some reason, Kennedy did not want Kennan as an ambassador—perhaps because Kennedy had noticed and not been impressed by the way Kennan had retreated from his famous Long Telegram and subsequent "Mr. X" article about the proper way to deal with the Soviet Union. I argued that next to Chip Bohlen, whom Kennedy greatly admired, Kennan was the Foreign Service's most distinguished member and that he ought, at the very least, to be offered an embassy. The offer—of Yugoslavia—was eventually made and accepted. So George went to Belgrade, though not for long, for he grew moody there—always a serious danger with George—and succeeded in simultaneously enraging the State Department, the Congress, and the president as well as the resident American press. It was what you might call a ten-strike.

My other contribution was to lobby the president-elect to give a place to Harriman, who had supported him for the nomination and no doubt contributed a tidy sum to his campaign. These benefits of Harriman's might have been overlooked since Kennedy had a dislike for discussion with deaf persons and, more generally, for the company of the aged. It was I who then gave Harriman a nickname that many other people used thereafter: "the old crocodile." Averell, I told Kennedy, had perfected the act of appearing to be half-asleep, looking like a log in the water, until his objective—or prey—came close enough, whereupon the huge jaws would snap. So Harriman was made a roving ambassador. He was perfectly content to be a fifth wheel, being confident of his ability to make a real place for himself in the Kennedy administration later on.

That brings me, at long last, to the very oddest and most unexpected party I ever hosted, which was on John F. Kennedy's inauguration night. Precisely because I had been personally engaged in Kennedy's election, I was also drawn into his inauguration in a way unique to my experience before or after. The whole week struck me as dazzling. Washington seemed rejuvenated. A great many attractive younger people had come to town for the fun. Among them were two women whom I had met in Los Angeles—Flo Smith, the wife of Earl T. Smith, a great friend of John Kennedy's from Palm Beach; and Flo's friend, a beautiful Venetian Afdera Fonda, a formidable person who had once been married to the actor Henry Fonda and was reputed to be named after a mountain peak in Mexico.

These women come into my story of that week for an odd reason. At one of the innumerable preinauguration parties around town, I inevitably let my enthusiasm run away with me to the point of saying to Afdera and Flo that if the lights were on in my house, there would be champagne to be drunk there for anyone who had had enough of the formalities of the inaugural balls. This promise to Flo and Afdera amounted to a time bomb that was already ticking when Phil and Kay Graham, with considerable additional company, dined at my house before the inaugural ball, where we had been allotted a box on the floor.

As I look back, I suppose that evening was the last during which I felt like a young man. Dinner was glorious fun, and so was the journey in the big car that Phil had ordered to take our party to the ballroom. The city looked dazzlingly beautiful under a blanket of snow. Snow fell continuously, and the trip downtown took so long that our company drank several more bottles of champagne during the course of our journey.

Perhaps because I do not dance, the ball itself struck me as painfully boring, and I made ready to leave long before the others had had their fill of the party. I maintained a vague hope of finding someone in a car outside preparing to go home. A foot or so of falling snow had accumulated by that time, and I had difficulty negotiating the sidewalk in my pumps. I was turning forlornly back to the ballroom when I ran into Averell Harriman's stepson Peter Duchin, who offered me a lift to Dumbarton Avenue.

Peter's sudden appearance struck me as a godsend—a very helpful and good-humored godsend. The trip through the snow to Georgetown was not easy, but since there was little traffic on the streets, we reached Dumbarton Avenue in about twenty minutes. Pulling up, I was horrified and instantly reminded of my own weakness for scattering invitations, for there, in their full ball-going regalia, were Flo Smith and Afdera Fonda beating on my door knocker in a determined manner. Begging Peter to help me, I rushed up the steps and let Flo and Afdera into the house, where Peter and I lighted the fire and sat them on each side of it. Luckily, in anticipation of further entertaining in the days to come, I had a considerable quantity of champagne on ice. I found the glasses, and Peter opened the first bottles. Before long we were able to settle down by the fire with Flo and Afdera.

Had the evening ended there, it would have made a pleasant finish, but it by no means ended there. Indeed, it soon became clear that Flo and Afdera had told all sorts of people, including the about-to-be-inaugurated president, that there would be champagne at my house, if the lights were on. Consequently, a line of cars delivered what seemed to me an endless stream of guests. Peter, who had assumed the role of co-host, was beginning to worry about the champagne supply when I heard a storm of hard knocking on the front door. I rushed to open it. The scene in the open doorway was unforgettable. Dumbarton Avenue was solidly blocked by a vast Secret Service cortege of black cars and limousines. Every one of my neighbors' windows was open and lighted, and in every window people in their dressing gowns were clapping and cheering.

I can still summon the picture of the new president standing on my doorstep. He looked as though he were still in his thirties, with snowflakes scattered about his thick, reddish hair. Exhilaration always rejuvenated him, and he had been greatly exhilarated by his inauguration and all that surrounded it. The burdens of his office had not yet settled across his shoulders, and there was a bounce in his manner, a light in his eye that would not be so prominent later. He explained that Jackie had been so tired after her last visit to one of the several inaugural balls, she had simply fallen into bed in the White House. He, however, had become hungry but could find no one in the White House who could give him anything to eat.

This confession horrified me, for I did not have so much as an egg in the house and could offer him nothing except the terrapin I had brought in from Baltimore for the same reason that I had loaded the icebox with champagne. Hoping against hope, I offered the president a bowl of terrapin along with a bottle of champagne. He took the wine but needed no more than a glance to reject what had formerly been the greatest delicacy in the United States. It hardly mattered. I soon observed that what he really wanted was one last cup of unadulterated admiration, and the people crowding my living room gave him that cup freely, filled to the brim.

Propelled by the new arrival, fueled by my dwindling supplies of champagne, the impromptu gathering continued on for a good while longer until, at last, the president returned to the White House. One of the young women who had come to the house and perhaps had had one glass too many succumbed to near hysterics in the garden rooms, wailing, "I'll not see him again; it's the last time I'll see him"; and so on. Flo Smith managed to get the wailing lady to go home with her. Peter Duchin most generously helped me transfer the worst of the mess from the living room to the pantry. We were concluding our chores when the guests who were staying with me came in from their postball party, to which I had not been invited. I could not resist telling them of the company they had just missed; and, human nature being human nature, the husband—who would later serve the Kennedy administration with some distinction—promptly blamed his wife for this social calamity, and she promptly retaliated in kind. So the evening might have ended in ill humor had there not been one last half bottle of champagne to share among the three of us, which we did while nursing the dying fire.

23

Kennedy's Washington

In the numerous memoirs and personal accounts of President Kennedy and his time in Washington, one almost always finds descriptions of the rich, intoxicating atmosphere that settled over the capital—and, indeed, around the country—during those early months of the administration. These narratives invariably convey a sense that this was a breathless time, full of promise and energy and, oddly enough, glamor, which is not a quality usually associated with Washington. Try as I might, I cannot contradict these accounts, nor can I look back at that period without the most unabashed feelings of romantic nostalgia and delight.

The truth is that after the staid Eisenhower years, the Washington that was invaded by the members of the Kennedy administration was suddenly enormously festive and gay. A good many of these men and women were well enough off to take big houses and to give many lively parties. Later on, Jackie and the president gave occasional small dances at the White House that were as good as any parties I have been to. In general, the president and his wife made every attempt to remain close to their old friends and connections. They were a visible and charismatic couple, and the obvious relish with which they took up their new roles in Washington had a curiously invigorating effect on the rest of the city.

Next to the impromptu rally at my own house on inauguration night, the oddest and most memorable party I have ever gone to was the first such gathering President and Jackie Kennedy held for friends at the White House. It took place on a Sunday night at the end of the long week of inaugural and postinaugural festivities that mark the beginning of all new administrations in Washington. The Eisenhower White House, after its evacuation by its occupants, presented a stark contrast to the White House I remembered from the Roosevelt years. Everything halfway pretty appeared to have been put into storage. Friends had told me that the display of the president's innumerable military souvenirs and handsome wartime decorations did something to lighten the gloom, but all of that was gone by that Sunday night in January 1961, when I, along with the Franklin Roosevelts, Leonard Bernsteins, and one other couple, arrived at the Kennedy White House for dinner. Indeed, the place looked like an enormously enlarged and not-quite-as-attractive version of the presidential suite at the Muehlebach Hotel in Kansas City.

By Sunday night, Jackie had rummaged through the entire house, encountering a good many surprises. "Do you know," I remember her exclaiming, "I've found a whole room of calligraphers busily at work in the cellar." These were, of course, the skillful people who spent their days writing out White House invitations and place cards in perfect script. Other contemporary features of the White House proved just as surprising. Among these were a pair of large portholelike contraptions built into the wall on either side of the door leading from the oval sitting room into the main upstairs hall. I had never seen anything like them and asked what the devil they might be. The president rang, and one of the ushers appeared as though by magic. The president asked the usher by name—he had already learned the names of all the members of the White House staff—what the portholes concealed. The usher opened one of them to show a television screen, and he explained that in their last year or so the president and Mrs. Eisenhower liked to dine on television suppers, each watching a different television show. Two portholes were necessary because the president preferred Westerns and Mrs. Eisenhower preferred soaps.

Jackie had found an enormous gold bucket, as big as a milk pail, and this was waiting for us in the oval sitting room upstairs filled almost to the brim with ten pounds of fresh caviar that a vague Palm Beach acquaintance of the Kennedys had sent for no reason at all except that he was delighted by their move into the White House. I had never seen ten pounds of caviar—much less fresh caviar—in one bucket before, and I have never seen it since. This did not, however, prevent our little dinner party from finishing this load to the last egg. I do not know what happened to the others, but I know that as a result I was sick as a dog the next day and unable to eat caviar in any form for another four years. But since the caviar was accompanied by bottle after bottle of Dom Perignon, it seemed good while it lasted and the party was jolly, indeed.

As for other particulars of that evening, I can only recall the peculiar combination of vomit-green and rose-pink that Mrs. Eisenhower had chosen for her bedroom and bathroom, plus the embarrassment of having to tell my cousin Franklin Roosevelt, Jr. that he could not go on calling the president of the United States "Jack," however close they had been in the past—a point he ought to have known. The Dom Perignon was almost too plentiful and certainly too tempting for me to have a clear memory of anything more except the conviviality and intimacy of the occasion and the gleam of the great golden bucket with its load of caviar.

So began what I still look back upon as the most enjoyable period of my life. Although personal matters have only a narrow place in political memoirs, it is, nevertheless, a real place. I shall break off the thread here to pay brief tribute to my wife, Susan Mary Jay, whose arrival in Washington coincided with John Kennedy's inauguration. Susan Mary was a family connection to begin with. Stewart had been her first Alsop admirer when she was a beautiful young girl just coming out in New York, and she had liked Stew well enough to go with him and Johnny often to Avon, where both Mother and Father prayed nightly that she and Stew would come to an arrangement.

Susan Mary was a courageous and witty woman who I came to know during the first years of the war, following her marriage to my friend Bill Patten. Before the war ended, Bill was named an attaché of the newly forming embassy in Paris. I had found them both there when I was en route home from China with General Chennault. Accompanied by the general and his dachshund Joe, we had a wonderfully cheerful and eccentric meal together. Thereafter, whenever I went abroad, the Pattens gave me a room and a glorious time in Paris.

Even then, Bill's years were numbered by his chronic emphysema, an illness he bore with unimaginable courage. He died, after a long battle, in the year of the Kennedy campaign. I was beginning to feel lonely, as single men often do. I cared greatly for Susan Mary, and, therefore, I wrote her from the convention in Los Angeles, proposing that she form a new partnership—with me, headquartered in Washington. She came to the capital shortly after the inauguration to make her decision, and, fortunately for me, it was a favorable one.

Marriage is a daunting prospect at any time, but never more so than late in life, when one has established the solitary and often self-indulgent habits of living alone. I was fifty years old at the time of my marriage to Susan Mary and can honestly declare that I had not considered such a step until the death of my old school friend Bill Patten. In point of fact, I had been blessed throughout my life with a number of deep and sustaining friendships. Thus far, my work had been continuously hectic and rewarding to the point where the gaps in my life, such as they were, seemed relatively few. The most conspicuous gap—and, indeed, this must be true for many bachelors, no matter how active and successful—was the lack of an immediate family. Being a member of an extended and exceedingly close clan, I had begun to feel this absence all the more keenly as I approached middle age. So when the opportunity arose to slip into the role of companion and father to a family I had known intimately for so many years, I eagerly volunteered.

Susan Mary's and my plans for a secretive wedding were dashed when Walter Lippmann's wife Helen announced to Susan Mary that she had already bought a new hat for the occasion, a signal that any idea of a tiny, superquiet ceremony was wholly impractical. We were married in a church in Chevy Chase because the Maryland laws then allowed weddings on short notice, while the laws of Washington did not. Following the ceremonies, my new bride returned at once to Paris to wind up her considerable household there. And after following her there for a short wedding trip to Greece, I came home again to plan the expansion of the house on Dumbarton Avenue to accommodate a wife and two stepchildren.

I should be leaving a serious gap in this story if I did not write something about the enormous fun both Susan Mary and I had in Kennedy Washington and the excitement it gave both of us to have the only private house to which the president and Jackie came fairly regularly. We were asked again and again to small gatherings in the White House (I had to watch myself carefully at dinner because the Kennedy wines were so good and so plentiful), and we were regular guests at all the other most envied houses in town, particularly David and Sissy Harlech's at the British embassy and Hickory Hill, Robert Kennedy's home, which was always wonderfully good fun and eccentric while Bobby was still alive.

Susan Mary and I enjoyed our social success, although I was well aware that it came to us less for our hospitality than it did because I was thought to be close to the president and, therefore, possessed of a fugitive importance. In any case, the president and Jackie came to Dumbarton Avenue; and by presidential standards they came often. According to one of the researchers at the Kennedy Library, the president and his wife dined with us once every six weeks while he was in office; and in summer, when Jackie was usually away, the president came a few times by himself when he was bored at home.

Whenever he was expected for dinner, Susan Mary and I always got out the best we had, including bottles of the generous supply of 1945 Lafite Rothschild, which Aline Berlin, Isaiah's wife, had given us for a wedding present. I don't think the president had a good palate, for our Lafite was extremely tannic and quite obviously not ready to drink. But he always read the labels and knew that Lafite was a good label.

Because of the contrast with the aging and self-righteous Eisenhower administration, the first period of the Kennedy era was, as I have said, downright exhilarating—perhaps more exhilarating than it ought to have been. In part, this exhilaration derived from the comparative youth and energy of all the principal players. From the Roosevelt years onward, I had been accustomed to thinking of myself as one of the younger men in Washington—as, indeed, I had been. Now I was confronted with a new government in which everyone, beginning with the president, was substantially younger than I.

Then, too, so many of these young officials had an air of brilliant competence of a kind I had not seen in public service since the Roosevelt years. I don't think I had met Bob McNamara before he became secretary of defense, but I quickly learned that he had been on the staff of K. B. Wolfe, the first commander of the B-29s when they came into China. With prodding, I dimly remembered an interstaff meeting called to discuss the workings of the difficult system by which the planes of the Fourteenth Air Force were made to be self-supplying at their new, semibuilt bases. All of us on the Fourteenth Air Force staff believed this system, which relied heavily on the B-29s to transport supplies, to be an impossible dream until we heard the presentation delivered by an obviously competent-seeming young man. He proved to be Bob McNamara, and in the end he was uniquely responsible for making the self-supply system a working reality.

When I met McNamara again in Washington, I had no recollection of this first encounter half a world away. Bob struck me as an altogether American type—an intellectual from the ranks of the industrialists, a group that had not supplied any intellectuals to any of the preceding administrations. He had been an executive at the Ford Motor Company but chose to live in the university town of Ann Arbor instead of the executive mansions in the Detroit suburb of Grosse Pointe. With his earnestness and his puritanical side, he also struck me as a bit priggish, but I had no doubts about his remarkable powers of mind.

The new secretary of defense and I cannot be said to have made a good start together. I had no trouble getting an appointment to meet him at the Pentagon. Unfortunately, when he received me in his vast, imperial office across the Potomac, I found his public-relations people waiting for me en masse complete with notebooks and tape recorders. In those days, I had a private rule (it would be completely unenforceable today) not to talk to any high government official, if at all possible, with PR persons present. The presence of these witnesses, I reasoned, plainly implied that the person receiving me either did not trust me or did not trust himself. Under such circumstances any confidential discussion of real value would never be possible. So, on that morning of our first meeting, I explained my rule to McNamara as politely as I could and left his office.

In the end, it took the president's own intervention to bring us together—or so Kennedy hinted to me when he suggested I ask Bob to come to a quiet breakfast at Dumbarton Avenue. We made our connection at one of the innumerable social events that characterized that opening year of the Kennedy administration. Thus, toward the end of that winter, Bob duly came to breakfast at Dumbarton Avenue—with most embarrassing results.

In those days, I used to indulge my liking for having birds in the house. Besides a parrot that belonged to Jose and Maria, the chief ornament of the garden room was a beautiful but loud-spoken toucan. He was a messy creature, for toucans are soft feeders and have a way of spitting unwanted and undigested bits of their fruit diet on the floor around their cages, a practice at which this particular bird excelled. Bob arrived at the appointed hour, and, as the sun came in through the garden-room skylight, we sat down to breakfast in a most amiable fashion. The ice had been broken. We were beginning to become friends and on the verge of discussing what in Washington is called "substance," when the toucan, strategically positioned at the secretary's back, gave a deafening shriek and, with unerring aim, spat at least half of a well-chewed banana onto McNamara's bald spot.

I leapt to my feet, horrified by the indignity to which the new secretary of defense had been subjected at this, our first real meeting. With little help from me waving napkins about in a frenzy, Bob quickly tidied himself up with a damp towel provided by an ashen Jose. It was an easy mess to clean up but a deeply embarrassing one. Breakfast continued, but I had not ceased apologizing when Bob left the house in apparent good humor. Despite this incident, the secretary and I managed to solve any of the differences we had, and our professional relationship proceeded smoothly from that point onward. That afternoon, to end the story, I exchanged the toucan at the pet shop for two pairs of mourning doves, and their cooing would accompany my mornings until I sold my big house and retired thirteen years later.

Bob and I went on to become friends, and as I watched him in action during those first years of the Kennedy presidency, I came to admire him more and more. From the beginning, I supported the administration's move away from what I considered to be a dangerously one-dimensional reliance on the nuclear deterrent—as had been the case in the Eisenhower years—toward a tougher, more modernized conventional force able to adapt and respond in numbers to an overseas crisis, should the need arise. Unlike Eisenhower's strict budget balancers, Kennedy's men thought this country's economy would not be irreparably harmed by an increase in defense spending. In large part, the doctrine of "flexible response," as it was then being called, owed its initial fiscal success to McNamara, who, in a relatively short period of time, managed to double U.S. armed strength effectively, while increasing the cost of the defense establishment by hardly more than 20 percent. Indeed, before his downfall in Vietnam, I used to think of McNamara as the best defense minister the Western world had known since Louvois, who effectively invented the profession for Louis XIV and was largely responsible for the French army's domination of seventeenth-century Europe.

By the same token, the competence of Douglas Dillon at the treasury, the toughness that Bobby Kennedy soon began to show at the Justice Department, and the brilliance of McGeorge Bundy, serving as what amounted to the president's in-house secretary of state with authority like that of Harry Hopkins during Roosevelt's time, were all beyond contest. Furthermore, I found myself excited both in their company and, more importantly, by their presence in Washington. Indeed, I often thought, during those first months of the Kennedy administration, that in McNamara, Bundy, and all the others this country had at last found successors to the "Wise Men":

civil servants as able, as tough-minded, as national-minded, and as self-denying as those men had been—and as courageous, too.

Despite this glittering beginning to Kennedy's administration, it seemed to me that several clouds hung over the scene. For some months during the spring of 1961, I had known that an operation such as the Bay of Pigs invasion was being contemplated and would be attempted. I also knew that some in the administration were whittling down support in the U.S. armed services for the operation. I wrote nothing about any of this for the same reason I had written nothing in 1954 when the CIA removed Jacobo Arbenz Guzmán as president of Guatemala or even earlier, when Mohammed Mossadegh was removed as leader of Iran. This type of journalistic discretion—or complicity, if one prefers that word—was never fashionable and today would likely come under bitter attack. However, it was then—and it is still now—my conviction that if the leaders of the U.S. government decide that all the risks and perils of a major covert operation are required to further the interests of the United States, it is not the business of individual newspapermen to put professional gain over that of country.

My trouble with the Bay of Pigs was not so much the aim of the mission (I thought Fidel Castro was well worth getting rid of), but rather the incessant and impractical whittling, which, over a period of months, had greatly jeopardized the operation's chances for success. The government should never embark on a major operation if it is not united on the need for the operation and not ready to back up fully the persons engaged in it. I foresaw trouble in this regard, and I purposely used my marriage to Susan Mary as an excuse to join her in Paris over the first two weeks of April. The news of the bungled mission broke on April 17, while I was still in France.

It proved even more grim than I had expected. My colleagues in the newspaper business were indignantly—and, I think, rightly—vocal about the disaster. But since almost all of my official friends in Washington—from Kennedy to Dick Bissell (who was in charge at the CIA)—were deeply involved in the operation, this was a chorus I was glad I did not have to join.

As I look back, the Bay of Pigs disaster provides evidence for the argument, ignored by many historians, that President Kennedy was not historically prepared to deal with the enormous burdens of the presidency of the United States. Indeed, in those months following the inauguration, it did not seem to me that the president was fully aware of the enormous responsibility inherent in his new office. At that time, the Soviets still enjoyed an established advantage over the United States in the area of conventional forces. Although the first reconnaissance satellite revealed no missile gap, no satellite was needed to reveal the enormous Soviet program of construction of medium-range missiles just as deadly as the ICBMs and capable of blanketing targets in Europe. The evidence was clear that these missiles had been built "to hold Europe in pawn," the phrase Khrushchev himself used when, later that year, he led British ambassador Sir Frank Roberts to the rear of his opera box at the Bolshoi for a confidential chat.

The Soviet leader had already begun the year by declaring his support for so-called "wars of liberation," of which several were under way in 1961. At the Bolshoi, he would point out to the ambassador that he could destroy the British Isles with one nuclear strike. When serious national leaders talk in tones like these with more than enough means to back up their threat, it is sensible to take them seriously. What is more, Khrushchev had long been threatening to liberate Berlin from any Western presence, a threat that was very much alive in the early spring of 1961.

These first months of the Kennedy presidency, then, were, from an international standpoint, a grim and dangerous time, and I felt the grimness myself, perhaps to an excessive degree. Shortly after the election, I had been moved to write the president a short letter, which must have been one of the first in which an old friend addressed him as "Mr. President." In it, I ventured to tell him that I felt both overjoyed and a little saddened by his victory since I had "lost a friend but gained a President." To this, I added the true statement that "no President can ever hope to have any friend but history" and that I believed and prayed that history would prove his friend. Kennedy, as I learned later from Kenny O'Donnell, was downright offended by this declaration, although I think he could see that it came from the heart.

I do not think, however, that John Kennedy felt the full weight of his responsibility until his first personal confrontation with Nikita Khrushchev at the Vienna summit in June 1961. I traveled with Kennedy to Vienna, like most of the other newspapermen in Washington, but I did not try to see the president there because my column was still being written on Mondays for Wednesdays, Wednesdays for Fridays, and so on. I was sure that one of my competitors among the daily newspapermen would get the real story first and publish it before I could. Furthermore, I knew that I was to see Kennedy anyway in London, where he went immediately after Vienna to attend the christening of the child of his sister-in-law Lee and her husband Stash Radziwill. And it was that occasion that left upon my mind an unforgettable impression.

The summit itself was, from President Kennedy's perspective, an altogether desperate and unnerving event. Those of us on the outside had no idea of just how badly the talks between Khrushchev and the president had gone. On levels of substance, the two sides could come to no accommodation save for a tentative agreement to explore mutual solutions to the conflict then boiling in Laos. Any hope for an agreement banning the testing of nuclear weapons in the atmosphere seemed lost, and the Soviet leader once again had raised the ominous issue of Berlin, this time presenting Kennedy with a hard deadline for the withdrawal of Western troops from the city. On a personal level, too, this was the president's first taste of Khrushchev's erratic and bullying behavior, and it left him visibly shaken.

The christening, which took place at the Radziwill's sun-filled flat in London, might well have been taken bodily from one of the novels of Ouida, the late nineteenth-century writer of romances and high life. Susan Mary came from Paris for the event and brought along a dazzling bright-pink silk dress from Dior that caused much envy. We lunched very grandly with my friends Tony and Bindy Lambton, and from their house we went on to the Radziwill flat, which was by then so full of flowers that there was hardly room for the numerous English grandees gathered there. The entire Cavendish and Cecil clans were on hand, including Prime Minister Harold Macmillan and his wife Lady Dorothy, who had been a Cavendish. Randolph Churchill was on hand, too, with more than a little champagne under his belt.

The crowd was large, so I found myself a place near the door. I was standing there idly drinking champagne when the door opened and the young president burst in. He was a little late and looked strangely preoccupied. Since I was the first person who met his eye, he half-pinned me to the wall and declared, "I want you especially, Joe, to know that I am not going to give up and I am not going to give in no matter what dangers we may have to face." What he was referring to, I soon learned, was the naked military ultimatum that Khrushchev had handed him in Vienna. It was a chilling way to begin such a dazzling party.

If I had been shrewd enough to deduce the next phase from what the president said to me at that extraordinary festivity in London, I might have known—I might even have foretold—that he would go home to take the grim measures he took in response to Khrushchev's ultimatum. These measures were not nearly as grim as Dean Acheson, whom Kennedy had called in as an adviser during the crisis, would have wished, for Dean was in favor of a stiff military stand in Berlin. The young president refused to back down to Moscow, however, and by late July had proposed a modest increase in the defense budget ($3.2 billion), sent an additional 40,000 troops to Europe, and announced a partial mobilization of reserve and National Guard units at home. Khrushchev would soon respond with a similar statement, declaring Soviet intractability on the matter and calling up his own reservists. And there the matter stood until the night of August 13, when East German security forces began construction of the wall that would partition East from West with an apparent glum finality.

In retrospect, Khrushchev's behavior from the Vienna meeting forward was an obvious prelude to the building of the Berlin Wall. For over a year, the Soviet's East German satellite had been in danger because of the continuous hemorrhage of its ablest older men and most competent and ambitious young people to the West through Berlin. Khrushchev, in fact, had only three alternatives by the time of his Vienna meeting with Kennedy. He could frighten the new president into accepting Soviet control of West Berlin; he could accept the gradual death of the loathsome Walter Ulbricht's regime in East Germany; or he could stop the hemorrhage. The wall was simply a measure to accomplish the latter. I did not believe that the United States had a duty to risk a world war in order to guarantee freedom of movement to the population of East Germany. So I wrote a column that, I think, stood alone at the time, when virtuous indignation was the general note in American newspapers and on television. In it, I came as near as I dared, in view of the prevailing atmosphere, to welcoming the erection of the wall as horribly ugly, to be sure, but nonetheless necessary in order to drain off the worst inflammations of the Berlin crisis. Evidently, the president felt the same way, for I got a letter complimenting me on the column. I note this because I am proud of it and not because I believe that the wall actually did liquidate the Berlin crisis. That did not happen until Khrushchev took his gamble with the missiles in Cuba one full year later.

As it happened, I would get some glimpse of President Kennedy's mood during his last great test as well, for he dined with Susan Mary and myself on the eve of the Cuban missile crisis in October 1962. The Cuban crisis would bring to a climax a foolishly violent controversy that, at the time, had been raging for some months within the Kennedy administration. Republican senator Kenneth Keating of New York—whether as a result of a masterly guess or special information I have never known—had publicly charged the Soviets with placing nuclear missiles in Cuba. CIA analysts convinced themselves that this was not true. They did so, moreover, with inappropriate violence, threatening to organize some sort of movement against Kennedy's new CIA chief John McCone, who had refused to sign off on the analysts' estimate. Both McGeorge Bundy and Secretary of Defense McNamara treated the Keating claim as partisan nonsense. McCone, however, went privately to the president and persuaded him that he was running a fearful risk by not trying to find out for sure. Consequently, the president ordered U-2 flights over Cuba despite the reluctance of McNamara and Bundy.

Meanwhile, Kennedy had just named Chip Bohlen as his ambassador-designate to France. It was then among the touchiest of our high-profile diplomatic posts, thanks to Charles de Gaulle, who was at the height of an anti-American period and on the verge of withdrawing his country's forces from NATO. I had planned a farewell dinner for Chip and Avis the night before they were due to leave for Paris and suggested to the president that if he came to the small dinner it would likely strengthen the new ambassador's hand there. He was delighted by the suggestion, and the French ambassador of those days, Hervé Alphand, was, therefore, invited, along with his wife Nicole and one or two other couples.

Everyone arrived on time, and everyone looked festive, as did the house, for Mrs. Paul Mellon had just sent Susan Mary one of her extraordinary boxes of flowers, and its contents had been scattered artfully about the rooms. From the beginning, however, the festivity was all on the surface. The president hardly said a word of greeting before he led Chip down to the end of the garden and began a long argument with him. Their exchange was watched with intense attention by Hervé Alphand, who could see them gesticulating at one another but could not guess what they were saying. Finally, the two men came back from the garden, still plainly not in agreement.

Dinner was announced. When we got to table, it became clear that the president was in the first deep brown study I had ever seen. Susan Mary, who always got on with him like a house on fire once she discovered that the only feminine conversation he really enjoyed was straight-out gossip, did her best to lighten the president's mood.

However, through four courses—the Washington rule in those days—President Kennedy hardly spoke a word. The men and women separated after dinner, and I hopefully led the men into the garden room for conversation and drink. Our talk ran on history and its unforeseen chances. It was the sort of subject the president liked. All the same, the president continued in his brown study. Indeed, we had come perilously close to the kind of forced conversation that my brother Stewart used to call "beebly-babbly," when Kennedy looked up and said quietly, "Of course, if you think simply about the chances in history, you have to quote the odds as somewhere near even that we shall see an H-bomb war within the next ten years."

This observation caused Hervé Alphand to turn the color of an uncooked biscuit. In my mind's eye, I could see him preparing his cable for Paris the next morning and only dared to hope that the fact that the dinner was in honor of Chip would not be forgotten. Once the president had thus spoken, moreover, I did not see much profit in continued "men's talk" in the garden room. So I arose, and we glumly joined the ladies, whereupon the president again took Chip into the lamplit garden, and again we could see them arguing vigorously with one another. Finally, the two men came in, and the president, apologizing that he had a hard and early day tomorrow, took his leave, although not before having one last argument with Chip on the front steps. Both Susan Mary and I were bursting with curiosity to know the subject of the argument. But when Avis asked Chip, he brushed her aside. We pursued it no further, and the party broke up.

The next day, however, I learned the facts—both of the president's vile mood and of the mysterious arguments between him and Chip. Earlier in the week, one of the U-2 flights had brought back photographs that left no doubt that the Soviets were placing nuclear missiles in Cuba. The president's remark on the odds in favor of H-bomb war thus fell into place as part of his own internal dialogue, touched off by the ill-omened photographs. In his arguments with Chip, he had been trying to induce his ambassador to stay on in Washington as a member of the Executive Committee, or Ex Comm, as they called the advisory committee gathered by the president to sit during the crisis.

Chip had refused the offer to stay on, arguing in his splendidly self-denying way that for the administration's principal Soviet expert to break from his scheduled arrival at a crucial diplomatic post such as Paris would likely signal to the Soviets that they had been found out. The president wanted Chip so badly that Chip was prepared to request Avis to take to her bed with a serious though unexplained malady in order to provide a cover for his remaining in Washington. But Chip quite rightly decided that the cover would soon be blown by the suspicious Soviets. And so we said farewell to Chip and Avis, bound for the most difficult diplomatic job they ever had.

Save for my knowledge of the existence and cause of the missile crisis, I had no notion at all of what went on from day to day within Ex Comm. All I can remember of it now is the almost intoxicated excitement that everyone felt when the crisis was successfully liquidated.

These social glimpses were the closest I came to the internal world of White House politics, although the president allowed me to argue with him on a number of occasions after he took office. My arguments usually were quite fruitless. I believed, for example, that no good purpose was being served by the way he and McGeorge Bundy regularly harassed and even teased the virtuous Adlai Stevenson. The president disliked Stevenson nearly to the point of contempt. Whatever Adlai's faults, however, he was the president's representative at the United Nations and might be needed at times of crisis—as, indeed, he was during the row over the Congo, when he performed splendidly. The president had beaten Adlai in a fair fight for the presidential nomination in 1960, and it did not seem to me good style or, above all, useful to take delight in making him miserable.

"Liberals" more generally did not have much influence on the president—at least in foreign-policy matters. On this topic, it is wise to read with cynical care my friend Arthur Schlesinger, Jr.'s elegant and generally thorough account of the Kennedy administration, *A Thousand Days*. Throughout his book, a body Arthur refers to as "the liberals" keeps cropping up with good advice on foreign policy. Care in reading is desirable because the fact is that the advice offered by these liberals was almost never taken. Professor John Kenneth Galbraith in India was one of the major advice givers, capable of producing at least one long letter of adjuration every week. I am prepared to bet any amount of money that the president replied to these letters in ways that caused Professor Galbraith to flush with pleasure, for he is a man with an easy response to flattery. However, I also remember the president reading some of them aloud with comic emphasis at small dinners at the White House as samples of the sort of thing presidents had to put up with.

John Kennedy was a man adept at flattery, and I suppose I, as a member of the press, was at times as much a target of his considerable and manipulative charm as Professor Galbraith. Bobby Kennedy was my more frequent confidant, however, although rarely did he—or others in the administration, for that matter—seek my advice on issues of shattering importance.

The most memorable of my meetings with Bobby took place over a meager lunch at the Justice Department, and the subject, oddly enough, was President Eisenhower's ex-chief of staff Governor Sherman Adams, who by that time was prospering as the head of a ski resort in New Hampshire. President Eisenhower had asked for Adams's resignation in September 1958 because, as he beautifully it, he could stand for no one in the White House who was not as clean "as a hound's tooth." At the time, Governor Adams was universally considered only mildly unclean because he had accepted small presents, like a vicuña coat and a Persian rug, from New England industrialist Bernard Goldfine.

Goldfine was a most curious man who, as I came to know after Bobby asked my advice on the matter, had the rather lunatic hobby of buying New England politicians. Senator Styles Bridges of New Hampshire, for example, was unquestionably the recipient of a number of financial favors from Goldfine, and, according to Bobby, one or two other key New England Republicans had also benefited from the financier's generosity.

When Goldfine's taxes were questioned in the summer of 1958, causing him to bring Governor Adams into the picture with nationally scandalous results, there had been, however, only one voice to speak up with the astonishing information that the president's chief of staff, far from being content with trifles like vicuña coats, had in fact been receiving $15,000 a month in cash. This testimony came from Goldfine's deeply devoted secretary, Miss Mildred Paperman.

I had no concern about the public relations of the Eisenhower White House by the time the Adams case began to break, and I had not challenged the decision made at the time that this totally unsupported testimony was not likely to stand up in court and would, therefore, be filed and forgotten. It was not quite forgotten, however. Adams, it seemed, was an exceedingly mean man and had a knack of making people with whom he did business dislike him—including his landlady from whom he rented a house on Capitol Hill. Not long after the Kennedy inauguration, the landlady had apparently written to Bobby to say that she had extremely confidential information that she could impart only to the attorney general himself.

Bobby was sufficiently curious to put fifteen minutes for the landlady on his own schedule, and at the appointed hour the landlady arrived bearing a list of the numbers, the dates, and the issuing banks of the certified checks with which Adams had always paid his rent. She said she had never been paid in this manner before and had kept a careful list of the check numbers and their place of issue because she smelled a rat, something she had obviously been only too ready to do. Bobby was naturally a little puzzled, too, and turned the matter over to the FBI. The FBI, in turn, sent out its own agents to the banks around the country to ask the responsible tellers whether they could identify Governor Adams as having purchased certified checks from their institutions during his time at the White House.

The pattern that then emerged was extraordinary. It appeared, according to Bobby, that whenever Adams accompanied President Eisenhower out of town or could otherwise get away from Washington, he would visit a long list of banks and at each one purchase certified checks either in sums needed to pay large bills like that for his rent or else in sums of $500 or less. The total amount of certified checks that the FBI found the governor to have purchased ran to near $400,000, perilously close to the total of $15,000 a month in cash Miss Paperman claimed the governor had received while in the White House.

With this evidence in hand, Bobby wrote the governor, requesting an explanation and pointing out that this information raised questions that might have to be put before the IRS. Bobby then showed me the governor's reply. The letter was long, self-righteous, and repetitive. The thrust of it was that Governor Adams, during his time at the White House, had the strange experience, while in railway stations and airports, of having people rush up to him and thrust into his pockets huge rolls of bills with the cry, "This is to help you clean up the mess in Washington." The same words, had come up in Miss Paperman's story: she claimed Adams had asked Goldfine for the $15,000 in cash each month on the grounds that he needed it to "clean up the mess in Washington."

The story seemed to fit together all too well, and as I ate the kind of dank luncheon that the Justice Department specialized in, I thought about it. Bobby finally asked me what he ought to do. I suggested he should forget about it on the grounds that nothing was to be gained either politically or morally by dragging out of obscurity from New Hampshire an already broken old man and putting all this cruel evidence on the record. Bobby said he would take my counsel under advisement, and we parted after lunch. The drama did not end there, however, for Jackie and her sister Lee Radziwill have since described to me the dinner that evening at the White House when the next episode occurred.

The two women were having supper alone with the president when Bobby came in with the same evidence that he had shown me. Jackie and Lee, as they both told me later on, vociferously seconded my advice of that afternoon because they thought persecuting the old and broken was never a good idea. I think, however, the president knew that the law did not allow evidence to be swept under the bed. Perhaps for this reason or perhaps because he simply wanted President Eisenhower on his side in case of future need, he sent an emissary to Gettysburg to lay the evidence before the retired president. The emissary recited a beautiful little speech, saying that President Kennedy held President Eisenhower in the highest possible regard and that Kennedy was reluctant to prosecute Governor Adams if only for that reason. President Kennedy did not feel, however, free to make the decision to prosecute or not to prosecute without consulting President Eisenhower because, after all, the former president was the man who had been betrayed.

The old general apparently asked for a few minutes to think this over, in which, one may assume, he considered his image with great care. In time, he sent back his message giving warm thanks for President Kennedy's thoughtfulness, adding that he was against prosecution.

Ever after, President Eisenhower was like one of those old fire horses who try to visit every fire long after their retirement. His fire visiting, less often in person than in the form of public statement, occurred only when great issues of foreign and defense policy were before the country and always took the same form—that the country ought to support its president.

So Miss Paperman was never publicly justified, and the charge against Governor Adams was never brought. The governor died peacefully in October 1986. Only after it became fashionable in the newspaper business to become so exact about public morality did I begin to think that the only president except Roosevelt whose death made me weep—and, indeed, the only president who I counted as a close personal friend—had, in fact, been guilty of suppressing evidence, which is not a light offense. Furthermore, as I still think about such matters in terms of hard, practical politics, I believe to this day that President Kennedy and his brother handled the matter just as it should have been handled.

24

Last Days

I cannot recall a single broad area of policy on which I really disagreed with President Kennedy while he was in the White House. The Kennedy administration was perhaps slow to tackle the great civil-rights issue head-on. The movement in some degree forced his hand, but when he and Bobby did finally address the questions eloquently posed by Dr. Martin Luther King and his supporters, they performed with prudent determination and style. Indeed, I have long thought that if we had had a different and less courageous president in office, the civil-rights issue would have been handled with less effect. As it was, real progress was made during the Kennedy years, which would be crowned by Lyndon Johnson's great Voting Rights Act, the single political reform in my lifetime from which, as far as I know, every result has been good.

I have always been convinced that on the domestic front the Kennedy presidency made a great difference. The power, population, and wealth of the United States had grown apace through the years after the Second World War. But this growth had been uneven. It had failed to benefit one-tenth of our people. It had created many new problems, such as the sprawl of the suburbs and the decay of our great cities at their centers. For all these reasons, a shocking backlog of unfinished business—of business not even begun, in many cases—awaited Kennedy when he entered the White House.

All this unfinished business was tackled in a pragmatic, hopeful style. For the first time in the postwar period, the problems of poverty, of racial discrimination, of the new and hideous effects of industrial civilization on the environment began to be identified and discussed in a wholly new way. Through the 1950s, the remaining members of the old New Deal were still repeating the same slogans they had used since 1948, when they ceased their mystic postwar chant of "Revive the OPA!" (the Office of Price Administration, which was founded in 1942 to regulate prices during wartime and was disbanded by President Truman under pressure from the Republican Congress). Under President Kennedy, the old liberal ideals began again to acquire some practical content. The momentum of the so-called "Great Society" programs would be carried through by Lyndon Johnson. It was Kennedy, however, who first framed the issues and, through his own particular vision of this country's greatness, conveyed their importance to the rest of us.

President Kennedy's management of foreign policy was novel in several respects, but above all because he saw nothing contradictory in rearming while preparing for negotiations. Indeed, I would guess that he regarded energetic rearmament as the best possible preparation for negotiation. In the immediate aftermath of the Cuban missile crisis, the Soviets were eager to negotiate, and President Kennedy seized the opportunity with enthusiasm. The signing of the Limited Test Ban Treaty, which halted the detonation of nuclear weapons in the atmosphere, underwater, and in space, followed shortly thereafter. This is the one major arms agreement with the Soviet Union that, as far as I know, has never been breached, has provoked a minimum of public twaddle, and has produced precisely the result it was designed to produce.

However, the final great foreign-policy crisis of the Kennedy administration was never fully realized or resolved. It was, of course, the widening conflict in Vietnam. Nothing so engrossed me during the Kennedy years—and after—as this. If my successive visits to Vietnam during the French regime, during the Eisenhower and Kennedy administrations, and finally when the United States was openly at war under President Johnson were added up, the time I spent working in Vietnam would absorb nearly two-and-a-half years of my life.

When John Kennedy took office, the prospect of the United States fighting a full-scale war in a land as distant and divided as

Vietnam was by no means unthinkable. Indeed, a good portion of the president's first months in office were devoted to solving a tangential crisis in Laos. This obscure little landlocked country had been in a precarious way since General Giap's first Viet Minh incursions there during the battle of Dien Bien Phu in 1954. Thanks in no small part to the aggressive patronage of Moscow, the confused and divided royalist forces in Vientiane were now subject to outright harassment from their ambitious neighbor as well as the increasingly effective Communist-supported guerrilla group, the Pathet Lao. Before his departure from office, President Eisenhower had recommended full-scale intervention in Laos in the event of an imminent takeover by the Communist forces there. In the end, President Kennedy rejected this option and chose instead to bolster the "counter insurgency" capabilities of U.S. forces, while allowing Averell Harriman to pursue some form of neutral settlement to the problem.

Harriman was much applauded for establishing a supposedly neutralist government headed by Prince Souvanna Phouma—with some cooperation from his Communist brother Prince Souphanouvong—and for making the whole look prettier by extracting a Soviet promise to stay out of Laos. However, the real problem in Laos was the construction of the Ho Chi Minh Trail as a supply line for Communist insurgents in South Vietnam. It was not mentioned at the Geneva meetings in June 1961. In any case, the Geneva Accords had no deterrent effect whatever on the extension, improvement, and constant use of the route by the government in Hanoi.

Hanoi, as early as 1959, had begun working to open a supply path into the south via the eastern border region of Laos. I had been a witness, in part, to these first efforts, for I had traveled to Laos in the late summer of 1959 to report on the situation from Vientiane. The capital itself was a dusty, provincial place with little to recommend it save for one or two startlingly good French restaurants left over from the colonial years. Through the U.S. military attaché in Vientiane, I had arranged, with the few other members of the foreign press corps who were present in the country, to accompany the brigadier general in charge of the Laotian army—a less-than-impressive man named Ouane Rathikoune—on a tour of some army positions upcountry, along the border in the northern province of Sam Neua.

I shall never forget the landing at the tiny provincial airfield. Laos is a mountainous, jungle-covered country, and the strip where we were to land lay in a short, narrow valley wholly surrounded by steep mountains and craggy hills. Approaching by air, we saw bright emerald rice paddies on the valley floor below mountain slopes shrouded in great forest trees and plumes of giant bamboo. It was a dazzling picture that, upon further inspection, appeared literally to merge with the runway itself. The little field was bracketed at both ends by grassy peaks, causing the landing strip to begin with a gentle hill, go upward over a considerable hump, and then trickle downward into a hollow, a landing that seemed to the uninstructed passenger to consist of flying straight into a hill.

What struck me as equally unusual was the simple fact that, once safely on solid ground, our party found no one at the landing strip to meet us. Neither the brigadier general nor the U.S. military attaché who had accompanied our little group showed any concern; and so the rest of us did our best to do the same. Since no transport of any kind was visible, we set off on foot toward the town, which supposedly contained the headquarters of the provincial commander. This proved to be a miserable promenade, for we had to cover two-and-a-half miles under blazing sun, along a road with a surface of shifting sand about two feet deep. We did not see another human being or, indeed, so much as a vagrant water buffalo along the road. What is more, when we reached the town, such as it was, we found it almost entirely evacuated.

In time, our awkward little group located the command headquarters. The provincial commander, who was also a general, motioned the rest of our apprehensive little group to take seats, while he led General Ouane to the opposite side of the long, almost cathedral-like anteroom of his headquarters. The two generals thereupon plunged into a most obviously absorbing and significant conversation, accompanied by many a grand gesture. As this conversation developed across the room, the military attaché became more and more agitated, and the newspapermen became obviously uneasy. At intervals, the attaché would rush to the door to check on the town's dwindling population, and, finding fewer and fewer people in the street with each visit, he finally asked me (I was the only member of our party who spoke French) to ask the two Laotian generals what the situation was outside.

The local commander, a dark man at least six feet tall, answered my question reflectively and in what I can only describe as ponderous tones. "Ah, monsieur," he said, "hier soir, tous nos postes ont été attaqués, et tous sont perdus" ("Yesterday evening, all of our posts were attacked, and all have fallen.") This statement struck me as more than a might chilling as I translated it for our military man. Before we had time to consider the full meaning of this news, General Ouane led us into a standard military briefing room, where he listed the four doomed posts and described the timing of the attacks. The emerging pattern made it abundantly obvious that the attackers, who were either North Vietnamese or, in all cases, North Vietnamese–inspired, aimed to control the frontier and, probably in short order, the town where we were then sitting.

General Ouane ended our briefing with a quick patter of orders to his provincial commander, and our grim little group started the sandy march back to the airstrip, where we hoped to find our plane waiting for us. In this, we were disappointed, and we spent a rather unsettling half hour loitering about the strip before the little aircraft hove into view from Vientiane. It was plain that the pilot had had no great wish to return to our abandoned airstrip. He probably knew what was dawning on us—that "native guerrillas" had little to do with this particular offensive. Indeed, Hanoi, at that point, had torn up the Geneva Accords and was briskly invading northern Laos— something it had attempted a fortnight before. That time "nos postes" had not fallen, so the North Vietnamese commander had simply ordered reinforcements and come again.

One year after this operation, Ho Chi Minh and his followers had taken the decisive step of publicly supporting the "liberation" of all of South Vietnam. It is worth noting that a primary motive for expanding the conflict was the respect and even, to some degree, the fear the Communist leaders in Hanoi felt for Ngo Dinh Diem, the South Vietnamese president. Although the North Vietnamese had left secret caches of arms and a small network of supporters in the south following the partitioning of the country in 1954, they had ceased any major activity below the dividing line between north and south. When full authority was in his hands, however, President Diem began to make significant progress in the south against the local insurgents, who by that time were called the Viet Cong. His means were brutal, and admittedly he had considerable American assistance. By 1959, the Hanoi leaders feared that the progress Diem was making might be irreversible unless measures were taken to support and expand the Communist effort in the south.

Not long thereafter, Diem's government began to feel the increased pressure from the north. Beginning in 1960, as the so-called "autumn cadres" began to move south (during that year, army intelligence estimated that there were some 10,000 Communist insurgents in the south, a five-fold increase in three years), the Viet Cong made considerable gains against the South Vietnamese army in the countryside. Furthermore, Diem, a practicing Catholic, found it increasingly difficult to manage and placate the innumerable factions and sects (principal among these were the Buddhists) competing for some say in his country's rule. One of President Diem's forgotten peculiarities was an obstinate resistance to increases in the early American military presence in Vietnam. However, as the situation in Saigon grew more and more urgent, American offers of direct armed assistance took on a commanding tone, and Diem's reluctance to accept outside support soon melted away.

I came to know President Diem fairly well during this period and I did not find him a brilliant man. He was, rather, a man of deep religious faith and great solidity of character who had made his whole career as a passionate Vietnamese nationalist. Like Chiang Kai-shek, who operated also in a precarious, faction-ridden environment, he was an isolated man. His weakness was that he was stubborn and lonely and, therefore, unduly subject to the influence of his much less well-balanced brother Ngo Dinh Nhu. Nhu, who held the title of counselor to the president, operated the government's myriad—often corrupt—security agencies from his office in the basement of the old royal palace in Saigon. He was slim, with the kind of gutta-percha–colored skin that, in the Far East of those days, indicated heavy opium use. Despite profound intellectual limitations, Nhu considered himself to be a thinker; and all too often, as I will later explain, his schemes ended by further complicating his brother's already tenuous political position.

President Kennedy, meanwhile, offered President Diem all the support his government could gather. The American president, of course, considered the stupidly named "brushfire" conflicts in the Third World to be of vital importance in maintaining a balance of power with the Soviets. A main feature of McNamara's new "flexible response" defense program would be the development of a force able to counter threats of insurgency in Third World countries like Vietnam. Then, too, as the cease-fire in Laos quickly deteriorated after the 1961 agreement (as I had thought it would), President Kennedy became sufficiently disenchanted with Hanoi and, by inference, with the Soviets, who had come to regard North Vietnam as one of their principal clients, to make a fixed decision to stand in support of Diem in South Vietnam.

Thus developed the underlying story of the Vietnam War during the Kennedy years: the progressive Americanization of South Vietnam. By the early summer of 1962, the U.S. government had already sent some 5,500 American combat advisers and supporting staff to South Vietnam along with countless helicopters and other supplies. By this time, President Kennedy regarded any suggestion of surrendering South Vietnam to the Communists as impermissible, and so did all his closest advisers, from McGeorge Bundy and

Dean Rusk downward. The same view was then held by even the most critical American reporters in Saigon. Consequently, the U.S. Army and its representatives almost always carried conviction when they said that if we go just this little bit further toward full involvement, we can solve the problem.

By 1963, however, President Diem was being maliciously and constantly traduced by the American newspapermen in Saigon. In my view, there is no more foolish fault, either in the newspaper business or in ordinary life, than to grow obsessed by the pimples of your friends simply because you see them every morning for breakfast, while forgetting the hideous ulcers of your enemies skulking out of view in the shrubbery. This, it seems to me, is a peculiarly American weakness. In China, Chiang Kai-shek may not have been the ideal moral man, but he most certainly was not the egomaniacal madman that Mao Tse-tung turned out to be. In Vietnam, Ngo Dinh Diem certainly did not cut an altogether heroic figure. Like Chiang, he was a man of many weaknesses—above all, the weakness of intense suspicion. However, as I have said, Diem was an honest and true nationalist, and as such he held a unique position among likely leaders in the South.

Furthermore, as the situation in South Vietnam continued to deteriorate, the support of the United States became President Diem's key asset. Every time another rash of viciously derogatory stories appeared in the American press, the reality of this asset was called into question by every soul in Saigon. Doubt could be heard from the Palais Gialong, where Diem had his office, to the ambitious generals of the army (several of whom were openly promoted by anti-Diem newspapermen) down to the barbers in their barber shops and the vendors along rue Catinat. In this fragile and fairly incendiary environment, the aimlessly crusading American press had the effect of an uncontrolled elephant in a French drawing room. In time, these reports would take their toll on Diem, for toward the end of his time in power, the harassed president had so isolated himself from the business of politics and, indeed, from the routines of everyday living, that his ability to govern the country was severely limited.

I could see that Diem and his half-mad brother Nhu were in serious political trouble when I revisited South Vietnam in September of 1963. Saigon was in a state of turmoil; demonstrations by the Buddhists, in which a number of monks had immolated themselves on the streets of the city, were still fresh in everyone's mind. In the provinces, where the fighting had dramatically increased in scale and intensity over the past year, some American advisers had begun to complain openly of the ineffectiveness of the South Vietnamese forces in battle. On this occasion, however, my perception of the trouble ahead came from two astonishing visits to the Palais Gialong in Saigon—the first of these with Nhu and the second with the president over lunch the next day.

My interview with the counselor, as Nhu was officially known in those days, was easily the most bizarre I have conducted in my entire career as a newspaperman. We met in the afternoon at Nhu's basement office, which was a very long, narrow room with a large desk at one end. The desk was surrounded by a complete and nearly purposeful clutter that, in turn, ranged down the long walls on shelves full of books, files, and other ornaments from Nhu's odd career. Nhu greeted me cordially enough and motioned me toward a chair near his desk. Pacing before me and lighting one cigarette after another, he began an angry attack directed not only against the American newspapermen in Saigon and the American government as a whole, but against his own brother, who, at that very moment, was sitting upstairs in the office of the president.

I was not surprised by Nhu's accusations against the newsmen, for I had heard them before. The counselor had somehow gotten the idea into his head that the United States Information Service (USIS) was controlling the hostile U.S. newspapermen in Saigon. I protested, not for the first time, that this notion was utterly untrue. From there, however, to my great astonishment, Nhu went on to discuss his own situation in Vietnam in terms that came close to suggesting paranoia. He proclaimed himself to be the world's greatest expert on combating guerrilla warfare. Even despite this obvious expertise, he complained, he still had the utmost difficulty in realizing his programs within his own government and in getting a hearing for his insights. This, Nhu claimed, was due to American obstruction and, I was shocked to hear, since the man was both his direct superior and his closest relative, the stupidity of his own brother the president.

Still pacing back and forth, Nhu proceeded to develop these two themes at some length until, after a good deal of bluster, he made the startling announcement that he was in the process of conducting negotiations with Hanoi. These negotiations—which, he assured me, would effectively end the Vietnam conflict—were proceeding, thanks to the French, who had made constant overtures to Nhu through their ambassador in Saigon, Roger Lalouette. Nhu went on to tell me that he hoped to reach an acceptable settlement with Hanoi before long, although he was greatly embarrassed to have to do so behind the backs of the Americans, who had, after all, given his country such generous help.

At this juncture, I asked Nhu what he would do if President Diem would not agree to a settlement with Hanoi. Nhu then launched into another spirited discussion of Diem's slowness and stupidity, and ended with the confident assertion that he, Nhu, could bring his brother around to his way of thinking in the end. I then asked Nhu what he would do if Hanoi, as had happened so often before, proved unfaithful to its promises and turned upon him after an agreement had supposedly been made. The counselor thereupon reverted, in tones that can only be described as half-crazed, to the earlier theme of his role as the leading expert on guerrilla warfare. He concluded that it would not really matter whether Hanoi sought to betray him because he would, if threatened, go into the countryside himself and, simply by giving the signal, raise 1 million men to fight for his cause.

Our conversation continued in this vein for a good two hours until I stood and, quite literally, begged permission to leave. At the door of his office, Nhu, whose vanity clearly had led him to this unbalanced extreme, gave me repeated injunctions to say nothing to anyone about what he had told me. I would later learn that the contact between Lalouette and Nhu had, indeed, taken place and that the counselor had expressed interest in a bargain of some kind with Hanoi. Just what kind of bargain this might have been remains unclear, although my guess is that if Nhu had been at all serious about reaching an agreement with the north, I would have been the last to know about it. In any case, I ended up publishing the story, but not until I had left South Vietnam and was safely in Hong Kong. Most likely, Nhu wished to let the Americans know that he was thinking of playing this altogether desperate card in the hope that Washington would not hesitate to offer more help to the Diem regime.

I had been asked to lunch the next day with President Diem and accordingly reported to the palace for my second official meeting there in as many days. Although the president seemed as sturdy and as courageous as always, I found him much harder to talk to than in the past. The theme of the plots against him by the USIS and its supposedly dependent newspapermen began to be heard at the beginning of lunch, and any attempt to explain to the president that this odd theory had no basis whatever in fact was completely useless. Worse still, on most subjects (I did not mention Nhu's negotiations with Hanoi), Diem's view turned out to be Nhu's view. Indeed, any suggestions of mine that Nhu's views were incorrect might as well have been whispered to a stone-deaf man. As I wrote in my column and later told President Kennedy, talking to Diem had become like talking to a perfectly sane person with plenty of guts and character, who despite all his virtues, saw with the borrowed eyes and listened with the borrowed ears of a madman.

As it turned out, this part of the Vietnam story would end with the assassinations of both Nhu and President Diem on November 1, 1963. I was horrified by news of this event, for even if the two men had ceased to become effective as leaders, their political murder was an unjustifiable criminal act. In the shooting and its aftermath, I came to revise my assessment of Diem and, indeed, felt some measure of guilt for having turned against him. At that time, I was one of the few members of the press in the United States who still retained a measure of sympathy for President Diem. I believe that President Kennedy also respected my views on the subject of Vietnam since he asked me, upon my return to Washington late in September, to come and talk with him at the White House about what I had seen in Indochina. My conclusion—that Diem had lost his ability to govern—may, therefore, have had some effect on the president's thinking and on the thinking of other officials within the Kennedy government, although I cannot be sure of this.

If the historical accounts of the incident are at all dependable, the background of the coup that finally deposed President Diem and his brother most sordidly discredits certain members of the Kennedy foreign-policy apparatus. The first concrete suggestions by U.S. officials that Diem and his government be abandoned seem to have been made in late August, well before my own meetings with Nhu and Diem in Saigon. Evidently concluding that maximum pressure should be placed on the South Vietnamese leaders to reform their ways, Roger Hilsman, who was head of the East Asia Bureau at the State Department, drafted a cable instructing Henry Cabot Lodge, Jr., then our ambassador to South Vietnam, to inform Diem that he must remove his brother from government or risk the loss of American support. Cabot, who, I knew, had lost faith in the Diem regime long ago, was also instructed to inform the anti-Diem elements within the South Vietnamese army, with whom he was in close touch, of this threat on the part of the U.S. government. Since both Cabot and Hilsman undoubtedly knew that President Diem would never, at that late stage, be persuaded to jettison his brother from power, this communication had the dual effect of increasing Diem's own isolation and paranoia, while signaling to Diem's opponents that they were legitimate in the eyes of Washington and could, therefore, expect tacit support.

Apparently, Hilsman's infamous cable was hastily drafted and sent to Saigon over the weekend of August 24 with the inexplicably confused result that some members of the Kennedy circle saw and passed on its contents while others did not. Whether the president, who was then spending the weekend at Hyannis, read the State Department cable or understood the implications of it is still a matter of debate among historians. I was not there and cannot judge. It is fairly certain, however, that Washington's instructions to Cabot Lodge almost certainly sealed the political fate of President Diem and his brother, although I do not believe that either Cabot or any of the officials responsible for the bungled cable from Washington wished to see the South Vietnamese leaders killed. As far as I could judge from his public reaction, President Kennedy was shaken to his very marrow by the assassinations in Saigon; and unless he was a marvelous actor, fit to play any role on any stage, he was free of any conscious share in the deaths of Diem and Nhu.

Even more important than the parceling of blame, however, was the fact that the alternatives to Diem favored by his official enemies Cabot Lodge, Averell Harriman, and Roger Hilsman as well as by most of the American press turned out to be flat busts in a matter of months. The assassination of Diem left South Vietnam without any sort of government for a considerable period and can now be judged as a grim and perhaps decisive turning point for the worse in the Vietnam War. The structure of authority that Diem established in the countryside collapsed at once, leaving a vacuum that was quickly exploited by the Communists. It would be a long and toilsome business to break this new authority.

Within a few short weeks, however, any memory of the murders of Ngo Dinh Diem and his brother Nhu—indeed, any debate over the responsibility for the event and its larger implications for the conflict in Indochina—was all but forgotten in Washington, obscured by a far greater tragedy. I was in the garden room on Dumbarton Avenue when Susan Mary came in to give me news of the shooting in Dallas. The early reports of the president's assassination were not decisive, and I do not think I was wholly convinced by what Susan Mary told me. It was not until I had made several agitated telephone calls to the White House and to other reporters around Washington that the terrible certainty of the event set in.

Of the grim days that followed, I can only say that it was a shattering sensation to discover quite abruptly that one had lived the best years of one's life between the ages forty-eight and fifty-three. I had never known I loved the president (for one does not think of this kind of relationship in those terms) until I felt the impact of his death. The fact is that Jack Kennedy had an extraordinary knack for capturing people and changing them. To me, this was his most inexplicable quality. With the sole exception of Harry Hopkins,

President Roosevelt did not command love from those who were close to him: he was loved by the millions he helped and sought to serve, but not by Ben Cohen or Jim Forrestal or any of the others who lived and worked around him. President Kennedy, in contrast, was genuinely loved by an astonishing number of the people who served him—not just the very able men like Ted Sorensen and Kenny O'Donnell, who gave their whole lives to him, but many others like Bob McNamara and McGeorge Bundy, and still others further out on the fringe like myself.

Of the funeral services, held on a bitterly cold Monday afternoon, I can add little. Alice Longworth, who, although well into her eighties by then, had experienced something of a social renaissance during the Kennedy time, accompanied Susan Mary and me to St. Matthew's Cathedral, where the eulogies were given. Mrs. L had an acidly unsentimental side, and she seemed to take the young president's death in a more resigned way than the rest of us. The eulogies presented in President Kennedy's memory were uniformly heartfelt and elegant, although I do not think I paid them much attention. I was nearly in shock. After the services, Susan Mary and I left Mrs. L, and together we trudged up the hard, bare hill in Arlington Cemetery to witness the final interment of the coffin. In my column of that day, I paid tribute to John Kennedy as a man "perfectly formed to lead the United States of America," who, taking over the country in a time of violent change, had succeeded profoundly, only to be "cut off before his task could be half done." No doubt this was true, and it has been repeated countless times since in words far more articulate than my own. Standing by the president's grave, however, my thoughts were not of country or of patriotism, but rather of simple, personal friendship.

For a time after Jack Kennedy's death, the sense of emotional loss was so staggering among those who had known and worked with him that the Washington landscape seemed to me to be littered with male widows. McNamara's deputy secretary Roswell L. Gilpatric, a man with a long experience in the world and not given to easy emotion, told me days after the event, "You know, Joe, when the President died, I suddenly realized that I felt about him as I've never felt about another man in my life." Mac Bundy admitted to me that President Kennedy's death struck him more deeply than the loss of his own father, who had passed away just months before. I felt much the same way. Why I should so irrationally mind the president's loss, and mind it much more than the loss of my own father, I cannot say. But, clearly, after that bright, blustery November day, nothing would be quite the same in my life again or, it hardly needs saying, in the life of this country.

I was one of many who pleaded for continuity between the old Kennedy White House and the new administration of Lyndon Johnson. In retrospect, however, I think that President Johnson was far too eager to keep on President Kennedy's men. In Lyndon Johnson's eyes, John Kennedy was everything that he felt excluded from—a particular kind of good looks, a particular kind of style, a particular kind of wife, a particular kind of connection. In fact, Lyndon Johnson had something of an obsession about John Kennedy—and a very sad one. Although he felt no personal allegiance to men like McNamara and McGeorge Bundy, the new president was clearly horrified by any appearance of mass exodus on the part of the glittering old guard. He, therefore, convinced them all to stay, fearing their absence would in some way diminish his own standing in the eyes of the public. So the old guard stayed on in body, if not entirely in spirit, with results that were predictably mixed.

Lyndon Johnson was a great politician, and, as president, his keen political instincts would, for the most part, serve him well. He was also a man of some considerable vision. As an example of this, I would cite his genuine concern about the race problem, which in those days was very rare, indeed, among politicians who came, as he did, from parts of the country where concern about race was highly unpopular. However, during those first crucial years in office, Johnson was limited in several significant ways. Successful leaders are invariably true to themselves. However, in the areas of foreign policy in general and Vietnam in particular, Johnson lacked any kind of internal compass; for guidance in these areas, he relied on the leftovers from the Kennedy time. And when these men failed him, he was left, in the case of Vietnam, to pursue a policy that he neither believed in nor understood.

The waging of war in a democratic society requires a good deal of political preparation on the part of the leaders who wish to fight. As Franklin Roosevelt well knew, the public must be persuaded of the necessity for battle long before the battle begins. To my mind, John Kennedy would have been a superb war president. He was a decisive leader who never looked back after a decision was made and had a special knack for communicating his resolve to the public at large. What is more, from Vienna to the Cuban missile crisis, President Kennedy, like FDR, showed a unique ability to learn from past decisions and mistakes, and, like FDR, he never ceased to grow in both stature and in confidence as his presidency moved forward.

President Johnson had no such knack. Schooled in the rough world of Texas politics, his instinct for leadership was of a pragmatic, political kind. Given to political manipulation and intrigue in private, his public style was far more reactive and malleable than President Kennedy's. In the case of Vietnam, when he was presented with the policy choices of the old Kennedy advisers, Lyndon Johnson chose, characteristically and fatally, to talk peace while making war. When speaking to the American public on the subject of the Vietnam War, he often placed the responsibility for ordering larger troop commitments on his commanders, adding, in relatively passive tones, that his force could not "be defeated" and would "stand in Vietnam." At no time that I was aware did President Johnson or his advisers seek to prepare the American people for the grim consequences of a protracted military battle, nor did they adequately explain to the public the reasons for the fight.

Given the view of this country's world role that then prevailed (during the first years of the Johnson presidency, the majority of polls showed fairly overwhelming public support for the war in Vietnam), it would have been far more effective for President Johnson to run Old Glory up the flagpole and declare, in effect, "Now we have a war on our hands. Let's go out and win it." As it actually happened, however, the decision to join in the Vietnam fight was not made all at once, but in a nearly ridiculous kind of salami-slicing way. With considerable political skill, the Johnson administration ordered over 150,000 ground troops to Vietnam before the *New York Times* ever admitted the United States was in a major war. The result, although a feat of great political craft, was almost wholly counterproductive for it left the public both divided and confused.

For my part, I was never confused about what policy this country should pursue in Vietnam. I continued, during the Johnson years, to make regular reporting trips to that country. The conditions I observed there through the 1960s in no way changed my conviction that the war in Vietnam was winnable and that, from the standpoint of U.S. interests—not to mention those of the South Vietnamese population—it was desirable for the U.S. military to win. These views of mine were nothing if not consistent, and President Johnson (whom I supported in his run for office against Barry Goldwater) was aware of them until the day he left office. At times, as has happened before during my career as a newspaperman and political columnist, I became perhaps too passionately involved with the events I was seeking to cover. I admit this now, although I do not apologize for it, for in Vietnam, as elsewhere, I continued to do my best to follow the rule I had set long ago in China: to go and see for myself the weather in the streets.

As I look back, there is one further point I would add. I do not think I was wrong about the importance of Indochina to the general balance of power. It seems obvious to me, in view of immediately subsequent history, that the American decision to accept defeat in Vietnam when we had never accepted defeat anywhere before rather naturally provoked an immense recalculation of risks in the Kremlin. Beginning with Angola, in fact, the Soviets took a long series of steps of a quasi-aggressive or, in the case of Afghanistan, directly aggressive and previously unprecedented character. At that early stage, moreover, no one could foretell—and no one did—that we would be saved from the consequences of our withdrawal by the simple fact that the Kremlin would thereby be tempted to overextend itself very badly. In consequence, we are not just back at square one, we are now in unknown country, and all the old landmarks formerly usable in judging the situation have entirely disappeared from view.

This much said, I must admit that the Johnson period and the years that followed until my retirement in 1974 were for me an increasingly bitter and bewildering time. The immediate postwar period, as I believe, was a time for all Americans to be proud of. Great worldwide tasks of reconstruction were undertaken by this country. Other toilsome burdens were assumed, and costly wars were fought in order to prevent the postwar period from merging into a new prewar period. All the American leaders of the time remembered how the British and the French had not done particularly well in this respect after World War I and how the postwar period that began in 1918 merged into a prewar period after 1930.

The great Americans of the post–World War II period were the leaders I followed. Theirs were the ideas I shared (and still share). However, as the debate over Vietnam lengthened from a purely political struggle into a personal and vindictive one, it became clear to me that the old ideas I so cherished had lost much of their meaning for the new generation. The postwar period was at an end, and my old bearings were of little use. The truth is, I could no longer understand what was happening in America, perhaps because I had finally become an old man, frozen in the viewpoints of the past. The pleasures the young indulged in during the 1960s seemed to me strikingly unpleasurable. The work of the younger artists struck me as thoroughly ridiculous or boring or, more often, both. And the chatter of the newly fashionable writers and so-called intellectuals began to drive me mad.

Increasingly, it seemed to me, the tragic defeats of this country—whether abroad in Vietnam or at home, as in the case of Richard Nixon's Watergate scandal—were greeted with unseemly crowing among members of my old trade. This crowing made me feel isolated and suddenly out of fashion. And it was not long before I began to hear the voice of the mysterious figure in T. S. Eliot's "The Waste Land," who calls out in a rather different context, "Hurry up please it's time." The voice came loudest when Stewart fell sick with leukemia and, after a lengthy and bravely met illness, died in May of 1974. By a chance that I count my great good fortune, my brother needed me while he lived, for our blood types were perfectly matched. And so I was drafted, on a number of occasions, to provide him with the nourishing white blood cells so crucial in battling his illness. Only when he died, therefore, could I do just as I chose. At the moment of his death—and, indeed, for months afterward—I felt not just the pain of loss and the decrepitude that is natural if you were born in 1910; I felt a final failure of all the zest and gusto and eagerness to know what will happen next that are the impelling motives of any good reporter. Not long after Stewart's death, I decided to end the column.

The plain truth is, alas, that the reporter's trade is for young men. In order to become a successful reporter, sturdy feet are nine times more important than a good head that fits the facts into a coherent pattern. After forty-two years in the business, my feet were gone and my head, quite clearly, was elsewhere. My lack of gusto, my sense of generational disorientation, was a problem that my brother and I already had begun talking about in the last year of his life, when I was able to see so much more of him. Oddly, Stew, who was doomed to die, felt no loss of zest at all. In many ways, he was a more receptive man than I, more settled in spirit and, therefore, more comfortable with outward change. He sensed my uneasiness with the new face of the world and diagnosed my very different feeling quickly and correctly. "You belong to the past much more than I do," said Stew. I am now sure that he was right.

Retirement, to be blunt, always requires a man to cash in his savings. My savings, somewhat eccentrically, have gone into my much-loved house and garden and into the house's endlessly pleasurable contents. Long ago, I concluded that I should probably do better buying the things I knew about and could use and care for instead of all the conventional things that people put their savings into. Mercifully, this turned out to be quite true. While in China during the war, I had begun to collect works of art in a rigorous, passionate way. I kept up the practice until it came time, after I ended the column, to sell off those pieces in my collection that had increased in value. Parting with objects, no matter how beautiful and valued, proved surprisingly easy. But leaving a house I designed myself, built myself, and had enjoyed since the Truman times proved far more difficult, and in the end I felt like a hermit crab leaving its shell.

In retirement, as in my active professional life, I have been a lucky man, for I have had good friends and good work to nurture me in my old age. Much of my energies have been spent in the completion of a labor of scholarship started in 1964. The project began as a history of art collecting as a social habit in China, the West, and the Muslim world, although it did not take me long to discover that this subject was vastly more complex and significant than I had imagined. In all, it took a full eighteen years for this vague theme to grow into a large and perhaps too laboriously notated volume. As has invariably been the case, I relished the scholarship and study but loathed the act of writing. My fits of despair were always passionate, however, and in the end, this passion saw the work through to completion. *The Rare Art Traditions,* as the book was finally called, is the only one of the eight volumes I have written or co-written that remains in print today. It is still my proudest piece of work.

My experience in marriage, as I look back, was a curious one, for Susan Mary and I loved one another very much but irritated one another far too often for a really successful partnership. Susan Mary, therefore, decided, in 1972, that we must separate. We divorced three years later because the Internal Revenue Service suggested we do so or pay much larger taxes after Susan Mary inherited her mother's fortune. But we still love one another. She lives only four blocks from me in her mother's house, which used to be one of the gloomiest I have ever known and which Susan Mary has now made one of the envied houses of the city. When I have friends in my house, she is still my hostess; and when she has a dinner, I am still her host.

On the whole, I should say that we are closer to one another than most married couples I know. And so the story, which still continues, has a happy ending, although the breakup was painful for us both, as breakups, I suppose, always are. Even now, when I am an old man, the partnership continues, for we see one another often every week. I still think of my stepchildren Anne and Bill as the nearest that I have to children of my own. And although I never let them call me anything but my first name out of respect for Bill Patten, I have given up the struggle for correctness and allow both Anne's children and Bill's to call me Grandfather, a title that, I must add, gives me immense satisfaction.

So let me end these memoirs here, on an altogether abrupt and sentimental note. My view is simple: I have seen the best of it. Stew said the same during the last days of his life, and I agreed with him then; I agree with him still. As one grows old, one succumbs to the altogether fatal tendency of praising the past. I am guilty of this, I know, but I do not worry much about it. I was born into a slow, settled world that was unique, in a special way, to the history of this country. I worked and flourished professionally during the long apex of what many have called this "American Century." That century has passed and will likely not come again. Likewise, the special manners and attitudes that shaped the world I knew so well when I was a boy and young man have all but vanished. I am aware that this is not an altogether bad thing. Still, this does not keep me from celebrating the uncommonly rich pleasures of my own special time and place, or from lamenting their passing.

Epilogue

Joseph Alsop remained a nationally syndicated columnist until December 1974, when he retired from full-time political writing. "When you are not awfully far off half-a-century in the same job," he wrote not long before his official farewell, "it is time to stop." During the last full decade of his professional life, Alsop continued to work at the hectic pace he was used to. Three columns were produced each week along with a steady flow of magazine pieces, books (an archaeological study of Crete called *From the Silent Earth* was published in 1964), and private correspondence. He began work on an ambitious volume of art history—eventually published in 1982 as *The Rare Art Traditions*—a project that would engross him on and off for the next two decades. Each year, there were also extended and, by the standards of most practicing journalists, grand processions abroad: Saigon, London, and Kenya in the spring of 1964; London again in May of the next year; followed by another stop in Saigon and visits to Hue, Pleiku, and the new U.S. marine base at Da Nang.

This itinerary gives some idea of Alsop's chief preoccupation during this last portion of his working life. He continued to cover

domestic events assiduously, writing often on the civil-rights movement; the presidential elections in 1964, 1968, and 1972; Nixon's
visit to China. But no subject so obsessed him during this period as
the U.S. war in Vietnam. By his own estimate, Alsop spent more
than two years of his professional life in South Vietnam, from the
time of his first visit to Saigon in the winter of 1953 to the last
column he composed in the country in April 1972. Joe was an obsessive man by nature, and this was an obsession that, in the end, got
the better of him. "An old monster with a commitment" is how he
described himself in a letter to a much younger colleague in the
summer of 1971.

The nature of this commitment is impossible to describe in a
wholly objective way. For all of his professional life as a columnist,
Joseph Alsop was a passionately subjective writer. Although he always advertised the fact that his column was based on primary reporting, he never pretended not to have opinions. In fact, he was
fiercely and consistently opinionated. Once he took a public stand,
he rarely relinquished it. In both his public and private life, disagree-
ments on matters of politics or policy could quickly become personal. He made enemies as easily as he did friends, and he relished
conflict, often cultivating it. He had a reputation as a pundit for an
insistent, almost excessive, pessimism. In part, this was a product of
Joe's personality. He was a worrier who liked to operate in a crisis
environment. On a more subtle level, he wanted to insure that readers continued to pay attention to what he wrote.

From an early date, Joe framed his reporting from Indochina in
the most severe terms. "A defeat at Dienbienphu, or even a fairly
mild French reverse at Dienbienphu, will cause the same kind of
reactions in Paris that Yorktown caused in London 171 years ago,"
he wrote in January 1954, shortly after his second visit to Southeast
Asia. "The future of Asia," he concluded in the same column, "may
well be at stake in this remote and obscure engagement."

For the next two decades, Joe never abandoned this view that
the conflict in Vietnam was part of a much greater struggle between
communism and the West, totalitarian rule and democracy. He advocated sending U.S. troops to bolster the French efforts against the
Viet Minh. When the French departed not long after the signing of
the Geneva Accords in July 1954, he drew parallels with the Munich
agreement of 1938 and baldly announced the abandonment of Indochina. This worry was animated by a staunch belief that the world
balance of power was a very real and fragile thing. Like other members of his World War II generation, Alsop argued that weakness
generally invited war and military strength prevented it. In his view,

the advent of nuclear weapons voided the old rules of imperialism, telescoped confrontation, and made the democratic world a smaller, more vulnerable place. During this "complex and dangerous" time it was the duty of his country, Joe believed, to counter Moscow's hand, to steady tottering allies—to take up the role, in short, of a great power.

"All rules of history can be put in one sentence," Alsop told a gathering of the Yale Political Union in November 1971: "nothing endures, because there is always change and there is always war." One can assume, as I am sure Joe did, that this assertion startled his correctly liberal audience. "Meanwhile," he continued, "the object of any society is in fact the unattainable object of enduring. And the problem is, what do we need in America to endure? It isn't enough to say that we are very numerous, or that we are vastly rich in proportion to everyone else in the world. Being that rich simply makes us a target, if you think about it. Everybody else would like to divide up our goods. They'd like to chew us up like a dead whale on a beach, if we'd let them do it. And I have the warmest sympathy for that desire. It is perfectly understandable, and we mustn't complain about it."

The specific reasons for supporting the American effort in Vietnam Joe laid out in a 1967 letter to a social friend, Mme. Philippe de Rothschild: "I should not support the Vietnamese war if I did not think that U.S. interests were served by it. Two main interests are concerned. On the one hand, there is the preservation of our major position as a Pacific power—for which we had already fought two very big wars before Vietnam came along. On the other hand, there is the vast and highly unsettling change in the whole world balance that now so clearly looms ahead in the Pacific. Japan, please remember, is already close to being the world's third industrial power, with a population twice that of France and a per capita income that will be about equal to that in France in less than a decade. When China breaks free of dogmatism to follow Japan—and all China experts now agree that this must happen soon—her development should also be very swift. . . . The Pacific, therefore, is soon (maybe within thirty years) due to become another great world lake, quite on a par with the Atlantic. And the U.S., a land bridge between the two world lakes, cannot really afford to opt out of history in the Pacific."

This conviction that the United States must act forcefully in a rough world was widespread among Americans during the Kennedy time and during the early years of Lyndon Johnson's presidency. Vietnam was generally seen as a beachhead in the battle against Communist expansion. Even so, when Alsop began to cover the story intensively in 1964 (he would make biannual trips to the field until 1972), he had a clearer knowledge than most that his country was going to war. In May 1964, he spent several days traveling in the provinces outside of Saigon. Six months later, he was back in-country, accompanying South Vietnamese army rangers on helicopter flights over Ben Tri, a provincial capital south of Saigon in the Mekong Delta. The scope and intensity of these forays only increased after President Johnson's decision, in July 1965, to commit 175,000 U.S. combat troops to the fighting. Joe was bent on covering this war the old-fashioned way. Like his colleagues during the Second World War and Korea, he believed in reporting the action, in getting the story. Like them, he also wanted to see his side win.

A schism between Joe and the majority of the younger American journalists in Vietnam developed early on and only widened as the war progressed. Part of the reason was Alsop's privileged VIP status. Although he spent rigorous days in the field, Joe, in his fifties now and fast leaving middle age, was used to coddling and rarely turned down preferential treatment when it was offered. When in Saigon, he often stayed as a houseguest of the U.S. ambassador. The army placed its vast transport system at Joe's disposal, whisking him from one destination to the next in specially assigned helicopters. On the ground, he was provided with high-ranking uniformed guides and, often enough, a personal trailer in which to rest. Official sources were supplied on command. The itinerary of a trip he made to South Vietnam in March and April 1968, shortly after the Tet offensive, gives an idea of the access Alsop enjoyed to those who ran the war:

> *Monday, 18 March*
>   Air France 191, arr. Saigon 5:05 PM
>   Dinner with Amb. Ellsworth Bunker
>   Stay with Amb. Bunker
> *Tuesday, 19 March*
>   Morning at American Embassy
>   2:30 PM—Gen. Philip Davidson [chief of
>   intelligence, Westmoreland's staff]
>   7:00 PM—Dinner with Gen. Westmoreland

Then, following time in the field:

> *Wednesday, 27 March*
>   9:00 AM—Pres. Thieu

10:00 AM—Vice Pres. Ky
Lunch with E. Lansdale
Dinner with Amb. Bunker and Chaisson [Marine
    Brigadier General John Chaisson, director,
    Combat Operations Center]

Naturally enough, programs like this were noticed by members of the press corps in Saigon. Many of Joe's younger colleagues thought he took advantage of his status as celebrated columnist to serve as a high-profile conduit for the government line. There was some truth to this claim, although not as much as Joe's detractors supposed. Once full-blown war was under way in Vietnam, Joe believed with many in the U.S. military that, given the proper logistical and political support, the conflict could be won, albeit with a "Korea-like result." He never lost this belief. Like many in Washington and Saigon, Joe also underestimated the toughness and tenacity of the North Vietnamese. Although his reporting was rarely grossly inaccurate, he was guilty on any number of occasions of cheerleading. He routinely drew exaggerated conclusions from what were, in hindsight, relatively modest gains on the part of the U.S. and South Vietnamese forces. During 1966 and 1967, the years of General William Westmoreland's "big unit" drives, he reported several times that the enemy was being ground down and peace was imminent. He was one of the few journalists to portray the Tet offensive, in January 1968, as a flat military defeat for Hanoi—"a play," as he put it, "from weakness rather than strength." This analysis has been supported by a number of historians since the war. Characteristically, however, Joe's conclusions after Tet—that the conflict was winding down and Hanoi could be forced to sue for peace before the November 1968 elections—proved absurdly optimistic.

Alsop was well aware, by the mid 1960s, that the war in Vietnam was not going well at home. "The President," he wrote in February 1966, "is still presenting the Vietnamese War to the country with techniques quite visibly borrowed from Madison Avenue." He believed, as he says in these memoirs, that Lyndon Johnson never adequately prepared the country for the consequences of a prolonged national fight. There is little doubt that Joe tried, in his column, to goad Johnson publically into adopting a more decisive military strategy in Indochina. Privately, Alsop blamed John Kennedy's old advisers, specifically Secretary of Defense Robert McNamara and McGeorge Bundy at the National Security Council, for leading LBJ out into the deep water and leaving him there to flounder. "Johnson is not at home with foreign affairs," he wrote glumly to Richard Rovere of the *New Yorker* in 1965, months before the first major deployment of U.S. troops. "The Kennedy machine for managing affairs, with Dean Rusk as non- or even anti-Secretary of State, is quite remarkably ill-adapted to Johnson's needs. And if the outcome in Vietnam is what now seems foreseeable, this alone may be sufficient to poison our national life for a generation."

Much of Joe's increasing gloom and bile during this period was reserved for members of his own profession. Throughout the Vietnam conflict, Joe considered the general tone of the coverage by the U.S. print and electronic press to be overly sensational, unprofessional, and, at worst, unpatriotic. He was not afraid of saying so. His correspondence from the early 1960s until his retirement in 1974 is full of squabbles and accusations with colleagues, many old friends of his, over the editorial treatment of this incident or that. He was especially incensed by the coverage Tet had received, along with the concurrent North Vietnamese siege of a U.S. marine base near the Laotian border at Khe Sanh. "Lurid, sentimental, hogwash," was Joe's assessment of the sensational parallels hastily drawn in the U.S. press between the predicament of the U.S. troops socked in at Khe Sanh and the French who were overrun at Dien Bien Phu in 1954. "Nothing is happening," he obstinately reported in a dispatch from Khe Sanh published on April 8, 1968, some weeks after the most severe fighting had ended. "The sun is shining fiercely. Running, even walking briskly in a flak jacket is precisely like doing the hardest kind of exercise in a preambulating sauna bath. This important fact, plus the general peacefulness, are the first things one notices about 'the agony of Khe Sanh.' "

It was also Joe's view that the U.S. press refused to admit that it had grossly overplayed the import and effect of the Tet offensive in South Vietnam. In a letter written in February 1971 to Richard Harwood, then national editor of the *Washington Post*, he recounts the story of Charles Mohr, the respected correspondent for the *New York Times*, who reported several months after the Communist attack that the Tet offensive had in fact been a "military and political disaster" for the enemy. Any losses, however, were outweighed by the clear "psychological success" of the attack in America, a success that, Joe maintained, was greatly facilitated by the reporting of the event in the United States. I include the following excerpt not to bolster any of Joe's claims, but as evidence of his thinking on the subject of the press and Vietnam, and of his personal outrage over the issue—something he held, in one form or another, until the end of his life: "If I am correctly informed, the 'Times' people had a considerable argument about whether and how to run Mohr's distinctly honest and courageous report. Finally, it was put on the front page, below the fold, with the smallest possible headline, in sharp contrast to the five-, six- and eight-column heads that were over the stories mis-reporting Tet, day after day, in the earlier period. Since then, 'Time' and other publications that shared the guilt of the 'Times' have picked up and repeated Mohr's formula of a 'military and political defeat but a psychological success.' The whole business strikes me as plain shameful, for a newspaper may grossly mislead its readers by accidents of circumstances and incomprehension. But if this has happened, the newspaper or publication in question has a plain duty to say so, prominently, and with editorial and news emphasis."

As the divisions over Vietnam deepened in Washington and around the country, Joe began to cultivate running feuds with prominent liberals, some of them former friends. "Although I may, therefore, merit your objections, I do not merit your contempt," Richard Goodwin, a Johnson speechwriter and no friend, wrote Joe in 1966. "When an intelligent man begins to regard other intelligent and patriotic men with disdain he had best begin to look to his own soul." Others were less polite. In his short-lived Broadway play *Sheep on the Runway,* the columnist Art Buchwald featured a bombastic, overwrought newspaperman named Joe Mayflower. Buchwald, an early critic of the war, plainly meant Mayflower to be a lampoon of his old adversary, and all of Washington knew it. Responding to a typical Alsopian attack on his views, John Kenneth Galbraith, who was still serving as the U.S. ambassador to India, declared that, along with Lyndon Johnson, Alsop was the "leading non-combatant casualty of Vietnam." Concluded Galbraith, "From a much-feared columnist, warrior and prophet he has become a figure of fun. It was the war that did him in."

By the early 1970s, this kind of fashionable denigration had begun to take a personal toll on Joe. His old public allies, men like Acheson and McNamara, had long since fled the field. Social friends grew weary of his monologues from the front. In letters to friends, he habitually referred to himself as an "aging, increasingly out-of-date newspaperman." This characterization, he knew, was not far from the truth. "I am well aware of my own loss of fashion in recent years," he wrote his old friend Katharine Graham, "and well aware, too, that this time it [is] going much deeper than [on] the other . . . occasions."

Still, he refused to waver in his hard headed, increasingly unpopular views. Although his predictions of victory became less frequent, he never publically disparaged the U.S. military effort. "As reporters we have a duty to refrain from dealing in what may be called the counterfeit coins of modern public discourse" he told a group of Nieman Fellows at Harvard University in December 1969. "These counterfeit coins are so numerous that I have no time to describe or analyze them all. International control commissions; peacekeeping forces; neutralization in the sense in which that word has been used about Vietnam; negotiations as the best way out of wars; and arms races as causes of wars—that is a pretty good short list. No International commission has ever controlled anything at all, except for things like locusts, whose control is in the interests of all concerned. No peacekeeping force has ever kept the peace, except perhaps in the special case of Cyprus, where one side has been slowly ground down while the other was protected. No seriously contested region of the globe has ever been neutralized, except by its own hard, native determination. Nor has any bitterly contested war, in all of history, ever really been settled by negotiations. Negotiations merely register the result; they do not produce it."

Predictably enough, Joe saw little use in pursuing the peace talks with Hanoi, under way in Paris since May 1968. He offered grudging editorial support for President Nixon's plan for a "Vietnamization" of the conflict but predicted that this approach would ultimately end in defeat. The White House decision, taken in April 1970, to expand the war into Cambodia he supported, going so far as to draw a parallel with MacArthur's landing at Inchon. A friend and sometime confidant of Henry Kissinger, he applauded rapprochement with China in 1972 (he would write glowing dispatches from the country the next year for which, given his past hard-line views on China, he was roundly criticized) but continued to fret over the situation in Southeast Asia. As Hanoi's forces began to press the Saigon regime and the Khmer Rouge advanced in Cambodia after the Paris peace accords in January 1973, Alsop began to parcel out blame. The Democratic Congress, which had voted to cut off funding for all U.S. military activity in Indochina in June 1973, received a large measure of abuse. The Vietnam War was the "worst managed serious war in United States history," he wrote and continued to warn, albeit with less frequency, of the dire consequences of Saigon's defeat.

Nixon's Watergate debacle, which some have argued hastened Saigon's fall, only increased Joe's personal sense of isolation and alarm. A practiced traditionalist in respect to the presidency, he was ultimately shocked by Nixon's transgressions (Joe never understood nor much admired the man) and puzzled by the glee with which the president's enemies, particularly those in the press, took in bringing him down. "I get rather angry, when I see large numbers of people who actually elected Nixon in 1968, and also made his election a dead certainty in 1972, behaving rather like hyenas around a corpse," he wrote the *Washington Post* cartoonist Herbert Block in 1974. "After all, he is our President, son of a bitch 'though he may be. And although nobody seems to remember the fact except myself, his misfortunes may very well be our misfortunes."

As he says in these memoirs, Joe's decision to retire became clear with the death of his brother Stewart from leukemia in the spring of 1974. At the age of sixty-three, Joe had begun to feel an old man. "Mine has been a straight line career marked by really golden luck until about three years ago, just as Stew's career was marked by golden luck, and our whole family's life was marked by golden luck until about three years ago," he wrote his old friend Isaiah Berlin in June 1974, not long after the death of his brother. "I sometimes think we lost our luck when my mother died [in 1971]. In the same way, I frequently think that the United States lost its luck when President Kennedy was shot. But I suppose that's superstition. And one must not give way to whining or gloom. The thing to do is to find a new way of pegging away, and thereby to create a reasonably satisfactory fin de carrière."

Joe wrote his final column on December 30, 1974, four months before the fall of Saigon. He would die on the twenty-eighth of August, 1989, only three months before the collapse of the Berlin Wall. If he had any thoughts on Hanoi's final victory, none was published. He never changed his general views on the subject, as far as I could tell. Nor did he live to see the cold war declared officially over, although he professed to being pleased with *glasnost,* albeit highly wary of it. The remainder of his life Joe devoted to family, to friends, and to scholarship. Always there was time for pleasure: "I can't resist confronting you with a zoo party," he wrote the playwright Lillian Hellman on the eve of one of her rare visits to Washington from her home in New York. "The hyenas laugh, the jackals whine, the vultures circle, and everyone waits for the lions and tigers that don't exist in our human zoo."

By her own account, Lillian Hellman confronted the Washington animals and found them charming. "I can't tell you what a really nice time I had," she wrote Joe by way of thanks for the weekend. "All the way home I asked myself what makes me comfortable and what, too often, even with close friends, causes me to flit about or sulk. I have no answer except your good manners, your good feeling, your nice house. Your dinner party—only gossip travels fast—

is now being talked about here. But, more important, I think, I hope, I have a new friend, and one I like."

There would be plenty of zoo parties during the last decade of Joe's life in Washington. Foremost, however, Joe Alsop was a man of action. In retirement, he dearly missed the high-stakes rough-and-tumble of his old public life. "Ohhhhh, I hate it!" he would say of his old age. He was well aware that he had lived a rich and peculiarly American life, and his work with me was a conscious way of reliving this. To the very end, he kept himself immersed in books. His personal library, which all but enveloped three large rooms of his Georgetown home, contained over 9,000 volumes. He never learned to drive, and he owned no television on the grounds that it corrupted new minds and left old ones soggy. Ideas animated him, and these were always opinionated, sometimes contrary, and often original. But he missed being a reporter for reasons he explained in the last two paragraphs of his final column of Christmas 1974. For a man whose public reputation for controversy and conviction often overshadowed a true devotion to craft, these words are as good an epitaph as any: "Getting the facts and publishing them, in turn, are major public functions because they are essential to the working of our brand of society. In my working lifetime, I have known a whole series of alleged American elites, definable as groups of people who inform themselves. I have never known any alleged American elite to be right about any subject whatever, except, arguably, subjects like the correct manufacture of soufflés. Meanwhile, I have never known the American people to be really badly wrong, if only they were correctly and fully informed. To be sure the reporter's trade cannot inform the country singlehandedly—if the ghastly groves of academe are talking unanimous, rancid twaddle, for instance. Nonetheless, I am deeply proud to have been a reporter so long. In the reporter's trade, we have a serious job to do."

—Adam Platt

Index

Page numbers in *italics* indicate illustrations.